# CRITICAL INSIGHTS

## The Poetry of
## Edgar Allan Poe

# CRITICAL INSIGHTS

# The Poetry of
# Edgar Allan Poe

Editor
**Steven Frye**
*California State University, Bakersfield*

Salem Press
Pasadena, California    Hackensack, New Jersey

*Cover photo:* ©Alexeyzel/Dreamstime.com

Published by Salem Press

© 2011 by EBSCO Publishing
Editor's text © 2011 by Steven Frye
"The *Paris Review* Perspective" © 2011 by Juliet Lapidos for *The Paris Review*

∞ The paper used in these volumes conforms to the American National Standard for Permanence of Paper for Printed Library Materials, Z39.48-1992 (R1997).

**Library of Congress Cataloging-in-Publication Data**
The poetry of Edgar Allan Poe / editor, Steven Frye.
   p. cm. — (Critical insights)
  Includes bibliographical references and index.
  ISBN 978-1-58765-705-4 (v. 1 : alk. paper)
   1. Poe, Edgar Allan, 1809-1849—Poetic works. 2. American poetry—History and criticism. I. Frye, Steven.
  PS2642.P63P64 2011
  811'.3—dc22
                               2010029144

PRINTED IN CANADA

# Contents_____

## The Poetry and Author_____

## Critical Contexts_____

## Critical Readings_____

# Resources

# About This Volume

Steven Frye

This collection contains a diverse array of essays discussing the work of one of the most important American literary figures of the nineteenth century. In his short career, Edgar Allan Poe worked as an editor, a critic, a short-story writer, and a poet, and he was one of the major arbiters of American letters. He prized the role of the poet especially, and though the merit of his verse is a matter of some controversy, its influence is beyond question, leading to much discussion and consideration over time. The first section of this volume contains a number of new essays that deal with issues ranging from formal poetics and prosody to critical reception and thematic concerns. These essays serve to orient readers to the poetry itself and to the topics that have preoccupied critics, many of whom have attempted to come to terms with Poe's verse in the context of the radical shift in poetic sensibilities that took place in the late nineteenth and early twentieth centuries. The second section contains a rich variety of republished essays by major scholars who have worked in detail with Poe's poetical works and, in doing so, have discovered a diverse array of both thematic and formal subjects to explore, ranging from the poet's psychological interests and dreamscapes to his concern with gender. Of particular interest to many renowned critics has been Poe's influence on later poets such as Charles Baudelaire and the Brownings, as well as the impact of his work internationally. In addition, the volume contains a chronology of the author's life, a comprehensive list of his works, and a brief biography, as well as a bibliography, an index, and a perspective from *The Paris Review* provided by Juliet Lapidos. I have also written a brief introduction to the volume dealing primarily with Poe's concept of the poetic as it appears in theory and practice, particularly relating to the interior realms of human psychology, as well as the effect of verse on the reader's mind and heart.

In the "Critical Contexts" section, Brian Yothers explores the role of the exotic in Poe's poetry, contextualizing it within the broader field of early-nineteenth-century travel literature. Jeffrey Scraba deals with the complexities of memory, paying special attention to how formal poetics functions to illuminate themes in Poe's poetry. Matthew J. Bolton works with the poetry in the broad context of its reception in the nineteenth and twentieth centuries, dealing with those figures Poe influenced domestically and abroad, especially in relation to form. Finally, Robert C. Evans comprehensively assesses the critical treatment of Poe as a poet in his own time and our own.

The "Critical Readings" section presents essays from eminent scholars in nineteenth-century literature and aesthetics, all of whom have worked extensively with Poe's writings, in particular, though not exclusively, his poetry. Dave Smith, G. R. Thompson, Richard Godden, and Daneen Wardrop work in detail with the poems themselves in inquiries dealing with individual poems as they explore the interrelationships of poetic language, the imagination, the dream self, and other systems of meaning and signification. Jonathan Culler, Burton R. Pollin, and Francis B. Dedmond establish the influence of Poe's work on subsequent poets, many of them tremendously significant themselves, clarifying his influence and importance as a precursor to later poetic figures and movements. Leland S. Person, Jr., Eliza Richards, and James Postema consider Poe within a set of broader cultural, intellectual, and political contexts, approaching the poetry productively and unconventionally in its relationship to time, place, and philosophical texture. Keiji Minato works to clarify the connection between Poe's verse and the concept of the poet in modern-day Japan. In each of these thoughtful treatments, Poe emerges as a poet preoccupied with the distinctive form and language of poetry and its capacity to express realms of thought and experience in unique ways, as well as its ability to illuminate not only the poet himself but also the dense historical complexities of his time.

# THE
# POETRY
# AND
# AUTHOR

# On Poe's Poetry

Steven Frye

Edgar Allan Poe was a "literary figure" in the most eclectic sense of the term: a writer of criticism and epistolary correspondence that doubled as literary theory as well as satire, tales, and even a novel titled *The Narrative of Arthur Gordon Pym*, he was also a magazine editor and a poet of significant renown in his time. In many ways his early death, the circumstances of which are themselves surrounded by conjecture, contributes to the myth of Poe, the tortured poet who, unsuited to the mundane realities of the physical world, was nevertheless attuned however briefly to the sublime and cursed by a visionary capacity that offered him only fleeting glimpses of the transcendent. His poetry in particular invites these speculations. "Tamerlane," "Al Aaraaf," "The Lake," "Sonnet—To Science," and "Israfel" all imagine the dream as a visionary state in which the poem becomes a beautiful but inadequate rendering of regions ambiguously psychological and metaphysical, in which the persona is transformed by a "Supernal Beauty" that recedes from human understanding.

Unlike William Wordsworth, Ralph Waldo Emerson, and Walt Whitman, all Romantics of a different sensibility, Poe offers little hope of apotheosis, no expectation of understanding in a normative sense. In terms of structure and form, he is more conventional than many of his later contemporaries, but in his forthright ambiguity on matters metaphysical and psychological he is distinctively modern. Though to all appearances he retreats from traditional religious orthodoxies, he retains an allegiance to a quasi-religious humanism, an implicit belief in the unique qualities of human consciousness and the transformative power of the soul, however inadequately it is defined. The imagination, its ability to glimpse the ultimate, even in a universe of pervasive darkness, seems to be Poe's central preoccupation. His poetic vision is sobering and melancholy, at times unsettling and frightening, especially to readers accustomed to the comfort of certitude. As a "Romantic," he challenges the boundaries of the imagination in the term's most restricted Wordsworthian sense, and he follows after Samuel Taylor Coleridge, who, in his critical treatise *Biographia Literaria* (1817) and in poems such as "Kubla Khan" and "The Rime of the Ancient Mariner," explores the extraordinary realms of the preternatural, the encounter of human imagination with the sublime.

As a critic Poe was prolific, and his various theoretical pronouncements provide a key to his poetic sensibilities. In "The Rationale of Verse" (1848) and "The Poetic Principle" (1850), he considers the medium of language in unconventional terms, less as a means transmitting thought and more as an embodiment of beauty through sound. Implicitly, he draws from the ancient recognition that poetry and poetic language are rooted in song, in the lyric blending of words and music. Music becomes a common metaphor in his poetry, echoing Plato's *Ion* as the poetic persona experiences an enraptured though ephemeral state of heightened aesthetic consciousness, a kind of divine madness. However, one must not press the Platonic parallel too far, since in "The Philosophy of Composition" (1845) Poe recounts writing "The Raven" and in doing so rejects Plato's conception of poetic creation as an unconscious, irrational process. For Poe, the poet is a master of technique and architect of words and phrases, rhythm, meter, and tone. He begins with a desired "effect" in mind and works toward it through the rational application of principles, methods that can be clearly articulated and understood.

Poe's description of technique in "The Philosophy of Composition" is so precise and detailed, so incommensurate with conventional notions of the creative intellect, that it is reasonable to suspect comic irony and self-parody. If present, however, it is a "romantic irony." Peculiar as his ideas seem, he means them, which becomes clear in other works of criticism. In "The Poetic Principle," he argues that the best poem must be comparatively brief, readable in a single sitting, and makes the striking claim that Milton's *Paradise Lost* is not a poem at all but a lengthy collection of lyrics. Thus a poem's exclusive aim is to create a unique and deeply emotional response in the reader, a transitory but profound apprehension of "Supernal Beauty." Truth at best is ancillary, a random attendant lord to the single purpose of effect. When truth maxims become the goal, the poet fails, having capitulated to the "Heresy of the Didactic." In this precept, Poe the Romantic firmly rejects the neoclassicism of critics such as Samuel Johnson, who in *Preface to Shakespeare* (1765) rearticulates the Horatian platitude, arguing that literature should instruct by pleasing. Poe's emphasis on the musical quality of poetic language is linked to his attempt to heighten human consciousness and perception at an affective and spiritual level, not for the purpose of understanding, which in metaphysical terms is impossible to achieve, but to create a distinctive kind of psychological experience—the pure aesthetic response.

In his preface to *Poems* (1831), known as "Letter to B——," Poe distinguishes among the aims of science, music, and poetry and argues that the most powerful effects are achieved through indistinctiveness, indirection, and allusion. Poe's influence on the critical tradition can be seen here as he anticipates twentieth-century formalists, particularly in his attention to the unique quality of poetic language, especially as it contrasts with science and philosophy. In this emphasis on effect, he prefigures the aesthetic movement that would dominate late-nineteenth-century France and England, and poets such as Charles Baudelaire, Stéphane Mallarmé, Paul Verlaine, and Oscar Wilde, who openly acknowledged his influence. In notes for his uncompleted *The Living Writers in America*, Poe remains interested in the primacy of imagination as a means of enrichment and experience, arguing that the "distant subjects" that inspire imaginative reverie are preferable to immediate, tactile, and sensory apprehension.

Poe's first poetry volume was *Tamerlane, and Other Poems* (1827). The title poem tells the story of the Mongol conqueror and portrays his torture as he contemplates his past excessive pride and ambition. Anticipating many of Poe's later lyrics, the character is blighted by lost love, and his emotional state and the overall tone of the poem reflect

Byronic melancholy and ennui. The lyric is replete with dream imagery and explores in tortured terms human consciousness in full awareness of mutability and change. Brevity and loss characterize this and other poems in the collection, as Poe envisions the dream self and the imagination in alternating states of movement and loss, heightened and compelled by a transitory sense of the supernal. Poems such as "The Lake" employ the natural imagery typical of Romantic poetry in an evocative way, making nature beautiful yet terrifying, more imbued with the Burkean sublime than with the picturesque. The lake is "lovely," "lonely," and "wild," evoking "terror" but also a "tremulous delight." The persona achieves a state of intense sensual awareness and an existential isolation, both as exquisite as they are impossible to bear.

In his second collection, *Al Aaraaf, Tamerlane, and Minor Poems* (1829), Poe added a number of works to his first collection, including the title poem. "Al Aaraaf" combines an elaborate mythological framework and celestial imagery into a vision exploring the confluence of the cosmological and the aesthetic in which the divine, momentarily incarnated in the human mind, becomes manifest only through beauty and imagination. Striking a clearly Romantic note, the persona of the brief lyric "Sonnet—To Science" laments the lost explanatory power of myth in the modern scientific age, but as the poem proceeds the mythological realm returns in the figures of Elfin, Diana, the Hamadryad, and the Naiad, suggesting that even in an age dominated by supreme rationality the poetic imagination may enrich the soul through the rejuvenating power of myth. In all of these collections, the imagination, the sublime, and the dream self are evoked in a poetic exploration of psychic and cosmological mystery. In the 1831 volume *Poems*, Poe collects revised editions of earlier poems and a few newer works on similar themes, expressing a nightmare vision and an even more intense preoccupation with the fleeting nature of Supernal Beauty. In "Israfel" the angel who plays the lyre is in essence the poet himself as he creates a music that transcends mortality to reach the realm of a fathomless eternal. In his later poems, most notably "The Raven"

(1845), Poe explores themes common to his tales as he deals with the human propensity to self-torture and the peculiar delight that emerges from sorrow and inner torment, especially as it arises from the loss of a loved one, particularly a beautiful woman.

As a poet, Edgar Allan Poe occupies a distinctive position among his contemporaries. In form he is by no means rigidly conventional, but any experimentation is moderate in comparison to those of other poets of his era, especially those who follow him in the American tradition, such as Walt Whitman and Emily Dickinson. But the critical precepts he defines with prose he enacts through poetry, producing a rich body of work that explores the nature of human consciousness, the transformative power of the imagination, and the immense complexity of the dream self. His poems engage the mind as it encounters the objective reality of the world and as it carries sense experience into the ephemeral realm of myth and the unconscious, seeking with a singular focus the aesthetic experience at its deepest and most transformative. It is these emotional intensities, the embrace of beauty and transience for its own sake, that made him a subject of near reverence among the major figures of the aesthetic movement, the French Symbolists, and, even later, some European and American modernists. For Poe, if there is a compensatory balance in the universe, an answer to mortality and loss, it is found within the soul's flight on what John Keats called the "viewless wings of Poesy."

# Biography of Edgar Allan Poe_____

Mark Minor

Edgar Poe was born January 19, 1809, in Boston, Massachusetts, to parents who were professional actors. Poe always believed that he inherited his talents as a reciter of verse especially from his mother, Elizabeth Arnold Poe, and it is not far-fetched to see his lifelong concern for the effect of the poem on the reader as an outgrowth of this early exposure to the stage. One of the most important events of his early life was the death of his mother when he was not yet three years old, and his poetry bears the imprint of his various attempts to find an ideal woman adequate to her memory. His father, David Poe, Jr., abandoned the family about this time and probably died shortly thereafter, and young Edgar was taken into the family of John Allan, a merchant from Richmond, Virginia. It was from Allan that Poe took his middle name.

From 1815 to 1820 the family lived in England, where Poe acquired much of his early education as well as his first exposure to the gothic style that figures so prominently in the atmosphere and settings of his works. Back in Richmond, Poe studied the classics in several schools, and in 1826 he entered the University of Virginia, where he seems to have impressed his teachers and fellow students with his knowledge of languages. He ran up large gambling debts, however, which Allan refused to pay, forcing Poe to drop out of school. Thus began an estrangement from Allan that lasted until Allan's death six years later.

At eighteen Poe enlisted in the U.S. Army, where he would rise within two years to the rank of sergeant major. Already at eighteen he had managed to have a slim volume of verse published, *Tamerlane, and Other Poems* (1827), followed by another, *Al Aaraaf, Tamerlane, and Minor Poems* (1829), when he was twenty. At about that time he requested (with Allan's approval) a discharge from the Army so that he could apply to the U.S. Military Academy at West Point. He entered the academy in 1830 and did well, but when Allan again refused him necessary financial support, it is likely he felt that he had no choice but to get himself expelled in order to find a job. He left West Point for New York, where, with financial support from West Point friends, he published a third volume of poetry, *Poems by Edgar Allan Poe* (1831), when he was twenty-two years old.

Poe now set himself to making a career in the world of professional letters, which he pursued with mixed success until his death eighteen years later. His financial circumstances were often desperate as he moved from one eastern city to another looking for work as a writer or editor of literary magazines. In 1835 he received his first job as an editor at the *Southern Literary Messenger*, and in 1836 he married his cousin, Virginia Clemm. In 1839 he became an editor at *Burton's Gentlemen's Magazine*, but he left that position after a year to try to establish his own magazine. When his attempt proved unsuccessful, he became an editor at *Graham's Magazine* in 1841, a position he left a year later, again to attempt to found his own magazine. He returned to editing again in 1842 with the *New York Mirror* and stayed there until 1845.

The circulation of both *Burton's* and *Graham's* increased dramatically under Poe's editorship, and he published some of his most famous stories in these magazines' pages. Sometimes, however, his erratic behavior and frequent problems with alcohol cost him jobs even when his actual performance was adequate. The journalistic world of the 1830's and 1840's was characterized by fiercely polemical writing, full of vituperation and personal attacks—a style that Poe practiced with great zest and ability. Despite his attacks in print on his fellow writers, some of them aided him in his times of unemployment and stress.

In 1842 Poe's young wife burst a blood vessel, and her deteriorating health over the next five years added greatly to Poe's financial worries. His mother-in-law was an important source of strength to the couple during these years. Amazingly, he was able to turn out dozens of first-rate poems, reviews, and stories for the magazines even while fighting off financial and health problems. The publication of "The Raven" in 1845 made him famous, enabling him to begin earning good money as a public reciter of poetry. The same year, he moved to the *Broadway Journal* and quickly became its proprietor until it folded in 1846.

When Virginia finally died in 1847, Poe himself became desperately ill. Even after recovering, he never regained his old resilience, though in 1848 he managed to publish his famous *Eureka: A Prose Poem*. That same year he became engaged to one of the several women he was seeing, Mrs. Sarah Whitman, another poet who attempted with some success to help him overcome his problems with drinking. Whitman's family disapproved of Poe, however, and the engagement was broken off not long after it began. Poe then became engaged to a widowed childhood sweetheart, Sarah Elmira Royster. In what was to be the last year of his life he achieved a measure of security with Royster, a regular income from lecturing and writing, and some popularity in Richmond society.

On September 24, 1849, Poe delivered his final lecture, "The Poetic Principle," in Richmond. On September 27, he took a steamer to Baltimore en route to New York. On October 3, he was found senseless and apparently drunk in a polling place and taken to a hospital, where he died a few days later, on October 7, at the age of forty.

From *Critical Survey of Poetry, Second Revised Edition* (Pasadena, CA: Salem Press). Copyright © 2003 by Salem Press, Inc.

## Bibliography

Bittner, William. *Poe: A Biography*. Boston: Little, Brown, 1962. This volume is a reliable study of Poe's life and is suitable for general readers.

Bloom, Harold, ed. *Edgar Allan Poe*. New York: Chelsea House, 2006. Compilation of essays by leading Poe scholars on various aspects of the author's work, including the boundaries of the detective-fiction genre and its relationship to psychoanalysis. Bibliographic references and index.

Buranelli, Vincent. *Edgar Allan Poe*. 2d ed. Boston: Twayne, 1977. This study of Poe's life and works offers an excellent introduction. The book includes a chronology of his life and an annotated, select bibliography.

Carlson, Eric W., ed. *Critical Essays on Edgar Allan Poe*. Boston: G. K. Hall, 1987. This supplement to Carlson's 1966 volume (below) offers a cross section of writing about Poe from the 1830's to the 1980's. Many of the essays deal with short stories, illustrating a variety of interpretive strategies.

_____. *The Recognition of Edgar Allan Poe*. Ann Arbor: University of Michigan Press, 1966. This selection of critical essays from 1829 to 1963 is intended to illustrate the development of Poe's literary reputation. It includes a number of the most important earlier essays on Poe, including Constance Rourke's discussion of Poe as a humorist. Also includes several essays by French and British critics.

Hoffman, Daniel. *Poe Poe Poe Poe Poe Poe Poe*. Baton Rouge: Louisiana State University Press, 1998. A perceptive study of Poe's personality and work. As the title suggests, Hoffman finds many Poes, a man and artist of many masks. He traces the coherence of the poet's work through the unity of his images.

Hyneman, Esther F. *Edgar Allan Poe: An Annotated Bibliography of Books and Articles in English, 1827-1973*. Boston: G. K. Hall, 1974. The quantity and variety of writings on Poe make it exceedingly difficult to compile complete lists. This volume, supplemented by *American Literary Scholarship: An Annual* for coverage of subsequent years, will provide an ample resource for most readers.

Kennedy, J. Gerald. *A Historical Guide to Edgar Allan Poe*. New York: Oxford University Press, 2001. Considers the tensions between Poe's otherworldly settings and his representations of violence, delivers a capsule biography situating Poe in his historical context, and addresses topics such as Poe and the American publishing industry, Poe's sensationalism, his relationships to gender constructions, and Poe and American privacy. Includes bibliographic essay, chronology of Poe's life, bibliography, illustrations, and index.

Meyers, Jeffrey. *Edgar Allan Poe: His Life and Legacy*. New York: Charles Scribner's Sons, 1992. Biography focuses on Poe's influence on other authors.

Peeples, Scott. *Edgar Allan Poe Revisited*. New York: Twayne, 1998. An introductory critical study of selected works and a short biography of Poe. Includes bibliographical references and index.

Perry, Dennis R. *Hitchcock and Poe: The Legacy of Delight and Terror*. Lanham, Md.: Scarecrow Press, 2003. This work discusses the thematic and stylistic parallels between Alfred Hitchcock's films and Poe's writings, both in general terms and through comparisons of specific works. Bibliographic references and index.

Quinn, Arthur Hobson. *Edgar Allan Poe: A Critical Biography*. Baltimore: Johns Hopkins University Press, 1998. This comprehensive biography of Poe, with a new introduction by Shawn Rosenheim, is devoted to setting out the facts of Poe's life and dealing with the legends surrounding Poe that have been misconstrued by other biographers.

Silverman, Kenneth. *Edgar A. Poe: Mournful and Never-Ending Remembrance.* New York: HarperCollins, 1991. A close reading of the writer's life and work.

Sova, Dawn B. *Edgar Allan Poe, A to Z: The Essential Reference to His Life and Work.* New York: Facts On File, 2001. A thorough guide to the life and works of Poe.

Whalen, Terence. *Edgar Allan Poe and the Masses: The Political Economy of Literature in Antebellum America.* Princeton, N.J.: Princeton University Press, 1999. A brilliant study of Poe that provides an inventive understanding of his works and his standing in American literature.

## The *Paris Review* Perspective

Juliet Lapidos for *The Paris Review*

Edgar Allan Poe was one of the first American writers to support himself entirely with his literary endeavors—a bona fide "professional" at a time when most authors had independent incomes or else supplemented their meager paychecks by teaching. He did not, however, set an encouraging example. His first book, the 1827 collection *Tamerlane, and Other Poems*, garnered no reviews and brought in no money. His second, published two years later, did poorly as well. Subsequently he turned to prose, supporting himself, his young wife, and his mother-in-law by churning out magazine stories and criticism. Forever on the brink of poverty, he drank too much, never learned to cope with failure, and antagonized the very friends who might have helped along his career. His poem "The Raven," published in 1845, was his only real popular and critical success, but he was unable to convert this accomplishment into financial reward. Throughout his nasty, brutish, and short professional life—he died in 1849 at age forty— he was the very definition of a *poète maudit*.

Nor can it be said unequivocally that, in death, Poe's abilities were finally recognized. His own literary executor, Rufus Griswold, downplayed his talents and propagated brazen lies about his private life— claiming, for instance, that Poe was a drug addict. Henry James argued that "enthusiasm for Poe is the mark of a decidedly primitive stage of reflection," Aldous Huxley gave special attention to the poet in his essay "Vulgarity in Literature," and the critic Harold Bloom has called Poe "a great fantasist whose thoughts were commonplace and whose metaphors were dead."

Yet this supposedly vulgar, commonplace thinker is read to this day and—contrary to the opinions of many expert naysayers—his verse in particular is of lasting value. His poetic body of work is relatively small, just sixty-three poems in number. (He was, quite simply, too busy with hackery to produce much more.) And his early efforts, in truth, are undistinguished—highly derivative of the European Romantics and larded with clunky rhymes, such as this couplet from the 1827 "Spirits of the Dead": "Thy soul shall find itself alone/ 'Mid dark thoughts of the gray tombstone." His style, however, improved as he grew older.

In his essay "The Poetic Principle," Poe defines poetry as "*The Rhythmical Creation of Beauty*" and argues that "in the union of Poetry with Music . . . we shall find the widest field for the Poetic development." It is therefore fitting that Poe's best, later works are musical in character. Take, for example, "The Bells," a four-part ode written in 1848. Each section describes the ringing of a different type of bell—sleigh, wedding, alarm, funeral—and, through meter, rhyme, and repetition, seems to replicate the sound in question. Thus Poe captures the tinny, rhythmic jingle of silver sleigh bells with "While the stars that oversprinkle/ All the heavens seem to twinkle/ With a crystalline delight;/ Keeping time, time, time/ In a sort of Runic rhyme." Similarly, the justly famous "Annabel Lee," which Poe referred to as a ballad, is songlike in that it circles back to the refrain "In this kingdom by the sea" and to variations on the phrase "the beautiful Annabel Lee."

One mark of a great poet is distinctiveness; it is impossible, for instance, to confuse Lord Byron for John Keats, even though they wrote in the same time period, or T. S. Eliot for his friend, editor, and fellow poet Ezra Pound. Part of what makes Poe's work immediately recognizable is its subject matter. Influenced, no doubt, by his wife's struggle with tuberculosis, Poe argued in "The Philosophy of Composition" that "the death . . . of a beautiful woman is, unquestionably, the most poetical topic in the world." He demonstrated his conviction by returning to the topic over and over again. "The Raven," "Annabel Lee,"

"Ulalume," "To One in Paradise," and "Lenore" are all narrated by a bereaved lover. Another identifying characteristic of Poe's work is a melancholy atmosphere—the sun shines too briefly or, more likely, not at all. The sky in "Ulalume" is "ashen and sober"; in "The City in the Sea," the "rays from the holy Heaven" never "come down"; and the narrator of "Annabel Lee" blames a "chilling" wind for his lover's fatal illness.

Given his obsessive morbidity, it is unsurprising that Poe's most intriguing narrators are, to put it kindly, unbalanced. The speaker of "Ulalume," for example, characterizes his soul as something external to himself, conversing with "Psyche" en route to his dead lover's tomb. His mental state is quite literally fractured. But Poe's most sensitive portrayal of a mind unhinged is found in "The Raven." The speaker, who is napping over old books when a raven raps at his chamber door, believes that the black bird is a prophetic supernatural agent. He peppers it with questions he wants answered in the affirmative: Will he ever get over the pain of bereavement? Will he at least join his lost love in heaven? At each juncture, the bird answers, "Nevermore," infuriating and upsetting the narrator to the point of madness. The bird, however, is not responsible for the narrator's derangement. There is no objective evidence to suggest that he is anything other than an escaped house pet, and his refrain, "Nevermore," seems ominous only because of the nature of the questions that the speaker chooses to pose. "The Raven" is not the story of a cursed, haunted man but the story of a nervous breakdown.

Perhaps Henry James was on to something after all when he wrote that enthusiasm for Poe indicates a "primitive stage of reflection," for there is a primal streak to the poet's work. A musical lilt makes his poetry memorable, even catchy; his morbidity and interest in madness provoke elemental fears. He was not, in truth, a poet of needless sophistication, but something better: a poet of the senses.

## Bibliography

Ackroyd, Peter: *Poe: A Life Cut Short*. New York: Doubleday, 2008.

Bloom, Harold, ed: *Edgar Allan Poe*. New York: Chelsea House, 1985.

Poe, Edgar Allan. *The Complete Tales and Poems of Edgar Allan Poe*. New York: Vintage, 1977.

# CRITICAL CONTEXTS

# Poe's Poetry of the Exotic_____

Brian Yothers

Edgar Allan Poe is not well known primarily for his depictions of travel. His late novel *The Narrative of Arthur Gordon Pym* was not terribly popular when it was first published, and his shorter pieces, like "MS. Found in a Bottle," "The Journal of Julius Rodman," and "The Unparalleled Adventure of One Hans Pfaall" remain relatively obscure even today when compared to his gothic tales of terror and his seminal exercises in detective fiction. A careful consideration of his critical reviews, essays, and poetry reveals, however, that Poe was obsessed with the idea of place, and particularly with examining locales that, in the nineteenth century, were deemed exotic, inaccessible, strange, or mysterious. He was not only engaged with the popular nineteenth-century genre of the prose travel narrative—writing reviews of such popular narratives as John Lloyd Stephens's *Incidents of Travel in Egypt, Arabia Petraea, and the Holy Land* (1837) and Washington Irving's *The Crayon Miscellany* (1835)—but he also adapted the genre's sense of place to meet his own goal, expressed in his "The Poetic Principle," of "elevating the soul" through poetry (*Poetry* 1431).

In order to understand Poe's interest in travel and place, it is necessary to consider the role that travel played in antebellum American literary culture. American travel writing in its earliest years was largely a part of British travel writing; for example, the man who is often considered the first major American travel writer, John Ledyard, became famous for his narratives of his travels with the British captain James Cook (Ziff 20). American travel writing began to develop its own identity in the two decades preceding Poe's birth. First, the 1790s American war with the Barbary Pirates meant that narratives of captivity in North Africa, both nonfictional and fictional, became particularly popular and resonant. Newspapers such as the *Philadelphia Minerva* regularly reported on American sailors taken captive by the Barbary Pirates, and before long numerous allegedly factual captivity narratives were appearing in print in the new republic.

It was in this atmosphere that American writers of fiction began to engage with the possibilities of fictionalized travel narratives. Royall Tyler, for example, wrote a picaresque novel, *The Algerine Captive* (1797), that satirized the foibles of early American society, inquired into the religious controversies between Christianity and Islam, and attacked the practice of slavery in the United States by using the captivity of white Americans in North Africa as a foil. The two writers Poe reviewed and who are discussed in this essay, Washington Irving and John Lloyd Stephens, both participated in the tradition of American writing about the Near East that the Barbary captivity narratives initiated. Irving, early America's most famous man of letters, researched and wrote widely about Muslim cultures around the Mediterranean and even went so far as to attempt a lengthy biography of the Prophet Muḥammad. Stephens, meanwhile, combined wide reading about the Near East with a personal voyage to the Holy Land.

Stephens and Irving thus participated in nineteenth-century Orientalism—the tradition of Western European and North American writing about the Near East that Edward Said criticizes for its imperialist proclivities in his influential study *Orientalism*. Said argues that the voluminous European writing about the Near East from the nineteenth century tended to reflect the imperial interests of European powers and to represent the Near East as a cultural "Other" against which European civilization could define itself. By inserting themselves into the very substantial European tradition of writing about the Near East, Irving and Stephens created works that can now be seen as American counterparts to the tradition critiqued by Said. These works also raise the question of the degree to which Said's analysis of British and French texts from the nineteenth century applies to nineteenth-century American works, and the degree to which American writers such as Irving and Stephens can be distinguished from their British and French contemporaries.

Literary culture in the nineteenth century was not bound by national literatures in any case, and, as a result, Poe's influences in choosing travel and the exotic as backdrops for his poetry were not simply American. One of Poe's literary heroes, particularly early in his career, was the great British Romantic poet George Gordon, Lord Byron, who had become famous in part by writing the verse travelogue *Childe Harold's Pilgrimage* and even parodied the genre of the verse travelogue in *Don Juan*, which is perhaps his most enduring work. Another of Poe's major influences, particularly in regard to his theory of art, was another of the great British Romantic poets, who was also an important theoretician on the nature of art, Samuel Taylor Coleridge. Coleridge used the idea of travel and the exotic most spectacularly in poems such as *The Rime of the Ancient Mariner* and "Kubla Khan." If Poe drew on Washington Irving and John Lloyd Stephens in finding travel to be a legitimate subject for fiction and literary essays, he found particular justification in the works of Byron and Coleridge for making the invocation of exotic locales a staple of his poetry. The nature of Poe's poetry of the exotic becomes clearest, however, when it is considered in relation to his incisive reviews of Stephens and Irving.

Poe reviewed Stephens's narrative, the first of a long series of American travel narratives about the Near East to gain widespread popularity,[1] in *The New York Review* in the year of its publication. The narrative was distinguished both by Stephens's respectful curiosity about the various Muslim, Jewish, and Eastern Orthodox Christian cultures he encountered and by Stephens's effort to build a vigorous, "masculine" persona that would make him seem the perfect guide for a difficult and dangerous journey through unfamiliar lands. Poe's extended response to Stephens's work is instructive. He begins by noting Stephens's "fresh manliness of feeling" (*Selected Writings* 936), in an evident nod to Stephens's carefully crafted masculine persona, but he largely evades a discussion of Stephens's more concrete observations of the lands through which he traveled. Rather, Poe focuses on the spiritual associations of Stephens's journey, and particularly on Stephens's convoluted discussion of whether or not he had transgressed a biblical curse by traveling through the land of Edom, a region south of the Dead Sea in what is now Israel. Poe's extended treatment of this question does not bear revisiting in this context, but it is noteworthy that Poe focuses specifically on the inward, spiritual meaning of Stephens's journey rather than on his concrete, outward travels.

Poe demonstrates a similarly otherworldly instinct in relation to place in his 1835 review of Washington Irving's *The Crayon Miscellany* for the *Southern Literary Messenger.* The part of *The Crayon Miscellany* that Poe reviewed, "Legends of the Conquest of Spain," in contrast to Stephens's nonfictional account of a single voyage to the Near East, is a collection of accounts of Spanish life under Muslim rule for which Irving does not claim absolute veracity. In a reflection on Irving's work, Poe observes:

> We feel it almost an act of supererogation to speak of this book, which is long since in the hands of every American who has leisure for reading at all. The matter itself is deeply interesting, but, as usual, its chief beauty is beauty of style. The Conquest of Spain by the Saracens, an event momentous in the extreme, is yet enveloped, as regards the motives and actions of the principal *dramatis personae*, in triple doubt and confusion. To snatch from this uncertainty a few striking and picturesque legends, possessing, at the same time, some absolute portion of verity, and to adorn them in his own magical language is all that Mr. Irving has done in this present instance. But that he has done this little well is needless to say. (*Selected Writings* 614)

Poe's description of Irving's method is quite close to the principles he outlines in poetic manifestoes such as "Letter to B——" and "The Poetic Principle." In these pieces Poe argues that poetry's prime allegiances are to beauty and pleasure rather than to truth and duty. Central to this argument is the idea that the music of poetic language is the defining trait of poetry. As he succinctly puts it in "The Poetic Principle":

I would define, in brief, the Poetry of words as *The Rhythmical Creation of Beauty*. Its sole arbiter is Taste. With the Intellect or with the Conscience, it has only collateral relations. Unless incidentally, it has no concern whatever either with Duty or with Truth. (*Poetry* 1438)

Poe's argument here that, for a poet, the creation of beauty through sound is more important than conceptual content dovetails nicely with his remarks on travel writers such as Stephens and Irving. As his attention to the spiritual aspects of Stephens's journey indicates, Poe is interested in place insofar as its evocation elicits a psychological response from his reader. Further, like Irving's, Poe's evocations of place depend on a mix of scant factual detail and possibly spurious picturesque associations, all of which are transformed and given meaning by Poe's own "magical language."

Poe's first volume of poetry, as its title indicates, highlights travel and the exotic on a grand scale. *Tamerlane, and Other Poems* (1827) takes as its muse the great medieval Mongol conqueror Timur (known as Tamerlane in Europe), and in its title poem offers a Byronic account of both Tamerlane's earthly conquests and his inner journey toward self-knowledge. This volume must be regarded primarily as juvenilia, since Poe published it as a teenager and in the preface claims that the poems were composed when he was thirteen years old. Nonetheless, Poe established some patterns in this collection that would hold good for much of his later work. In one of the more brief poems from *Tamerlane*, "O, Tempora! O, Mores!" Poe seeks to present himself as a world-weary traveler on the Byronic model:

> Of all the cities—and I've seen no few;
> For I have traveled, friend, as well as you—
> I don't remember one, upon my soul,
> But take it generally upon the whole.
>
> (41-44)

---

Poe's lines here are both an exaggeration of his experience and a useful reminder that his life was shaped by early experiences of travel. Born in Boston, raised in Virginia, and educated in part in England, Poe could reasonably claim to be a young man who was at the least well on his way to seeing the world. Nonetheless, the lines almost certainly represent a pose more than a factual comment on Poe's still-modest travels. The lines' primary thought is the tendency of travel to blur together distinct places and cultures. The abstract concept of the unfamiliar and new becomes more important than any concrete details—a tendency that also appears frequently in Poe's more poetic short stories, such as "Ligeia" and "The Fall of the House of Usher." This tendency to blur boundaries of time, place, and culture also appears in the title poem from the collection, "Tamerlane," in which the speaker, Tamerlane himself, is shown making his confession to a priest, despite the fact that the historical Tamerlane was Muslim. Like Poe's speaker in "O, Tempora! O, Mores!" (who seems closely identified with the poet himself) this Tamerlane is more strongly defined by the abstract concept of a movement out into the world of experience than by the concrete details associated with the actual historical figure. It is the glamour of Tamerlane's name and of the places associated with him, like Samarkand, not the historical truth, that contribute to the "elevat[ion] of the soul" that Poe claims to seek to elicit from his readers.

Perhaps the best illustrations of Poe's blending of the factual voyages appearing in his reviews and essays into his own poetic journeys of the imagination are his early poems that, like the travel-writing traditions in which Stephens and Irving participate, invoke the Muslim Near East. "Al Aaraaf" (1829), perhaps the earliest of Poe's poems to show a truly distinctive voice, considerably extends the interest in the wider world evident in "Tamerlane." "Al Aaraaf" is a complex narrative poem that comprises both a philosophical dialogue between God and disembodied spirits associated with artistic creation and a love story that culminates in the destruction of the lovers because of the intensity of their emotions. It is set both in outer space and in the spiritual world of the afterlife as depicted in the Koran, the central sacred text of Islam. The poem is both global and cosmic in its range of references: it uses imagery associated with Islam, particularly incorporating images from George Sale's introductory notes to his 1734 translation of the Koran, to give itself a global dimension in relation to human culture, and it uses, improbably, the idea of life in outer space to extend itself beyond the sublunary sphere of Earth. Tracking the otherworldly locales alluded to in the poem, one finds the entire circuit of the Mediterranean—from Turkey and Greece to the south of France, North Africa, and Palestine—as well as lands farther afield, such as Persia and India.

On a metaphysical and cosmic level, "Al Aaraaf" moves back and forth between the Muslim idea of a middle ground between Earth and Heaven—analogous to the Christian Purgatory but distinct because, in Poe's version, it leads not to ultimate purification but to annihilation—and the idea of a fading supernova, observed by Danish astronomer Tycho Brahe in 1572 (see Poe's note, *Poetry* 38), that provides a temporary home where true poetry can be realized. The two locations are identified with each other in the poem, but they can also be clearly seen as different places. Poe makes both the spiritual location associated with the Koran and the cosmic location associated with Tycho Brahe's supernova metaphors for the elusive, indefinable power of art. Poe's "Al Aaraaf" is characterized particularly by the presence of extremes of pleasure, including the intoxicating pleasure of grief. These emotional experiences, Poe explains in a footnote, are the source of the ultimate annihilation of the souls in Al Aaraaf. The pleasures of Al Aaraaf, which are attenuated precisely by their intensity, are comparable to the escapist experiences afforded by poetry, which are derived from the distance between what a poem can suggest and what it can ultimately assert in concrete terms. In "Al Aaraaf," then, specificities of place serve to stimulate the poem's language and are ultimately overwhelmed by the poetic power of the imaginative tropes they call up.

Poe's 1831 poem "Israfel" offers a more concise version of the theory of poetic emotion and creation presented in "Al Aaraaf," and, as its presence in numerous anthologies indicates, it is among the most resonant of Poe's poems. "Israfel" contrasts the title character, an angel who is able to sing with immeasurable beauty because of his position as an immaterial creature living among the stars, with the speaker, an earthbound human being who will never be able to match the transcendent beauty of the angel's song because of the constraints of mortality. As with "Al Aaraaf," Poe combines Koranic references with those from other sources to create his own interpretive overlay of the figure of the Islamic angel Israfel. As scholar Arthur Hobson Quinn points out in his 1941 biography of Poe, Sale's "Preliminary Discourse on the Koran" identifies Israfel as the angel who will "sound the trumpet at the resurrection" (180). Quinn also notes that the central conceit of the poem, that Israfel's heartstrings are a lute, is derived not from the Koran but from the poetry of one of Poe's contemporaries, Thomas Moore (180).

Further, the conceptual structure of "Israfel" overlays Islamic cosmology with Poe's poetic intent of "elevating the soul," making use of place and the exotic in several important ways. First, Israfel's status as a Koranic angel means that Poe can invoke the early-nineteenth-century Near East in a particularly rich manner. Early-nineteenth-century Americans writing about the Near East tended to emphasize the region's imaginative possibilities, with its non-Christian religious tradition and non-Western artistic and literary traditions. By making his ideal poet a Muslim angel, and thus associated with a religious tradition both closely related to Christianity as a monotheistic religion and distinct from Christianity in its historical and cultural development, Poe is able to capitalize on these imaginative possibilities by spiritualizing art and emphasizing the element of the uncanny (the simultaneously familiar and strange) in artistic production. And by associating Israfel with the cosmic, he can re-create the ideal world of beauty and art of "Al-Aaraaf" as he simultaneously dramatizes his own predicament as a literary artist who, unlike Israfel, cannot escape the confines of earthly place and therefore cannot sing so "wildly well" as the disembodied spirit (48). As with "Tamerlane" and "Al Aaraaf," it is the capacity of Poe's language to create beauty that transfigures the sparse but essential geographical associations of the poem.

Another of Poe's poems with Near Eastern associations, "The City in the Sea," depends particularly on an exotic sense of place, and it is a measure of the degree of mystery associated with Poe's city that scholars have never been able to agree with certainty on its location. Thomas Ollive Mabbott argued confidently in 1945 that the city is the biblical city of Gomorrah, which the author of Genesis locates near the Dead Sea, and G. R. Thompson seconds this identification in the 2004 Norton Critical Edition of *The Selected Writings of Edgar Allan Poe*. On the other hand, Dwayne Thorpe, following Killis Campbell, argued with equal aplomb in 1979 that the location must be Babylon as it is imagined in the biblical book of Revelation (395). However one resolves the dispute over the city's identification, what is clear is that in his descriptions of it Poe again mixes a series of physical details that seem evocative of a specific place, only to retreat to a spiritualized understanding of the city that leaves its specific location uncertain. What matters here, as in Poe's review of Washington Irving, is the felicity of Poe's style, the magic of his language, which leaves readers tantalized by the mix of strangeness and familiarity in the poem's hellish cityscape.

But what of Poe's many poems that largely exist in clearly imaginary locations? What, for example, of "Dream-Land" or "Ulalume"? The title of the former clearly suggests that the poem is primarily set in a mental landscape, but this landscape is also dependent in part on more particular geographical associations. Of particular import is Poe's invocation in line 6 of the "ultimate dim Thule." While, in the context of the poem, this line refers to the state one enters into immediately prior to dreaming, it gains much of its metaphoric force from its long association, beginning with ancient Greek geography and lasting through the nineteenth century, with the Arctic regions north of Britain.

"Ulalume" provides a particularly compelling example of how the concept of travel resonates in Poe's work, even (and perhaps especially) when he is writing at a remove from any easily recognizable map of the world. The sets of coordinates that Poe provides to locate this poem are on the one hand polar—Yaanek has been identified with the Antarctic volcano Mount Erebus (Wolosky 260)—and on the other hand artistic—the "dank tarn of Auber" has been seen as referring to the French composer Daniel François Esprit Auber (Mabbott, "'Ulalume'" 57) and the "the misty mid-region of Weir" to the American Hudson River school painter Robert Walter Weir (Leary 25).[2] By locating the poem in this way, Poe conjures up not only the forbidding aspects of the polar regions for his readers but also the imagined fairyland of Auber's operas and woodlands and of Weir's imagined New York countryside. The poem thus has as one of its themes a meditation on the capacity of language itself to create a sense of place.

Poe's late poem "Eldorado" provides a more compressed example of conflation of multiple exotic landscapes to create a specific effect. The term "Eldorado" refers, of course, to a mythical site of great wealth in South America, and Burton R. Pollin has linked Poe's reference to South America to his sardonic response to the California gold rush of the 1840s (12), a linkage G. R. Thompson endorses in the Norton Critical Edition of Poe's selected works. Despite the brevity of the poem, however, Poe's geographical references once again strain toward both the global and the cosmic. The poem begins with a "gallant knight" (2) who eventually inquires of a "pilgrim shadow" the way to Eldorado (15). The stranger directs the knight on an oddly circuitous route:

> "Over the Mountains of the Moon,
> Down the Valley of the Shadow
> Ride, boldly ride"
> the shade replied,
> "If you seek for Eldorado."
>
> (19-24)

These lines capture with remarkable compression Poe's blending of the terrestrial exotic, the cosmic, and the spiritual. The Mountains of the Moon can be read as either a place that Poe had reason to believe might actually exist (although its existence was conclusively demonstrated only after his death), the rumored mountain range at the source of the Nile, or mountains on the moon itself, or both. And the Valley of the Shadow can be linked to the valley of the shadow of death in the Bible's Twenty-third Psalm. Even in this rather slight poem, Poe finds travel to be a rich source of metaphor.

We might consider a still further question. Can Poe's expansive geographical vision be useful to an understanding of even his most famous poem, "The Raven"? At first glance, the answer would appear to be a resounding no. After all, "The Raven" takes place entirely within the confines of the narrator's chamber, and the end of the poem strongly hints that the speaker will never leave his chamber again. Characteristically for Poe, however, "The Raven" is far from being bereft of references to the wider world. As G. R. Thompson's copious notes to "The Raven" in the Norton Critical Edition of *The Selected Writings of Edgar Allan Poe* illustrate, ravens have been associated with mythical Scandinavian, Greek, and Roman figures, and Poe reinforces these geographical connections by referencing the Roman god of death and the underworld with the phrase "the Night's Plutonian shore" (47) and the Greek goddess of wisdom and war with the "bust of Pallas" (41). Moreover, the narrator's plaintive query "Is there—*is* there balm in Gilead?" (89) calls up associations with the Bible and with the Holy Land narratives of John Lloyd Stephens and others that were so popular in the mid-nineteenth century. Finally, the reference to "some distant Aidenn" (92) in the antepenultimate stanza has the effect of combining Jewish and Christian associations with the Garden of Eden with the exotic associations many nineteenth-century Americans had with Arabia and Islam. This mingling of northern European, Mediterranean, and Near Eastern images is, as we have seen, quite characteristic of Poe's poetry. It is also characteristic of some of his most striking short stories, including "Ligeia," and is thus a strand that connects his poetry with his broader body of published work.

What appears through this rapid survey of Poe's poetic career is that although Poe's use of place seems maddeningly vague—"Out of Space—Out of Time," to use his own phrase from "Dream-Land" (8)—it is also utterly dependent on the very particular associations that nineteenth-century readers had with specific places. There is thus an aura of specificity about Poe's use of place that grows out of his wide reading and curiosity about a range of exotic and, for an often impoverished nineteenth-century American writer, unreachable locales. Without this aura of exotic specificity, Poe's poetry would dissolve into abstraction. Because of the ambiance the specific places add, however, Poe's work has the capacity to haunt its readers and to evoke from them a sense of wonder, an accomplishment that would be impossible without the grand sweep of the poet's geographical imagination.

Understanding the use of exoticism in Poe's poetry can also inform our critical understanding of the wider significance of Poe's body of work. For some modern-day critics, Poe's penchant for the exotic can take on sinister overtones, particularly when Said's critique of Western Orientalism is taken into account. John Carlos Rowe, for example, has described Poe as a "carny barker for the Empire" (25) because of the global expansiveness of his vision in *Eureka* and the work's dedication to the famous German explorer of Latin America, Alexander von Humboldt. I would suggest, however, that a global vision is not imperialist by default. Although it would be difficult and somewhat anachronistic to argue that Poe embraces a Mark Twain-style anti-imperialist ethos, it seems unnecessary (and perhaps even more anachronistic) to assume that Poe's eclectic use of European, Near Eastern, Latin American, Asian, and African sources constitutes an expression of a political will to dominance. Put simply, tropes are not natural resources, and the sort of zero-sum game that applies in relation to gold, silver, and hydrocarbons is less applicable to cultural transactions. Poe's invocations of the diversity of the world's cultural and artistic traditions serve not to subordinate non-European traditions to European norms, as in imperialist works, but rather to relativize the position of European norms in relation to the broader field of human culture and aspiration. To assume that the invocation of non-European traditions is necessarily in the service of an imperial ethos is, paradoxically, to diminish the power and resonance of those very traditions.

Indeed, the international reception of Poe's poetry over the past century and a half suggests that Poe's embrace of the wider world is frequently and enthusiastically returned. The long-standing devotion to Poe among the French Symbolist poets (who themselves exercised influence on noted Poe denigrator T. S. Eliot) is well known, as are Fyodor Dostoevski's admiration for Poe's psychological fiction and Vladimir Nabokov's invocations of Poe in novels such as *Lolita*. Less well known is Poe's prominence outside of Europe and anglophone North America, which does not end with his adoption by Jorge Luis Borges, Argentina's canonical experimental poet and fiction writer. Regard for Poe's work extends even to Mexico City, where a street is named for him.

Nor is Poe's international appeal limited to the Americas and Europe. The late Sri Lankan intellectual Regi Siriwardena titled one of his works from the 1990s *The Lost Lenore*—a clear reference to "The Raven." A postcolonial novel written and published in Sri Lanka, for Sri Lankans, and dealing with the particular fears and desires of the island's war-torn inhabitants, its title shows that its author, who opposed British colonialism in his native Sri Lanka (then Ceylon) in his youth and continued to be an advocate for human rights throughout his life, found sufficient intellectual and imaginative nourishment in Poe to borrow from his work.

Siriwardena's example should give us pause when we consider the political significance of Poe's poetry. If Poe made use of materials drawn from a substantial range of locations and cultures in his works, he also, by the same gesture, made his own work available to a substantial range of locations and cultures. Poe's yearning for the distant, the surprising, the unusual, and the exotic is a feature of his work that makes it accessible to readers from around the world and ensures that his poetic devices can be reinterpreted by readers with the same gusto that Poe employed in reinterpreting his poetic materials. If the presence of the exotic in Poe's poetry signified for Poe his own efforts to embrace the world, this same presence of the exotic in Poe's work has helped the world, over the past century and a half, to embrace Poe's poetry.

## Notes

1. For an extended discussion of both Stephens's narrative and of the Holy Land travel narrative more generally, see my study *The Romance of the Holy Land in American Travel Writing, 1790-1876*. For briefer considerations of Stephens's place in Holy Land writing, see Hilton Obenzinger's *American Palestine* and Malini Johar Schueller's *U.S. Orientalisms*. Schueller also provides an overview of Orientalist elements in Poe's prose fiction. For a good contextualization of how Americans represented Islam in the nineteenth century, see Timothy Marr's *The Cultural Roots of American Islamicism*.

2. For a reading of "Dream-Land" and "Ulalume" that highlights the significance of the polar regions for both poems, see J. O. Bailey's 1948 essay "The Geography of Poe's 'Dream-Land' and 'Ulalume.'"

## Works Cited

Bailey, J. O. "The Geography of Poe's 'Dream-Land' and 'Ulalume.'" *Studies in Philology* 45.3 (1948): 512-23.

Campbell, Killis. *The Poems of Edgar Allan Poe*. New York: Ginn, 1917.

Leary, Lewis. "Poe's 'Ulalume.'" *Explicator* 6 (Feb. 1948): item 25.

Mabbott, Thomas Ollive. "Poe's 'The City in the Sea.'" *Explicator* 4 (Oct. 1945): item 1.

_____. "Poe's 'Ulalume.'" *Explicator* 6 (June 1948): item 57.

Marr, Timothy. *The Cultural Roots of American Islamicism*. New York: Cambridge UP, 2006.

Obenzinger, Hilton. *American Palestine: Melville, Twain, and the Holy Land Mania*. Princeton, NJ: Princeton UP, 1999.

Poe, Edgar Allan. "Al Aaraaf." *Poetry, Tales, and Selected Essays*. Ed. Patrick Quinn and G. R. Thompson. New York: Library of America, 1984. 38-52.

_____. "Dream-Land." *Poetry, Tales, and Selected Essays*. Ed. Patrick Quinn and G. R. Thompson. New York: Library of America, 1984. 79-80.

_____. "Eldorado." *Poetry, Tales, and Selected Essays*. Ed. Patrick Quinn and G. R. Thompson. New York: Library of America, 1984. 101.

_____. "Israfel." *Poetry, Tales, and Selected Essays*. Ed. Patrick Quinn and G. R. Thompson. New York: Library of America, 1984. 62-64.

_____. "O, Tempora! O, Mores!" *Poetry, Tales, and Selected Essays*. Ed. Patrick Quinn and G. R. Thompson. New York: Library of America, 1984. 21-23.

_____. *Poetry, Tales, and Selected Essays*. Ed. Patrick Quinn and G. R. Thompson. New York: Library of America, 1984.

_____. "The Raven." *Poetry, Tales, and Selected Essays*. Ed. Patrick Quinn and G. R. Thompson. New York: Library of America, 1984. 81-86.

_____. *The Selected Writings of Edgar Allan Poe: A Norton Critical Edition*. Ed. G. R. Thompson. New York: W. W. Norton, 2004.

_____. "Tamerlane." *Poetry, Tales, and Selected Essays*. Ed. Patrick Quinn and G. R. Thompson. New York: Library of America, 1984. 24-31.

_____. "Ulalume." *Poetry, Tales, and Selected Essays*. Ed. Patrick Quinn and G. R. Thompson. New York: Library of America, 1984. 89-91.

Pollin, Burton R. "Poe's 'Von Kempelen and his Discovery': Sources and Significance." *Études anglaises* 20.1 (1967): 12-23.

Quinn, Arthur Hobson. *Edgar Allan Poe: A Biography*. New York: D. Appleton-Century, 1941.

Rowe, John Carlos. "Space, the Final Frontier: Poe's *Eureka* as Imperial Fantasy." *Poe Studies/Dark Romanticism* 39.1-2 (2006-2007): 19-27.

Said, Edward. *Orientalism*. New York: Vintage, 1979.

Schueller, Malini Johar. *U.S. Orientalisms: Race, Nation, and Literature, 1790-1890*. Ann Arbor: U of Michigan P, 1998.

Siriwardena, Regi. *The Lost Lenore*. Colombo, Sri Lanka: Author, 1996.

Thorpe, Dwayne. "Poe's 'The City in the Sea': Source and Interpretation." *American Literature* 51.3 (1979): 394-99.

Wolosky, Shira. "Poetry and Public Discourse, 1820-1910." *The Cambridge History of American Literature*, vol. 4, *Nineteenth-Century Poetry, 1800-1910*. Ed. Sacvan Bercovitch and Cyrus R. K. Patell. New York: Cambridge UP, 2004.

Yothers, Brian. *The Romance of the Holy Land in American Travel Writing, 1790-1876*. Aldershot, England: Ashgate, 2007.

Ziff, Larzer. *Return Passages: Great American Travel Writing, 1780-1910*. New Haven, CT: Yale UP, 2000.

# Repetition and Remembrance in Poe's Poetry_____

Jeffrey Scraba

Of the many controversial statements made by Edgar Allan Poe during his career, perhaps none is more notorious than his claim that "the death . . . of a beautiful woman is, unquestionably, the most poetical topic in the world" ("Philosophy" 19). Taken together with the morbid content of many of his poems and stories, Poe's stated preoccupation with dead and lovely women has encouraged many of his readers to see his work as pathological. For example, in his recent biography of Poe, Peter Ackroyd maintains that "in his art and in his life, [Poe] fell in love with dying women" (144). Poe was an alcoholic, a drug addict, a manic-depressive, a misogynist, and/or a troubled orphan, so these interpretations go, and therefore his works reflect his diseased mind. As Eliza Richards observes, "The recurrent centrality of women in Poe's poetry, particularly dead women, is often considered a product and a sign of a psyche shattered by the repeated early loss of significant female figures" (30). As Richards also argues, however, this view of Poe obscures the fact that "some of the seemingly more peculiar traits of Poe's poetry are variations on conventional themes in nineteenth-century poetry, particularly in the poetry of women" (31). What looks like strangeness to us, especially in Poe's representations of dead women, would look familiar to readers in Poe's day. Perhaps less conventional in Poe's poetry is his fascination with the mind of the mourner. As Poe also explains in the same essay, the "lips best suited for" depicting a beautiful woman's death "are those of a bereaved lover" ("Philosophy" 19). In other words, Poe is not primarily interested in the dead woman but in the experience of the "lover lamenting his deceased mistress" (19).

Poe wrote "The Philosophy of Composition," which was published in *Graham's Magazine* in 1846, supposedly to explain how he put together his most famous poem, "The Raven." Readers have since had difficulty interpreting what Poe meant when he wrote that he composed the poem with, as he claims, "the precision and rigid consequence of a mathematical problem": the essay has been taken as everything from a straightforward account of Poe's poetics to an attempt to quiet his turbulent subconscious to one of his many hoaxes (or as some combination of these aims). However seriously we take Poe's claims in "The Philosophy of Composition," the essay clearly demonstrates the author's meticulous attention to detail and craft in his poems. The essay also stresses that Poe constructed his poetry to produce a certain effect on the reader's mind; as Rachel Polonsky puts it, "Every creative choice the poet makes is made 'for effect,' rather than to satisfy some transcendent inner compulsion of his enraptured soul" (51). As with "The Raven," the "effect" Poe hopes to produce in much of his poetry is an association of the reader's mind with the speaker's: he wants his readers to understand the thought processes of the fictional characters who speak the words of his poems.

These thought processes, as Poe's interest in mourning demonstrates, often involve the possibilities and problems of memory. Many of Poe's most important poems, like "The Raven," have to do with the memory of loss. His poetry recurrently represents the imagined repetition of a painful experience. For Poe, the emotions connected with such recollection and repetition are constitutive of the highest aesthetic experience: "Beauty of whatever kind, in its supreme development, invariably excites the sensitive soul to tears. Melancholy is thus the most legitimate of all the poetical tones" ("Philosophy" 17). Melancholy is the state ideally shared by the speakers in and readers of much of Poe's poetry. This feeling is generated through the conflicts involved in recollecting something lost—such as that infamous beautiful woman—in the past: one wants to overcome the pain involved in losing something one values, yet one wants to preserve the memory of the lost object. As Sigmund Freud explains the conflicts of mourning (for a loved one or for a loved abstraction such as freedom): "Reality-testing has shown that the loved object no longer exists, and it proceeds to demand that all libido shall be withdrawn from its attachments to that object. This demand arouses understandable opposition" ("Mourning" 253). While the rational mind can acknowledge the loss of the loved one, the unconscious tries to keep the loved one alive. As we shall see, this tension between withdrawal and attachment structures many of Poe's most famous poems.

Poems such as "Tamerlane," "The Raven," "Ulalume," and "Annabel Lee" also develop a closely related duality of memory. As Paul Ricoeur observes, memory is both a *praxis* and a *pathos*, or both constructive and affective. In other words, memory can be considered as an activity (the techniques of searching for and representing something that has happened in the past) or as an experience (the emotions that accompany the act of remembering). Just as memory can oscillate between rational withdrawal and passionate attachment, so it can fluctuate between the analysis of the past and the affective connection to it. We can see this process of remembrance, of repeating something that one has already lived through, as the effort to place something properly in the past and look toward the future. This process is most clearly evident in the mourner's efforts to accept the death of a loved one. In Ricoeur's view, memory is defined by the "temporal mark of the before": memory works only when one recognizes that the event one is recalling has happened in the past (58). When one fails to recognize the "before" of an event, when something from the past seems like something from the present, memory fails in its function. Poe is compelled by such failures in his poetry. The "death" of a beautiful woman remains an event suspended in a perpetual present: the lover does not reach the point of "remembering" his beloved as someone who lived in the past. In Poe's poems, such failures of memory are often signaled by repetition—of content, of action, of sound, of rhythm, of theme. George Santayana's famous aphorism holds that "those who cannot remember the past are condemned to repeat it"; Poe's poetry, we might say, dramatizes this play between remembrance and repetition.

---

## "Tamerlane": Memory as Nostalgia

Poe's first significant poem, "Tamerlane," appeared in his first collection of poetry in 1827. Though published when Poe was only eighteen (and likely written several years earlier),[1] "Tamerlane" displays many of Poe's lifelong poetic concerns: the psychology of loss, the problems of memory, and the compulsion to repeat the past. Unusually for Poe, "Tamerlane" takes the form of a dramatic monologue, in which the Asian emperor of the title makes a deathbed speech to a priest. Because Poe has placed the words of the poem in the mouth of a historical figure, it is easier for us to understand that Poe is not simply expressing his own pain brought on by the loss of women in his life but rather is exploring the ways in which people think about and deal with their pasts.

In his speech to the priest, Tamerlane makes a strange sort of confession. He refuses to repent of his sin of "[u]nearthly pride," but he does admit to "the secret of a spirit/ Bow'd from its wild pride into shame": his "craving heart" mourns for "the lost flowers/ And sunshine of [his] summer hours" (5, 13-14, 21-22).[2] What troubles Tamerlane as he approaches death are recollections of the "lost flowers" of his past. He is ashamed of these memories—he sees his yearning to relive his younger years as a sign of weakness—but he cannot avoid such reminiscences, since the memories of his youth insistently intrude themselves into his consciousness, like a death knell:

> The undying voice of that dead time,
> With its interminable chime,
> Rings, in the spirit of a spell,
> Upon thy emptiness—a knell.
>
> (23-26)

In Tamerlane's perception, he is not actively trying to recollect his past, but he is passively experiencing that past as repeated bell chimes.

As memory can be either active or passive, so the past can be remembered as remote or experienced as immediate: a memory may seem like something that occurred a long time ago, or it may seem like something that one is living through again. This duality of memory is captured in Tamerlane's paradoxical description of "[t]he undying voice of that dead time": the past is both alive to him (an "undying voice") and impossible to recapture (a "dead time"). While this paradox (as we shall see) structures many of Poe's most celebrated poems, in "Tamerlane" the duality of memory takes the particular form of nostalgia. As Svetlana Boym defines it, "Nostalgia (from *nostos*—return home, and *algia*—longing) is a longing for a home that no longer exists or has never existed. Nostalgia is a sentiment of loss and displacement, but it is also a romance with one's own fantasy" (xiii). Tamerlane keeps the fantasy of his childhood home alive, but at the price of losing that home forever; his nostalgia makes his home both undying and dead.

When Tamerlane describes his youth to the priest, he explains that his wild upbringing nurtured his martial ambitions. Though he boasts of the "proud spirit" and "kingly mind" developed in his youth, Tamerlane ironically misses the woman who "E'en *then* . . . knew this iron heart/ In woman's weakness had a part" (33, 32, 73-74). Nearing the end of his life, having realized all his ambitions for power, Tamerlane finds his thoughts turning to the love of his youth. He seems both to revere and to resent her for revealing his "woman's weakness." Yet his memories of her are fleeting:

> Nor would I now attempt to trace
> The more than beauty of a face
> Whose lineaments, upon my mind,
> Are—shadows on th' unstable wind
> (77-80)

While the passive memory of the "undying voice" makes Tamerlane keep returning to this dead and beautiful woman, his active recollection fails him: the images of his love and of his home are fantasized through his melancholy reflections as he nears his own death. While he tries to re-create his time with his young lover, Tamerlane realizes that he has "no words—alas!—to tell/ The loveliness of loving well" (75-76). His failures of memory are, for him, akin to misreading:

> Thus I remember having dwelt
> Some page of early lore upon,
> With loitering eye, till I have felt
> The letters—with their meaning—melt
> To fantasies—with none.
>
> (81-85)

Tamerlane suggests that the truth of his past is there to be read, like words on a page, but his mind "loiters." The "meaning" of his youth has become a fantasy, and the repetitions of nostalgia erode, rather than strengthen, his understanding of the past.

As Tamerlane slowly recognizes, the worst distortion of his memory has been to confuse ambition with love, to think that he wanted to conquer the world for the sake of his beloved: "And so, confusedly, became/ Thine image and—a name—a name!/ Two separate—yet most intimate things" (120-21). When he has gained his "name" through military conquest, the fallacy of confusing the image of his lover with fame becomes clear. Tamerlane recalls the moment after he reached his highest aspirations, when his hope turned from ambition to love:

> When Hope, the eagle that tower'd, could see
> No cliff beyond him in the sky,
> His pinions were bent droopingly—
> And homeward turn'd his soften'd eye.
>
> (187-90)

As he arrived back in his native village, however, he realized that his beloved was dead, and that he could no longer return: "I reach'd my home—my home no more—/ For all had flown who made it so" (213-14). The "undying voice" of his early love, misremembered and misunderstood as he conducted his military campaigns, is betrayed by his "dead" home.

For Tamerlane, the moral of this deathbed recollection is contained in the closing lines:

> How was it that Ambition crept,
> Unseen, amid the revels there,
> Till growing bold, he laughed and leapt
> In the tangles of Love's very hair?
> (240-43)

In his preface to the 1827 collection, Poe maintains that "Tamerlane" was designed to "expose the folly of even *risking* the best feelings of the heart at the shrine of Ambition" (*Poetry* 9). Since this poem is the first major effort of a very ambitious young writer, Poe's assertion should be taken with a grain of salt. What Tamerlane's confession does reveal is the ways in which remembrance can falsify and idealize the past. As Boym argues, nostalgia is a failure of memory in that it tries to destroy time: "The nostalgic desires to obliterate history and turn it into private or collective mythology, to revisit time like space" (xv). By repeating his return home, trying to revisit the past as space, Tamerlane illustrates the process of retelling through which memory becomes nostalgia.

## "The Raven": Memory as Interpretation

Though Poe published "Tamerlane" in each of his first three volumes of poetry (in 1827, 1829, and 1831), it was never a popular or critical success. When Poe failed to launch his career through collections of his poetry, he turned to the periodical press; beginning in the early 1830s, he made his living largely through contributions to and editorships of magazines. His poems and stories were constructed on particular aesthetic principles, but they were also designed to be successful in the ephemeral periodicals of the 1830s and 1840s, under the conditions of what Meredith McGill has called "the culture of reprinting."[3] It might be claimed, in fact, that Poe's inveterate recycling of material for various publications constitutes another exploration of the problems and possibilities of memory: Poe desperately desired lasting fame as a writer, but he was obliged to publish most of his work in magazines that were quickly forgotten. The reprinting of his work was a kind of repetition by which he meant to secure his place in cultural memory. Because Poe was more successful at placing tales and reviews in periodicals, he largely abandoned poetry following the publication of the 1831 volume. His greatest literary triumph, however, the work that did in fact ensure his lasting reputation, came with "The Raven," a poem he explicitly wrote to achieve popular success, or, as he put it in a May 4, 1845, letter to Frederick William Thomas, "for the express purpose of running" (qtd. in Thomas and Jackson 531). As Kenneth Silverman notes, "The reception of 'The Raven' might be compared to that of some uproariously successful hit song today" (237). That "The Raven" was by far the most popular poem in America in 1845 again illustrates that its dramatic situation—the bereaved lover lamenting his dead and beautiful beloved—was by no means bizarre to contemporary readers.[4]

The famous opening stanza of "The Raven" establishes many of the key elements of the poem: the speaker's isolation, the burdens of memory, and the repetition that signals the speaker's melancholy. In the very first line of the poem, the internal rhyme of "dreary" and "weary" makes the external world a reflection of the speaker's emotional state: the world has become bleak due to his mental exhaustion. Like Tamerlane, the student who tells the story of the poem "loiters" in his reading: he is trying to remember the "forgotten lore" of his "quaint and curious volume[s]" but finds himself "nearly napping" (2-3). And as Tamerlane's distraction produces his meaningless fantasies, so the action of "The Raven" unfolds like the dream—or nightmare—of the speaker. The intrusions of the external world, as indicated by the second internal rhyme of "napping" and "tapping," will be subsumed into the speaker's reverie. The "tapping" also gives us our first clue to the speaker's obsessive mental state. He repeats his evaluation of this noise three different times: "''Tis some visiter,'" "''[o]nly this,'" and "''nothing more'" (5-6). This uncertain returning to the same simple idea prepares us for the subsequent repetitions that are symptoms of the speaker's failures of memory.

In the second stanza, the source of the speaker's sadness is made apparent. This stanza opens by more clearly specifying the moment of the action: "Once upon a midnight dreary" (which might remind us of the opening of a children's story) has become "distinctly I remember it was in the bleak December" (7). As we will later discover, this is a particular recollection that the speaker is somehow compelled to repeat, and this repetition is closely associated with his lost love, Lenore. The speaker's failure to recollect the "forgotten lore" of his books brings back the pain of her death: "vainly I had sought to borrow/ From my books surcease of sorrow—sorrow for the lost Lenore" (9-10). As the speaker emphasizes, Lenore is "nameless *here* for evermore," meaning that she can no longer be called in this world (12); he is therefore looking both back to her life and forward to his death, when he can once more be with her. This stanza also prepares us for the association between death and haunting in the description of the dwindling fire: "each separate dying ember wrought its ghost upon the floor" (8).

As we discover by the fifth stanza, the speaker's mind is very much occupied with the afterlife of Lenore. Having reassured himself several more times that the tapping is a commonplace "visiter," the speaker opens his door to find only darkness. This incongruity between sound and sight plays upon the speaker's mind, causing him to "[dream] dreams no mortal ever dared to dream before" (26): that Lenore's ghost has come back to him. Of course, the dream of being visited by the ghost of a loved one is a dream that almost every mortal *has* dreamed before; it is easy for the reader to identify with the mournful student. When he tentatively calls out to her in the darkness, the sound is described in the passive voice: "the only word there spoken was the whispered word, 'Lenore?'" (28). We might take the passivity of this action as an indication that the memory of Lenore has overtaken the speaker, so that he begins to lose control of his voice and his thoughts. This whisper is met by an echo from the darkness, which answers his interrogative with an exclamatory: "'Lenore!'" (29). The exclamation point indicates that his imagination has confirmed the supernatural existence of Lenore, setting the stage for the encounter with the Raven.

Even before the Raven makes an appearance, then, we are prepared for the strange encounter by the strange mental state of the speaker. We are also subtly introduced to one of the key elements of the poem—the effect of mourning on time—by the poem's meter. Poe was quite proud of the novelty of his stanza form, which he describes as follows: "The feet employed throughout (trochees) consist of a long syllable followed by a short: the first line of the stanza consists of eight of these feet—the second of seven and a half . . . —the third of eight—the fourth of seven and a half—the fifth the same—the sixth three and a half" ("Philosophy" 21). The effect of the trochaic meter, as one discovers if one reads the poem aloud, is to hurry the reader along: each unstressed syllable encourages the reader to jump ahead to the next stressed syllable:

/ ˘ / ˘ / ˘ / ˘ / ˘ / ˘ / ˘ / ˘
Once up | on a | midnight | dreary, | while I | pondered, | weak and | weary

Further, the unstressed syllables that end the first and third lines of each stanza cause the reader to hurry ahead to the stressed syllables that begin the following lines. The meter of the poem, as it were, pushes the reader on through the series of events that occur in it.

In contrast to the impulsive movement of the trochaic rhythm, the series of rhymes that begin with "lore" and "door" in the second and fourth lines cause the reader to stop and look back. The catalectic second, fourth, and fifth lines of each verse—the lines with "seven and a half" feet—create a natural pause on the final accented syllable, and all of these lines in the poem, along with the final lines in each stanza, rhyme. The key words in this sequence of rhymes, of course, are "Lenore" and "Nevermore": once the rhyme scheme is established, the two ideas of the speaker's dead lover and "never again" converge in the speaker's and the reader's minds. As suggested by the trochaic rhythm, the speaker is being pulled into the future by the natural course of events: he cannot resist time's flow. But, as suggested by the insistent "or" rhyme, the speaker's mind insistently returns to the past through his memories of his lost love and his fear that she is "nevermore." We might say that the speaker's active memory is trying to help him overcome the loss by returning to his studies, and his passive memory keeps thwarting his plans by forcing Lenore into his consciousness. Or we might say that the speaker's rational attempts to withdraw his love from the dead Lenore are meeting with considerable opposition from his unconscious. This conflict is dramatized in the two essential words of the poem: to the speaker's hopeful unconscious question "Lenore?" the rational and terrible answer is "Nevermore."

In "The Philosophy of Composition," Poe explains that he used the word "Nevermore" as a "refrain" in order both to strike a "key-note" and to give the reader the pleasure of "repetition" (17). His innovation in the use of the refrain, according to Poe, was to "produce continuously novel effects, by the variation *of the application* of the *refrain*—the *refrain* itself remaining, for the most part, unvaried" (17). The interest of the poem, in other words, lies in the changing meaning of the repeatedly uttered "Nevermore." We might say that once the Raven has arrived on the scene, "The Raven" develops as a problem of interpreting the bird's only word. As Barbara Johnson maintains, "The plot of 'The Raven' can be read as the story of what happens when the signifier encounters a reader" (46). Of course, the speaker is not just any reader: his interpretive strategies are determined by his memories of loss.

The speaker is at first amused by the Raven and begins to ask him questions in a quizzical tone, beginning with "'Tell me what thy lordly name is on the Night's Plutonian shore!'" (47). While the speaker is surprised to hear the reply "'Nevermore,'" he invests it with emotional meaning: "as if [the Raven's] soul in that one word he did outpour" (56). The speaker thus forms an immediate empathetic bond with the raven, a bond that is represented by his odd idea that the Raven will leave him, as "'Other friends have flown before'" (58). The Raven's reply, as expected, is "'Nevermore.'" By asking the question that will condemn the bird to stay with him always, the speaker thus ironically brings about his own curse. The speaker's first interpretation of the Raven's reply is seemingly sensible: he thinks that the word was "'[c]aught from some unhappy master whom unmerciful Disaster/ Followed fast and followed faster till his songs one burden bore—'" (63-64). The irony is compounded as we realize that the speaker is here describing himself, and the bird and burden (in both senses of "refrain" and "load to carry") will become his own.

The burden of "Nevermore" becomes weightier as the speaker asks ever more important questions that are sure to meet with this same reply. As Poe explains, the speaker "experiences a phrenzied pleasure in so modeling his questions as to receive from the *expected* 'Nevermore' the most delicious because the most intolerable of sorrow" ("Philosophy" 19). While the speaker gradually increases his own torment in the remembrance of his dead lover, part of him still wishes to forget and move on with his life. He begins to hallucinate the arrival of angels who have come to relieve him of his pain: "'Wretch,' I cried, 'thy God hath lent thee—by these angels he hath sent thee/ Respite—respite and nepenthe from thy memories of Lenore'" (81-82). The rational desire to forget the past is sabotaged by the speaker's "phrenzied pleasure": he knows that the Raven will deny him respite by answering "Nevermore." Finally, the speaker dares to ask his most momentous question: "'Tell this soul with sorrow laden if, within the distant Aidenn,/ It shall clasp a sainted maiden whom the angels name Lenore—'" (94-95). Because he knows the answer, we might conjecture that the speaker either loses his faith in eternal life or that he becomes convinced of his own unworthiness to enter heaven. We can be certain, though, that the speaker has magnified his loss so greatly that he will never recover from his separation from Lenore.

The speaker's paralysis of grief is emphasized by his desire to keep the Raven with him. Knowing the bird's inevitable reply, the speaker exhorts the Raven to "'[t]ake thy beak from out my heart, and take thy form from off my door!'" (101). By the end of the poem, the speaker's past-tense recounting of the Raven's arrival has become a perpetually suspended present tense. In the never-ending moment in which the speaker is telling his story, this suspension is signaled by the Raven's immovable presence: "And the Raven, never flitting, still is sitting, *still* is sitting" (103). The repetition of "still" reminds us that the Raven is both "not moving" and "continuously" there. The time of the poem is the no-time of what Poe calls "*Mournful and Never-ending Remembrance*," which is symbolized by the Raven ("Philosophy" 25). The Raven casts a shadow that buries the speaker's soul, and the speaker's napping has led to an endless nightmare:

> And his eyes have all the seeming of a demon's that is
> dreaming,
> And the lamp-light o'er him streaming throws his shadow
> on the floor;
> And my soul from out that shadow that lies floating on the
> floor
> Shall be lifted—nevermore!
>
> (105-8)

The speaker's attempt to "forget"—to remember Lenore successfully so that she properly belongs to the past—has been overmastered by his unconscious desire to keep her alive, a desire that is represented by the dreaming Raven/demon. "Nevermore" encapsulates the speaker's failure of memory in his inability to imagine a future.

## "Ulalume" and "Annabel Lee": Memory as Melancholia

Two of Poe's most celebrated late poems, "Ulalume" and "Annabel Lee," are similar to "The Raven" in their explorations of bereavement. The mourning lovers in these poems, however, exceed the speaker of "The Raven" in their disturbed memories. While the speaker of "The Raven" is at least partially aware of the events that led to his profound sorrow, the speakers of "Ulalume" and "Annabel Lee" are perplexed by their inability to comprehend the past. In his famous essay "Mourning and Melancholia," Freud distinguishes between remembrance, which acts to situate a past experience as properly belonging to the past, and repetition, which emerges from repressed desires and acts to relive the past experience as a new experience in the present. Whether or not we concur with Freud's hypothesis (of which he himself was not entirely convinced) that such repetition demonstrates the desire for an organism to return to an inanimate state (what is often referred to as the "death drive"),[5] we can understand that the repetition of a past event constitutes a failure to comprehend and contextualize the event. Such repetition, for Freud, was a symptom of what he called "melancholia": a malfunction of memory that creates a debilitating attachment to a lost object. (Freud's "melancholia" is thus a pathological version of the profound sadness Poe called "melancholy.") Two key distinctions separate melancholia from mourning, to which it is closely related. First, the lost object in melancholia is not simply a person but is some kind of ideal: the melancholic has made the lost love into an abstract value ("Mourning" 253). Second, in melancholia, the libidinal connection to the lost object is withdrawn into the ego, creating an "*identification* of the ego with the abandoned object": the melancholic internalizes the lost object, making it part of his or her own consciousness ("Mourning" 258). As a result, the melancholic keeps the love alive by incorporating the loved object, but at the price, as we shall see, of continuing to repeat the past.

Like "The Raven," "Ulalume" tells a story that will be constantly retold. And as in "The Raven," the poem begins with the external world reflecting the speaker's mental state: "The skies they were ashen and sober;/ The leaves they were crispéd and sere—/ The leaves they were withering and sere" (1-3). In the third line's echo of the second, an atmosphere laden with death and dying is evoked, and we are subtly introduced to the key idea of recurrence. As the speaker specifies the time (October) and place ("the ghoul-haunted woodland of Weir") of his story, he also explains that it took place in his "most immemorial year" (5). "Immemorial" is an odd word to describe a recollection: it might indicate "ancient beyond memory" (and thus something established in perpetuity) or "unable to be remembered" (and thus something that might be repeated again and again). As we will see, "Ulalume" captures both these senses of forgetfulness.

Once the scene is set, most of "Ulalume" is taken up with a dialogue between the speaker and his soul, which he calls "Psyche." Their dialogue is introduced by an emphasis on the fallibility of memory. The speaker and his Soul share a sickness of mind: "our thoughts they were palsied and sere—/ Our memories were treacherous and sere" (21-22). Not only do these lines introduce an element of unreliability into the poem, but they also reinforce the connection between the external world and the speaker's mind by the repetition of "sere," used earlier to describe the dying landscape. As Richard Kopley and Kevin J. Hayes note, the speaker's forgetfulness "reinforces the difficulty he has distinguishing between external reality and his interior mental state" (201). Though the speaker and his soul *should* remember the place and time of their wandering, they do not:

> . . . we knew not the month was October
> And we marked not the night of the year—
> . . . . . . . . . . . . . . . . . . . . . . . . . . . . . . .
> We noted not the dim lake of Auber,
> (Though once we had journeyed down here)
>                                    (24-27)

Their previous visit to the "ghoul-haunted woodland of Weir," it seems, has become immemorial.

This forgetfulness leads to a brief interlude of hope, a moment of solace such as the speaker of "The Raven" seeks in vain. Near the end of the dying ("senescent") night, the speaker and his soul see the crescent of the rising Venus, which he identifies with Astarte, the Phoenician goddess of fertility. Symbolizing a hope of new love, Astarte compels the speaker to follow the star's beams. The speaker trusts that the goddess has taken pity on him: "'She has seen that the tears are not dry on/ These cheeks where the worm never dies'" (42-43). This is the first indication that the speaker, like the speaker of "The Raven," seeks to forget a lost love in the "'Lethean peace of the skies'" (46). No longer in sympathy with the speaker, Psyche shrinks from the "pallor" of the star in terror, but the speaker "conquer[s]" her "scruples and gloom" just as the two stumble upon the tomb of Ulalume, the speaker's lost love (74). The sight of the tomb kills the speaker's evanescent hope, as he remembers that he buried his beloved exactly a year ago:

> . . . I cried—"It was surely October,
> On *this* very night of last year,
> That I journeyed—I journeyed down here!—
> That I brought a dread burden down here—
> On this night, of all nights of the year,
> Ah, what demon hath tempted me here?"
>
> (85-90)

Finally, the speaker recognizes the place in which he finds himself:

> "Well I know, now, this dim lake of Auber—
> . . . . . . . . . . . . . . . . . . . . . . . . . . . . . . . . .
> Well I know, now, this dank tarn of Auber—
> This ghoul-haunted woodland of Weir."
>
> (91-94)

---

The emphatic repetition of "now" in the speaker's moment of clarity seems to indicate that he has successfully remembered his Ulalume. But the "now" of his realization is a past present, a moment of recollection that belongs to a previous time. The speaker's remembered discovery of the tomb, which merges him with the dying landscape, also echoes the opening lines: "Then my heart it grew ashen and sober/ As the leaves that were crispéd and sere—" (82-83). The circularity of this dying image pattern, as the adjectives "sober" and "sere" describe the forest then the speaker's memories then his heart then the forest again, leads us to think that this journey will be constantly repeated. Moreover, after the horrifying re-realization of Ulalume's death, the speaker and his soul slip back into a state of forgetfulness. Ultimately, they think that the "'woodlandish ghouls'" have "'drawn up the spectre of a planet'" that will help them to forget—and subsequently to rediscover— Ulalume's tomb (96, 101). By the end of the poem, the tomb itself is not a site of revelation but an unnamed horror: the "pitiful" and "merciful" ghouls are trying "'To bar up our way and to ban it/ From the secret which lies in these wolds—/ From the thing that lies hidden in these wolds" (97-100). While the speaker tries properly to remember Ulalume's death and so situate the events of the poem in the past, the poem suggests that he is doomed to repeat this journey again and again. As Eric W. Carlson argues, "The narrative is not an objective retelling of what is done and gone, but an experience of great emotional intensity relived in a dreamlike trance of feeling and realization" (26). "Ulalume" is, in fact, a reliving of the reliving of the event of Ulalume's death: it describes the kind of repetition that is symptomatic of the delusions of melancholia.

Poe's final poem, "Annabel Lee," can be read as a companion piece to "Ulalume."[6] While the speaker in the latter poem is condemned to a cycle of forgetting and remembering his beloved's tomb, the speaker in "Annabel Lee" finds himself perpetually trapped in the tomb of his love. "Ulalume" is subtitled "A Ballad," but "Annabel Lee" is much closer in form to a traditional ballad. Though "Annabel Lee" contains many anapests, the poem is predominantly composed of iambic tetrameter alternating with iambic trimeter: the common meter of thousands of traditional ballads. And, at least in the first half of the poem, "Annabel Lee," like most traditional songs, tells a generic story with which many might identify: the speaker remembers his childhood love who met with a tragic early death. These first three stanzas develop through a kind of fairy-tale past perfect, characterized by vague setting ("In a kingdom by the sea" [2]) and imprecise time ("It was many and many a year ago" [1]). The legendary quality of this section of the poem is typified by Annabel Lee herself, who is never described but "whom you may know/ by the name of Annabel Lee" (102). While "Ulalume" seems largely to take place in the landscape of the speaker's mind, "Annabel Lee" opens in the immemorial realm of songs passed down for many generations.

"Annabel Lee" becomes stranger and more personal in the final few stanzas, however. Rather than acknowledging the natural death of Annabel Lee (who seems to have succumbed to an illness borne by the "chilling" wind), the speaker thinks that some agent has intervened to separate them. He first blames her family, who may have resented him: "her high-born kinsmen came/ And bore her away from me" (17-18). Then he speculates that her death was caused by the angels in Heaven who envied them:

> . . . that was the reason (as all men know,
> In this kingdom by the sea)
> That the wind came out of the cloud, chilling
> And killing my Annabel Lee.
>
> (23-26)

In his insistence that "all men know" about the supernatural reason for Annabel Lee's death, the speaker takes a turn toward the misinterpretations of melancholia: he fails to remember his beloved's death properly. By the concluding stanza of the poem, the speaker, like the speaker of "The Raven," is trapped in an eternal continuous present: "For the moon never beams without bringing me dreams/ Of the beautiful Annabel Lee" (34-35). Unlike the "mournful and never-ending remembrance" experienced by the speaker of "The Raven," however, the speaker of "Annabel Lee" is trapped in a perpetual fantasy of joining his love in her grave:

> And so, all the night-tide, I lie down by the side
> Of my darling, my darling, my life and my bride
> In her sepulchre there by the sea—
> In her tomb by the side of the sea.
>
> (38-41)

Not only does the speaker fail to remember his past properly, but he also cannot live in the present: wherever he is, he is always *there* in the "tomb by the side of the sea." "[M]y Annabel Lee" of the first part of the poem has become "the beautiful Annabel Lee": the speaker has internalized and idealized his lost love, trapping him forever in a sort of "death in life."

## Conclusion: "The Bells"

While "Annabel Lee" was probably the last poem Poe wrote for publication, in the nineteenth century "The Bells" was widely considered to be Poe's final poem.[7] Published about a week after Poe's death, "The Bells" seems a fitting epitaph for his career. The poem's four stanzas describe a sleigh ride, a wedding, a fire, and a funeral. Each stanza ends with the insistent repetition of "the bells, bells, bells, bells/ Bells, bells, bells" (12-13, 33-34, 67-68, 110-11). As with the "Nevermore" of "The Raven," the sound of the bells is heard differently depending on the character of each of the events it concludes. But the funeral bells, which initially provoke "solemn thought" "[a]t the melancholy meaning of the tone" (72, 75), devolve into meaningless sound. The funeral is presided over by a band of fiends who delight in human suffering:

> They are neither man nor woman—
> They are neither brute nor human,
> They are Ghouls:—
> And their king it is who tolls.
>
> (86-89)

In the hands of this king of misrule, the bells, which should give final meaning to human existence and allow mourners to understand the deaths of their loved ones, become a senseless repetition of noise: "Keeping time, time, time,/ As he knells, knells, knells,/ In a happy Runic rhyme,/ To the rolling of the bells" (104-7). In "The Bells," repetition of the memory of loss has a kind of magical incantatory power, but the memory has lost any rational significance.

In the progression of the problems of memory we have traced, "The Bells" seems like a logical conclusion. Throughout his career, Poe was preoccupied with the psychology of loss and the problems of remembrance. From the slightly distorted nostalgia of Tamerlane to Annabel Lee's lover's melancholic fantasy of life in the grave, Poe charts the ways in which people try to remember what they have lost and the patterns of repetition that mark the failure of their remembrances. Tamerlane's ringing "undying voice" has become, in "The Bells," a habitual repetition signifying the meaninglessness of mourning. Looked at another way, these struggles between withdrawal and attachment, or between remembering and reliving the past, describe the existential frustration of the human condition. In "The Poetic Principle," Poe proposes that poetry gives us a glimpse of what lies beyond human limitations, of the transcendent that would release us from human suffering: "When by Poetry . . . we find ourselves melted into tears—we weep then—not . . . through excess of pleasure, but through a certain, petulant, impatient sorrow at our inability to grasp *now*, wholly, here on earth, at once and for ever, those divine and rapturous joys, of which *through* the poem . . . we attain to but brief and indeterminate glimpses" (77). In illustrating the pain of loss and remembrance, Poe also aims to give us a glimpse of a "respite and nepenthe" from our sorrow.

## Notes

1. In his preface to the 1827 collection, Poe claimed that "the greater part of the Poems which compose this little volume, were written in the year 1821-2, when the author had not completed his fourteenth year" (*Poetry* 9).

2. All citations of Poe's poetry are from *Poetry, Tales, and Selected Essays*.

3. McGill argues that the 1830s and 1840s constituted a distinctive era in American letters, in which "legal and political resistance to tight controls over intellectual property produced a literary marketplace suffused with unauthorized publications. Not only was the mass-market for literature in America built and sustained by the publication of cheap reprints of foreign books and periodicals, the primary vehicles for the circulation of literature were uncopyrighted newspapers and magazines" (1).

4. Kenneth Silverman also sees Poe's obsession with death and mourning as reflective of American culture in the 1830s and 1840s: "American culture of the time fostered such a preoccupation, preaching from every quarter the duty of remembering the dead. This so-called cult of memory helped to allay anxieties about the continued vitality of Christian ideas of immortality, and concern that commercial and industrial values had begun to prevail in personal and domestic life" (72). Yet, as Silverman also observes, Poe's attitudes toward this cultural obsession were perverse: "[Poe] neglected principal elements of the consolation literature of the time" (73).

5. At the end of "Beyond the Pleasure Principle," in which Freud first elaborates his theory of the death drive, he writes: "It may be asked whether and how far I am myself convinced of the truth of the hypotheses that have been set out in these pages. My answer would be that I am not convinced myself and that I do not seek to persuade other people to believe in them" (332).

6. As Mabbott notes in his commentary on the poem in the *Collected Works of Edgar Allan Poe*, "At least in the form in which Poe submitted it for publication, 'Annabel Lee' was his last poem, and he seems to have thought it would be" (469).

7. Mabbott cites an introduction to "The Bells" written by N. P. Willis when he reprinted the poem in the *Home Journal* some two weeks after its first appearance: "*Poe's Last Poem*. The *Union Magazine* for November contains the following remarkable poem by the late *Edgar A. Poe*. We do not know of a piece of fugitive poetry in the English language that will be more likely to be more generally read" (in Poe, *Collected Works* 433).

# Works Cited

Ackroyd, Peter. *Poe: A Life Cut Short*. London: Vintage, 2009.

Boym, Svetlana. *The Future of Nostalgia*. New York: Basic Books, 2001.

Carlson, Eric W. "Symbol and Sense in Poe's 'Ulalume.'" *American Literature* 35.1 (Mar. 1963): 22-37.

Freud, Sigmund. "Beyond the Pleasure Principle." *On Metapsychology: The Theory of Psychoanalysis*. Ed. Angela Richards. Harmondsworth: Penguin, 1991. 269-338.

_____. "Mourning and Melancholia." *On Metapsychology: The Theory of Psychoanalysis*. Ed. Angela Richards. Harmondsworth : Penguin, 1991. 245-68.

Johnson, Barbara. "Strange Fits: Poe and Wordsworth on the Nature of Poetic Language." *The American Face of Edgar Allan Poe*. Ed. Shawn Rosenheim and Stephen Rachman. Baltimore: Johns Hopkins UP, 1995. 37-48.

Kopley, Richard, and Kevin J. Hayes. "Two Verse Masterworks: 'The Raven' and 'Ulalume.'" *The Cambridge Companion to Edgar Allan Poe*. Ed. Kevin J. Hayes. New York: Cambridge UP, 2002. 191-204.

McGill, Meredith. *American Literature and the Culture of Reprinting, 1834-1853*. Philadelphia: U of Pennsylvania P, 2003.

Poe, Edgar Allan. *Collected Works of Edgar Allan Poe*, vol. 1, *Poems*. Ed. Thomas Ollive Mabbott. Cambridge, MA: Belknap Press of Harvard UP, 1969.

_____. "The Philosophy of Composition." *Essays and Reviews*. Ed. G. R. Thompson. New York: Library of America, 1984. 13-25.

_____. "The Poetic Principle." *Essays and Reviews*. Ed. G. R. Thompson. New York: Library of America, 1984. 71-94.

_____. *Poetry, Tales, and Selected Essays*. Ed. Patrick F. Quinn and G. R. Thompson. New York: Library of America, 1984.

Polonsky, Rachel. "Poe's Aesthetic Theory." *The Cambridge Companion to Edgar Allan Poe*. Ed. Kevin J. Hayes. New York: Cambridge UP, 2002. 42-56.

Richards, Eliza. *Gender and the Poetics of Reception in Poe's Circle*. New York: Cambridge UP, 2004.

Ricoeur, Paul. *Memory, History, Forgetting*. Trans. Kathleen Blamey and David Pellauer. Chicago: U of Chicago P, 2004.

Silverman, Kenneth. *Edgar A. Poe: Mournful and Never-Ending Remembrance*. New York: HarperCollins, 1991.

Thomas, Dwight, and David K. Jackson. *The Poe Log: A Documentary Life of Edgar Allan Poe, 1809-1849*. Boston: G. K. Hall, 1987.

# Rhyme and Reason in Poe and His Predecessors_____

Matthew J. Bolton

As the bicentennial of Edgar Allan Poe's birth, 2009 witnessed a series of critical appraisals and appreciations of the author. In popular magazines and academic journals alike, essayists mused on Poe's place in American literature and on the relative merits of his fiction and verse. Such essays tend to follow a common arc: they tell some of the more colorful anecdotes from Poe's difficult and tragic life, run through a list of his most famous stories and poems, detail how various Poe societies have celebrated the bicentennial, and make their claim for what Poe has contributed to American literature and culture. In general, these retrospectives tend to put forward Poe's horror stories in the gothic genre as his most enduring work. The reputation of the short stories seems secure, in part because the best of these retain their uncanny, cloying power, and in part because one can so readily see their influence on novels and films of the past century. Poe's work gave birth to whole genres, including the horror story and the detective novel. As Stephen King writes in the 2009 collection *In the Shadow of the Master: Classic Tales by Edgar Allan Poe*, "We are all the children of Poe" (190). More than two hundred years after his birth and one hundred sixty years after his death, Poe's legacy as a short-story writer is rarely challenged.

Poe's reputation as a poet, however, is a different matter. Reading the various bicentennial assessments of the author, one gets the distinct feeling that most critics do not quite know what to say about the poetry. Poe wrote a handful of poems that have become among the most popular and widely known in the English language, foremost of which is, of course, "The Raven." But to rework Machiavelli's adage, being loved is not the same as being respected, and Poe's verse has always been dogged by the question of whether it is actually any *good*. As Jill Lepore asks in her 2009 article about Poe in *The New Yorker*, "Was the man an utter genius or a complete fraud?" (para. 34). Poe's very popularity seems to work against him: poems such as "The Raven," according to some arguments, are appealing precisely because they are so accessible. While some of Poe's later contemporaries, such as Emily Dickinson and Walt Whitman, were relentless innovators who reshaped the poetic forms that they inherited, Poe, by contrast, worked within conventional, closed forms, and in this respect, his poetry can seem to be lacking in formal innovation.

It is perhaps because of his relative conventionality that he is so popular, easily loved by schoolchildren as well as by adults who have never passed beyond a schoolchild's appreciation of poetry in its most insistently rhythmical and relentlessly rhyming form. Certainly this has been the opinion of several important twentieth-century critics. Aldous Huxley argues that Poe's lines "protest too much" their own poetic worth and that "it is when Poe tries to make it too poetical that his poetry takes on its peculiar tinge of badness" (161). According to Huxley, Poe is a lockstep, unmusical poet, one who pours his ideas into ready-made poetic forms: "All he has to do is to shovel the meaning into the moving stream of the metre and allow the current to carry it on waves that, like those of the best hairdressers, are guaranteed permanent" (161). Yet Huxley may be voicing a fundamentally modernist bias against the sort of closed forms in which Poe worked. Because Eliot, Pound, Stevens, and other poets of the twentieth century broke from conventional forms, Huxley seems to assume that Poe's use of those forms is "too poetical" and hence too limited in artistry and sophistication. Huxley might well level the same charges against Shakespeare, Milton, or any number of poets who worked within the demanding constraints of closed forms. Poet and critic T. S. Eliot, who himself is largely responsible for the twentieth-century movement from closed form to free verse, takes issue as much with Poe's subject matter and worldview as with his prosody. Eliot argues: "That Poe had a powerful intellect is undeniable: but it seems to me that it is the intellect of a highly gifted young person before puberty. The forms which his lively curiosity takes are those in which a pre-adolescent mentality delights" (35).

Huxley and Eliot's criticisms are corrective, aiming to put into perspective a poet whose work, they argue, has been overestimated. Interestingly enough, however, both critics are concerned less about American attitudes toward Poe than they are about French ones; Poe was translated by Charles Baudelaire and subsequently exerted a tremendous influence over the nineteenth-century Symbolist poets, including Paul Verlaine, Arthur Rimbaud, and Paul Valéry. Huxley and Eliot seem rather annoyed that the French have given pride of place to an English-language poet who, in their estimation, is not particularly good.

In talking about Poe's poetry, issues of mass culture and high culture inevitably push themselves to the forefront of the conversation. This may say as much about the state of contemporary poetry as it does about Poe's actual work. Poetry has become as rarified a form in the twenty-first century as it was a popular one in the nineteenth. After all, while a collection of short stories in tribute to Poe—with a foreword by Stephen King, no less—seems to have the makings of a best seller, we would be baffled by a similar collection in which contemporary poets pay tribute to "Ulalume" and "The Bells." That the market for poetry has been eclipsed by the market for fiction is all the more reason one should not take the popularity of Poe's verse for granted. Instead, teachers, writers, and others who are invested in seeing poetry remain alive and well might ask how students' and readers' appreciation of Poe can lead them to appreciate other poets as well. Aficionados of Poe's verse understand and accept a connection between form and content: they see the insistent rhyme, repetition, and rhythm of his poems as giving voice to their speakers' fevered obsessions. Poe's verse may therefore serve as a form of induction, leading a reader to appreciate the work of other poets. By comparing and contrasting Poe's use of rhyme, meter, the structure of the poetic line, and the lyricism and musical quality inherent in closed form with that of several great poets who came before him, such as Shakespeare, Milton, and Swift, one might come to a better understanding not only of Poe but also of poetry itself.

In a famous scene from director Alfred Hitchcock's 1929 film *Blackmail* (adapted by Hitchcock from a play by Charles Bennett), a murderer listens as her gossiping neighbor unwittingly recounts the details of her crime. The sound in this scene is edited so that the neighbor's recitation becomes an incomprehensible drone out of which only a single word can, again and again, be heard: "knife." This scene serves as an expressionistic representation of the guilty woman's consciousness. She hears this one word precisely because it speaks to her deepest, guiltiest secret, and the repetition of the word enacts her fixation on the object it represents—the murder weapon. This scene writes large the connection between repetition and obsession, and can offer a framework for how Poe's verse functions. In many of Poe's poems, a narrator repeats a word or a sound because he is fixated on the object the word represents, and the poem might therefore be read as his consciousness cast into a concrete form.

Several of Poe's most famous poems feature rhyme schemes that are built around the name of an absent woman. The effect is to link all of the narrator's thoughts back to the name of his loved one, making the poem, like his consciousness itself, fixated on the departed lover. The first stanza of "Annabel Lee" (1849), for example, establishes the rhyme scheme that will dominate the poem as a whole:

> It was many and many a year ago,
>> In a kingdom by the sea,
> That a maiden there lived whom you may know
>> By the name of ANNABEL LEE;
> And this maiden she lived with no other thought
>> Than to love and be loved by me.
>
> (1-6)

The same three words will echo across each subsequent stanza: "sea," "me" (or sometimes "we"), and "Annabel Lee." The poem therefore features not only a rhyme scheme but also what we might call a "repetition scheme." In the narrator's mind, the name of his dead lover is inextricably linked with his own consciousness ("me") and with the place where she is buried: ". . . her sepulchre there by the sea—/ . . . her tomb by the side of the sea" (40-41). Rhyme and repetition are an enactment of the narrator's grief and of his fixation on the deceased Annabel Lee.

The first several stanzas of "Annabel Lee" each contain an unrhymed line, such that the rhyme scheme of the sestet might be written *ababcb*. At first consideration, one might assume that this unrhymed line serves as a poetic and psychological safety valve, that the narrator has an occasional thought that does not bring him back to his obsessive musing over the sea and his loved one. Yet listing all of the unrhymed words across the poem's six stanzas creates a telegraphed version of the narrator's story: "thought," "heaven," "chilling," "came," "sepulchre," "know," "night," "soul," "dreams," "eyes." These words provide no relief, for they, too, speak of Annabel Lee. Moreover, as the poem progresses, both its lines and its stanzas become longer: a sestet that alternated between ten and eight lines gives way to an octet that alternates between twelve and eight. There is a fevered quality to this expansion, as if the narrator is getting carried away by the act of speaking and remembering. And as the lines grow longer, they feature internal rhymes or internal repetitions that makes them sound against themselves. In one stanza, for example, the narrator repeats the word "love" three times: "But we loved with a love that was more than love" (9). The line feels compulsive, as if his first intonation of the word "love" sets off a series of echoes.

The final stanza of the poem is a tour de force of internal rhymes and end rhymes:

> For the moon never beams without bringing me dreams
> > Of the beautiful ANNABEL LEE;
> And the stars never rise but I see the bright eyes
> > Of the beautiful ANNABEL LEE;
> And so, all the night-tide, I lie down by the side
> Of my darling, my darling, my life and my bride,
> > In her sepulchre there by the sea—
> In her tomb by the side of the sea.

(34-41)

If in the first stanza the rhymes were to be found at the end of the lines, now nearly half the lines feature internal rhymes ("beams . . . dreams," "rise . . . eyes," and "tide . . . side"). There is a process of acceleration here, as if the narrator's thoughts and words intensify over the course of the poem. Note, too, how many times lines repeat themselves: the second and fourth lines are identical, while the last two are nearly so. As the poem comes to its close, the narrator gives full vent to his *idée fixe*: Annabel Lee has died and lies buried by the sea, and he might as well be buried with her.

Turning from "Annabel Lee" to "The Raven" (1845), one finds a similar relationship between rhyme, repetition, and fixation. The first stanza establishes a pattern of internal and end rhymes that will hold true throughout the poem:

> Once upon a midnight dreary, while I pondered, weak
> > and weary,
> Over many a quaint and curious volume of forgotten lore,
> While I nodded, nearly napping, suddenly there came a
> > tapping,
> As of some one gently rapping, rapping at my chamber door.
> "'Tis some visitor," I muttered, "tapping at my chamber door—
> > Only this and nothing more."

(1-6)

---

As in the latter part of "Annabel Lee," internal rhyme helps to structure these very long lines. If we were to put parentheses around the letters representing internal rhymes rather than end ones and brackets around those representing repetitions rather than rhymes (here, the words "rapping" and "door"), the rhyme and repetition schemes would look something like this: (*a*), *a*/ *b*/ (*c*), *c*/ (*c*), ([*c*]), *b*/ [*b*]/ *b*. This stanza, then, is a remarkable little echo chamber; the words dropped into it will sound and reverberate across the poem.

In the first stanza, we hear echoes of a name that will not appear until the end of the second: "lore," "door," "door," and "more" move insistently toward the name of the narrator's lost love, Lenore.

> Ah, distinctly I remember, it was in the bleak December,
> And each separate dying ember wrought its ghost upon
>     the floor.
> Eagerly I wished the morrow;—vainly I had sought to
>     borrow
> From my books surcease of sorrow—sorrow for the lost
>     Lenore—
> For the rare and radiant maiden whom the angels name
>     Lenore—
> > Nameless *here* for evermore.
>
> > (7-12)

Like the narrator of "Annabel Lee," this narrator is fixated on the name and image of his dead lover, who dominates both his thoughts and the text of the poem. While the initial end rhyme of each stanza changes (from "dreary" and "weary," in the first stanza, for example, to "remember" and "December" in the second), the second end rhyme does not. All of the words occupying that *b* position rhyme with "Lenore," and hence each stanza ends with a series of echoes of her name. To return to the schema from above, we might label the sounds that change from stanza to stanza as *x* and *y*, while leaving a *b* label on the constant

"-ore" sound: (*x*), *x*/ *b*/ (*y*), *y*/ (*y*), ([*y*]), *b*/ [*b*]/ *b*. This begins to look algebraic—which is exactly the point. Just as the memory of Lenore is a constant in the narrator's consciousness, so her name is a constant in the rhyme scheme of the poem. She is his *idée fixe*, and he can no more escape her than he can escape his own consciousness.

There is a moment midway through the poem when the narrator writes large the process through which the world reflects back to him only his own thoughts:

> But the silence was unbroken, and the darkness gave no
> token,
> And the only word there spoken was the whispered word,
> "Lenore!"
> This I whispered, and an echo murmured back the word,
> "Lenore!"
> Merely this and nothing more.
>
> (27-30)

The echo casts back to him the name Lenore, offering nothing else to take her place. Grief and loss have locked the narrator into a prison of the mind, and his world is as circumscribed as the rhyme scheme of his poem.

In Poe's verse, rhyme serves to reflect a narrator's obsessions and fixations. Words echo and reverberate across the poem just as thoughts and memories do across the narrator's consciousness. The reader who enjoys "Annabel Lee" or "The Raven" is, on some level, taken both with the sound of the poems and with the relationship each poem establishes between form and content. He or she accepts as valid Poe's linkage of rhyme and repetition with fixation, and in so doing accepts the underlying principles of poetry as a whole. Poe himself articulated these principles in several essays on versification. In "The Poetic Principle," for example, he mounts a defense of lyric verse and of the centrality of rhyme and rhythm to poetry, arguing, "Music, in its various modes of metre, rhythm, and rhyme, is of so vast a moment in Poetry as never to be wisely rejected—is so vitally important an adjunct that he is simply silly who declines its assistance" (77). Poe's concept of poetry is grounded in the importance he places on rhyme, rhythm, and meter. He writes, "I would define, in brief, the Poetry of words as *The Rhythmical Creation of Beauty*. Its sole arbiter is Taste. With the Intellect or the Conscience it has only collateral relations" (78). Poetry appeals directly to a reader on a sensual and aesthetic level, because it is at its core a form of music. Poetry should not be first and foremost a matter of ideas or morals, but one of sound. Poe's earlier essay "Letter to B——" amplifies this definition of poetry: "Music, when combined with a pleasurable idea, is poetry; music without the idea is simply music; the idea without the music is prose from its very definitiveness" (11).

Poe may therefore serve as an introduction to a basic element of poetry: the relationship between sound and sense. A reader who appreciates Poe's treatment of rhyme ought to turn his or her attention to other canonical poets, most of whom write in a closed form and are aware of the relationship of form and audience response. By considering how poets from the sixteenth, seventeenth, and eighteenth centuries use rhyme, one may be better able to situate Poe in the poetic tradition.

\* \* \*

In Shakespeare's sonnets and plays, rhyme serves not as a marker of fixation but as one of finality. Rhyme—and particularly the rhyming couplet—is a form of closure and concentration in which a speaker puts a fine point on the thought processes that have preceded it. This is certainly the effect in Shakespeare's sonnets, where three quatrains of alternating rhyme are followed by a rhyming couplet. There is a measured deliberation to the quatrains, as here in the opening of Sonnet 18:

Shall I compare thee to a summer's day?
Thou art more lovely and more temperate,
Rough winds do shake the darling buds of May
And summer's lease hath all too short a date.

(1-4)

In Poe, rhyme indicates the distraught lover's fevered state of mind. The Shakespearean sonneteer, on the other hand, is as much a logician as a lover. The alternating rhyme scheme allows the poet enough space to mount and develop his argument. Here in this first quatrain, for example, he can pose his question ("Shall I compare thee to a summer's day?"), answer it, and then provide two images that help explain why his beloved is better than a summer's day. In Shakespeare's hands, the sonnet is at once a playful and precise poetic form. In Sonnet 18, the sonneteer challenges the rhetorical conventions of the sonnet—specifically the one in which a lover is supposed to draw all manner of hyperbolic comparisons about his loved one—yet he does so by working within its metrical conventions. Shakespeare understands how great a range this poetic form allows him.

Whereas the Petrarchan or Italian sonnet consists of an octet and a sestet, Shakespeare's sonnet features three quatrains and a couplet. The rhyme scheme of the Shakespearean sonnet can therefore be represented this way: *abab*, *cdcd*, *efef*, *gg*. By ending his sonnet with a couplet, Shakespeare is able to gather and comment on all of the ideas and images that have come before it. The couplet is an act of concentration in which the sudden proximity of the rhyme signals the sudden insight of the sonneteer. In the third quatrain of Sonnet 18, for example, the sonneteer has argued that while a summer's day fades, his lover's beauty will not, for he has immortalized her in the sonnet itself. The couplet drives this idea home: "So long as men can breathe or eyes can see,/ So long lives this, and this gives life to thee" (13-14). In the quatrains, rhyming words were separated by an off-line; here, however,

---

the two lines rhyme with each other. The effect is like pulling tight a knot—the sonneteer has clinched his argument.

In a poem that has already structured itself around a series of rhyming words, Shakespeare in the couplet looks for other rhetorical devices by which he might amplify his meaning. As Poe later would, he uses repetition to amplify rhyme. The two lines of the couplet both begin with "So long." The first line uses parallel structure, balancing two alternatives—"men can breathe" and "eyes can see"—on either side of "or." The last line is like a funhouse mirror as the first and second halves of the sentences cast distorted reflections of each other. "This," signifying the sonnet itself, appears in each clause. But the words around "this" shift and change: one clause features "lives," a verb, while the other offers "life," a noun, and the rhyming word "gives." Moreover, Shakespeare underscores the iambic rhythm of the lines— and of the sonnet as a whole—by composing his couplet entirely of monosyllabic words. In the quatrains, we see any number of lines that feature polysyllabic words or that deviate, to one extent or another, from the unstressed-stressed pattern of iambic pentameter. Here at the poem's conclusion, however, Shakespeare atomizes the materials of his poem to work with the smallest possible units of sound. The couplet is a rhetorical tour de force in which rhyme, repetition, and rhythm bring a sense of finality and closure to the stanzas that have come before.

In the sonnet, the couplet serves to gather together and put a fine point on the poetic images and logical arguments that have preceded it. Couplets serve a similar purpose in Shakespeare's plays, where they often come at the end of blank-verse monologues. Blank verse—lines of unrhymed iambic pentameter—allowed Shakespeare to compose with a freedom and range of effect that rhymed verse would have limited. By ending a monologue with a couplet, however, he could exploit some of the effects of rhyme that are missing from blank verse. This offers the best of both worlds, and the couplet is all the more powerful for coming on the heels of unrhymed verse. In the prologue to *Henry V*, for example, the chorus delivers a long, unrhymed address to the audience that concludes with a couplet:

> Think, when we talk of horses, that you see them
> Printing their proud hoofs in the receiving earth;
> For it is your thoughts that now must deck our kings,
> Carry them here and there; jumping o'er times,
> Turning the accomplishments of many years
> Into an hour-glass; for the which supply,
> Admit me Chorus to this history;
> Who prologue-like your humble patience pray,
> Gently to hear, kindly to judge, our play.
>
> (26-34)

As in the sonnets, the couplet serves as a conclusion to everything that has come before it.

In the context of a stage play, the couplet serves the additional duty of signaling to the audience and the other actors that a particular speech has come to a close. The Lord Chamberlain's Men and other theater companies of Shakespeare's time mounted new plays with remarkable speed. The actors generally were given copies of their own lines but not those of their fellow actors. The actors may not have known the specific words with which the speeches of others would end, but they knew that when they heard rhyming couplets, that would be their cue to take the stage and speak.

Like Shakespeare, John Milton found blank verse to be an ideal form in which to compose his poetry. Whereas Shakespeare used rhyming couplets to punctuate or draw to a close his blank-verse passages, however, Milton tended to abjure rhyme altogether. In his apology for *Paradise Lost* (1667), the poet famously declared his position on rhyme:

The measure is English heroic verse without rhyme, as that of Homer in Greek and of Virgil in Latin; rhyme being no necessary adjunct or true ornament of poem or good verse, in longer works especially, but the invention of a barbarous age. (6)

The "barbarous age" began with the fall of Rome, and in rejecting rhyme Milton reached back to the traditions and conventions of classical literature. Since Homer and Virgil did not rhyme, neither would Milton.

Given Milton's statements concerning rhyme in *Paradise Lost*, it is fascinating to see how he used rhyme elsewhere in his body of work. In *Samson Agonistes* (1671), Milton's neoclassical play about the Old Testament hero, the title character tends to speak in blank verse, as here in the opening passage:

> A little onward lend thy guiding hand
> To these dark steps, a little further on;
> For yonder bank hath choice of Sun or shade,
> There I am wont to sit, when any chance
> Relieves me from my task of servile toil, . . .
>
> (1-5)

Though blinded, imprisoned, and made to labor, Samson retains some modicum of freedom. He may move about, may be visited by his father and his tribesmen, and may speak freely. Such free speech, interestingly enough, is unrhymed.

The Chorus of the Israelites, on the other hand, tends to speak in rhyme. When Samson and the Chorus interact, the effect can be jarring. Compared to Samson's blank verse, the Chorus speaks in an echoing singsong:

God of our Fathers, what is man!

That thou towards him with hand so various,

Or might I say contrarious,

Temperst thy providence through his short course,

Not evenly, as thou rul'st

The Angelic orders and inferior creatures mute,

Irrational and brute.

(667-73)

The chorus's language is constrained and circumscribed in a way that Samson's is not. This is only fitting, since the Chorus counsels restraint and submission. Samson's Philistine captors have ordered him to attend a feast in honor of their god Dagon. Samson bridles at being led into the temple of his enemies and contemplates what his refusal will mean for him and for his people. Ever cautious, the Chorus urges Samson to do what he is told so as not to bring further retribution on the Israelites. As the voice of the people, the Chorus is invested in conformity and the status quo. By casting the Chorus's words into rhyming couplets, Milton implies that rhyme itself is part of this status quo.

When Samson, midway through the Chorus's visit, begins to despair, his words, too, begin to rhyme:

O that torment should not be confin'd

To the bodies wounds and sores

With maladies innumerable

In heart, head, breast, and reins;

But must secret passage find

To th' inmost mind.

(606-11)

Rhyme therefore is a signal of conformity and submission. When Samson is in a state of desolation, his words become as shackled as his body. The chains of rhyming sounds in this speech signal his loss of hope and freedom. At the play's conclusion, however, when Samson has decided that he will destroy the temple of Dagon rather than worship his enemy's god, he again speaks in blank verse. The blind strongman Samson therefore becomes a stand-in for the blind poet Milton: while the former rejects the counsel of the Chorus, the latter rejects the rhyme scheme in which that counsel is couched.

* * *

Whereas Milton abjured rhyme, John Dryden, Alexander Pope, Samuel Johnson, Jonathan Swift, and other poets of the next generation were enamored with it—and in particular with the couplet. Shakespeare had used rhyme to signal closure, Milton had equated it with confinement, but the eighteenth-century poets exploited an entirely different aspect of rhyme, seeing in it the stuff of comedy. Indeed, one cannot separate the content of eighteenth-century poetry from the verse forms that it employed: this was an age of biting wit, and the heroic couplet was the sharp tooth of such wit. A pair of end-stopped lines of iambic pentameter ending in an exact masculine rhyme, the heroic couplet was a form that defined an age.

Jonathan Swift's 1730 poem "The Lady's Dressing Room" shows how the heroic couplet can be put into service as a comic device. The poem centers on an act of transgression: while a young woman named Celia is away, her admirer, Strephon, steals into her dressing room. Strephon is a romantic who has assumed that Celia is an ethereal creature, "sweet and cleanly" (18). Consequently, the reality of the dressing room shocks him:

> But, oh! it turn'd poor Strephon's bowels
> When he beheld and smelt the towels,
> Begumm'd, bematter'd, and beslim'd,
> With dirt, and sweat, and ear-wax grim'd;
> No object Strephon's eye escapes;

Here petticoats in frouzy heaps;
Nor be the handkerchiefs forgot,
All varnish'd o'er with snuff and snot.

(43-50)

This passage might still be funny even were it unrhymed—bodily fluids and bad smells are, after all, staples of comedy—but rhyme certainly amplifies and concentrates its comic effect. The couplets serve as a form of comic tension and release, for the first line of each couplet sets up a level of anticipation on which the next line delivers. Each rhyming line is also a punch line.

Changes in pronunciation between Swift's time and our own may help to illustrate the degree to which the humor of "The Lady's Dressing Room" is bound up with its rhyme scheme. Looking about the disordered room, Strephon "swears, how damnably the men lie/ In calling Celia sweet and cleanly" (17-18). This line may fall a little flat at first, and might even strike the reader as rather cruel and judgmental—until one realizes that in Swift's time this couplet would have been an exact rhyme. In the eighteenth century "cleanly" was pronounced "clen-lie" rather than "cleen-lee" (*Oxford English Dictionary*). Somehow, seeing exact rhyme in this couplet empties it of cruelty; it becomes, instead, wholly comic, much as an act of violence that would be appalling in real life is funny in the context of a slapstick film. This line is one of several instances in which Swift rhymes two words in one line with a single word in the other. The poem opens with "Five hours (and who can do it less in?)/ By haughty Celia spent in dressing" (1-2), while later Swift uses a similar construction as Strephon inspects ". . . greasy coifs, and pinners reeking,/ Which Celia slept at least a week in" (53-54). Lines like these are a form of metrical sleight of hand, and the effect is surprising and witty, as if Swift has pulled off a particularly dexterous feat.

* * *

Returning to Poe after surveying the work of some of his greatest predecessors, one can see that his use of rhyme both engages with and departs from the poetic tradition. Like so many English-language poets before him, Poe works within the poetic conventions he inherited, writing verse in which the rhythm and rhyme scheme are regular and exact. To a twenty-first-century reader, who has read Eliot and Pound and the other great innovators of the last century, Poe's closed forms may at first seem too conventional. Yet Poe was himself an innovator, one who worked brilliantly within the forms he inherited rather than subverting or discarding them. In several of his best-known poems, Poe puts his own stamp on exact rhyme by making it an index of his speakers' fevered and obsessive imaginations. Understanding this relationship in frequently anthologized poems such as "The Raven" helps one to identify more nuanced relationships between sound and sense in other of Poe's poems.

In "Al Aaraaf," the long poem that Poe wrote as a teenager, he creates one musical effect after another. In the opening stanza, Poe creates the textual equivalent of an echo: "Joy's voice so peacefully departed/ That like the murmur in the shell/ Its echo dwelleth and will dwell" (8-10). Because "murmur" is itself an onomatopoeic word, its own two syllables re-creating the hushed tone it denotes, Poe enacts the echo of the murmur. The effect is repeated as the word "dwelleth" is answered by the fainter, truncated "dwell"—the longer word comes early in the line and the attenuated echo rings against it as well as the earlier "shell." It is an ingenious instance of Poe expressing a musical idea through the skillful deployment of rhyme, rhythm, and repetition.

Elsewhere in the poem, Poe exploits the musical nature of rhymed iambic pentameter to slow the pace of his line. Here the spirit Nesace attempts to transport herself across the cosmos:

Away—away—'mid seas of rays that roll
Empyrean splendor o'er th' unchained soul—
The soul that scarce (the billows are so dense)
Can struggle to its destin'd eminence—
(20-23)

Poe uses the natural weight and speed of English words to create the illusion of slowness and heaviness. In the third of these lines, Poe's use of eight single-syllable words and a parenthetical aside re-creates in the reader a sense of the effort that Nesace herself must expend on her journey. The reader, like the spirit, must struggle to get through this passage. Poe has not deviated from his closed form—these lines are still in regular iambic pentameter—rather, he has worked within this form and in so doing has shown how versatile it really is in the hands of a master.

The equating of rhyme with obsession is therefore only one of Poe's contributions to the field of poetry. Perhaps more important than his mastery of rhyme, rhythm, and repetition, however, is Poe's creation of a handful of poems that have remained popular for more than a century and a half. Poems like "Annabel Lee" and "The Raven" exert a fascination over readers precisely because of the musicality that Poe cultivated in his own work and prized in the work of others. For younger readers in particular, Poe's verse may be the first time they respond not to plot or character but to the sounds of words themselves. Poe may therefore be the means by which new generations of readers come to appreciate a wider range of poets and poetry.

## Works Cited

Eliot, T. S. "From Poe to Valéry." *To Criticize the Critic and Other Writings*. Lincoln: U of Nebraska P, 1992. 27-42.

Huxley, Aldous. "Vulgarity in Literature." *The Recognition of Edgar Allan Poe: Selected Criticism Since 1829*. Ed. Eric W. Carlson. Ann Arbor: U of Michigan P, 1969.

King, Stephen. "The Genius of the Tell-Tale Heart." *In the Shadow of the Master: Classic Tales by Edgar Allan Poe*. Ed. Michael Connelly. New York: Harper-Collins, 2009. 189-90.

Lepore, Jill. "The Humbug: Edgar Allan Poe and the Economy of Horror." *The New Yorker* 27 Apr. 2009. 18 Nov. 2009. http://www.newyorker.com/arts/critics/atlarge/2009/04/27/090427crat_atlarge_lepore.

Milton, John. *The Complete Poetry of John Milton*. Ed. John T. Shawcross. New York: Anchor Press, 1971.

_____. *Paradise Lost*. Ed. Gordon Teskey. New York: W. W. Norton, 2004.

Poe, Edgar Allan. "Letter to B——."*Essays and Reviews*. Ed. G. R. Thompson. New York: Library of America, 1984. 5-12.

_____. "The Poetic Principle." *Essays and Reviews*. Ed. G. R. Thompson. New York: Library of America, 1984. 71-94.

_____. *Poetry and Tales*. Ed. Patrick Francis Quinn. New York: Library of America, 1984.

Shakespeare, William. *The Riverside Shakespeare*. Ed. G. Blakemore Evans. Boston: Houghton Mifflin, 1974.

Swift, Jonathan. *The Complete Poems*. Ed. Pat Rogers. New York: Penguin, 1989.

# The Poems of Edgar Allan Poe:
## Their Critical Reception_____

Robert C. Evans

Most critics have been willing to celebrate Edgar Allan Poe's stature as a writer of short fiction, but there has been much less agreement about his skill as a poet. Although Poe himself aspired to be remembered primarily as a writer of great verse, many commentators have been quite reluctant to grant him this status. Of course, Poe the poet has always had vigorous champions, but often they have been readers whose first language is not English. French authors and critics, in particular, have frequently been admirers of Poe, and indeed Poe is often widely praised outside the United States—although, once again, more for his tales than for his poetry. The United States, paradoxically, has long been home to many of Poe's severest critics, especially critics of his verse. Harold Bloom, for instance, calls Poe "the worst" of significant American authors, although he concedes that together "with Walt Whitman, Poe continues to be the most influential of American writers on a worldwide basis, eclipsing even Eliot and Faulkner" (xi). Even genuine admirers of Poe often show little intense interest in his poetry; thus Dwayne Thorpe noted in 1996 that "academic criticism provides a striking picture of neglect" and commented that in "any given year, critics produce dozens of analyses of Poe's fiction but almost none of his poetry; and most essays are analyses of single poems, not attempts to view the poetry as a whole" (89-90). While noting the paucity of books devoted exclusively to the poems, Thorpe also commented on the "contrast between Poe's passion for his poems and his critics' indifference to them" (90). Indeed, Poe's critics have often been downright hostile rather than merely indifferent; still, Poe the poet has had vigorous champions ever since his verse was first published.

From the beginning, critical opinion of Poe's verse has been divided. The favorable reviews of his early poems saw evidence of a developing talent and vivid imagination, but other critics censured Poe

---

for poor taste and nonsense. A Baltimore reviewer highly praised *Al Aaraaf, Tamerlane, and Minor Poems* (1829), finding in the poems "a rich vein of deep and powerful thought, clothed in language of almost inimitable beauty and harmony" (in Walker 70). He found Poe's "fancy . . . rich and of an elevated cast; his imagination powerfully creative. There is no labored attempt at effect; no immoderate use of epithets; no over-burdening the idea with words, no cant, no nonsense" (70-71; see also 72). John Neal likewise praised Poe as "evidently a fine genius" in his review of *Al Aaraaf* but faulted Poe for lacking "judgment, experience, [and] tact" (in Walker 69). An anonymous reviewer of Poe's 1831 *Poems* was far less complimentary, suggesting that although the book "occasionally sparkles with true poetic expression," sometimes "a conflict of beauty and nonsense takes place" in which the latter often wins out (in Walker 75). Neal reviewed this book as well, finding "pure poetry in one page—pure absurdity in another," and he advised Poe not to "mistake oddity for excellence" or uniqueness for superiority (76).

Poe's most famous poem, "The Raven," met an enormously enthusiastic reception when it was first published in January 1845 in the *New York Evening Mirror* and, despite some later critics' reservations, it has remained popular ever since. Writing in 1845, Nathaniel Parker Willis called it "the most effective single example of [American] 'fugitive' poetry" and "unsurpassed in English poetry for subtle conception, masterly ingenuity of versification, and consistent, sustaining of imaginative lift" (in Walker 140). James Brook was equally positive; he praised the poem's tone of melancholy and despair and ended by declaring, "In power and originality of versification the whole is no less remarkable than it is, psychologically, a *wonder*" (Walker 143). Meanwhile, Elizabeth Barrett, the great English poet, found the poem powerful, praising in particular its rhythm and refrain, and thought it had "uncommon force and effect." She told Poe that it had become a sensation in England and was admired by Robert Browning, who was then courting her (in Walker 144), though she did remark that the poem could be improved by a clear indication of its speaker's insanity, which would remove any danger of the poem missing the eerie and instead falling into the absurd. One early commentator seems to have seen a similar danger and preemptively defended the poem from charges that it was "flat nonsense" and lacked serious meaning (in Walker 146).

An especially important early valuation of Poe's career came a month after "The Raven" was published from James Russell Lowell, who praised Poe's early verses as "the most remarkable boyish poems that we have ever read" (in Walker 161). Lowell commended the "melody" of the famous sonnet "To Helen" (161), extolled Poe's "*genius*" (162), and called him "the possessor of a pure and original vein" (166). Less enthusiastic was William Gilmore Simms, who alleged in November that Poe "seems to dislike the merely practical, and to shrink from the concrete," thus making his poetry "too intensely spiritual for the ordinary reader" (in Walker 171). Simms, however, did defend Poe against some of his northern critics (171-73).

When Poe published *The Raven, and Other Poems* in 1845, the response was somewhat mixed. George Pope Morris praised Poe's ability to make his "dream-land" seem "more touching than the actual life we had left," and he defended "The Raven," with its "exquisite versification," against any charge of being "aimless and unsatisfactory." Morris celebrated that poem for an "indescribable charm" produced by "the shadowy and indistinct implied resemblance of the material and immaterial throughout" (in Walker 225). Less impressed, however, was Margaret Fuller, who found most of the poems (except "The Raven") unsatisfying "fragments," although she did single out a few, such as "To One in Paradise" and "The Haunted Palace," for praise (in Walker 228-29). Likewise, Thomas Dunn English extolled "The Raven" but found many of the other poems less consistently impressive (in Walker 231, 233). He called Poe the poet of the idler, the scholar and dreamer. He has nothing to do with every day life. He is of the ether, ethereal. . . . He is neither the poet of outdoor nature; nor the poet of every day humanity. He is the poet of the ideal; and sings to his own soul, having no care to sing to the souls around him. (234-35)

Many other critics have leveled this same charge.

An anonymous reviewer writing in the *Boston Post* praised "The Raven" condescendingly and singled out "The Bridal Ballad" for commendation, but concluded that the rest of the works in the 1845 volume "range from mediocrity to absolute nonsense," calling the book "a parcel of current trash" (in Walker 236). Slightly more nuanced was the response of John Sullivan Dwight, who praised the poems for their power, beauty, thought, rhythm, diction, originality, and dramatic effect but concluded that "if they attract you to a certain length, it is only to repulse you the more coldly at the last. There is a wild unearthliness, and unheavenliness, in the tone of all his pictures, a strange unreality in all his thoughts. . . . Indeed the impression of a very *studied* effect is always uppermost after reading him" (in Walker 238). Dwight considered Poe a poet who offered "the fancy which is merely fancy, the beauty which springs from no feeling, which neither illustrates nor promotes the great truths and purposes of life" (238).

In stark contrast, Freeman Hunt in 1846 extolled Poe's genius and fancy and said that his verse "is, while seemingly riding havoc in thought, meter and harmony, restrained throughout by a skilful rein," so that it never "border[s] upon the ridiculous, or ill-judged sublimity." Interestingly, Hunt found "The Raven" to be "rather a production of artistic cleverness than genius," but he highly praised the genius, passion, imagery, and power of the following poems (in Walker 240). In the same year, however, Lewis Gaylord Clark mocked Poe as an "infant rhythmist" and found his works thoughtless, puerile, and extremely vague (in Walker 241, 242-43).

Also writing in 1846, Lucius Alonzo Hine emphasized Poe's "wildness" and "ethereality" but saw these as signs of Poe's "genius," and he considered "The Raven" in particular "a perfect original" that would "live longer than its author" (in Walker 247). Nevertheless, Hine found some flaws even in that poem, and he ended his review by condemning some works (such as "The Valley of Unrest," "The Sleeper," and "Israfel") but extolling others (such as "The Coliseum," "Dream-Land," "To One in Paradise," and "The Conqueror Worm") (249-50). Meanwhile, the Englishman Thomas Kibble Hervey accused Poe of imitating the oracular obscurity of recent British poets and ended by advising Poe to "be simple and natural" and to take his inspiration from American subjects (in Walker 252-53). Similarly, another English critic also found Poe's verse too much influenced by non-American writers (in Walker 261; but see also 395 and 399).

More general comments on Poe's poetry by English-speaking critics in the mid-nineteenth century broke little new ground. "The Raven" was praised repeatedly (in Walker 269-70, 292, 299, 301, 305, 316, 320, 323, 349-51), Poe's sense of rhythm was constantly extolled (in Walker 275, 327, 353, 395, 399), and other aspects of his artistry were singled out for commendation (in Walker 275, 301, 305, 320, 352, 354, 398). Nevertheless, doubts about the worth of his poems were also often expressed (in Walker 320, 322, 332, 353), and the alleged defects of his verse were often linked to its supposedly narrow scope, lack of fundamental seriousness, or varied shortcomings of vision (in Walker 334-35, 337-38, 366, 402). Sometimes even the praise Poe received was ambivalent, as when George Washington Peck in 1850 wrote that "Poe succeeded, marvellously succeeded, yet we cannot find it in our heart to wish what he accomplished ever to be undertaken again" (in Walker 353). One unsympathetic reviewer—John Moncure Daniel— even called an edition of Poe's writings "the rawest, the baldest, the most offensive, and the most impudent humbug that has ever been palmed upon an unsuspecting moon-calf of a world" (in Walker 358), yet even Daniel finally expressed admiration for "The Raven" and defended it from various detractors (370-71). In an especially ambivalent sentence, Daniel asserted that Poe "left very little poetry that is good; but that little contains traces of merits transcendent—though undeveloped" (371). If there tends to be any point of agreement among Poe's admirers and detractors, not only in the nineteenth century but also later, it is that "The Raven" is an unusually memorable and even accomplished poem.

Although in the English-speaking world enthusiasm for Poe's verse has always been somewhat uneven, this has been far less true in France, where his poetry has had vigorous champions. First and most influential among these was Charles Baudelaire, himself a major poet, who in 1852 called Poe a "solitary spirit" and almost the only American representative of "the Romantic movement." Baudelaire considered Poe's "profound and plaintive poetry . . . finely wrought, pure, correct and brilliant as a crystal jewel," and he said that although Poe "loved complicated rhythms, he shaped them in a profound harmony, no matter how complicated they were," and he praised "The Raven" as "a pure work of art" (in Alexander 115). Later, in 1857, Baudelaire extolled Poe's "natural, innate poetic gift" and credited him with the central belief that the best poems are those "written solely for the pleasure of writing a poem" (in Carlson 55-56). Baudelaire admired Poe's attention to technique, including his facility with rhythm, refrains, rhyme, and repetitions, and he asserted that Poe's verse "always creates a powerful effect," describing it as "something profound and shimmering like a dream" (in Carlson 58-59).

Less enthusiastic was a Frenchman named J. Barbey d'Aurevilly, who in 1858 called Poe "certainly the finest literary product" of the United States, a nation he nevertheless regarded as the "cream of the scum of the world" (in Alexander 145). He considered Poe's poems "abortive but showing the signs of extraordinary capacity on every page," and he remarked that Poe's mind "was accessible only to inferior emotions"—namely, "curiosity and fear" (146-47). Writing in 1863, Charles de Moüy, while conceding Poe's gifts, called him a strange poet "who did not know how to speak in verse," arguing that he "succeeded only moderately" because "poetry, which seems essentially destined to express the nebulous, cannot endure too much of it" (in Alexander 158-59). On the other hand, Armand Renaud in 1864 commented that although "a sort of monotony results" from Poe's use of repetition, it is "a monotony so artistic that instead of causing boredom it becomes something strange which fascinates and lulls the reader" (in Alexander 169-70). Renaud called attention to a "tenderness that mingles with the most somber despondency" in Poe's verse, and he also praised Poe's "gift of evocative description" and his ability to "transport" readers into a land of dreams (172-73).

Stéphane Mallarmé's praise of Poe's poetry in the closing decades of the nineteenth century was perhaps the most decisive in France because Mallarmé himself became such a highly respected poet. Indeed, his lyric tribute titled "Le Tombeau d'Edgar Poe" (in Carlson 64-65) is often reprinted, despite its somewhat obscure phrasing. There is nothing obscure, however, about Mallarmé's claim that each of Poe's best poems "is a unique masterpiece" (in Alexander 216). In particular, Mallarmé admired "The Raven," singling out the "mysterious dread and the subtle mechanics of the imagination that seduces our spirits" (217). A more critical opinion, however, was offered early in the twentieth century by Remy de Gourmont, who contended that even "when impassioned and despairing, Edgar Poe's poetry has an ironic coldness. There is too much of the well chosen and willed . . . in the expression of his anguish and his dreams." De Gourmont faulted Poe for never achieving "the oratorical line, freely moving, limpid, fiery" (in Alexander 224). For the most part, however, French opinion sided with Baudelaire, Mallarmé, and other admirers of Poe rather than with such naysayers as de Gourmont, de Moüy, or d'Aurevilly, and the prestige of Poe in France grew even greater when Paul Valéry, himself a highly regarded poet, joined the ranks of Poe's admirers in the early twentieth century (in Alexander 233-43). For many writers in the United States and England, however, this French enthusiasm for Poe's poems was somewhat mystifying.

Henry James, for instance, in 1876 famously referred to Poe's "very valueless verses" and remarked that "to take him with more than a certain degree of seriousness is to lack seriousness one's self. An enthusiasm for Poe is the mark of a decidedly primitive stage of reflection" (in Carlson 65-66). In 1879, Thomas Wentworth Higginson offered more detailed, more nuanced, and more appreciative comments (in Carlson 68-70), but he still concluded that Poe was "the patron saint of all willful boys suspected of genius, and convicted at least in its infirmities. He belonged to the melancholy class of wasted men" (72). Meanwhile, Walt Whitman in 1880 praised Poe's technical skills yet called his poems "brilliant and dazzling, but with no heat," finding them uncongenial and terming them "lurid dreams" (in Carlson 74-75). Across the Atlantic, William Butler Yeats, one of the greatest of all modern poets, in a private letter of 1899 found Poe's fame "puzzling," noting that although he admired "a few of his lyrics extremely," he found much of Poe's writing "vulgar and commonplace." Even of "The Raven" Yeats said, "Its rhythm never lives for a moment, never once moves with an emotional life. The whole thing seems to me insincere and vulgar" (in Carlson 76-77). Later, however, during the 1909 centenary of Poe's birth, Yeats publicly called Poe "the greatest of American poets, and always and for all lands a great lyric poet" (76). This extreme shift suggests either that Yeats had radically changed his privately expressed opinion over the course of the intervening decade or that he was being extremely diplomatic.

As the twentieth century dawned, Poe the poet found both admirers and detractors in the English-speaking world. Edwin Arlington Robinson, himself a significant poet, wrote a sonnet praising Poe's "*wondersongs*" (in Carlson 81), although Robinson did not print this sonnet in his own collected poems. George Bernard Shaw, the great dramatist, praised Poe extravagantly, calling his poems "exquisitely refined" and ranking even Poe's failures above any success by Tennyson. Shaw claimed that "Poe constantly and inevitably produced magic where his greatest contemporaries produced only beauty," and he claimed that

"The Raven," "The Bells," and "Annabel Lee" are "as fascinating at the thousandth repetition as at the first" (in Carlson 98). Poe's poems, Shaw asserted, "always have the universe as their background" (99); his "verse sometimes alarms and puzzles the reader by fainting with its own beauty; but the beauty is never the beauty of the flesh" (100). In contrast to Shaw, however, D. H. Lawrence found Poe's poetry somewhat mechanical and lacking in life (in Carlson 114-15). William Carlos Williams, on the other hand, thought it full of soul and fresh in its phrasing (in Carlson 131), although later in the same essay he expressed doubts about Poe's poetic success (141).

Writing in 1926, the great critic Edmund Wilson found Poe a precursor of symbolism, and although he thought the poetry "rarely quite successful," he nevertheless considered it "of first-rate importance." Wilson found problems in many of the poems, both early and late, considering some of the "tricks" in the latter even "a little trashy," but he nonetheless claimed that "all of Poe's poetry is interesting, because more than that of any other Romantic (except perhaps Coleridge in *Kubla Khan*), it does approach the indefiniteness of music—the supreme goal of the symbolists." Thus, "from the ordinary point of view," Poe's verse often seems exceptionally "nonsensical," but in this respect it foreshadowed the achievements of the Symbolists and other more modern poets (in Carlson 150). Poe understood, according to Wilson, the importance of conveying feeling and creating an effect, and no one knew better than he "that the deepest psychological truth may be rendered through phantasmagoria" (151). Meanwhile, among the English, the esteemed critic George Saintsbury in 1927 called Poe "absolutely alone" as a poet and especially praised the music of his verse and his diction (in Carlson 154). Saintsbury highly extolled "For Annie" and "Ulalume," although he thought they could have been improved a bit by judicious trimming, and he considered "Annabel Lee" nearly perfect (158).

Three years after Saintsbury celebrated Poe, however, Aldous Huxley issued one of the most stinging denunciations of Poe's verse ever composed. He began by asking whether Poe was a major poet and then answered his own question: "surely it would never occur to any English-speaking critic to say so," since Poe's work, except in such poems as "City in the Sea" and "To Helen," is spoiled by a "taint of vulgarity" (in Carlson 160). Those poems, Huxley felt, showed "what a very great artist perished on most of the occasions when Poe wrote verse." Yet Huxley felt he had to account for Poe's lofty status in France, and he did so by suggesting that the French, for whom English could only be a second language, were "incapable of appreciating those finer shades of vulgarity that ruin Poe for us." Poe was "one of Nature's Gentlemen" but was "unhappily cursed with incorrigible bad taste," like someone who would wear "a diamond ring on every finger" (161). Examining the first two stanzas of "Ulalume," Huxley found them overwrought and unsubtle (162), and the rhythmic effects that so many other readers have praised Huxley considered innovative in highly inflexible ways. Poe and others like him "tortured and amputated significance into fitting the ready-made music of their highly original metres and stanzas." Baudelaire, relatively ignorant of English versification, could not appreciate how bad Poe's verses are—at least according to Huxley (165).

Even more stringent in commenting on Poe's poetry was the noted American critic Yvor Winters, who felt that too many scholars had devoted far more attention to Poe's verse than it came close to deserving. A familiarity with English, Winters thought, "ought to render his crudity obvious," especially since Winters believed that for Poe "exaltation of spirit is merely a form of nervous excitement" (in Carlson 177, 180). According to Winters, "Poe appears never to have grasped the simple and traditional distinction between matter (truth) and manner (beauty)" (182; see also 186), and indeed he considered Poe "an explicit obscurantist" whose obscurity is deliberate, not accidental (187-88). For him, Poe's verse is marred by "clumsiness and insensitivity," so that his rhythms soon "disgust, because they are untrained and insensitive and have no individual life within their surprising mechanical frames" (189). Poe preferred "a heavy, unvaried, mechanical beat" and "had an ear for only the crudest of distinctions" in his rhythms. Winters considered only six poems—"The City in the Sea," "The Haunted Palace," "The Conqueror Worm," "Ulalume," "The Raven," and "The Sleeper"—to be "ambitious efforts; the others, even if one grant them a high measure of success, are minor" (192). Even the better poems, however, were flawed (192-94), and indeed Winters judged Poe so weak in so many ways and in so many genres (194-201) that the only sensible conclusion was to acknowledge that "his influence could only have been a bad one," so that "to assert that he exerted an influence is not to praise him" (201).

Far more ambivalent than Winters was T. S. Eliot, himself both a great poet and an important critic. In 1948 he began a noteworthy lecture by declaring that Poe's works seem to contain "nothing but slipshod writing," "puerile thinking," and "haphazard experiments," but he immediately conceded that this was not the whole picture. Though he found Poe's rhythms "incantatory" but unsubtle and thought that Poe often sacrificed sound to sense—as in the allegedly inaccurate use of the word "immemorial" in "Ulalume" (a usage, however, that has been praised and defended by others)—Eliot contended that if Poe's body of work is viewed from a distance, it presents "a mass of unique shape and distant size to which the eye constantly returns." Like Huxley before him, Eliot attempted to explain why Poe's poetry has been better received in France than in England and the United States. In part, he seconded Huxley—the great French writers' knowledge of English was imperfect, and this caused them to misjudge Poe. Eliot even claimed that Baudelaire's and Mallarmé's French translations were better than Poe's original poems (in Carlson 213-14). But Eliot also argued that the French writers tended to overvalue Poe because of his personality, theories, and techniques, which outshone his actual poems (214-15). In any case, Eliot had little good to say about any particular poems—he remarked that even "The Raven" contains several words that "seem to be inserted merely to fill out the line to the required measure, or for the sake of a rhyme" (209-11)—although he did finally concede "the importance of [Poe's] *work* as a whole" (219). Poe had a "powerful intellect," Eliot allowed, though a rather childish one, the "intellect of a highly gifted young person before puberty" (211-12).

Writing in 1950, the poet W. H. Auden found Poe's most typical poems, such as "Ulalume" and "The Raven," the most problematic (in Carlson 223-25), while another significant poet, Allen Tate, in 1951 judged Poe's diction to be merely vague rather than intriguingly complex (in Carlson 240). In 1959, the poet Richard Wilbur, who is now widely considered one of Poe's best critics, argued that Poe's two great subjects are "first, the war between the poetic soul and the external world; second, the war between the poetic soul and the earthly self to which it is bound" (in Carlson 259). Wilbur paid Poe the compliment of giving his poetry serious and sustained attention, and by the 1960s the same was becoming increasingly true among academic scholars and critics. In 1961, for instance, Roy Harvey Pearce, in a major book, devoted a number of pages to Poe, calling him "quite obviously the poet of dream-work" but also remarking that Poe's "obviousness makes for a kind of over-insistence which to American readers at least must seem no less than vulgar" (141). Pearce repeated many of the standard charges against Poe's verse—that it is too filled with unreality, obscurity, and egocentrism—but, as is true of many of Poe's critics, he did not feel he could ignore Poe (141-53). If for no other reason than its popularity, Poe's poetry is work critics have often felt the need to attack rather than completely disregard.

Perhaps the most surprising aspect of Poe's modern reputation as a poet is that his champions have not been more vigorous or more thorough in demonstrating his excellence and skill, especially in the face of all the negative criticism he has received. Even Floyd Stovall, one of the best modern scholars of Poe, was relatively defensive in a 1963 article meant to argue for Poe's status as a major poet. Stovall conceded that "a large part of Poe's writing . . . is trivial, artistically crude, and often in bad taste," but he nevertheless claimed that "the rest is of literary importance and merits detailed study" (418). Stovall's article, however, offered little of the detailed analysis it called for, nor is there much to be found in his excellent 1965 edition of Poe's poems. Much of the commentary there, even in the introduction, is purely objective; Poe's importance as a poet is assumed rather than demonstrated with much specificity. Likewise, Thomas Ollive Mabbott, in his splendid 1969 edition of Poe's poetry, opened by declaring that although Poe wrote only a small number of poems, "the proportion of excellence is surprisingly high, and, as is not always true of lyric poets, his powers never waned; they increased" (xxiii). Yet Mabbott, like Stovall, spent most of his introduction outlining the objective features of Poe's poetry without really making a strong or explicit case for his poetic talent. Mabbott noted, for instance, that Poe's poetic vocabulary contains relatively few words, and common ones at that; that his syntax is largely common and conversational; that most of his innovations involved meter and sound, particularly rhyme; and that he was less influenced by classical and European literature than by earlier and contemporary English writing (xxiv-xxx). All this information is, like so much else in the edition, helpful, but both the Mabbott and Stovall editions tend to take Poe's importance as a poet for granted rather than argue forcefully on his behalf.

Much the same seems true of many of the studies summarized in Esther F. Hyneman's excellent annotated bibliography of 1974, which surveys studies published between 1827 and 1973. Many of the books and articles covered by Hyneman deal with the themes, meanings, and sources (indeed, especially the sources) of Poe's poems, with relatively few writers, apparently, trying to make any sustained or detailed case for Poe's poetic talent, and this often seems to be the case in subsequent commentary as well. In fact, commentary on Poe the poet (as opposed to Poe the writer of short stories) has been surprisingly sparse in the past fifty years, as becomes immediately obvious from a search of the annual surveys printed in *American Literary Scholarship*. Excellent overviews of the poems can be found in recent work by such scholars as Vincent Buranelli, Benjamin F. Fisher, Kevin J. Hayes, Bettina L. Knapp, Richard Kopley, Scott Peeples, Elizabeth Phillips, and Dwayne Thorpe (to mention just a few).

Of these overviews, perhaps the most valuable and comprehensive are the ones by Phillips and Thorpe, who both offer fairly detailed discussions of a wide variety of individual poems as well as a good sense of recent critical trends in thinking about Poe's poetry. Focusing mainly on Poe's early verse, Phillips emphasizes the "trials by which Poe tested and proved himself as a poet," arguing that the "lines of force in the evolution of the work are not consistent or continuous; there are starts and stops and returns for rewriting." Phillips stresses "the experimental quality of the verse from 1825 and 1835" and warns against the temptation to read this verse in light of Poe's later pronouncements as a critic (67). Instead, each of the early poems should be read as an attempt by Poe to find his way as a writer of verse. Phillips comments on recent critics who discuss such topics as developments in the rhetorical strategies of the early poems and their Platonic and Romantic aspects (67-68). In addition, she notes that recent commentators have explored such themes or issues in the early poems as "a preoccupation with death and the afterlife" (68), the importance of rhythm in poetry, and the relationship between the real and the ideal (69). Phillips herself argues that "Poe seems to have begun writing verse primarily for amusement," but she explores the ways in which even his earliest poems anticipate some of his later preoccupations (69). She concedes that the quality of the early poems is "uneven," and she cites other recent critics who emphasize their nature as experiments in various poetic conventions (71). Commenting in particular on the poems published in 1827, she suggests that while "their influences show," they served Poe as "exercises in thinking for himself and making poems that were recognizably his own" (71).

The poems published in 1829 reveal, according to Phillips, a new maturity and a more distinctive voice (74) than some of the earlier works, and they often have genuine interest as "experiments in tone"

(77). Later poems show Poe experimenting with different techniques (including blank verse and poetic drama), and indeed Phillips thinks that Poe was a better writer of drama than he is often seen as being (86). All in all, she contends that the "verse from 1825 to 1835 reveals not only the frustrated hopes but also the exceptional gifts of the poet," and she emphasizes Poe's interest—and success—in exploiting a wide "*range* of styles" (87). Phillips provides perhaps the best one-chapter survey available of the early poems and of the diversity of critical commentary those poems have provoked.

Much the same can be said of Dwayne Thorpe's overview of the later poetry. He opens by discussing the general neglect of Poe's verse by academic critics before he then stresses the "insistent musicality" of Poe's poems and comments on the ways Poe's poetry "explores longings for the eternal in a world of time" (90). Thorpe discusses the relations between the poetry and the prose fiction (90-91) and also emphasizes such important themes as "despair and nihilism" (93) and such techniques as suggestiveness, which he sees as the "hallmark of Poe's verse" (94). Other important themes discussed by Thorpe include dissolution, mutability, and isolation, while other significant techniques include irony, the use of expletives, and "passionate repetition" (95). Thorpe comments that "if time in Poe's poems is a shapeless force that first divides soul from thought, then swallows self, universe, and God, its opposite, the ideal, may offer no solace" (95). He suggests that many recent critics see Poe as a disillusioned romantic whose "mature poetry, like his fiction, contains many indications that the dream may be a trap" (95). Thorpe stresses the importance of realizing that the speakers of Poe's poems should not necessarily be identified with Poe himself—a fact that many recent critics have been willing to concede when discussing "The Raven" but have not always emphasized when commenting on some of Poe's other poems (96-97).

Although Thorpe tends to offer less detailed discussions of other recent critics than Phillips provides, his essay is still highly useful in this regard. He notes, for instance, how "Ulalume" has been approached recently from allegorical, psychological, phenomenological, and philosophical perspectives (100)—to mention just a few—and Thorpe's own readings of individual works are always clear, sophisticated, and up-to-date. His more general comments are also valuable, as when he suggests that once "Poe had used a form, stanza, or effect, he rarely returned to it, and his revisions almost always replace regular stanzas with novel effects" (105). Thorpe concludes by suggesting that Poe's poems are best read against the background of his entire corpus of texts, and in fact Thorpe's own essay, like the companion essay by Phillips, displays the very sort of comprehensive vision that it encourages others to cultivate. Anyone seeking a solid overview of the best recent work in studies of Poe's poetry could hardly do better than consult these two fine contributions to the field.

What is most needed, however, is a comprehensive volume that patiently makes the case, line by line and sometimes word by word, for the skill and power and beauty of the best examples of Poe's verse. Such a volume would be valuable for many canonical writers, but it would be especially useful in the case of Poe, since the merits of his poetry have been denied so strongly, and so often, by so many significant writers and critics. A critical variorum edition of Poe's poetry would be even better, since readers of such a volume could then follow, in precise detail, the particular critical and analytical points that have been made about Poe's poetry, both pro and con, over the many decades since it was first published. A major poet surely deserves such an edition, at least for his very best poems.

## Works Cited

Alexander, Jean. *Affidavits of Genius: Edgar Allan Poe and the French Critics, 1847-1924*. Port Washington, NY: Kennikat Press, 1971.

*American Literary Scholarship*. Durham, NC: Duke University Press, 1965-    .

Bloom, Harold, ed. *Edgar Allan Poe*. New York: Bloom's Literary Criticism, 2008.

Buranelli, Vincent. *Edgar Allan Poe*. 2d ed. Boston: Twayne, 1977.

Carlson, Eric W., ed. *The Recognition of Edgar Allan Poe: Selected Criticism Since 1829*. Ann Arbor: U of Michigan P, 1969.

Fisher, Benjamin F. *The Cambridge Introduction to Edgar Allan Poe*. New York: Cambridge UP, 2008.

Hyneman, Esther F. *Edgar Allan Poe: An Annotated Bibliography of Books and Articles in English, 1827-1973*. Boston: G. K. Hall, 1974.

Knapp, Bettina L. *Edgar Allan Poe*. New York: Frederick Ungar, 1984.

Kopley, Richard, and Kevin J. Hayes. "Two Verse Masterworks: 'The Raven' and 'Ulalume.'" *The Cambridge Companion to Edgar Allan Poe*. Ed. Kevin J. Hayes. New York: Cambridge UP, 2002. 191-204.

Pearce, Roy Harvey. *The Continuity of American Poetry*. Princeton, NJ: Princeton UP, 1961.

Peeples, Scott. *The Afterlife of Edgar Allan Poe*. Rochester, NY: Camden House, 2004.

Phillips, Elizabeth. "The Poems: 1824-1835." *A Companion to Poe Studies*. Ed. Eric W. Carlson. Westport, CT: Greenwood Press, 1996. 67-88.

Poe, Edgar Allan. *Complete Poems*. Ed. Thomas Ollive Mabbott. Urbana: U of Illinois P, 1969.

_____. *Poems*. Ed. Floyd Stovall. Charlottesville: UP of Virginia, 1965.

Stovall, Floyd. "The Conscious Art of Edgar Allan Poe." *College English* 24.6 (1963): 417-21.

Thorpe, Dwayne. "The Poems: 1836-1849." *A Companion to Poe Studies*. Ed. Eric W. Carlson. Westport, CT: Greenwood Press, 1996. 89-109.

Walker, I. M., ed. *Edgar Allan Poe: The Critical Heritage*. London: Routledge & Kegan Paul, 1986.

# CRITICAL
# READINGS

# Edgar Allan Poe and the Nightmare Ode_____

Dave Smith

When I left home for college at the University of Virginia, I must have imagined history was something confined to textbooks and roadside commemorative markers, which occur in Virginia nearly as often as azaleas and daffodils. Among the splendid benefits of college nothing outweighs awakening to the presence of the past as it shapes and changes one's life. In 1963, for example, I lived in a cottage next door to James Southall Wilson, the founder of the *Virginia Quarterly Review* and a Poe scholar. He was also husband to the formidable granddaughter of President Tyler. He seemed to me, and I think he was, in accent, courtesy, rose gardening, and tales about Poe, an embodiment of the Southern gentleman, a type parents, preachers, and teachers invoked freely for my moral edification. Professor Wilson embodied the lost world of Southern refinement, principle, and neoclassical culture our schools proclaimed our due heritage. He was nothing like the men in my family, for whom being a Southerner meant only raising the stars and bars with a liquid rendition of Dixie.

Perhaps we find ourselves in the men that history isolates. Once, dawdling by the serpentine wall which Mr. Jefferson, as we were taught to call our founder, had built with slave labor, I exchanged pleasantries with a man who had written books I read in my classes, a man named Faulkner. Almost daily I walked to class by the brick pavilion where Edgar Allan Poe had lived in 1826. Poe was as great a Southern presence to me as Faulkner, for I had read his stories and poems. My school teachers were assiduous in noting that Poe was a Virginian like all of us, not merely a name in a textbook. Poe and Faulkner suggested to me I was not wholly outside a history found in textbooks. I was of it and of them.

I don't think I much considered what I was until my first-year English class read Robert Penn Warren's *All the King's Men*, a book which made me so aware of "Southernness" that I remember *where* I read almost every page. I felt I was reading about family. Mine was the sort of family made mobile and modestly prosperous after the Second World War. I spent summers with my grandparents, often taking Sunday rides in a green Hudson automobile, meandering through the woody burgs of Yorktown and Williamsburg. These were places people lived in, not the toy villages they are now. I played on Virginia's much bloodied battlefields, but I did not trouble myself to know exactly whose blood was spilled or why.

Even as I began to see myself connected to others in the Southern story, I grew aware I also stood outside the official Virginia history, for I belonged to no patrician family and no prep school, hardly knew what an Episcopalian was, let alone a Catholic, and could point to no cultural ancestry which I possessed or whose loss, with family ground, shadowed me. I grew up in a subdivision where backyards debouched onto farms that had always been there, farms tended some by tractors, some by black laborers with names like "Peanut." They seemed to think my name was "Mistuh." Those farms are gone. Those who called me "Mistuh" are gone. Not gone with the wind but with the developers who bulldozed eighteenth- and nineteenth-century houses and schools for shopping centers, who made our Baptist Church an anachronism like Philip Larkin's in "Church Going." Change in the South is the relentless bastard of greed. Its peculiar violence, so characteristic of a place in metamorphosis, leaves the Southerner orphaned, intensely aware of *being there* and simultaneously *not being there*.

That awareness marks Poe's writing, as actively in his poetry as in his fiction. Poe's university room, in 1963, was identified by a plaque that made it officially historic, yet a student lived in the room. I don't believe I ever saw its interior and so I could think of Poe, despite my old teachers, as a disembodied creator of tales, not a man. But I could also think of him as alive behind that door, a student with a university life not radically unlike my own. In this way, too, I was both in and out of Southern history. It did not then occur to me that Poe may have felt the same.

Today, the memorializers at the University have erected a barrier to this awareness. An impervious Plexiglas door seals his room, into which the monied visitor, that coveted pigeon, may gaze as if into Poe's soul. What the visitor will see is historically correct: a wooden bed, small desk, a few chairs, a rug, living accoutrements. Oddly, a raven (can it be *plastic*?) is perched on a branch as naturally as if it were a poster of Def Leppard. No stereos, no rack of books and tapes, no knickknacks, no letters from home, no photographs of mom and pop and favorite girl. The black-and-white prospect is sterile and chilling. They have buried Poe in plain view to a greater extent than Poe himself managed. University administrators seem to believe history is a containable pollutant. Undefiled, tourists come and stand and look for Poe as if he were Elvis, Sinbad, or Madonna. Some have read Poe and others have seen the Vincent Price movies. They want to see Poe, the bard of our nightmare of dispossession.

To be banished from the garden is western civilization's most painful sanction. It is recorded in the Genesis case of Adam and Eve vs. God. It is recorded in a long literary tradition of gardens and exiles. The intellectual historian of the South, Lewis P. Simpson, explains the garden image in *The Dispossessed Garden*. He calls it a "pastoral plantation" and defines it as "a secure world redeemed from the ravages of history, a place of pastoral independence and pastoral permanence" (17) and "a homeland of the life of the mind" (23). Simpson believes there was little modernist alienation in the antebellum Southern mind which, as he says,

> was cut off from what affected the general stream of literary culture because of the involvement of the Southern man of letters in the politics of slavery. He could not participate in the opposition to society which distinguishes the function of the man of letters in Europe, and in New England, where it marks in important ways the writings of Emerson, Thoreau, and Hawthorne. (38)

The antebellum mind viewed the Jeffersonian garden as encompassing, perhaps engendering, a civilization whose classico-Christian values link individuals to supernatural continuity, a community of souls. Yet the garden was lost to the encroachments of the modern world, to commercialized values, a dispossession and outage dramatized by civil war and so intensely felt that it became the signature of Southernness. The Southern literary voice is that of an outcast, an orphan, an outsider cut off from communal support and, importantly, communal definition which he once had and which henceforth he carries like a threatening headache. Or a pastoral memory. Or myth. James Joyce causes Stephen Daedalus to declaim, on Irish soil, this modern, nationalist, pathology: "History is the nightmare from which I cannot awake." If Southerners could have thought it, they might have said it: *Alienation, c'est moi.*

The nightmare of half-being, half-knowing is that of not being and not knowing: dispossession. Until the twentieth-century so-called Renascence, Southern literature occupies only the garden of half-being and half-knowing, a netherland of knightly gentlemen, asexual ladies, and a contract Heaven. The divorce from reality experienced by protagonists is a denial of history, an orphaning. When the denial's lie festers sufficiently to invade the body of society, sickness requires treatment; writers probe the actual, becoming aware that historical conditions of ignorance, poverty, defeat, pain, brutality, hopelessness, self-delusion, and isolation from community have configured the South as different from the American ideal of positive change and credible hope.

That ideal empowered Jefferson to raise a university in the garden, to foster an enlightenment whose headache was slavery. The black man was, according to Simpson, "the gardener in the garden," as much founder as Jefferson himself. The absent hand that let his garden go to seed was, inevitably, the slave's. Who more than a slave was the orphan dispossessed of his garden? Who more than an orphan could chronicle the simultaneously personal and cultural nightmare of outage?

We might answer that the nineteenth-century voice would be, wouldn't it, Charles Dickens? Or his American peer born scarcely three years earlier, Edgar Allan Poe. Poe, I think, was also a gardener, a transplanter of the English garden of verse into dark American soil. From the first poems he published at age eighteen to his last, and in his remarks on form, Poe coveted an invariable, mechanistic prosody which might with legal force yield a predictable life, stable and evident, perhaps compensation for what his life lacked. His essay "The Philosophy of Composition" argues a dogmatic methodology he believes will lead him to improvisation and to an impression of platonic beauty which "The Raven" seems to many to have achieved. Even T. S. Eliot, no admirer, conceded Poe sometimes made the true magic of poetry. But Poe's rational blueprint of process tells us only what he thought *about* the poem; it does not tell us much of what he used to *think* the poem, or why.

"The Raven," unequivocally the most famous of Poe's small body of poetry, may be among our most famous *bad* poems. Americans are fond of saying we do not read and do not care for poetry. It may be so. Yet Americans commonly recognize Poe's bird as subject of a poem by a weird guy who drank himself to death. Written and published in 1845, in print steadily for 148 years, the stanzas of "The Raven" are sonic flashcards. We may not know Whitman, Dickinson, Frost, or Eliot. But we do know Poe. We know "The Raven."

A poem that might have been designed by Benjamin Franklin, "The Raven" purports to be explained by Poe's "Philosophy of Composition." Poe wrote his essay for crowds smitten by his bird. Interestingly, he does not justify poetry with morality, as Emerson and Whitman would. He pretends to expose the poet's trade. Some recent criticism has seen "The Raven" as a parody of Romantic poems of personal discovery. Perhaps. What Poe leaves unsaid peels, layer by layer, toward two questions answerable only by speculation. The first asks why "The Raven" has for fifteen generations commanded the imaginations of people who have often enough known it to be a bad poem. The second question asks if Poe is a Southern writer. They are related questions.

That "The Raven" is a bad poem is unacceptable to many readers, and Poe people are not swayed much by rational argument. Were they, the plot alone would convict Poe. A man sits late in a storm; he laments a lost lady love; a bird not ordinarily abroad at night, and especially not in severe weather, seeks entrance to the human dwelling; admitted, the bird betrays no fright, no panic, its attitude entirely focused on its host—an invited guest; the bird, then, enters into a ventriloquial dialectic with the host and is domesticated to become an inner voice; we might say it is the voice of the *innerground* as opposed to *underground*, which word means much to the American spirit with its reasons to run, to hide, to contain itself. Action then ceases.

Poe knew this one-man backlot production for the smoker it was. His embrace of gothic machinery includes a terrified, obsessed man, an inhospitable, allegorical midnight in December, a "gifted" animal, extreme emotional states, heavy breathing of both cadence and melodramatic signifiers (*grim, gaunt*), the supernatural presence of inexplicables (perfume, Pallas, bird), all to portray a psychic battle in the mind. Poe assembles a version of saloon theater for the mind's ear. But his poem's form emerges from the unbuckled ways of the ode, the loosened metrics of which Poe knew in the work of Keats, Shelley, Coleridge, and Wordsworth. Poe's editorial slush pile was full of their imitators. Odes attracted people because, as Gilbert Highet has said, they "soar and dive and veer as the wind catches their wing." The capacity for passion, personal experience, ambitious public utterance, and a celebrative finish defines the ode. The boosterism, self-infatuation, and lyceum podiums of nineteenth-century America made Poe and the ode a natural match.

Poe was drawn to what was left of the Pindaric ode with its systemically recurrent parts. The classical ode, both Horatian and Pindaric, implies fixity and continuity. The form manifests noble purpose, dignity of subject and demeanor; it is ordinarily public address with an encoded civics lesson. The same explosions of social change which scattered people over the globe loosened the metrical grasp of this lyric form until it is, in American practice anyway, not readily different from an elegy. Indeed, as comedians know, ode is a word suspect to both poet and reader, a synonym for what Ezra Pound meant by "emotional slither." Once, perhaps, the ode celebrated and the elegy lamented. Both are, in some measure due to Poe, less specialized in contemporary practice.

Poe was attracted to the ode because, as English Romantics had used it, a classical rigor was maintained while a daring shift had begun which would result in lyric, singular, interior expression. Paul H. Fry, in *The Poet's Calling in the English Ode*, points to Allen Tate's "Ode to the Confederate Dead," where Tate stands at the cemetery but cannot enter and be among that historical order. The ode permits Tate, Fry says, to dramatize that moment of *being there* and *not being there*, an awareness of visionary discontinuity prerequisite to pastoral. With "abysmal frustration," Fry says, the ode writer at that gate discovers there is "no threshold at all between the self and what is unknown, or other," and the ode of all forms "most boldly and openly tests the possibility of calling in the Spirit" (2). The intent of the ode is to marry the poet's voice with the God-voice in order to manifest reality—life, death, or other. The ode-voice identifies with, i.e., celebrates, all that it summons because whatever its various registers of discourse may be, it means to praise a "belonging-to" quality.

That the language strategies Poe employs, largely yoked under the braided tropes of reiteration and interrogation, are distantly related to the Pindaric tradition of triadic movement which desires aesthetic completion as well as to the Horatian tradition of monody seems obvious enough. It is not my intent to follow Poe's descent from either. Nor do I mean to examine the micrometrical features of the poem, but a look at a single stanza is helpful to establish Poe's chains of repetitions:

> Once upon a midnight dreary, while I pondered, weak and weary,
> Over many a quaint and curious volume of forgotten lore—
> While I nodded, nearly napping, suddenly there came a tapping,
> As of some one gently rapping, rapping at my chamber door.
> "'Tis some visitor," I muttered, "tapping at my chamber door—
>     Only this and nothing more."

Poe termed the meter of this quintet-plus-a-hemistich stanza "octameter acatalectic," with alternation of "heptameter catalectic" in line five and "tetrameter catalectic" in the bob, or sixth line. The norm is a duple foot, either trochaic (louder) or iambic (softer). Lines one, two, and three have sixteen syllables; lines four and five have fifteen, and line six has seven. Full lines are broken by a mid-caesura and halves of each line link internally by rhyme exact or slant. The half-line, a lyric staple, surges against the longer and outswelling rhythm of the full line. The full line is a prose rhythm by virtue of both its feet-patterns of ascent and descent and its unitary sprawl and self-containment. The sonic adventure of each stanza is like a contained body of water into which some weight is dropped, causing outward swelling of wave action. When these waves reach and rebound from the containing walls, they dash against each other. Narrative events create new waves. The result is a psychic chaos, a pace that stumbles, almost, upon itself, imitating panic, queasiness, and fear. Poe wanted a rhythmic trance he felt was conducive to an impression of beauty but wanted the trance to dispossess the reader from tranquil stability. He relies on the catalectic, or broken pattern, a missing syllable that "bumps" our progression. Poe exploits a ballad half-line, with its comfortable lyric expectations, its mnemonic power, and its narrative momentum to tell a virtually plotless story, a story entirely interior and psychological. He has telescoped the ballad line into the ode's stanzaic regularity, controlling tropes, public address, and mixed dictions to accomplish what appears a personal complaint, not the ode's meditational tone for imponderables such as art, beauty, life, and death. The tale served by his machinery is the dispossessing myth of lost love, which Poe routinely furnishes with classical allusions to establish eternal resonance.

Our affection for Poe's bird must be, in some measure, due to his adaptations, clunky and juryrigged as they appear. Poe thought his work daring, and it is, in the presentation of the nightmare of absent consolation, or belonging-to. "The Raven" reverberates not with the usual flight-to-vision, return-enlightened celebration, but with the psychic thrill of confronting despair, isolation, and the utter futility of lovely words. The nightmare vision made the poem an allegory of the darkest self in terror.

Robert Lowell, in "Skunk Hour," echoes Milton when he says "I myself am hell; nobody's here." Poe's parable of loneliness, like Lowell's, nudges the reader beyond the problem of man without woman. The condition of self's hell is an orphan sensibility. It does not require too great a leap to read Poe's poem as the figure of a dispossessed garden, an eroded Southern culture, in which Poe seeks to know what, in any real sense, we might belong to. If the poem centers the bereaved lover, it emphasizes his plight as outsider. Poe finds himself alone in the time and season of human intercourse at its lowest ebb; a time, indeed, when we remind ourselves that we had better change our ways, or else—as Dickens' Scrooge learns. A knock at his door should bring Poe a human visitor, if any, an emissary from the community; yet there is darkness, and then the Raven, the predator. And a predator who seems to know Poe is doomed to an absence of civil intercourse, a silence, and words which echo without effect. Poe understands and declares that even the bird will leave him, as all others have done, as hope has done. With this, Poe's poem has arrived at nightmare, the living isolation from fellowship that popular horror movies have turned into the ghoulish marches of the living dead. If Poe's bird seems deadly, the incantatory rhythms which evoked the birdspell are the forbidding stanzas which clank forth and enchant us as if the bird were enacting some chthonic ritual. The bird, in fact, makes no move after arrival. It does not threaten, seems entirely content, is a creature not unfamiliar to odes. Yet how different from, say, a nightingale so sweetly caged by a form which for Poe permits the witness to come close to his creature and yet keep safe, a glimpsed but not engaged threat. Still, having summoned the raven, Poe cannot so easily deny or repress it: he tells us the bird sits in the forever of that last stanza, a curse neither expiated nor escaped. The bird is, as Ted Hughes has seen and shown with *Crow*, a nightmare.

I had better, at this point, say a nightmare of alienation. Alienation from what? Lenore, the woman who is always *there* and constantly *not there*, of course. I remind myself, again, that the ode is a celebratory form, a public form, and I am not apt to think of the "raven" as either, so private is its agon from start to finish. Again what is dramatized is what doesn't happen, the human visit; a moment of social cohesion fails; but a visit occurs that shifts the abandoned speaker toward public experience. The erotic, aesthetic, and familial resonances Poe celebrates in the missing Lenore may be read as symbolic of community. It will be missing *eternally*, for Poe cannot lift his soul "from out that shadow that lies floating on the floor" and that in-escape is the nightmare of alienation.

Doubtless, for most readers, Lenore, whoever she might have been and may be in her *is-ness*, constitutes the drawing power of the poem. We have loved and lost, felt heartbreak, felt ourselves abandoned. This is a basic country-western song and it sells more than we may want to think about. Yet few country-western songs last in admiration or consciousness as "The Raven" does. Poe's addition of the nearly voiceless but intimidating bird employs Gothic machinery to touch unresolved fears of what's under the bed or behind the door. But Poe's bird has the power of knowledge—it knows *us*—and this makes the world a more slippery place than we had thought. It exposes our inside. That is a problem for Poe, and for all of us, because he knows that the inside without connection to an outside is an emptiness, a desert. No self can supply love's support, community sustenance, or the hope we once drew from an outside system. Poe's terrible fable sticks with us because no matter what our intellects conceive, our hearts believe we are alien, each of us, and there is a god-bird that knows it, too.

But alienation from Lenore seems, finally, not enough. Poe is paralyzed, room-captured, divorced from books, ideas, poetry itself, and in the last stanza from the goddess of wisdom, Pallas, who has until this minute sat Virgil-like over Poe's bower. Not Pallas now; now the Raven. Why? Can being dumped by hard luck account for this depth of despair? Poe, in some important ways, has a modern's existential attitude. He has understood the relentless industrial rapacity which Dickens so brutally knew. The connection between them is that both were dispossessed. Poe may have gotten his bird, as some argue, from Dickens. He got his alienation from hard times.

Poe loved women who died, often violently, diseased. His mother went first; he was two and an orphan. He was taken in and raised as ward of John Allan and his wife Frances, a sickly woman who would die on him, but first there would be Jane Stanard, on whom he had a fourteen-year-old's crush. She was thirty-one when she died insane. Poe suffered the death of three women before he finished being a moody teenaged boy. His foster father Allan wanted and had children by a second wife, who had little interest in Poe. Allan raised Poe as the squire-son of a rising businessman—to a point. But Poe was not Allan's blood son.

Poe felt he had second-class treatment from his foster family. He felt himself orphaned. At eighteen he went to the University of Virginia, where he was undercapitalized and made to feel his inferior circumstance. He was pushed outside that society, too. Returned to Richmond, he found himself an outsider, and he embarked on one of his secret journeys. Wandering, turning up, writing, editing, trying to establish a domestic community, then wandering off—this was the pattern of Poe's life. In every relationship and in every circumstance, he was the outsider, the orphan.

No one feels the powerful attraction of the *being there* and the *not being there* more than the orphan. Jay Gatsby shows it. Poe lived it. Americans are, by definition, orphans. We were all, at one point, come-heres, all by scheme equal in opportunity taken according to ability. The positive idea of national possibility underwrites the very imagining of the "new world." Poe's foster father, John Allan, a Scot, embodies the chance to make it, and one cannot doubt he would trumpet the values of American opportunity were he with us, no less than that great Kiwanian Walt Whitman. But with Poe the brilliant shimmer of hope brought by morning sun was leaden early on. It grew heavier all his life. He did not belong. He could not declare a belonging-to, as Gatsby would learn. And he could not lie about the world as he saw it. He was an artist, a truth-teller—nothing is more obsessive in his tales than that need. His truth was a nightmare.

If we read "The Raven," despite its absence of specific local details, as an "awareness" of the life of America in 1845, we see that Poe has conjectured the nightmare of the individual cut off from history, abandoned by family, place, and community love. He experiences personally what the South will experience regionally and the country will, down the long road, experience emotionally. Though he means to celebrate Lenore, what he most intensely celebrates is the union with community, the identity of place and people which Poe simultaneously *has* and has lost. In this, in 1845, he speaks for the Southern white and, paradoxically, for the slave paralyzed in his garden and also dispossessed. This story is still the nightmare. Having seen it, Poe celebrates the sensibility or imagination that suffers and knows simultaneously, ultimately the figure of the artist. This figure will sit in the lost garden, knowing its lostness, without explanation, but aware that the change is hopeless and continuous. This poem will, in its late variations, become our outlaw song of the renegade, the cowboy in black, the rebel without a cause. "The Raven" is the drama of nightmare awakening in the American poetic consciousness where there is no history which is not dispossession, little reality to the American promise, and nothing of consequence to place trust in except the song, the ode of celebration. Poe knew that he stood, like Tate, who called him cousin, at the gate to the answers. But he could not go beyond it. Like Tate, he sought to form a culture (because one did not exist) out of the English poetic baggage, but too often it failed. "The Raven" is the croaking and anguished nightmare ode of allegiance, and we have been finding ourselves in it ever since Poe began hearing "Nevermore."

From *Southern Humanities Review* 24, no. 1 (1995): 1-10. Copyright © 1995 by Dave Smith. Reprinted with permission of Auburn University and the author.

# The Visionary Paradox:
## Poe's Poetic Theory

G. R. Thompson

The following essay is adapted by its author from a lecture originally presented before the Edgar Allan Poe Society of Baltimore and
published by the Society as *Circumscribed Eden of Dreams:
Dreamvision and Nightmare in Poe's Early Poetry.* Endnotes have
been revised to correspond to redacted text and renumbered; references to Poe's critical essays are keyed to the standard Harrison edition of 1902; Thompson's edition of *Essays and Reviews* (Library of
America, 1984) was published later in the same year as this mono-
graph.

In the late poem "Dream-Land" (1844-49), Edgar Allan Poe evokes
a world "Out of Space—Out of Time":

> Haunted by ill angels only,
> Where an Eidolon, named Night,
> On a black throne reigns upright . . . .

Its dreamscape is of:

> Bottomless vales and boundless floods,
> And chasms, and caves, and Titan woods,
> With forms no man can discover
> For the dews that drip all over;
> Mountains toppling evermore
> Into seas without a shore;
> Seas that restlessly aspire,
> Surging, unto lakes of fire;
> Lakes that endlessly outspread
> Their lone waters—lone and dead . . . . [1]

---

The apocalyptic dreamscape is what most of us remember when we think of Poe's poetry and his prose poems: the imaging of the torment of the bereaved lover in "Ulalume" (1847) as an ice-locked volcano at the South Pole ceaselessly rolling sulphurous fires down its frozen steaming sides; the lurid light streaming hellishly up from "The City in the Sea" (1831); the "flowering" of volcanoes on a newly formed world just "spoken" into existence in "The Power of Words" (1845); the nightmare dream of Arthur Gordon Pym.

Poe's announced poetic vision is not of such nightmare landscapes—in fact, it is directly antithetical. The poetic vision described in Poe's essays is of an indefinitive, indescribable, supernal loveliness. The supernalist harmony of another world, however, is rarely captured in Poe's poetry, though occasionally we have glimpses of its vague contours in Poe's first two books *Tamerlane* (1827) and *Al Aaraaf* (1829), which comprise all save two of his earliest extant poems. These two volumes are especially instructive in seeing the development, and the destruction, of the mythos of Poe's poetic world. They are also instructive in placing Poe in the tradition of romantic poetry in both Europe and America.

Poe's principal European models are Byron, Shelley, and Thomas Moore; and he stands out in America from the Emerson-Whitman school of romantic "ideal realism," wherein the poet sees the physical world, the concrete "real," as possessing within it, and as one with it, the spiritual.[2] Poe finds the physical world a prison-house, an impediment to attaining spirituality, a punishment. In this, he is more orthodoxly Christian than, say, Emerson, though his version of the Godhead is aesthetic, not moral. God, for Poe, lies in supernal beauty that transcends the concrete reality of the earthly. Both the supernalist and realist schools of poetry are "transcendental"—but in very different ways—and between these antipodes vibrates the major dynamic of romantic poetry in America.

Within this large dichotomy, there is another dichotomy in Poe's writings, between the poetic theory and the rendered vision of the poems. Poe's lecture at the end of his career on "The Poetic Principle" (1848), a summary of the theory he had been developing for twenty years, asserts that the "sense of the Beautiful" is an "immortal instinct" deep within the spirit of humankind and that the "Poetic Sentiment" is an innate desire to apprehend "supernal Loveliness."[3] The idea that the "ultimate object of all Poetry is Truth" and that every poem should "inculcate a moral" he calls "the heresy of *The Didactic*" (XIV, 271). A poem conveys whatever "truth" it has through its art, through the experience of the poem itself. Nothing more dignified or supremely noble exists than a "poem written solely for the poem's sake" (XIV, 272). Only in the "contemplation of the Beautiful" can we attain "elevation, or excitement *of the soul*" (XIV, 275; cf. 290). Poe ends with a catalogue of elements that induce the "true poetical effect" (XIV, 290), for which rhythm and song are essential. He moves from, first, the stars, through indefinite objects of nature, vague sights, indistinct smells, and gentle tactile sensations like wind, to the sense of the undiscovered, the distant, the unworldly, concluding with the beauty and love of woman (XIV, 290-91).

Within the poetry itself, as partially illustrated by the opening quotations, is another dichotomy—that between the gentler visionary dreamscapes and the nightmare landscape that rapidly comes to dominate the poetry as well as the tales. At the beginning of his career, Poe had attempted to write ideal poetry of supernal beauty and mystery—indistinct and dreamlike, out of space and out of time—though these early poems are suffused with romantic melancholy and contain the threat of the sinister. In "Al Aaraaf," Poe evokes a mythic star world beyond earthly space and time.

> O! nothing earthly save the ray
> (Thrown back from flowers) of Beauty's eye,
> As in those gardens where the day
> springs from gems of Circassy—
> O! nothing earthly save the thrill
> Of melody in woodland rill—

. . . .
O, nothing of the dross of—
Yet all the beauty—all the flowers
That list our Love, and deck our bowers—
Adorn yon world afar, afar—
The wandering star.

In the far star world of "Al Aaraaf," poetic myths, banished from earthly realities, still have ethereal existence in an otherworldly mid-region, where all is initially counterpoised in static sleep before the call to awake comes from Ligeia, the spirit of harmony. In Part II of the poem, Poe attempts a delicate and indefinite dreamscape:

Young flowers were whispering in melody
To happy flowers that night—and tree to tree;
Fountains were gushing music as they fell
In many a star-lit grove, or moon-lit dell;
Yet silence came upon material things—
Fair flowers, bright waterfalls and angel wings—
And sound alone that from the spirit sprang
Bore burden to the charm the maiden sang:
  "'Neath Blue-bell or streamer—
    Or tufted wild spray
  That keeps, from the dreamer,
    The moonbeam away—
  Bright beings! that ponder,
    With half closing eyes,
  On the stars which your wonder
    Hath drawn from the skies,
  Till they glance thro' the shade, and
    Come down to your brow
  Like—eyes of the maiden
    Who calls on you now—

> Arise! from your dreaming
>> In violet bowers,
> To duty beseeming
>> These star-litten hours—
> And shake from your tresses
>> Encumbered with dew
> The breath of those kisses
>> That cumber them too . . . ."[4]

This dreamy vision through "half closing eyes" of "star-lit grove" and "moon-lit dell," of fountains "gushing music," of "angel wings" and the dew-kissed tresses of a maiden, radically contrasts with the nightmare vision of the works first quoted. Yet these images are trite conventions of romantic verse. This part of the poem is not particularly successful in suggesting an ideal world of supernal beauty; characteristically, the more effective is the latter part of the poem, where the star world is annihilated.

But Poe will not, in theory, give up the concept of poetry as the vision (even if glimpsed merely) of supernal loveliness. He pushes the supernalist poetic to its limit in a review (1844) of R. H. Horne's *Orion.* He writes that the aim of poetry is to exalt the sensitive reader's soul into "a conception of pure *beauty*" by appealing to his

> sentiment of the beautiful—that divine sixth sense which is yet so faintly understood—that sense which phrenology has attempted to embody in its organ of *ideality*—that sense which is basic of all Cousin's dreams—that sense which speaks of *God* through his purest, if not his *sole* attribute— which proves, and which alone proves his existence.[5]

One might feel that poetry used as the only proof of God is taking the spirit of romanticism rather far, even though the romantic age made the poet tantamount to a god. But Poe puts a limitation on the divine powers of poesy.

In his early (1836) review of the poems of Joseph Rodman Drake's *The Culprit Fay* and Fitzgreene Halleck's *Alnwick Castle*, Poe remarks that poetry has an "intangible and purely spiritual nature" so ethereal that it cannot even be defined. It "refuses to be bound down within the widest horizon of mere sounds," that is, of mere earth-bound words.[6] Yet, although poetry cannot be defined, it can be recognized:

> If, indeed, there be any one circle of thought distinctly and palpably marked out from amid the jarring and tumultuous chaos of human intelligence, it is that evergreen and radiant Paradise which every true poet knows, and knows alone, as the limited realm of his authority—as the circumscribed Eden of his dreams. (VIII, 281)

In what ways this "authority," this "circle" of thought, this "horizon" of sounds, is "limited" and "circumscribed" is the question I wish to explore here in connection with the two kinds of dreams in Poe's fictive world: the hellscape of the nightmare; and the evocative, indefinite visions of supernal loveliness in his earliest poems. The visionary lyric impulse of Poe's earliest poetry gives way rapidly to the dramatization of nightmare. But the theory remains the same, though refined and elaborated: Poetry is an expression of the religious instinct. The most salient feature of the theory is the idea of a transcendent supernal beauty just out of reach, glimpsed merely, by the earth-bound visionary poet struggling with some "ill demon" in himself or in nature. The *Tamerlane* poems embody a consistent development of a tension between visionary experience and a double limitation or circumscription of that experience. This tension generates the eventual triumph of the dark imagination in an evocation of the aesthetic process itself in the final poem. This poem is an icon of the nine shorter lyrics of the volume and a direct bridge to Poe's second volume, *Al Aaraaf*, in which the sad celebration of the "dreaming" imagination gives way to the final nightmare of total annihilation.

* * *

In April, 1831, the New York publisher Elam Bliss brought out *Poems by Edgar A. Poe*, Second Edition. The volume has a critical prefatory essay, "Letter to Mr.——," which begins "Dear B——," probably an invented person, possibly his publisher, Bliss. This is Poe's first critical statement; in it he states a poetic credo derived in part from Coleridge and, as well, unwittingly identifies what will be the major problems for a full comprehension of his poetry and poetics. These include an uncertain relation of the earthly to the unearthly; the disconcerting presence of flippancy, humor, satire, and irony; and an almost schizophrenic tension between the beautiful and terrifying.

A poem, Poe asserts, is opposed both to a work of science *and* to a work of romance.

> A poem . . . is opposed to a work of science by having, for its *immediate* object, pleasure, not truth; to romance, by having for its object an *indefinite* instead of a *definite* pleasure, being a poem only so far as this object is attained; romance presenting perceptible images with definite, poetry with indefinite sensations, to which end music is an *essential*, since the comprehension of sweet sound is our most indefinite conception. Music, when combined with a pleasurable idea, is poetry; music without the idea is simply music; the idea without the music is prose from its very definitiveness.[7]

This particular passage is remarkable for its succinct setting forth of the concerns regarding the nature and function of poetry that will preoccupy Poe to the end of his life: the relation of the true to the aesthetic (pleasure); the implication of the possibility of an undercurrent of the true in the poetic (*immediate* vs. secondary object); the theory of the necessity for indefinite rather than definite (and therefore earthly) images; the distinction of prose from the poetry of words on the basis of its integration with the musical. Poe's emphasis on music, as the most abstract and mathematical, the least earthbound of the arts, becomes more insistent in later essays. In addition to this abstract indefinitiveness, however, another element, also indefinite, but terrible rather than supernally beautiful, lurks in the background.

This other element emerges in a roundabout way in "Letter to B———" via, first, a humorous excoriation of Wordsworth, followed by contrastive praise of the fiery darkness of Coleridge. The polemic is quite revealing. Although Wordsworth in youth may have had "the feelings of a poet," these now "have the appearance of a better day recollected" (VII, xxxix-xl). This remark is doubtless a jab at Wordsworth's famous definition of poetry in the preface to *Lyrical Ballads* (1800) as powerful feelings "recollected" in tranquillity. The "glimpses of extreme delicacy in his writings," says Poe, "at best, are little evidence of present poetic fire." The specific cause of this judgment is Wordsworth's criticism of what Poe regards as a beautiful passage in James MacPherson's "Ossian" poem, *Temora* (1763). Poe's admiration for this passage is absolutely characteristic. Wordsworth, he says, objects to the beautiful beginning of the poem, where "'The Blue waves of Ullin roll in light; the green hills are covered with day; trees shake their dusky heads in the breeze.' And this—gorgeous, yet simple imagery, where all is alive and panting with immortality—this, William Wordsworth, the author of 'Peter Bell,' has *selected* for his contempt" (VII, xli, Poe's italics).

Poe then pretends to select a passage from Wordsworth's "The Idiot Boy" in order to "see what better he, in his own person, has to offer" (VII, xli). Actually, Poe mangles Wordsworth, slightly misquoting, reversing and dropping lines so that mismatched phrases are jammed together:

> "And now she's at the pony's head,
> And now she's at the pony's tail,
> On that side now, and now on this,
> And almost stifled her with bliss—

A few sad tears does Betty shed,

She pats the pony where or when

She knows not: happy Betty Foy!

O Johnny! never mind the Doctor!"

The contrast with the ethereal supernaturalism of the landscape of the Ossian poems could hardly be greater. Poe follows with a second example, from Wordsworth's "The Pet Lamb," adding dashes at the wrong places to make the verses look absurd as well as simple-minded. He comments that "no doubt" the description of the lamb tethered to a stone "is all true; we *will* believe it, we will, Mr. W. Is it sympathy for sheep you wish to excite? I love a sheep from the bottom of my heart . . ." (Poe's ellipsis).

After this mild sarcasm, Poe lapses into heavy ridicule, conceding, ironically, that "there *are* occasions, dear B——, there are occasions when even Wordsworth is reasonable," as in the following extract (with Poe's interpolations) from the preface to *Lyrical Ballads*:

"Those who have been accustomed to the phraseology of modern writers, if they persist in reading this book to a conclusion (*impossible!*) will, no doubt, have to struggle with some feelings of awkwardness; (ha! ha! ha!) they will look round for poetry (ha! ha! ha! ha!) and will be induced to inquire by what species of courtesy these attempts have been permitted to assume that title." Ha! ha! ha! ha! ha! (VII, xlii)

He then contrasts Wordsworth with Coleridge, of whom, despite his unfortunate immersion in metaphysics, Poe "cannot speak but with reverence. His towering intellect! His gigantic power! . . . In reading his poetry, I tremble, like one who stands upon a volcano, conscious, from the very darkness bursting from the crater, of the fire and the light that are weltering below" (VI, xlii). This disturbing sense of a fiery and awesome power struggling to emerge from the darkness parallels to a degree the "ill demon" of the visionary poet of the *Tamerlane* poems, which becomes an interior limitation on the attainment of a full vision of supernal beauty. This ill demon, moreover, seems to be connected with the general inability of humankind to perceive the supernal directly. In "The Poetic Principle," the section on man's immortal instinct and unquenchable thirst for beauty above ends with a lament over "our inability to grasp *now*, wholly, here on earth, at once and for ever, those divine and rapturous joys, of which *through* the poem, or *through* the music, we attain to but brief and indeterminate glimpses" (XIV, 274).

Another facet of the circumscription of the poet's power is the paradox that the poet's limitation is also his source of inspiration, as he emulates the indefinitive in an effort to capture the very indistinctness of his dream visions. The problem of the poet is to evoke the indefinite through earthbound words that by their earthly nature are too definite. Poe's *Marginalia* note on Tennyson (1844) clearly articulates the paradox. He proposes that, whether on a conscious level or not, Tennyson seeks from profound poetic instinct ("the silent analytical promptings of . . . poetic genius") a "suggestive indefinitiveness of meaning, with the view of bringing about a definitiveness of vague and therefore of spiritual effect" (XVI, 28). True poetry is musical, ethereal, dreamlike, as delicate as the "breath" of "faery"; it "floats" upon the "atmosphere" of the "mystic."

> I *know* that indefinitiveness is an element of the true music—I mean of the true musical expression. Give to it any undue decision—imbue it with any very determinate tone—and you deprive it, at once, of its ethereal, its ideal, its intrinsic and essential character. You dispel its luxury of dream. You dissolve the atmosphere of the mystic upon which it floats. You exhaust it of its breath of faery. It now becomes a tangible and easily appreciable idea—a thing of the earth, earthy. It has not, indeed, lost its power to please, but all which I consider the distinctiveness of that power. (XVI, 29)

Despite the disconcerting word play on "distinctiveness" in the last sentence, the statement is clear and definite about indefiniteness and perfectly consistent with "Letter to B——" thirteen years before. True poetry is otherworldly; the poet suggests the mystical by the least coarse of earthly matter. The implicit sense of a continuum between coarse matter, refined matter, and rarification toward atmosphere will later be more fully developed, altering to a degree Poe's sense of duality.[8]

The problem of the relation of the mystical (or supernatural conceived as the "divine") with the earthly (or natural conceived as the physical) is in fact given fuller development in the same section of "The Poetic Principle" we have already had recourse to. The "immortal instinct" of the beautiful "administers" to man's "delight in the manifold forms, and sounds, and odours, and sentiments amid which he exists" (XIV, 273). Poe is consistent (or predictable) in his choice of earthly objects. The impalpable is emphasized—sounds and odors—surrounded by abstract "forms" and "sentiments." There is no sense of touch, weight, pressure, heft—no gravity. Such a choice of objects is hardly the ideal "realism" of Wordsworth or Emerson, much less the revelling in the physical of Whitman.

To release the poetic even further from the earthly, Poe also rejects conventional concepts of truth and morality as legitimate objects of poetry, leaving only the aesthetic, if not solely in and for itself, as that which stands closest to the angelic. Much of the theory of "The Poetic Principle" had been outlined years before in practical reviews of new books, notably in his two-part review (1842) of Longfellow's *Ballads and Other Poems*, where Poe vigorously attacks the "mob's" conception of poetry as truthful or moral. Poe claims that Longfellow's "conception of the *aims* of poesy is all wrong. . . . His didactics are all *out of place*" (XI, 67). The "*general* tendency" of Longfellow's poems suggests that "he regards the inculcation of a *moral* as essential," though there are some "magnificent exceptions, where, as if by accident, he has permitted his genius to get the better of his conventional prejudice"

(XI, 69). Longfellow's "invention, his imagery, his all, is made subservient to the elucidation of one or more points (but rarely of more than one) which he looks upon as *truth*." For Longfellow, morality is truth; for Poe, it is a non-poetic conception. He suggests that one cannot "reconcile the difference between the obstinate oils and waters of Poetry and Truth" (XI, 70), a position that he will modify, to a degree, later.

As in "The Poetic Principle," between the "intellect" and the "moral sense" Poe places "taste." Aesthetic taste mediates between truth and moral duty—the paradigm of Immanuel Kant in the introductory section of *The Critique of Judgment* (1793).[9] But while Kant's notion of aesthetic judgment is abstract and austere, for Poe taste as the divine "sense of the Beautiful" is a "thirst unquenchable" that belongs to "the *immortal* essence of man's nature" as a "consequence and an indication of his perennial life" (XI, 71). Echoing Shelley, Poe says that this "burning thirst" is not "the mere appreciation of the beauty before us," but is instead "the desire of the moth for the star" (XI, 71-72). "It is a wild effort to reach the beauty above. It is a forethought of the loveliness to come. It is a passion to be satiated by no sublunary sights, or sounds, or sentiments, and the soul thus athirst strives to allay its fever in futile efforts at *creation*" (XI, 72).

This striving of the earthbound, unsatisfied soul of man is what gives birth to poetry. "Poesy is thus seen to be a response—unsatisfactory it is true . . . to a natural and irrepressible demand" (XI, 73) that is "inspired with a prescient ecstasy of the beauty beyond the grave." Poetry "struggles by multiform combination among the things and thoughts of Time, to anticipate some portion of the loveliness whose very elements, perhaps, appertain solely to Eternity" (XI, 72). These remarks are not only another statement of the circumscription of the earthly poet imprisoned in time, struggling to suggest the timeless. They also constitute a definitive statement of the indefinitive supernalist vision of the Godhead: it is not true, not moral, but aesthetic.

"Novelty," as that which departs from earthly norms, approximates, in its very divergence from existing time-bound, space-bound forms, the release from earthly constraints anticipated in the eternal. "Novelty" results from a creative act of imagination. Novel combinations in poetry attempt to satisfy the unsatisfiable human "thirst for supernal Beauty . . . not offered the soul by any existing collocation of earth's forms . . ." (XI, 73).

According to Poe, the two chief "attributes" of all definitions of poetry are "Creation" and "Beauty." The poet "creates" the "beautiful" by constructing a novel "fiction," as expressed by "the German terms *Dichtkunst*, the art of fiction, and *Dichten*, to feign" (XI, 74). Although the emulation of physical entities here on earth is a source of delight to human beings, mere mimetic "repetition" of them does not produce poetry. In a passage that he also uses elsewhere than in "The Poetic Principle," Poe writes:

> . . . just as the lily is repeated in the lake, or the eyes of Amaryllis in the mirror, so is the mere oral or written repetition of these forms, and sounds, and colours, and odours, and sentiments, a duplicate source of delight. But this mere repetition is not poetry. He who shall simply sing, with however glowing enthusiasm, or with however vivid a truth of description, of the sights, and sounds, and odours, and colours, and sentiments, which greet him in common with all mankind . . . has yet failed to prove his divine title. (XIV, 273).

This sounds suspiciously like an anti-romantic manifesto, at least as romanticism is conceived by Wordsworth, Emerson, and later Whitman. Poe seems implicitly to share Emerson's concept of art as nature intermixed with man's purposiveness.[10] But Poe's true poet is set far above ordinary humanity as an elitist seer of the "divine" beyond this world: out of space—out of time. For Poe, it is in the very "struggle" to reach the beauty beyond that we "sense" true poetry, knowing all the while that the effort cannot ultimately be completed by the earth-imprisoned poet.

In these struggles of the soul to achieve novel combinations, it is "not impossible that a harp may strike notes not unfamiliar to the angels" (XI, 75). The metaphor of music, though conventional, is crucial. The "highest possible development of the Poetical Sentiment is to be found in the union of song with music," as the "old Bards and Minnesingers" understood. That is, although music most nearly approaches unearthly ideal beauty, it needs the addition of words to become Poesy (as Poe says in "Letter to B———") and satisfy the urgings of the divine in the Poetical Sentiment. Sounds, odors, colors—the least tangible physical attributes—are joined with human "sentiment" in a creative fiction of the imagination. As perception is augmented by words, so words are augmented by the loveliness of music. The "Poetry of words" is not mere combinations of known mimetic forms, but the recreation of forms by the godlike aesthetic imagination of the poet attuned to melody, measure, quantity, accent, rhythm. Poetry is thus *"the Rhythmical Creation of Beauty"* (XI, 75; cf. "Poetic Principle," XIV, 275).

In this emphasis on the rhythmical, Poe not only hammers home the point that poetry has nothing intrinsically to do with truth or duty. He also establishes the ground for the integration of his poetics with the metaphysics of his philosophical essay on the universe, *Eureka*. This booklength prose essay, published 1848, the same year as "The Poetic Principle," Poe calls a "poem" which is (nevertheless) true because the fiction of the universe is beautiful. In this way, and only in this way, can the obstinate oils and waters be reconciled. In the preface Poe writes: ". . . I offer this Book of Truths, not in its character of Truth-Teller, but for the Beauty that abounds in its Truth; constituting it true" (XVI, 183). The essay is offered to "the dreamers and those who put faith in dreams as the only realities." To them he presents "the composition as an Art-Product alone:—let us say as a Romance; or, if I be not urging too lofty a claim, as a Poem." Nevertheless, *"What I here propound is true. . . ."* Whether Poe would accept Keats' "Beauty is truth, truth Beauty" ("Ode on a Grecian Urn," 1820) is uncertain, but he concludes the preface by the reassertion that even though true "it is as a Poem only that I wish this work to be judged after I am dead."

In *Eureka*, Poe proposes a monism that seems at variance with the apparent dualism of his early writings. The created universe is composed entirely of matter, extending outward toward the Godhead in infinite gradations of increasingly rarified matter. This conception has important implications for Poe's ideas about imagination, fancy, novelty, ideality. Moreover, although for Poe spirit is finally matter, it is by no means clear that the reverse is true; the old dualism between the earthly and the supernal to the earthly remains, the two ingeniously, if not logically, reconciled. Poe's material spiritualism shares few properties with Whitman's spiritual materialism.

The mythos of Poe's "poem" is that of a pulsating universe, alternately swelling into existence and collapsing into nothingness in an eternal cycle of creation and annihilation. This divine pulsation he likens to the systole and diastole of earthly organisms: it is a rhythmic cycle that is the divine "heart throb" of the cosmos. The poet's rhythmical creation of beauty on earth lifts the earthly from the mundane as he emulates this vast abstract cosmic rhythm.

The problem of the visionary earth-bound poet, seeking to suggest the intangibility of the other world and to achieve harmony with the cosmic rhythm, is clearly dramatized in Poe's early poem, "Israfel" (1831). The angel sings "so wildly well" that the stars and the moon cease their celestial "hymns" and listen "all mute" to Israfel. He has an advantage over the earthly poet, for he dwells in heaven, whereas in this world:

> Our flowers are merely—flowers,
> And the shadow of thy perfect bliss
> Is the sunshine of ours.

But if the earthly poet could dwell

---

Where Israfel
Hath dwelt, and he where I,
He might not sing so wildly well
A mortal melody,
While a bolder note than this might swell
From my lyre within the sky.[11]

We can see why writers like Drake and Halleck do not seem truly poetical to Poe. They are too earthbound, too "fanciful" merely, not "imaginative" enough; they fail in their mechanical combinations to suggest
the mystical, the ideal. In that earlier review, Poe parodies Drake's attempt to "accoutre a fairy" by rewriting several lines in which he mechanically substitutes different animal and plant metaphors, one-for-
one, with those of Drake's "Culprit Fay," concluding that "the only
requisite for writing verses of this nature, *ad libitum*, is a tolerable acquaintance with the qualities of the objects to be detailed, and a very
moderate endowment of the faculty of Comparison—which is the chief
constituent of *Fancy* or the powers of combination" (VIII, 293-295).
The difference between the poems of Drake and Halleck and those
poems that are truly poetic, such as Shelley's *Queen Mab*, Coleridge's
*Christabel*, Milton's *Comus*, Dante's *Inferno*, is the difference between
mere "Fancy" and true "Imagination."[12] Imagination, Poe writes with
Shelley in mind, is the "soul" of poetry and springs "from the brain of
the poet, enveloped in the moral sentiments of grace, of color, of motion—of the mystical, of the august—in short of *the ideal*" (VIII, 301).

Moreover, just as conventional concepts of truth and virtue are excluded from Poe's poetic, so also are passionate emotions. Agreeing
with what he takes Coleridge's position to be, Poe writes that the poetic
imagination may modify, exalt, enflame, purify, or control "the passions of mankind," but in poetry there is no "inevitable" or "necessary
co-existence" of true imagination and the passions. The passions are
earthly, while poetry is spiritual. Just as truths are not the *main* object
of poetry, neither is emotion. Only if beauty is the main object can truth

enter in. So also the only worthwhile "passion" is the divine passion of poetry, abstract, intellectual, rarified, unearthly.[13] Poe has apparently rejected all the major theories of the nature and function of poetry (or beauty) except the abstract idealism of Immanuel Kant, which he tries to take even farther into the infinite and divine.

Poe uses two phrenological terms to get at the essence of true poetry. The functions of "Veneration" and "Ideality" both point to some power or realm superior to our present earthly condition. Poetry, he says, is "the sentiment of Intellectual Happiness" on earth and "the Hope of a higher Intellectual Happiness hereafter," and he singles out Shelley's "Hymn to Intellectual Beauty" (1817) as the poem most nearly describing these aspirations and possessing such ideality (VIII, 282-283). The poem, in fact, provides a gloss on Poe's theory of poetry as well as on many of his early poems. "Hymn to Intellectual Beauty" opens with an indefinite landscape upon which "floats" a mysterious "unseen Power." The imagery is of shadow, moonbeam, flower, wind, water-spray, and distant mountain:

> The awful shadow of some unseen Power
>     Floats unseen among us,—visiting
>     This various world with as inconstant wing
> As summer winds that creep from flower to flower,—
> Like moonbeams . . . behind some piny mountain shower . . . .[14]

This power on "inconstant wing" is perceived only fleetingly:

> It visits with inconstant glance
> Each human heart and countenance . . . .

> (ll. 6-7)

It is indistinct (the hue of evening harmony, clouds in starlight, the memory of music no longer heard) and "dearer" for that mysterious indistinctness:

> Like hues and harmonies of evening,—
>    Like clouds in starlight widely spred,—
>    Like memory of music fled,—
>    Like aught that for its grace may be
> Dear, and yet dearer for its mystery.
>
> (ll. 8-12)

This "Power" turns out to be the "Spirit of Beauty," which passes away and leaves humankind hopeless:

> Spirit of *Beauty* . . .
>    . . . .
>       —where art thou gone?
> Why dost thee pass away and leave our state,
> This dim vast vale of tears, vacant and desolate?
>
> (ll. 13, 15-17)

For only:

> Thy light alone—like mist o'er mountains driven,
>    Or music by the night-wind sent
>    Through strains of some still instrument,
>    Or moonlight on a midnight stream,
> Gives grace and truth to life's unquiet dream.
>
> (ll. 32-36)

Poe's poetic vision is all here: the light of beauty alone gives meaning to the "dream" of life, but it is fleeting and intangible, like mist on the mountains, like the nightwind's music, like moonlight on water.

At the same time that Poe values indefiniteness and ideality, he also insists on a logical pre-established pattern for the whole work, as in his explanation in "The Philosophy of Composition" of the step-by-step ratiocination by which he constructed "The Raven." His concept of "unity or totality of effect" (after Schlegel) is noticeably geometrical and mathematical. In 1849, in an expansion of his essay on "Song Writing" ten years before, Poe links the ethereal, dreamlike sense of indefinitiveness in poetry not only with "melody," but also with the mathematical measurement of music.[15] He even goes so far as to assert that mathematical equality is the root of all beauty, ideas also elaborated in "The Rationale of Verse," and related to the technique of incantatory repetition to achieve the hypnagogic. As elsewhere, for Poe, the most abstract, the least earthbound, the most purely formal relationship (even to the mechanics of ratio) is identified with the spiritual. Like his basic understanding of the relation of intellect, aesthetic judgment, and morality, Poe's concept of such pure formal relationship without reference to natural forms is culled from Immanuel Kant, who names it the "arabesque."[16]

But this carefully pre-planned organization toward an arabesque effect in a poem operates hidden behind indefinitiveness. Once again, the paradoxical problem is to emulate the indefinite vision by definite earthbound means to give the *effect* of the spiritual. The design of a poem is not in itself spiritual; but pure logical design is at least a step away from earthly circumscription. It is clear in this context why overt didacticism and the use of allegory destroy, for Poe, the poetic quality of the poem: allegory is too heavy-handed, too definite and fixed, too this-worldly. Rather, a truly poetical work will have a mystical "undercurrent" of suggestivity.

By the 1840's, Poe's poetic theory had begun to develop in a slightly new direction under the influence of his developing monist philosophy. He had become troubled about the relation of the moral, the imaginative, and the true—or more concretely, about the relation between the poet's actual "creativity," his perception of the good, and his working with the actual materials of nature—the givens of the earthly. Some major modifications of his earliest critical positions begin to manifest themselves, though the supernalist aesthetic still dominates. In the Longfellow review cited earlier, Poe suggests that poetry can in fact "inculcate a moral" if handled with a sense of proportion: that is, the didactic element must not override the aesthetic. When the moral dominates the aesthetic, as in most of Longfellow's works and in most contemporary American poetry, it is a "heresy" against art (and therefore against the divine). The inversion of the usual connotations of "heresy" here is acute, resulting in the memorable phrase "the heresy of *The Didactic*." The implicit distinction in "Letter to B——" between an immediate object and a secondary one now becomes a distinction between "the truthful and the poetical modes" of inculcating a moral (XI, 70). The true can only occur through the poetical as an "undercurrent."

Poe's concept of the proper function of an "undercurrent" of meaning in a poem, its relation to the "mystic" and to "imagination," is developed at some length in his 1840 review of Thomas Moore's *Alciphron*. Revising his earlier opinion in his Drake-Halleck review, he now criticizes Coleridge's distinction in the *Biographia Literaria* between "Fancy" and "Imagination" ("the fancy combines, the imagination creates"). Poe defines a "*mystic*" work according to the concept of "Augustus William Schlegel, and of most other German critics." It is "that class of composition in which there lies beneath the transparent upper current of meaning an under or *suggestive* one. What we vaguely term the *moral* of any sentiment is its mystic or secondary expression." It is like "accompaniment in music" that "spiritualizes the *fanciful* conception, and lifts it into the *ideal*" (X, 65).

The earthbound artist patiently *combines*, by logic and laborious attention to detail, in order to create a work suggesting the ideal. Therefore Poe disputes Coleridge's distinction between the lower faculty of Fancy and the higher of Imagination. It is, Poe says, a distinction "without a difference." Neither really creates. "All novel conceptions are merely unusual combinations." A griffin or a sphynx, for example, is a compendium of limbs and features from known animals. In a way, this contention is consistent with his criticism of Drake in 1836, where he substitutes different parts for Drake's metaphors of leaves, acorns, and so on for his fairy knight's shield, clothing, and spear. Poe now claims that the imagination is fancy "*loftily employed*"; it is a matter of degree only.

The new definition of imagination as fancy loftily employed may at first seem inconsistent with his contention two years later in the Longfellow review that the true music of supernal beauty is not formed by an "existing collocation of earth's forms." The key is in the word "existing." Neither in the Longfellow nor in the Moore review does Poe say that the poet employs "nothing earthly"—rather, that the poet reshapes, re-combines, the "existing forms," transmutes them through his creative imagination (or high fancy). The new definition of imagination reflects the developing monism that results in *Eureka*, but Poe cannot give up the old sense of the dualistic split between the earthly and the supernal. Moreover, whereas once the struggling and striving seemed to Poe to give rise to the true poetical music, now his sense of the final futility of striving for the supernal intensifies. In the *Alciphron* review, he argues that vague loftiness of fancy will lift the work into the ideal by haunting suggestions of something just out of reach: "With each note of the lyre is heard a ghostly, and not always a distinct, but an august and soul-exalting *echo*. In every glimpse of beauty presented, we catch, through long and wild vistas, dim bewildering visions of a far more ethereal beauty *beyond*" (X, 66). The sense of bewilderment is present from the very first poems, but it has grown stronger. The image of the supernal through long and wild vistas, with a very slight altering perspective, could be seen, not as positive, but as negative, as infinite regress. In fact, such a shift had already taken place, as we shall see, in the poems.

Another philosophically troublesome area for Poe in the 1840's is the question of how the earthbound poet can transfer the glimpses of supernal beauty to earthbound language, the dream vision to conscious rational analysis. Poe's resolution to this problem is also ingenious, derived from certain theories of the German natural idealists; at the same time, we find an undercurrent suggesting another version of infinite regress. In a *Marginalia* note of 1846, Poe writes:

I do not believe that any thought, properly so called, is out of the reach of language. . . . For my own part, I have never had a thought which I could not set down in words, with even more distinctiveness than that with which I conceived it . . . the thought is logicalized by the effort at (written) expression.

There is, however, a class of fancies, of exquisite delicacy, which are *not* thoughts, and to which, *as yet*, I have found it absolutely impossible to adapt language. I use the word *fancies* at random, and merely because I must use *some* word; but the idea commonly attached to the term is not even remotely applicable to the shadows of shadows in question. They seem to me rather psychal than intellectual. They arise in the soul (alas, now rarely!) only at its epochs of most intense tranquility . . . at those mere points of time where the confines of the waking world blend with those of the world of dreams. I am aware of these "fancies" only when I am upon the very brink of sleep, with the consciousness that I am so. I have satisfied myself that this condition exists but for an inappreciable *point* of time—yet it is crowded with these "shadows of shadows"; and for absolute *thought* there is demanded time's *endurance*.

. . . I regard the visions, even as they arise, with an awe which, in some measure, moderates or tranquilizes the ecstasy—I so regard them, through a conviction (which seems a portion of the ecstasy itself) that this ecstasy, in itself, is of a character supernal to the Human Nature—is a glimpse of the spirit's outer world. . . . (XVI, 88-89)

Such a conception of dreamvisions was widespread in Europe, where poets like Novalis spoke of a condition of "involuntariness," a psychic, hypnagogic limbo or trance state: the half-conscious mind is open to the subconscious (the gate to the supernal), thus making its mystic perceptions available to the conscious mind.

Adverting again to the concept of novelty as suggestive of the unearthly, Poe suggests that such perception is an "instantaneous intuition" generated by the *"absoluteness of novelty"* in "psychal impressions" which no ordinary worldly impressions can even "approximate." "It is as if the five senses were supplanted by five myriad others alien to mortality" (XVI, 89). The poet seeks to control this state of perception, to "prevent the lapse from . . . the point of blending between wakefulness and sleep . . . from this border-ground into the dominion of sleep." Subsequently, Poe writes, "I can startle myself from the point into wakefulness–*and thus transfer the point itself into the realm of Memory*—convey its impressions, or more properly their recollections, to a situation where (although still for a very brief period) I can survey them with the eye of analysis" (XVI, 90).

Therefore, he does "not altogether despair of embodying in words at least enough of the fancies in question to convey, to certain classes of intellect, a shadowy conception of their character." This is the reason that he can say in the same essay that "so entire is my faith in the *power of words*, that, at times, I have believed it possible to embody even the evanescence of fancies such as I have attempted to describe" (XVI, 89). And this is the reason that the supernal, even the Godhead itself, is revealed to ordinary men through poetry, and through poetry alone. Poe concludes rather wryly with the implication that the poet of words is separate from ordinary human beings—a seer—by disclaiming to be able to judge whether or not the dream visions given to him are common to others. He knows merely that he has had such visions and hopes that one day he will be able to catch them in words.

But it is all still shadow-upon-shadow. The vision vouchsafed the earthly poet is rather dim. Poe's concept of the shadow-of-a-shadow vision is like the Platonic theory of copies. But it is even more like the concept of veiled reality of the ancient Egyptians and Hebrews. He who would look beneath the veil of Isis and see reality face to face is driven mad. In I Corinthians 13:12, we have the more hopeful Christian version: "For now we see through a glass darkly, but then face to face." The limbo state of half-vision is described in "Dream-Land." The traveller through Dream-Land:

> May not—dare not openly view it;
> Never its mysteries are exposed
> To the weak human eye unclosed;
> So wills its King, who hath forbid
> The lifting of the fringed lid;
> And thus the sad soul that here passes
> Beholds it but through darkened glasses.

Not only is human vision, even that of a poetic seer, dim; but also there is something dangerous in trying openly to view in dreams that other world.

* * *

The visionary spirit who would lift the veil were wise to look through darkened glass or with half-closed eye. Visions of the Other are purchased dearly. Mere mortals must be careful. Yet for the visionary, who wants to see clearly, this dim vision is agony. The *Tamerlane* poems present just such half-vision and just such a visionary paradox.

Poe's combination of mystical world-weariness in the figure of one of superior but dark vision in the early poems is blatantly Byronic. In *Manfred* (1816-17), for example, we read:

> From my youth upwards
> My Spirit walked not with the souls of men,
> Nor looked upon the earth with human eyes;
> The thirst of their ambition was not mine,
> The aim of their existence was not mine;
> My joys—my griefs—my passions—and my powers,
> Made me a stranger.[17]

But this picture of the visionary set apart from ordinary mortals owes as much to Shelley, whose "Sonnet," known as "Lift Not the Painted

Veil" (written 1818, pub. 1824), provides an example of the romantic veil trope and as well provides a gloss on Poe's Tamerlane figure, whose presence is felt not only in the title poem but also in the nine shorter lyrics of the volume.[18] The principal elements of Poe's *Tamerlane* are given concise embodiment in Shelley's poem:

> Lift not the painted veil which those who live
> Call Life: though unreal shapes be pictured there,
> And it but mimic all we would believe
> With colours idly spread,—behind, lurk Fear
> And Hope, twin Destinies; who ever weave
> Their shadows, o'er the chasm, sightless and drear.
> I knew one who had lifted it—he sought,
> For his lost heart was tender, things to love,
> But found them not, alas! nor was there aught
> The world contains, the which he could approve.
> Through the unheeding many he did move,
> A splendour among shadows, a bright blot
> Upon this gloomy scene, a Spirit that strove
> For truth, and like the Preacher found it not.
>
> (ML, p. 201)

The sense of unreality, the two opposite poles of human destiny (fear and hope), the solitary superior spirit among the many, searching futilely for love and truth, all inform the principal persona of Poe's volume.

The major themes of *Tamerlane* involve loss: lost joy, lost love, lost purity, and lost visionary experience of youth. The loss motif is coupled with desire for unworldly dreaming as a refuge from pain, dull reality, or the dimming of the inner vision; with scorn for one's own worldly pride and ambition; with an indefinite sense of some higher truth and purity residing beyond this world in the realm of the far stars. Hovering about all existence is a vague sinister threat—some "ill demon"—in nature, in the mind, in both.

Poe's 1829 poem, "Alone," provides a succinct statement of the troubled vision of the Tamerlane figure. The parallels with the passage earlier quoted from Byron's *Manfred* are clear.

> From childhood's hour I have not been
> As others were—I have not seen
> As others saw—I could not bring
> My passions from a common spring—
> From the same source I have not taken
> My sorrow—I could not awaken
> My heart to joy at the same time—
> And all I lov'd—*I* lov'd alone—
> *Then*—in my childhood—in the dawn
> Of a most stormy life—was drawn
> From ev'ry depth of good and ill
> The mystery which binds me still—
> From the torrent, or the fountain—
> From the red cliff of the mountain—
> From the sun that 'round me roll'd
> In its autumn tint of gold—
> From the lightning in the sky
> As it pass'd me flying by—
> From the thunder, and the storm—
> And when the cloud that took the form
> (When the rest of Heaven was blue)
> Of a demon in my view—

* * *

The nine shorter lyric poems of the rest of the volume (under the title "Fugitive Pieces") intertwine lost love with the infinite regression of all perception into one dream behind another. Even more prominent than in "Tamerlane" is the paradoxical celebration of the dreaming imagination, wherein visionary perception is always combined with a "dark alloy" that is "powerful to destroy" "The Happiest Day."

The final poem, "The Lake," has been generally regarded as one of the two best of the short "Fugitive Verses." It is certainly a significant piece. In addition to its lyric evocation of a dark dreamscape of the mind, it brings the themes of the volume—both the undercurrent of visionary dreaming and the undercurrent of the circumscribed powers of the poet—to an appropriate resolution. The ill demon of the imagination triumphs over *itself* by creating out of its own adversity a doubly visionary poem.

The poem is said to describe an actual place, the Lake of the Dismal Swamp in Virginia, whose waters are poisonous.[19] The biographically-oriented reading has the poem the embodiment of a local legend of the ghosts of two lovers who roam its shores. But it probably owes much to two poems by Thomas Moore: "A Ballad: The Lake of the Dismal Swamp," based on his visit to Virginia in 1803, and "I Wish I Was By That Dim Lake," set in Donegal, Ireland. The Virginia legend is that a bereaved lover, maddened by his loss, is deluded into believing that the girl is not dead but is lost in the Dismal Swamp; he disappears, apparently having gone in search of her. The speaker of Poe's poem says that in "youth's spring" he haunted a spot that he "could not love the less," for

> So lovely was the loneliness
> Of a wild lake, with black rock bound,
> And trees that tower'd around.
>                           (ll. 4-6)

When the black night throws a pall on that spot (and over all things) and when the wind passes in "stilly melody," then

> My infant spirit would awake
> To the terror of the lone lake.
>                           (ll. 11-12)

The "loneliness" itself is lovely, partially *because* of the faintly in-timidating if not outright sinister wildness of a lake circumscribed by masses of black rock and towering trees. As the stasis of night brings the sounds of silence, the solitary visionary spirit responds more ac-tively to the sinister element. The "terror of the lone lake" is also a "tremulous delight," a "feeling undefin'd, springing from a "darken'd mind" (ll. 14-16). The indefinitive takes the form of a thought of death in the "poison'd wave" and leads him to think the depths of the lake a "fitting grave" for one who could find "solace" in the scene by dream-ing, one whose "wild'ring thought" could make an "Eden of that dim lake" (ll. 21-22).

The poem is sometimes read as a direct statement from the speaker about his own darkened mind. But it is more complex. If the legend ap-plies, as it seems to, the speaker in his own mind makes the waves of the lake an appropriate symbolic grave both for the lady seeking solace from earthly anguish and for the lover who transformed it into an imag-inary Paradise where he preserved the memory of his lost love, thereby becoming another ghost of the lake. The awakened imagination of the speaker, creatively sharing the delusion of the lover while maintaining some distance from him in his dramatized imagining of him, can also transmute terror and sorrow and death into loveliness: the complex re-sponse to the physical scene results in the poem itself. In one sense the double imagining is like a dream of a dream. More generally, the am-bivalence of nature, of the creative mind, of pain and joy are the things that make a poet. "The Lake" in its slighter and much different way deals with the same subjects as Walt Whitman's great poem, "Out of the Cradle Endlessly Rocking": love, separation, death, and the poetic process. The poem appropriately concludes the volume with the imagi-native re-creation of a lost love and a bereaved lover, by a youth who in dreaming of them finds in life and art a terror that is yet a delight.

\* \* \*

The next stage in the evolution of Poe's poetic world, the poems of the 1829 *Al Aaraaf* volume, will darken the visionary experience even more. As mentioned, Al Aaraaf is a star, where the "spirits" of poetic imaginings have a temporary existence, in a limbo region between heaven and hell. It contains both the terrible and the beautiful:

> Spirit! that dwellest where,
> In the deep sky,
> The terrible and fair
> In beauty vie!

"Al Aaraaf" itself balances, with more overt tension than the *Tamerlane* poems, the benign with the apocalyptic—moving from the drowsy dreamscape of the spirits of flowers, nymphs, and music floating upon the air—to a vision of desolation and ruin as red winds burn and go out in the heavens—to a vision of the God-ordained destruction of earth—to a vision of the final destruction as the star extinguishes.

"Al Aaraaf" is a mid-world in a series of infinite regressive dreams of a higher reality—a half-realized Platonic idea of absolute Beauty. The divine is known only through beauty via the imagination, which is the godlike part of man. But even in this "deep sky," as in the yet deeper heaven, the "terrible and fair,/ in beauty vie," in an eternity of which we feel but the shadow. The spirit beings whom God's messenger, Nesace, has known have only dreamed of God's "Infinity" as a "model of their own" (I, ll. 104-105; cf. ll. 35-37). Through beauty (Nesace) and harmony (Ligeia) the will of God is indefinitely communicated to man. Understanding of such things is but faint on earth; earthly science confuses truth and falsehood; and fuller knowledge is refracted, through death, from God's infinity. Although the poetically imagined world of the angels hints of the true beauty, even in this star world, passion, which is too earthly for pure poetry and beauty, intrudes. The intrusion of earthly love destroys the two half-human, half-angelic spirits of Al Aaraaf.

Thus although the poem creates a cosmology of higher beauty, this world too is flawed; the only release is to sink into oblivion. "Al Aaraaf" is an invented myth codifying the implications of the earlier poems, "Evening Star," "Stanzas," and "A Dream." It anticipates Poe's later prose-poem dialogues about the creation and destruction of the earth, "The Conversation of Eiros and Charmion" (1839), "The Colloquy of Monos and Una" (1841), "The Power of Words" (1845). It anticipates as well as his booklength cosmological treatise, also a "prose-poem," *Eureka* (1848), in which Poe attempts to reconcile various contraries of existence under the proposition that the fundamental paradox of existence is that annihilation is built into the very springing forth of life in both the individual and the cosmos.

From this point on in Poe's poetry—except for the rather charming verses addressed to various ladies and a number of self-correcting parodies of romantic poetic excess—the indefinitive visionary aspect will give way almost entirely to the sense of loss, interior torment, infinite regress, and the world of nightmare. The journey from the music and song of blue-bells, fountains, and woodland rills to the landscape of nightmare is an incredibly rapid one—though hardly unlooked for given the implicit nightmare of the earliest poems. There is a very slight remission of the negative in *Poems* of 1831, especially in the new introduction to "Al Aaraaf," called "Mysterious Star," which emphasizes the supernal loveliness of the star world, with its dream gardens and dream maidens. All things, even sorrow, are gentle here: the "truest type of grief/ Is the gently falling leaf," and "sorrow is not melancholy" (ll. 26-29).

But the new "Introduction" to the volume as a whole reverts to the multi-toned Byronic note of the *Tamerlane* poems, in which satire, sarcasm, self-hate, pride, aspiration, despair are all mixed. This introduction speaks of "eternal Condor years" falling upon the visionary soul of the poet-narrator, robbing him of his ability to see the benign aspects of the world of spirit, so that the few calm hours that come to him must be spent in response to some dimly perceived horror lurking beneath. The "voice" of these poems is a fictive construct embodying the torment of the visionary spirit of the romantic poet, torn apart by the vision of possible supernal loveliness in an other world and the simultaneous recognition of the circumscription of the power of poetic vision that earthly existence presents. This is the "ill demon" of the world and the self. The never adequately imaged landscape of supernal beauty, just barely glimpsed in part of "Al Aaraaf," and merely invoked in *Tamerlane* and *Al Aaraaf*, gives way steadily to nightmare landscapes.

## Notes

1. References to the poems are to Vol. I of the *Collected Works of Edgar Allan Poe*, ed. Thomas Ollive Mabbott (Cambridge, MA: The Belknap Press of Harvard University Press, 1969); here, I, 343-345, lines 2-4 (cf. 52-54), 9-18. Mabbott in his introduction to the poems comments on the production of vast desolation by the denial of limitations (after A. H. Quinn), notes a similar effect in *Paradise Lost*, II, ll. 890-896 (after Richard Wilbur), and remarks parallels in *Arthur Gordon Pym*; other similarities are noted in "Fairyland," "The Sleeper," and "Ulalume." Milton's lines describe the first view Satan's legions have of the "infernal Pit":

> Before their eyes in sudden view appear
> The secrets of the hoary Deep—a dark
> Illimitable ocean, without bound,
> Without dimension; where length, breadth, and height,
> And time, and place, are lost; where eldest Night
> And Chaos, ancestors of Nature, hold
> Eternal anarchy, amidst the noise
> Of endless wars, and by confusion stand.
>
> (II, ll. 890-897)

Citations from the longer prose fiction and the essays and reviews are to *The Complete Works of Edgar Allan Poe*, ed. James A. Harrison (1902; reprint ed., New York: AMS Press, 1969).

2. The phrase "ideal realism" is Coleridge's, from Chapter XIII of the *Biographia Literaria* (1817): ". . . ideal Realism, which holds the same relation in abstruseness to

Plotinus as Plotinus does to Plato" (*Selected Poetry and Prose of Coleridge*, ed. Donald A. Stauffer [New York: Modern Library, 1951], p. 262). The Coleridge-Plotinus-Plato relation is complex and important for an understanding of romantic aesthetics. In discussing "the chain of realities" in *Ennead* III.viii, Plotinus sets up a four-fold reality, from the primal, all-encompassing One at the top of a vertical chain, through Intelligence, Soul, and Matter, thus doubly complicating Platonic dualism. Although not totally consistent, Plotinus generally regards the world of sense experience as an impediment to the soul's attainment of the One. Section 11 of III.viii contains passages that succinctly describe the shaping matrix of Poe's aesthetics and metaphysics. Intelligence, writes Plotinus, "is the most beautiful of things. It is illuminated by a pure light and shines with a pure splendor; it contains the intelligible beings of which our world, in spite of its beauty, is but a shadow and an image." This idea of multiple worlds in Byron, Shelley, and Poe is discussed in the main text momentarily. The world of Intelligence, Plotinus continues, "lies in full resplendence because it contains nothing unintelligent or obscure or indefinite"; as Poe would have understood this, the definitiveness of the world of Intelligence is opposed to the imprisoning realm of sense matter, which generates the soul's dissatisfaction with indeterminate glimpses of Intelligence, and through it of the One. Plotinus continues: "Wonder seizes him who sees it and who enters it properly and becomes one with it. Just as the view of heaven and splendor of the stars lead one to seek and think of their author, so contemplation of the intelligible world [i.e., of form and connection, not matter] and the admiration it induces lead one to seek its author. . . ." (*The Philosophy of Plotinus*, ed. and trans Joseph Katz [New York: Appleton-Century-Crofts, 1950], pp. 57-58). One way in which "ideal realism" is more "abstruse" than the philosophy of Plotinus is that the romantic task of the soul is to enter into and become one with both the realm of Intelligence and the realm of Sense Matter simultaneously, thus participating in the One. The passage in Coleridge is preceded by a discussion of "transcendental" vs. "transcendent" (after the German distinction) in Ch. XII, and followed by the famous definitions of the "esemplastic" power of the "primary" and "secondary "*Imagination* as opposed to *Fancy*. In addition to these specifically romantic influences, there should be added Milton, of whom Poe was quite appreciative, despite his criticism of the length of *Paradise Lost*.

3. *Complete Works*, XIV, 273-274. The poetic sentiment and supernal loveliness may manifest themselves (itself) in music, architecture, and landscape gardening as well. Although beyond the scope of the present essay, significant connections exist among Poe's landscape tales, "The Island of the Fay" (1841), "Morning on the Wissahiccon" (1844), "The Domain of Arnheim" (1847), "Landor's Cottage" (1849); the cosmic apocalypses, "The Conversation of Eiros and Charmion" (1839), "The Colloquy of Monos and Una" (1841), "The Power of Words" (1845); other tales employing major architecture-landscape settings and motifs; and landscape-architecture poems additional to those discussed in the present essay, such as "Fairyland" (1829), "The City in the Sea" (1831), "The Sleeper" (1831), "The Valley of Unrest" (1831), "The Coliseum" (1833), "Sonnet—Silence" (1840), "Dream-Land" (1844), "Ulalume" (1847).

4. *Collected Works*, I, 99-100, Part I, ll. 1-6, 9-15; Part II, ll. 60-87. Poe's note to the second passage cites Shakespeare, "Fairies use flowers for their charactery"

(*Merry Wives of Windsor*) and the Egyptian myth that the moon "has the effect of producing blindness in those who sleep with the face exposed to the rays . . ." (I, l. 108). In ll. 80-84, the word play on "inviolate" seems appropriate to the aesthetic purity of the dreamscape untouched by earthly concepts of morality, its only "duty" being that which is "beseeming/ These star-litten hours."

5. *Complete Works*, XI, 255-256. The locution "sole attribute" would seem to be a pun on "soul." For a fine discussion of the relation of Victor Cousin on Poe's poetic theory, see Glen A. Omans, "Victor Cousin: Still Another Source of Poe's Aesthetic Theory?" *Studies in the American Renaissance* (1982), pp. 1-27.

6. *Complete Works*, VIII, 281. See the tale "The Power of Words" (1845) for an interesting link between the material and spiritual through words; cf. note 8 below, the discussion in the text of the *Marginalia* note on words and "psychal impressions," and the monism of *Eureka*. For a brief summary of "the war of the spirit with the external world and the quest for Supernal Beauty" in Poe, see Donald Barlow Stauffer, *A Short History of American Poetry* (New York: Dutton, 1974), pp. 85-91.

7. *Complete Works*, VII, xliii. The citations to the critical essays are all to this edition, not to *Collected Works*, and henceforth cited in parentheses in the text.

8. These monistic ideas were current in German romantic philosophy, deriving in part from Leibniz's monadology and the "law of continuity" (cited by Poe, *Complete Works*, XVI, 46), and informing the principal treatises on *Naturwissenschaft* by Schelling and Hegel. Poe's developing monism, within an essential dualist frame, as he picks up the philosophical ideas in the air of his times, is discussed later in this essay with regard to the connection between Poe's aesthetics and the philosophy of *Eureka* (1848).

9. Glen A. Omans maintains that Poe is always closer to Kant than is Coleridge, who is generally (but mistakenly) regarded as the major English-speaking romantic exponent of Kantian aesthetics. Coleridge, according to Omans, continually veers toward Hegel—whereas Poe at the time is the only pure Kantian in the English-speaking world. See "'Intellect, Taste, and the Moral Sense': Poe's Debt to Immanuel Kant," *Studies in the American Renaissance* (1980), pp. 123-168, and "Victor Cousin," passim. See also George E. Kelly, "Poe's Theory of Beauty, "*American Literature*, 27 (1956), 521-526, and "Poe's Theory of Unity, "*Philological Quarterly*, 37 (1958), 34-44; Margaret Alterton, *Origins of Poe's Critical Theory* (1925; reprint ed., New York: Russell & Russell, 1965). Hardin Craig completed the American Men of Letters series volume, *Edgar Allan Poe*, begun by Alterton, the introduction to which gives a contextual overview of Poe's aesthetics (1935, rev. ed., New York: Hill and Wang, 1962). More detailed on critical theory (even though emphasizing the pragmatic) is Robert D. Jacobs, *Poe: Journalist & Critic* (Baton Rouge: Louisiana State University Press, 1969), esp. Chs. II, VI-IX, XII-XIII, XV-XVIII. More summary is Edd Winfield Parks, *Edgar Allan Poe as Literary Critic* (Athens: University of Georgia Press, 1964). The most brilliantly original discussion of Poe's aesthetics in terms of the creation of a poetic mythos is Richard Wilbur's "House of Poe" (Library of Congress Anniversary Lecture, May 4, 1959), reprinted in *The Recognition of Edgar Allan Poe*, ed. Eric W. Carlson (Ann Arbor: University of Michigan Press, 1966), 255-277; see also Wilbur's introduction and notes to the Laurel Poetry Series *Poe* (New York: Dell, 1959). But

Hyatt A. Waggoner, in *American Poetry from the Puritans to the Present* (Boston: Houghton Mifflin, 1968), has a point when he says that Wilbur, like Roy Harvey Pearce, mostly talks "about something else"; that is, Poe's poems are meaningful "only when read in terms of the myth Poe elaborated in his prose, particularly in *Eureka*," and thus Wilbur's commentary "gives more space to the prose than to the poetry" (p. 137). Waggoner's brief discussion raises essential evaluative questions about Poe's poems, Poe as a "minor" poet, and Poe's "crude" theory of poetry. Waggoner seems to me in the main to be right (though Poe's theory of poetry is hardly crude), but his strictures in no way reduce Poe's considerable historical interest—especially in the disjunctive congruence of poetry and poetics. See the concluding paragraph of Waggoner's Poe section ("Death is at the center of Poe's dreaming poetry") for a succinct overview of the tension of poetics and poetry in Poe and Emerson, and by extension Whitman (p. 146).

10. See the 1836 *Nature*, Chs. I-III. David Halliburton, in *Edgar Allan Poe: A Phenomenological View* (Princeton, NJ: Princeton University Press, 1973), says Poe regards human artistic endeavor as a necessarily inferior or degenerated mode, a complicated point insufficiently argued by Halliburton.

11. The phrasing of the 1845 version; *Collected Works*, I, 176-177, lines 42-44, 46-51.

12. *Complete Works*, VIII, 299. Others cited are Aeschylus, *Prometheus Vinctus*; Cervantes, *Destruction of Numanitia*; Pope, *Rape of the Lock*; Burns, *Tam O'Shanter*; Coleridge, *Ancient Mariner* and *Kubla Khan*; Shelley, *The Sensitive Plant*; Keats, *Nightingale*. It is notable how many of these works contain a demonic element.

13. A controversy in older scholarship is Poe on the "passions." On the one hand, Poe talks of poetry as a great passion; on the other, he will make such a declaration as ". . . we agree . . . with Coleridge, that poetry and *passion* are discordant . . ." (*Complete Works*, XI, 255; review of Horne's *Orion*). But Poe is not really so contradictory about the passions as some critics have suggested. He uses the terms "passion" (usually in the singular), "passionate," and "ecstasy" to describe the effect of "true" poetry and the generation of such poetry; this, obviously, is a higher passion, the true passion, not mere earthly emotions. The melancholy preface to *The Raven and Other Poems* (1845) can be read in such a way: "Events not to be controlled have prevented me from making, at any time, any serious effort in what, under happier circumstances, would have been the field of my choice. With me poetry has not been a purpose, but a passion . . ."; *"Tales" and "The Raven and Other Poems,"* facsimile ed., with introduction by Jay B. Hubbell (Columbus, OH: Charles E. Merrill Pub. Co., 1969). Humankind has in fact trivialized the passions: ". . . the passions should be held in reverence; they must not—they cannot at will be excited with an eye to the paltry compensations, or the more paltry commendations, of mankind."

14. *Selected Poetry and Prose of Shelley*, ed. Carlos Baker (New York: Modern Library, 1951), p. 367, ll. 1-5.

15. ". . . that merely mathematical recognition of *equality* which seems to be *the root of all Beauty*" (*Marginalia*, 1849, *Complete Works*, XVI, 136-140; cf. X, 41-45, 1839, rev. 1849 as "*National Melodies of America*. By George P. Morris").

16. See my discussion of grotesque and arabesque in *Poe's Fiction: Romantic Irony*

*in the Gothic Tales* (Madison: University of Wisconsin Press, 1973), pp. 103-110 and esp. p. 227 n2. For some mysterious reason, Poe scholars persist in misunderstanding the meaning of these terms in the romantic period in general and Poe's use of them in particular, assigning comic tales to the category "grotesque" and serious or sinister tales and poems to the "arabesque." The term "arabesque" in German romantic criticism means intricate design and derives from the proscription in the Koran regarding the reproduction in art of any natural forms that may have a soul. The Arab artist is circumscribed by that prohibition to a graphic art of mathematical, geometrical, symmetrical, and rational design, approaching organic forms only insofar as vines, tendrils, and foliage are suggested. In this feature, the arabesque becomes entwined in art history with the grotesque, which takes its name from the "grotto paintings" (*grottesco*) unearthed in renaissance Rome, and which Vitruvius described in the 1st century as a bastard or hybrid style of painting fusing animal forms with plant forms, or organic with inorganic. The German romantic critic, Friedrich Schlegel, applied the term "Arabesque" to the intricate narrative symmetries and frames of the new *Roman*, which Novalis called the "geometrical novel." Kant's concept of the arabesque not only parallels this sense of unearthly, unearthbound, abstract design but also influenced the romantic development of the concept.

17. See also Byron's *The Giaour.* In addition to generalized resemblances to *Manfred*, cf. the setting in the mountains and the figure of the chamois hunter (see Poe, ll. 42-43; "strife with chamois"); cf. also Manfred's speech to the abbot, III, ll. 66-78, with the opening address of Tamerlane to a "friar." It is striking, given the implied situation of so many of his prose tales, that Poe's first major poem is a death-bed confession in dramatic monologue form.

18. In the 1831 publication of *Poems*, Poe incorporates lines from some of the shorter lyrics following the 1827 "Tamerlane" into the new version of the poem. The whole of the last 1827 lyric, "The Lake," becomes Section VIII of the 1831 "Tamerlane," with the addition of other lines, and in line 95 the addition of the name of the girl, Ada (the name, incidentally, of Byron's daughter).

19. See Mabbott's introduction to the poem, I, 83.

# Poe and the Poetics of Opacity:
## Or, Another Way of Looking at That Black Bird_____

Richard Godden

I

Common to post-Saussurean accounts of language is the assumption that where the signified once stood, the signifier now stands, and that furthermore it is signifiers all the way down. The systematic assumption that language operates in the absence of an available signified has tended to produce practices of reading for which a certain dematerialization and abstraction are the inevitable concomitants of language's actual incapacity to refer. Yet it is arguable that where the absence of the referent is an easy assumption, too little concern may be shown for the residual vehemence with which signs attend to the world. To explore what may be in effect a turn towards reference by devious paths we must attend to opacities since it is in moments when meanings fail that, as psychoanalysis has insisted, the painful origin of that failure may be intimated. Of particular relevance here is the work of Nicolas Abraham and Maria Torok, who have focused on language as a barrier or obstacle to understanding within which what is being obstructed is a situation "whose interpretation consists entirely in evaluating its resistance to meaning."[1] The words in which the event resides, if only as the pressure points left by its refusal of expression, are "defunct," words "relieved of their communicative function," but not, paradoxically, of their force.[2]

Abraham and Torok describe a situation in which the impact of some traumatic event is such as to block the symbolic operation and to locate linguistic resistance to communication in phonic and graphic effects. Such effects obstruct direct articulation of the event, with heightened non-semantic features operating in the service of the need to conceal. One example chosen by Abraham and Torok in their exploration of Freud's Wolf Man case may serve to make the point: *tieret* (Russian, to rub) is taken to crystallize a four-year-old boy's trauma over witnessing his father fondling or rubbing his six-year-old sister.[3] At sixteen the sister commits suicide by swallowing mercury (Russian *rtut*). Abraham and Torok, noting two shared consonants ("r" and "t") and "the glottal pronunciation *t.r.t.*," hear *rtut* as an oblique enunciation of *tieret*.[4] The girl swallows the word, objectified as mercury, and the boy disguises the word *tieret* in a visual image of a nursemaid scrubbing a floor (*natieret*, to rub down, to scrub, wax, to scrape, wound oneself). The word, with its freight of occluded events, silent within the image of domestic rubbing, causes the boy to achieve orgasm "in his father's place, as it were."[5] Whether or not one is persuaded by the ingenuity of Abraham and Torok's reading is not finally the point: the example is intended to illustrate how absolutely the event—the early scene of child abuse—has taken on phonic and graphic substance. *Tieret* and *rtut* are both "defunct" semantically, at least in terms of the scene they finally address, and yet because of that occluded site elements of each term remain semantically over-charged—theirs is, we might say, a forceful opacity. This turn away from language as communication—away from the presentation of what we might call a knowable event and toward an experience of the past as a kind of indeterminate force—encapsulates that need to conceal which characterizes the discourse of trauma. The event is repressed at the level of direct expression and can make itself felt again only in what Abraham and Torok call the "antisemantic" features of language.[6] Yet in what ways can such textual items be read when they aggressively occlude those elements which are normally read, replacing them with elements which customarily do not carry semantic burdens?

One way to approach this set of questions is to consider the degree to which a particular linguistic opacity articulates or denies access to the originating event against which it provides a preliminary psychic defense. The kinds of opacity or linguistic dysfunction which result from what may be called the traumatic event should not be perceived as simply a stylistic option. Opacity here signifies a condition of language which is not a transhistorical and epistemological linguistic given, but rather registers the deforming effect of a specific historical event. Unless, at some level, that event is recognized, opacity features will amount to no more than a stylistic device which might properly be called a kind of decadence. Recognition is potentially available through those features described by Abraham and Torok as antisemantic. Each element of their term is operative because the force released by the initial event is itself divided, seeking semanticization in communicative language, even as it enacts its own occlusion through the deformation of that medium. This double movement inscribes a form of temporal play which in Freud's analysis of trauma has become known as "deferred action" or "retroaction."[7]

Deferred action is a product of the excessive character of the first event, which requires a second event of re-narration to release its traumatic force. John Forrester neatly defines this movement as "the articulation of two *moments* with a time of delay."[8] Articulation in such circumstances involves not simply the recovery of an original site but a restructuring and reworking of that site: the work in question, as most typically explored within the psychoanalytic tradition, involves a particular species of talk characterized by often extreme forms of condensation and displacement which assert the continuing force of the original traumatic moment but not its complete recoverability. The talking cure so expressed proposes readability without delivering a transparently readable first event. For Freud, the act of memory requires a deliberate and interminable "working through" of the closed forms of temporal and linguistic order on which modernity has been based.[9] Jean-François Lyotard's understanding of the interminability of such work is useful here since he gives particular attention to *anamnesis* as a type of memory which would exceed a narrative or discursive ordering of past "facts" in sequence.[10] "Working through" ostensibly releases us from argument, dialectic, and the hegemony of the will, relying instead on mechanisms of association which produce an unpredictable and ultimately therapeutic cross-weave of times and images. The linguistic extension of this cross-weaving is what is meant here by "opacity," entailing in its necessary tensions a radical unsettling of what Foucault terms the "philosophy of representation—of the original, the first time, resemblance, imitation, faithfulness."[11]

With the loss of any unproblematic notion of resemblance and imitation comes a necessary materialization of the sign. The first event seems both crucial to referentiality and unavailable to the act of reference: out of this stand-off between the event and its signification comes an exorbitation of the sign. Caught in the vector of the event which it articulates, the sign becomes excessive because it is under contradictory pressure to reveal what finally cannot be revealed, an unavailable first event "which cannot be assimilated into the continuity of psychic life."[12] A particular kind of semantics results from such circumstances, a semantics which should not be reduced to the simple absence of that which is being addressed, because the event remains somehow "encrypted" within a language which is wried from the norm by its apparent refusal to refer. Abraham and Torok speak of a process of "designifying" by which words even as they signify normally are felt more importantly to refer to some event which is inadmissible.[13] What is difficult here and what marks the force of the *de-* or *anti-* in "designifying" and "antisemantics" is the fact that the second reference puts a new and troubling angle on the first, while appearing to leave it intact. Hence the first or normative reference is made to encrypt the second reference, where "encrypt" means both "to bury" and "to render cryptic."

This set of terms belongs to a broader vocabulary of cryptonymy, central to which is the notion of incorporation as opposed to introjection. Whereas introjection responds to traumatic loss by assimilating to the self what is lost (and getting on with life), incorporation perpetuates the existence of the lost object as something alive and foreign within the self (effectively, getting on with death). The dead person is thus not an object of identification but a phantasmatic presence within the self which gives rise to a topography which Abraham and Torok call the "crypt":

> Inexpressible mourning erects a secret tomb inside the subject. Reconstituted from the memories of words, scenes and affects, the object correlative of the loss is buried alive in the crypt as a full-fledged person, complete with its own topography. The crypt also included the actual or supposed traumas that made introjection impracticable.[14]

Language is essential to the design of the crypt; indeed, there can be no crypt without a peculiar kind of word, the cryptonym. The cryptonym is opaque not because it does not refer but because it refers to too much, part of which is unacknowledged. What is unacknowledged is the dead event incorporated in the living event, the dead referent encrypted in the living referent. Derrida in his foreword to Abraham and Torok's *The Wolf Man's Magic Word* argues:

> Anasemia creates an angle, within the word itself. While preserving the old word in order to submit it to its singular conversion, the anasemic operation does not result in a growing explicitness, in the uninterrupted development of a virtual significance, in a regression toward the original meaning.[15]

What Abraham and Torok mean by *anasemia* is thus "a constant movement 'back up toward' (from the Greek *ana*) successively earlier sources of signification (*semia* that lie beyond perception)."[16] This kind of semantics occurs, as Derrida might put it, because the angled term carries "a past that has never been present."[17] For Derrida, the past or, we might say, the traumatic event is both ever immanent and never present. In the remainder of this essay I want to look more closely at this double condition, which produces a writing strongly marked by contradictory desires, turning toward opacity and the satisfactions of concealment even as it offers a cryptic promise of readability.

Poe's "The Raven" (1845) would be eminently readable, were it not that its remorseless trochaic rhythm, extended through one hundred and eight predominantly eight-foot lines, displaces attention from meaning. An iteration of trochees may cause us to hear, but not to listen to what the poem says. Indeed, Nicolas Abraham departs from just such an intuition, making sense of the rhythms of "The Raven" while "leaving aside the semantic aspects" of the poem.[18] Initially, at least, his preoccupation is with what I would call antisemantic features, in the form of catalectic lines as they recur within heptameters consisting of fifteen or sixteen syllables arranged trochaically. Abraham scans Poe in order to read absence made present only by rhythm; in terms of the catalectic lines—or lines wanting a syllable in their last foot—he articulates what is literally not there. Here is Poe's first stanza, followed by Abraham's scansion of it:

> Once upon a midnight dreary, while I pondered, weak and
>     weary,
> Over many a quaint and curious volume of forgotten lore—
> While I nodded, nearly napping, suddenly there came a
>     tapping,
> As of someone gently rapping, rapping at my chamber door.
> "'Tis some visitor," I muttered, "tapping at my chamber
> door—
>                     Only this and nothing more."

$$— \smile — \smile — \smile — \smile \ (a^1) \qquad — \smile — \smile — \smile — \smile \ (a^2)$$
$$— \smile — \smile — \smile — \smile \ (x) \qquad — \smile — \smile — \smile — \ (b^1)$$
$$— \smile — \smile — \smile — \smile \ (c^1) \qquad — \smile — \smile — \smile — \smile \ (c^2)$$
$$— \smile — \smile — \smile — \smile \ (c) \qquad — \smile — \smile — \smile — \ (b^2)$$
$$— \smile — \smile — \smile — \smile \ (x) \qquad — \smile — \smile — \smile — \ (b^3)$$
$$— \smile — \smile — \smile — \ (b^4)^{[19]}$$

Neither Abraham nor Poe sees "many a" and "curious" as sticky trochees, sticky in that prosaic delivery finds three rather than two syllables. In his essay on the constitution of "The Raven" ("The Philosophy of Composition" [1846]), Poe makes no mention of exceptional feet, emphasizing instead a reiterated metrical pattern:

> the feet employed throughout (trochees) consist of a long syllable followed by a short: the first line of the stanza consists of eight of these feet—the second of seven and a half (in effect two-thirds)—the third of eight—the fourth of seven and a half—the fifth the same—the sixth three and a half.[20]

Abraham focuses on the effect of the incomplete sixteenth foot, with its withheld weak syllable, as it interrupts compounded trochees. He notes:

> Toward the end of the second line we feel slowly overcome by drowsiness. This is when the incident occurs. Its immediate effect is to jolt us awake. But there is more: in suppressing the expected rhyme [b¹] as well as its retroactive reference to an inductive rhyme (x), the incident suggests that, while I was dozing, something developed behind my back.[21]

The incident recurs when the eight trochees of line three give way to the seven and a half of line four; this, despite the fact that the third line's rhymes ($c^1$ and $c^2$) are reinforced internally by the fourth line ($c^3$), as though lulling us towards a sleep which the line's catalectic conclusion dashes. Metrically, lines five and six serve to reiterate the tension between trochee-recurrent and trochee-interruptus, with the closing three-and-a-half-foot line being mainly interruptus.

The first stanza's pattern, in terms both of meter and rhyme, is a template for the eighteen stanzas of the poem. Abraham reads its movement as broadly typical and as involving "reiterated attempts to fall asleep, waking with a start and, in the end, the victory of an inexorable reality."[22] But he points to a dysfunction between semantic event and the emergent sequence of metrical incidents; at the level of overt meaning, someone knocks seeking entry from outside, but does so (line three) within a rhythmic series free of incident and inculcating drowsiness. The three catalectic breaks or omissions occur as the story speaks of reassurance. Consequently, there is a dissonance between meaning and rhythm which Abraham takes as exemplary:

> Of the fact that the reality breaking in upon the dream is not an external event but a harrowing wish whose specter reaches consciousness in the form of hallucinatory representations. . . . In the story, an attempt is made to reassure . . . in the rhythm, mounting anxiety. All the rhythm says is: a troubling obstacle is upsetting sleep. The discrepancy between the rhythm and the plot adds: there is anxiety, something like an affect of insomnia along with the projection of anguish-desire kept in check by a return to wakefulness. From the first stanza on, we are plunged into a nightmare.[23]

Having rested heavily on Abraham, I now wish to move beyond him by extending his exploration of "The Raven"'s under-announced opacities. Abraham does not mention that all the catalectic feet of the poem rhyme on variants of the syllable "or." Poe claims that, having made up his mind as to a single-word refrain, and having divided the hypothetical poem into stanzas which would foreground the refrain, he was "inevitably led . . . to the long o as the most sonorous vowel, in connection with *r* as the most producible consonant."[24] "Nevermore" is famously the vehicle required by Poe's preferred phonemes. At no point in his explanatory essay does he unite "*o*" and "*r*," which consequently remain for him antisemantic elements. However, readers of his commentary and its poem may be less willing to suspend semantic inference, particularly given that the sound "or" recurs seventy-two times as the first beat of a truncated trochee, and therefore prefaces an absence, whose presence is both rhythmically required by the surrounding iteration of trochees, and typographically marked by frequent exclamations and dashes. Such repetition begs the exclamatory question, "or / what?"

Answers might seem to turn on those rhyming words which most significantly or frequently carry the syllable in question. "Nevermore" because it is the refrain. "Lenore" because she is the subject of the refrain. "Door" and "more" by dint of sheer recurrence, fourteen times and eleven times respectively. These words are clues to a missing syllable. Poe's suggestion that, metrically speaking, the omission—in each instance prefaced by "or"—constitutes no more than one-third of the catalectic trochee, because presumably it is the weaker beat of the foot, draws further attention to what is left out by announcing a kind of repression.[25] "Nevermore," "Lenore," "door," "more," "or" . . . "or what?" I am close to saying "so what?," except that if the "door" to the missing "more" proposed by "or" is simply "Lenore" (dead and buried), and her harbinger comes back to say as much, surely—since this is what the poem overtly announces—there may well be an entirely different and much more disruptive "or" being proposed by the poem's *de*signifying factors?

Since the clues, so far, turn on metrical exceptions, I shall consider less systematically exceptional feet. These are few and far between, and I shall work backwards through them because initial instances are liable to seem arbitrary without the emerging and retroactive pattern that recurrence implies. The second line of the penultimate stanza (seventeen) apparently accords with other second lines, consisting of seven trochees followed by an incomplete eighth foot:

> "Get thee / back in / to the / tempest / and the / Night's Plu /
>     tonian / shore!"

However, the seventh foot is conventionally trochaic only if three syllables shift into two, so that "ton i an" (in "Plutonian," a four-syllable word) becomes "ton [y]an"; this, of itself, might pass as an aural convention were it not that two lines earlier (in stanza sixteen) metrical regularity is preserved by a similar elision of three into two:

---

"Clasp a / rare and / radiant / maiden / whom the / angels /
    name Len / ore."

Here, the third foot is trochaic because the syllable "i" is pronounced
"y" ("ra[i]d [y]ant"). In both cases, if "i" were sounded, the lines would
scan as having eight feet, though each with iambic exceptions.[26] The
same Plutonian play appears in line five of stanza eight, operating from
the seventh foot in a similar way; the difference in this case being that
the attendant "i" into "y" foot is reversed, so that in the first line of the
stanza, "ebony" can operate as a second trochaic foot only because the
three syllable word ("eb on y") is occluded into two ("eb ny"), where
the "y" of the new closing syllable is under alliterative pressure to yield
the phoneme "i" ("Then th*i*s / ebony / b*i*rd beg*ui*ling / my sad / fancy /
*i*nto / sm*i*ling,"). My point is not to restore the "i," but to suggest that
only because "i" vanishes into "y," or "y" into "i," can "or" constitute a
preface to an absence.

I am clearly being careful to retain an antisemantic emphasis, but the
strain begins to tell, particularly in stanza seventeen, where two exceptional feet in close proximity, and with a similar structure, create a liaison
between "radiant" and "Plutonian." Since "radiant" refers to the angelic
Lenore, while "Plutonian" is associated with the raven, light is juxta-
posed against dark even as "I" (first person pronoun) turns into "why"
(an interrogative term), so that "or" can beg the question "or what?,"
twice. "White," "black," "I," "why?," "Or—?" . . . more of this later.

In the fourth line of stanza fourteen, "memories" must be pronounced "mem'ries" to supply a trochee. The phoneme "o," spoken as
"or," is omitted just prior to an occurrence of the name Lenore, and its
omission allows the second syllable of the loved one's name to function catalectically. Once the sixth and eighth feet are seen as metrically
interdependent, "or" is suppressed in "memories" only to return propo-
sitionally attached to "Lenore," which now, in effect, reads metrically
"Lenore or?" It would seem that Poe can't keep a good exception
down. More, too, of this later.

In stanza twelve, lines four and five share in their repetition of "ominous," a contraction of three syllables into two so that a trochee, "om'nous," can be sounded. Again "i" is silenced, permitting "yore—," via its demonstration of omission, to advance a mute alternative. The letter "i" and the dash are metrically tied; the nature of their knot is implied at the site of excision which ties that knot—"om in ous" as it becomes "om nous." Division of the word syllabically produces a pun, and once more the antisemantic infers an alternative semantics. "Ominous" can be designified in two ways: "om in us" or "om i *nous*"; the prevalence of "i" in exceptional feet as a free-standing and easily dispersed phoneme favors the latter. In which case the presence of a French pronoun transposes "om" into "*homme*," which, translated, yields "man I we." But, as always with puns, the alternative won't go away, contaminating the French with its preposition and its English pronoun, to generate a hybrid, "man in us." Although one should not forget that this combination leaves "i" inappropriately high and dry, unless the man who is in us is taken as also in "I."

I offer in my defense two pieces of literary evidence. Poe was fond of punning, both in French and on the first person pronoun; witness his play on "Dupin" in "The Purloined Letter" (1845), in which the detective tricks the Minister D— by substituting a facsimile for the missing missive. The substitute is carefully forged by Dupin who, we are assured, "imitat[es] the D— cipher, very readily, by means of a seal formed of bread."[27] First pronounal plays are central both to "William Wilson" (1839) and "The Tell-Tale Heart" (1843). In the former, before a mirror at the "farther end" of a room, doubles fight it out until one kills the other; under a paternal pun, a son kills his all-but-brother so that by "will" he can assert his exclusive identity ("I am") as "Will's son."[28] In a region without primogeniture law, where plantations tended to be divided at the death of the planter, the pun is not without its politics.[29] In the latter story, the narrator kills and dismembers an old man, but remains at a loss over his own motive. He starts the tale with an exclamatory proposition, "I think it was his eye!," and adds that he killed to "rid myself of the eye forever."[30] Since the resilient beating of the victim's heart induces confession, and since apprehension implies execution, the closing of the old man's eye terminates the "I" of the narrator.

These have long been the commonplaces of Poe scholarship.[31] The "*nous*," "*homme*," and first-person, released antisemantically into the subsemantics of "The Raven," are not; their latencies lie as yet unread. "Ominous" recurs at a crucial moment in the poem's narrative: its repetition in stanza twelve literally marks the spot where the narrator initiates the process which ties bird to missing mistress. As soon as he "link[s]" "fancy to fancy" in pursuit of the meaning of the bird's word, he comes up with "ominous" twice. In the footsteps of Abraham, I would point to a further and more sustained "discord between meaning and rhythm"; at the level of narrated event, the narrator pulls up a "cushioned seat" from which to study the raven; at the touch of a cushion's "velvet lining" he recalls "*She*" who will press it no more (stanza thirteen).[32] Ergo, while he "sat engaged in guessing, but no syllable expressing," a happy coincidence of touch and sight gives rise to the female pronoun, though the narrator insists that "*She*" remains unexpressed "to the fowl." Perhaps his reticence can be explained by noting how the exceptions take exception via their release of a contradictory subplot which, by way of "ominous," puts a man, not "*she*," into an interior both singular and collective. Although the narrator does not enunciate the female pronoun (despite having fallen into the habit of talking aloud to the bird), the unuttered "she" is sufficient to produce spectral competition for the raven in the form of stanza fourteen's seraphic "footfalls" presaging the offer of a cessation of sorrow ("nepenthe")—all of which rises from "memories of Lenore." Single syllables appear to pack a lot of plot. You may recall that in the middle of the ghostly stand-off (stanza fourteen, line four), hesitation over whether to express or repress the syllable "or" in "memories" induces a metrical hesitancy as to whether the last syllable of "Lenore" (the "she" in question) should front a missing alternative, or foreclose on the reiterated question of that alternative. Seldom can the word "memory" have been under such pressure from one of its syllables to reveal the differences (the ors and the eithers) that generate its substance. I would stress that "or" can do all this because it takes its place among metrical events, activating phonic and graphic agents whose rhythm runs counter to narrated events. The lady Lenore serves to explain both the narrator's grief and his ornithological obsession; but the word "Lenore" disfigures that explanatory analogy by its rhythmically induced capacity to carry its own alterity. The discordant inference that the body of the "beautiful woman" may finally not be the raven's source requires the question, "who lies encrypted in her cryptic name?"[33]

I am close to exasperation, and I have not yet finished with stanza twelve, whose first line, in its echo of the first line of stanza seven, hints at an answer: "But the Raven still beguiling all my fancy into smiling." "Raven" (second foot, first line, stanza twelve) stands as a metrical correction of "ebony" (second foot, first line, stanza eight), but much would vanish were the earlier line changed to "Then this Raven fast beguiling my sad fancy into smiling." "Ebony" contains more than a play on "i" and "y" activated by a suppressed syllable; it is the first tinting of the raven who on entry settles on a bust of "Pallas" (line five, stanza seven). "Pallas" will later euphonically yield "pallid" and is doubtless the preferred perch (referred to three times) for reasons of color contrast. But "Pallas" contains another word, being an alternative name for Minerva, goddess of wisdom, who, it was popularly supposed, sprang from the split skull of her father, Jupiter, and who was fond of feathered forms.[34] Poe's ebony bird is an obscurely wise headache, particularly because the exceptional foot "ebony," proximate to "Pallas" and already metrically split and contracted, can be further redistributed to give "bone," which arguably foregrounds the cranial wound available within the word "Pallas." To recap: rhythmically persuaded to cast "ebony" into its antisemantic fragments, I find "i," and "y," and "ebon," which incline to "I," "why," and "bone," where the third term is drawn out by "Pallas"—a name which "bone" recasts *and* recolors, so that Pallas becomes Minerva at the same time that she assumes the form of a black bird sprung from the white head upon which it perches. Well might a white subject ("I"), faced with such a phantom scene issuing from "ebony," question its own integrity ("why?").

In order to complete my progress by way of exceptional feet towards an anthology of subsemantic whisperings, I must mention line one, stanza seven, and the second line of the first stanza. I shall work with the exceptions occurring in stanza one because that line shares the foot "many a" with stanza seven: "Over many a quaint and curious volume of forgotten lore—." Given that Poe's metrical intentions are not at this early stage clearly established, a failure to note that "many a" or "curious" are deviations from the trochaic rule leads to a scanning of the line which cancels the catalectic final foot and so occludes the interrogative inference of "or." Contracted to form a trochee "curious" becomes "cur[e] yus," "i" passing into "y" in a word that already invites enquiry. "[M]any a" reduces to "man ya," or more properly "m[e]n ya," which viewed retrospectively through the template of "ominous," as it turns towards "man in us," whispers of a connection between mankind and the indefinite article, or even between "men" and "are"; both enunciate a question.

The key exceptions are now in place, and by working through them I feel as though I have cracked a code where there was no code, merely a number of "rhythmic events" productive of designifiers which began systematically to infer a meaning that has yet to form. Were I to articulate that immanence, I would have reductively to say that the subject who narrated (i) is hesitant about his status (y) because of its sustained proximity to alterity ("or—," left catalectically open). But to say only this is to complement the poem's overt narrative of anxiety focused on an "other," in the form of a dead woman, whom the narrator appears to have "incorporated."[35] In Abraham and Torok's terms, the speaker has made of himself a crypt in which he encrypts Lenore, whose gnomic emissary (from within) is the bird. "i," "y," and part at least of "or" comply, but their effects in "ominous," "ebony," "Plutonian," and "radiant" amount to more because, taken together, they at least infer that the crypt contains not a woman but a man, and moreover, a man who is black. When the "other" in question darkens and switches gender, the "or" rhythmically drawn from Lenore's name (as "Lenore-or?") suggests that the event of her death operates in the poem as a first order of reference, containing and encrypting quite another referent.

Let us suppose that what lies buried in the poem's narrator is not a dead mistress whom he sustains, but a dead slave whom he cannot let die. At once I have both a formal and a historical problem which may yet prove to be part and parcel of one another. Formally, I have traced how a silent syllable metrically nominates an act of withholding, whose rhythmic effect in a number of exceptional lines encourages either a scansion that will obstruct that occlusion, or the suppression of a group of phonemes which, even as they are phonically wiped, leave a graphic residue—a residue that, despite being "relieved of [its] communicative function," retains through opacity a capacity to imply a buried referent. Indeed, by systematically going missing, these graphemes suggest that something has been missed. My formal problem can be simply stated: why should a group of sub-communicative effects, amounting to opacity, retain a semblance of transparency? In this instance, reading the unreadable, or trying to demystify textual effects as they stop short of articulation, might well start at the level of the poem's announced referent, Lenore or "the death . . . of a beautiful woman." The reasons why Poe found female mortality "unquestionably, the most poetical topic in the world" are traceable to an antebellum cultural pathology whose plot runs as follows: during the antebellum period, Southern white males of the owning class idealized womanhood by raising the female gentry on pedestals above the reality of interracial sex between slave women and slave owners. As the color line was criss-crossed in the quarters, so the pedestals soared at the plantation house. In the words of one Southern historian, the white woman became "the South's Palladium . . . —the shield-bearing Athena gleaming whitely in the clouds, the standard of its rallying. . . . She was the lily-pure maid of Astolat. . . . And—she was the pitiful Mother of God."[36] By means of her propriety husbands, fathers, and sons whitewashed their property and its sustaining institutions. The cult of Southern womanhood raised the standard of the unbreachable hymen precisely because miscegenation breached the color line throughout the prewar South.[37] Plainly much of the iconic resiliency of the lily-white figure derived from that which it stood to negate. "She" was only as beautiful, white, and impermeable as he was ugly, black, and permeating. I summarize a cultural narrative to demonstrate how an ideal of beauty, constituted by racial fear, may require the presence of that which it denies. That Poe's "beautiful woman" must also be dead and therefore available for melancholy ("the most legitimate of all the poetical tones") is a measure of his need to preserve her intact as his own strength; internalized and entombed she is safe as his property in perpetuity.[38] Of course, the subplot of my cultural narrative also requires that a black be in the psychic crypt to preserve both the purity and the relevance of the icon to which it gives birth. By this reading Poe's Pallas/Minerva has a Southern complexion; she is "wise" to the fact that the integrity of her form, indeed of her iconic substance (or bone), derives from the black—hence, Pallas a black bird sprung from a white head, and hence, also, that black bird as the all but silent and yet irrepressible mouthpiece of Lenore.

Again, my reading leaves a residue of the unreadable; specifically, "us" or "*nous*"—"ominous" stipulates "a man in us" not "a man in her." So far, my turn to historical referents has dealt in sexual fear, and in a region's history of miscegenation, but if the bird's terms encrypt a man, and if that man permeates men as well as women, an exchange other than the sexual is tacitly implied. Reading the raven as a dislocated expression of the trauma of miscegenation, necessarily displaced even as it colors the whitest of whited sepulchres, will explain neither why the offending "man" is in us (male *and* female), nor, and perhaps more importantly, why he should be both dead and alive, as well as hidden and apparent.[39] In the antebellum South, black bodies passed into white bodies in ways both more traumatic and more foundational than those proposed either by the specter or by the real fact of miscegenation. Southern labor is a site of physical exchange in which, I shall argue, the black is traumatically lodged within the generic body of the white owning class—he lodges there as a revenant, a man who is both dead and alive and whose presence must be denied. On these grounds the primal scene angling within the rhythmic incidents of "The Raven" is the scene of Southern slave labor. A brief historical gloss is necessary to establish the dynamics of that scene.

For the Southern slave owner, the slave was a chattel, a thing without a will, whose will along with his or her name belonged to the master. Historians of slavery note that masters typically allocated their slaves new names at time of purchase, thereby declaring them socially dead, since if slaves were things they could have no parent, wife, child, or social extension.[40] However, by dealing the slave a social death, the master threatened his own life. Here, Hegel is helpful. Hegel has it that the lord seeks absolute, because independent, authority. At the moment of his supremacy, however, he is troubled because he recognizes, in objects through which he represents that supremacy to himself, labor that is not his own. He knows that his lordship depends upon the labor of the bound man:

> Just when the master had effectively achieved lordship, he really finds that something has come about quite different from an independent consciousness. It is not an independent consciousness, but rather a dependent consciousness that he has achieved.[41]

The trauma of recognition involves him in an unpassable contradiction; the white lord must extract from his lordship those black materials which define it ("in order to become certain of [himself] . . . as a true being").[42] To do as much is impossible, since the master's mastery depends upon the body, labor, and consciousness of the bound man. And, as Jessica Benjamin has it: "if we fatally negate the other, that is if we assume complete control over his identity and will, then we have negated ourselves as well."[43] It follows that, should the master negate the slave, allowing him no independent consciousness, he will find himself enmeshed with a dead thing (a non-conscious being). And he, having deprived himself of the very goods and recognitions that represent his lordship, will discover himself close to death.

Many of Poe's narrators almost die, tangling with the almost dead: "almost" is the parabolic point. Alive, the slave exposes to the master that his mastery is a form of dependence. Dead, the slave cancels the master's means to mastery. Buried alive, the slave ratifies the master's mastery (underpinning the substance of the lord), without troubling his master's independent consciousness. The solution to the master's impassable contradiction is that the slave become a revenant *in language*, and in language of a particular kind.

Enough of parables—instead, an example of linguistic revenanting. Take the word "Lenore": with its first syllable concluding a trochee and its second triggering a catalectic foot, the name has been analyzed as inviting its own alterity; indeed, it declares itself an improper name, whose essence is present only as a withdrawal from nomination, prefaced by "or." One might say that from the missing syllable, proposed by the name, emerges the raven (both bird and poem). Attendant on the bird, and rhythmically dependent on the fact that the syllable stays missing, are a number of graphic incidents. "[y]," "i," "ebon [as bone]," and "—" imply (and no more than imply) that encrypted inside Lenore (as in her name) lies a black man, who, since the poem's narrator has incorporated his mistress, resides also in that narrator. All this occurs, quite literally, *in* language. The figure of the revenant slave, structurally central to a premodern regime of accumulation and to the *un*consciousness of an owning class, never forms, but makes itself felt at the lower levels of the narrator's consciousness and consequently at the outer semantic reaches of his language. Yet the revenant's trace must be *almost* readable, if the consciousness of the class that owns him is to retain its peculiar substance; consequently "Lenore," activated by the poem's exceptions, keeps "*Le noir*" down among its taciturnities.

## Notes

The first section of this paper was co-written with Peter Nicholls and presented as part of a joint paper at the Neo Formalist Circle Conference in Mansfield College, Oxford (1996). I am grateful to Peter Nicholls for his permission to publish it here.

1. Nicholas Rand, "Translator's Introduction" to Nicolas Abraham and Maria Torok, *The Wolf Man's Magic Word: A Cryptonomy*, foreword by Jacques Derrida (Minneapolis, Univ. of Minnesota Press, 1986), lx. The principal texts by Abraham and Torok in English translation are *The Wolf Man's Magic Word* and *The Shell and the Kernel*, vol. 1, ed. and trans. Rand (Chicago: Univ. of Chicago Press, 1994). See also Abraham, *Rhythms: on the Work, Translation, and Psychoanalysis*, trans. Benjamin Thigpen and Rand (Stanford: Stanford Univ. Press, 1995).

2. Abraham and Torok, quoted by Derrida in his "Foreword" to *The Wolf Man's Magic Word*, xxxv-xxxvi.

3. For abbreviated accounts of the narrative, see *Shell*, 132-34 (where the Russian word is spelt *teret*) and *The Wolf Man's Magic Word*, 16-19.

4. For Abraham and Torok's spelling, see *Shell*, 133.

5. Abraham and Torok, *Shell*, 133.

6. See for example *Shell*, 85, where Abraham and Torok speak of psychoanalysis as "this scandalous antisemantics of concepts designified."

7. For literary applications of Freud's concept of deferred action, see Peter Nicholls, "The Belated Postmodern: History, Phantoms and Toni Morrison," in *Psychoanalytic Criticism: A Reader*, ed. Sue Vice (Oxford: Polity Press, 1996), 50-74, and Richard Godden, "*Absalom, Absalom!* And Rosa Coldfield: Or What *Is* in the Dark House?," *The Faulkner Journal* 8.2 (1993): 31-66.

8. John Forrester, *The Seductions of Psychoanalysis: Freud, Lacan and Derrida* (Cambridge: Cambridge Univ. Press, 1990), 206.

9. On "working through," see Nicholls, "Divergences: Modernism, Postmodernism, Jameson and Lyotard," *Critical Quarterly* 33.3 (1991): 4-5.

10. See, for example, Jean-François Lyotard, *L'inhumain: Causeries sur le temps* (Paris: Editions Galilée, 1988), and *Heidegger et 'les juifs'* (Paris: Editions Galilée, 1988).

11. Michel Foucault, *Language, Counter-Memory, Practice: Selected Essays and Interviews*, ed. Donald F. Bouchard (Cornell: Cornell Univ. Press, 1977), 172.

12. Rand, "Introduction: Renewals of Psychoanalysis," in Abraham and Torok, *The Wolf Man's Magic Word*, 21.

13. See, for example, Abraham and Torok, *Shell*, 84.

14. Abraham and Torok, "Mourning *or* Melancholia: Introjections *versus* Incorporation," in *Shell*, 130.

15. Derrida, "Foreword," xxxiv.

16. Esther Rashkin, "Tools for a New Psychoanalytic Literary Criticism: The Work of Abraham and Torok," *Diacritics* (Winter 1988): 50.

17. Derrida, *Memories for Paul de Man*, rev. ed., trans. Cecile Lindsay and others (New York: Columbia Univ. Press, 1989), 58.

18. Abraham, *Rhythms*, 107.

19. Abraham, *Rhythms*, 125. For "The Raven" I have used the text available in *Selected Writings of Edgar Allan Poe*, ed. David Galloway (Harmondsworth: Penguin, 1978), 77-80.

20. Poe, "The Philosophy of Composition," in *Selected Writings*, 488.

21. Abraham, *Rhythms*, 125.

22. Abraham, *Rhythms*, 126.

23. Abraham, *Rhythms*, 127.

24. Poe, "Philosophy," 485.

25. See Poe "Philosophy," 488.

26. The scansion must run as follows:


"Gēt thĕe / bāck in / tō the / tēmpĕst / and thĕ /nīght's Plŭ / tonĭ / ăn shore!"
"Clāsp ă/ rāre and / rādĭ / ănt māid / en whŏm / thĕ ăn / gĕls nāme / Lēnore."


27. Poe, "The Purloined Letter," in *Selected Writings*, 347.

28. Poe, "William Wilson," in *Selected Writings*, 178.

29. See Richard Godden, "Edgar Allan Poe and the Detection of Riot," *Literature and History*, 8.2 (1982): 206-31.

30. Poe, "The Tell-Tale Heart," in *Selected Writings*, 277.

31. See, for example, J. J. Moldenhaur, "Murder as a Fine Art: Basic Connections between Poe's Aesthetic, Psychological and Moral Vision," *PMLA* 83.2 (1968): 284-97.

32. Abraham, *Rhythms*, 127 ("discord between meaning").

33. The phrase is drawn from Poe's infamous assertion that "the death, then, of a beautiful woman is, unquestionably, the most poetical topic in the world" ("Philosophy," 486).

34. Pallas/Minerva lends herself to the bird motif, being much associated with both Cock and Owl. However, I am aware that in pursuing this name play, I risk straining my reader's patience. I would offer in mitigation Abraham and Torok's psychoanalytic claim that trauma and its regression can so distort the signs through which it is represented that a "cryptonomy" forms. See Abraham and Torok, *The Wolf Man's Magic Word*, lviii. For an application of "cryptonomy" to Poe's "The Fall of the House of

Usher," see Esther Rashkin, "A Meeting of the Minds: Edgar Allan Poe's 'The Fall of the House of Usher,'" collected in her *Family Secrets and the Psychoanalysis of Narrative* (Princeton: Princeton Univ. Press, 1992), 123-55.

35. See Abraham and Torok, "Mourning *or* Melancholia." Abraham and Torok define "incorporation" as refusal to mourn, resting on an ingestion of the love object: "If accepted and worked through the loss would require major readjustment. But the fantasy of incorporation merely simulates profound psychic transformation through magic; it does so by implementing literally something that has only figurative meaning. So in order not to have to 'swallow' a loss, we fantasise swallowing (or having swallowed) that which has been lost, as if it were some kind of thing" ("Mourning *or* Melancholia," 126). What is swallowed lies in a psychic vault within the subject. Arguably, the catalectic feet, central to "The Raven"'s metrical effect and turning on the name Lenore, involve a related form of swallowing.

36. W. J. Cash, *The Mind of the South* (London: Thames and Hudson, 1971), 89.

37. See Joel Williamson, *The Crucible of Race: Black White Relations in the American South Since Emancipation* (New York: Oxford Univ. Press, 1984), 306-8.

38. Poe, "Philosophy," 484.

39. See Joan Dayan, "Amorous Bondage: Poe, Ladies and Slaves" (*American Literature* 66.2 [1994]: 239-73) for an intriguing and related reading of "Ligeia" as one expression of a secret history of miscegenation.

40. James Oakes, *Slavery and Freedom: An Interpretation of the Old South* (New York: Alfred Knopf, 1990), 4.

41. G. W. F. Hegel, *The Phenomenology of Mind*, trans. J. B. Baillie, 2 vols. (New York: Macmillan, 1910), 1:184.

42. Hegel, 1:176.

43. Jessica Benjamin, *The Bonds of Love: Psychoanalysis, Feminism and the Problem of Domination* (New York: Pantheon, 1988), 39.

# Quoting the Signifier "Nevermore":
## *Fort! Da!*, Pallas, and Desire in Language _____

Daneen Wardrop

We twentieth-century American readers have long seen Edgar Allan Poe's "Raven" as glumly recounting one more variation on his reaction to the death of a beautiful woman. There has endured, however, a Poe who offers in the poem a dramatic and exciting scenario of the desire that occurs in language formation. Perhaps modern scorn partly can be traced to an overstrong focus on the mathematician in Poe, the algebraic poet in "The Philosophy of Composition" who dryly proffers the metrical scaffolding of "The Raven," as if a computer had composed it. Such (purported) calculation is anathema to the American sense of individual passion and spontaneity and the romantic tradition of sublime poetic inspiration. Then, too, we may malign "The Raven" because we suspect it of old-fashioned allegorizing, because we balk at a line so broad as "'Take thy beak from out my heart.'"[1] To the extent, however, that the raven's beak can operate as a point or nub of a pen, and the heart as a convention of desire, the poem becomes a more postmodern allegory, integrating in this image the major elements of the desire *à la lettre*—the desire that initiates language. Indeed, "The Raven" can be seen as no less than the quintessential poem of desire in language, reenacting for us the entry of the subject into the signifying chain.[2]

The narrator of Poe's poem must gain his identity, as must all subjects, by interjecting himself into the chain of signification—that is, by experiencing the desire that makes signification inevitable, and thus entering into the symbolic realm of language.[3] As Jacques Lacan describes it, the subject is "defined in his [or her] articulation by the signifier."[4] Lacanian desire is inseparable from signification; it must travel through the defiles of the signifier. Perhaps Lacan's most beguiling contribution remains his understanding of how we begin using language, claiming and being claimed by the signifier. He asserts significantly that "the moment in which desire becomes human is also that in which the child is born into language" (*E*, 103). From the outset of "The Raven," we know that we stand at the brink of such a moment, that we have entered the realm in which Lacanian desire—desire *à la lettre*—prompts such a birth. Edward Davidson divides the poem into halves of nine stanzas each and suggests that it becomes interiorized in the second half, where the narrator "loses hold of himself" and reality.[5] An alternative division presents itself, however: a tripartite structure in which the six-stanza sections roughly correspond to three stages of linguistic development—a prelingual mode, the entry of desire and the signifier, and the attempt to resolve the Lacanian-style oedipal dilemma.

# 1

The first third of "The Raven" forms a quest for the pure signifier: the sign that stands only for itself, undeterred by the signified, heralding the desire for language. Surely it is no surprise that the pure signifier is "Nevermore," but the poem takes its own good time— again, a full third—to arrive at it. The preparation for that signifier warrants our investigation. From the inception of the poem, the narrator's lack of a proper designation for his lost love signals to the reader that we start at the site of absent language.[6] In the most crucial line of the first section, the narrator states that Lenore remains "[n]ameless *here* for evermore" ("R," 365; emphasis original). "*Here*": we stand at an important moment, as the italicization shows. We begin at a place where language is unavailable to the narrator, a land of signifier perdition or purgatory where only one word is worth saying—"Lenore," a word with "no" at its very center, a name given, not by the narrator himself in the symbolic mode where language is the father, but by the angels. "Lenore" can never be his word. Into this namelessness—a realm in which "the silence was unbroken, and the stillness gave no token" (365)—the raven will drop his one brash signifier.

Another salient feature of the poem's first third is the effect of repetition, which informs our initial contact with "The Raven" and is perhaps even the first thing we notice. Such an attention Poe would have welcomed. The narrator's desire *à la lettre* starts in a place before desire, and Poe evokes this place with waves of repetitive sound. These waves are not unlike the *chora* described by Julia Kristeva, where "rupture and articulations (rhythm)" come before "evidence, verisimilitude, spatiality and temporality."[7] The subject exists at a site where he experiences the rhythms of needs but not yet the desire that gives birth to the signifier. Although repetition of course remains indigenous to the poem throughout, it is never so insistent as at the outset; in fact, here it interferes with meaning to the extent that it renders many of the lines nearly nonsensical. In the first verse alone we encounter the following: "nodded," "napping," "tapping," "rapping," "rapping," "tapping" ("R," 364-65). Mutlu Konuk Blasing calls the room in which the narrator works—and, indeed, Poe's very use of language in this section—a veritable "echo chamber."[8] The narrator himself divulges that, in order "to still the beating of [his] heart, [he] stood repeating" (365). He next reports the reiterated line and then immediately reports it again, so that he speaks redundantly, repeating the repetition:

> And the silken, sad, uncertain rustling of each purple curtain
> Thrilled me—filled me with fantastic terrors never felt before;
> So that now, to still the beating of my heart, I stood repeating
> "'Tis some visiter entreating entrance at my chamber door—
> Some late visiter entreating entrance at my chamber door;—
> This it is and nothing more."
>
> (365)

The beating of his heart may be indistinguishable from all the tapping and rapping that rattles through the first stanzas.

The repetition in tandem with the annoyingly persistent rhymes—rapping, tapping, beating, entreating, repeating—creates a din of sonic effects. Much fun has been made, at Poe's expense, of such effects here and in the similarly cacophonous "The Bells." Being annoying, however, is not the same as being inept. Poe may have written "The Philosophy of Composition" in anticipation of just such unfair charges of ineptitude or banality. In that essay he asserts that the frequent repetition of the refrain forms a basic objective of the poet, aided by "some altogether novel effects, arising from an extension of the application of the principles of rhyme and alliteration."[9] Poe pursues his effects, chasing sound and not content in this case: "[t]he pleasure," he maintains, "is deduced solely from the sense of identity—of repetition," a remark that refers to the use of the refrain but that could be applied to any of the poem's repetitions. Poe goes on to explain that he chooses first sound and then word: "The sound of the *refrain* being thus determined, it became necessary to select a word embodying this sound, and at the same time in the fullest possible keeping with that melancholy which I had predetermined as the tone of the poem" ("PC," 17, 18). It is at this point that the algebraic Poe can help us, and we should take him seriously. The repetition, intentional and not ad hoc, forms a kind of prelingual rhythm into which desire and language might be introduced effectively.

We can find yet another, related, reason for the poem's compulsive rapping and tapping: repetition compulsion. Such behavior forms the concept from which Lacan launches the introduction of his definitive work, *Ecrits*, drawing an excerpt from his famous essay on "The Purloined Letter": "Our inquiry has led us to the point of recognizing that the repetition automatism (*Wiederholungszwang*) finds its basis in what we have called the *insistence* of the signifying chain."[10] Freud understood repetition automatism as "the effort to find an irretrievably lost object" that manifests not as memory but as a movement of repetition—a notion that Lacan appropriates to his analysis of language formation. In an overview of Lacan's essay, John Muller and William Richardson note that "the theme of the entire Seminar [on 'The Purloined Letter'] is that the automatism of repetition is accounted for by the primacy of the signifier over the subject."[11]

The compulsive repetition in the first third of the poem brings us tantalizingly close to the signifier "Nevermore." Though early on the narrator repeats several times the phrase "nothing more," this clearly is not the pure signifier; it only prepares us for that declarative arrival at the end of the eighth stanza. One of the seemingly idiosyncratic features of the refrain is that it does not occur until the second third of the poem—an odd feature unless we understand the need to set the stage: Before we can apprehend that "it is the symbolic order which is constitutive for the subject,"[12] we must experience the presymbolic state. We remain pre-oedipal in the first stanzas, experiencing a time prior to the articulation of desire as the narrator searches for a signifier.

## 2

The second section heralds the arrival of "Nevermore." Whereas the first third of the poem uses rhythm and repetition, the second third introduces, with "Nevermore," the inchoate articulation of syllables that stands on the verge of meaning, predicting entry into the symbolic mode. The sonority of the word dampens the chattering repetitions that precede it, and Poe chooses the word precisely for its monotonous quality ("PC," 18). Hence, the term gains effect both from its delayed entry and from the contrast of its sound with the sounds in the previous verses. The narrator marvels to hear a word spoken, "to hear discourse so plainly"; and though ostensibly he marvels at the fact that a bird can speak, given the sonic effects Poe creates he must also marvel simply at the existence of discourse itself. That "Nevermore" stands as a pure signifier important only in its quality of "signifier-ness" is suggested when the narrator reports that the word carries "little meaning—little relevancy" ("R," 366). The word attempts to offer us pure discourse, a representation of absence.

Much of the middle section, in fact, unfolds as an opportunity for the narrator to marvel at "[t]hat one word" ("R," 367) given to him by the raven. Signification begins to enter this previously language-barren place, and we see the narrator's astonishment at the phenomenon. After all, marveling is warranted; the entry of the pure signifier may be the most telling event in the linguistic life of any human being. Poe is working ironically when he has the narrator say:

> For we cannot help agreeing that no living human being
> Ever yet was blessed with seeing bird above his chamber door—
> Bird or beast upon the sculptured bust above his chamber door,
> With such name as "Nevermore."
>
> (367)

The irony inheres because the entry of "Nevermore"—the projected birth into language—happens to every human being capable of speech. Apprehending as new and singular an experience that forms a staple of development, the quintessential moment when desire becomes human, Poe's narrator reveals the depth of his amazement.

Repetition, again, informs the crucial position that "Nevermore" occupies in the poem's paradigm of language. We have already noticed the role of repetition compulsion in Freud's ideas of psychological development and Lacan's ideas of language acquisition. The child's earliest experience with such compulsion, found in what Freud called the *Fort! Da!* game, demonstrates for Lacan the vital link between repetition and linguistic being: "the conception of the signifying chain," he claims, can be seen "as inaugurated by the primordial symbolization (made manifest in the game *Fort! Da!*, which Freud revealed as lying at the origin of the repetition compulsion); this chain develops in accordance with logical links whose grasp on that which is to be signified . . . operates through the effects of the signifier" (*E*, 215). Freud first observed the *Fort! Da!* game when his grandson repeatedly played a version of peek-a-boo by throwing a spool at the end of a string over the edge of his cot, then pulling the spool by the string back to himself. When the spool was out of sight he let out a sound, "o-o-o-o-o," which Freud and the child's mother both interpreted as his attempt to say the German word *fort*, which means "gone." Once he pulled the spool back to himself he would happily pronounce *da*, German for "here." Freud reports that "[t]his, then, was the complete game—disappearance and return."[13] The boy would repeat his *Fort! Da!* game compulsively when out of the company of his mother, which Freud understood as a way to tolerate her absence.

In the *Fort! Da!* game, Lacan sees a paradigm for the rise of language, which he describes as a "presence made of absence." In this way the beginnings of language and of desire are coeval: "These are the games of occultation which Freud, in a flash of genius, revealed to us so that we might recognize in them that the moment in which desire becomes human is also that in which the child is born into language" (*E*, 65, 103). Before language, the infant feels a wholeness and boundlessness, a union with the mother experienced as undifferentiated drives, but upon discerning the mother's absence, s/he becomes aware of lack and replaces the drives with desire. The child apprehends lack as the "want-to-be" (*manque-à-être*); because the child wants to be one with the mother, s/he knows a "want of being."[14] The moment of want-to-be, the desire for the absent mother, announces the need for language. Only with the signifier can the child move from unexpressed drives to the articulation of desire that language comprises. The *Fort! Da!* game marks the child's desire *à la lettre*—the entry into the Law of the Father that constitutes the symbolic mode of language.

Lacan recognizes the negating effect of the child's vocalization of the opposites *fort* and *da*:

[The child's] action thus negatives the field of forces of desire in order to become its own object to itself. And this object, being immediately embodied in the symbolic dyad of two elementary exclamations, announces in the subject the diachronic integration of the dichotomy of the phonemes, whose synchronic structure existing language offers to his assimilation; moreover, the child begins to become engaged in the system of the concrete discourse of the environment, by reproducing more or less approximately in his *Fort!* and in his *Da!* the vocables that he receives from it. (*E*, 103)

Poe's signifier "Nevermore" owns exactly the dichotomous relationship between its parts "never" and "more" as *Fort! Da!*, and it in fact closely approximates the sense of the dichotomy Lacan describes. "Never" incorporates the idea of "gone" in an absolute and dramatic way, while "more" attempts to recall the absent figure back to presence. Poe's insistence that he selected "Nevermore" for its sound, especially prizing the long "o" as "the most sonorous vowel," further suggests that the word bears for him the inchoative property—the play of barely-meaning phonemes—that Lacan found necessary to the *Fort! Da!* game (see "PC," 18). One might go so far as to say that the quintessential site of "The Raven" is the Lacanian point of want-to-be, where a human being, through desire, stands poised to enter the signifying chain. Lacan's notion of desire begins with the kind of absent presence that the word "Nevermore" indicates. As the child does with *Fort! Da!* so does the narrator with "Nevermore": repeating the phonemes that make absence bearable, both play out their want-to-be. Poe's refrain evidences the dynamic of the subject struggling to be born into the signifying chain.

Through the signifier "Nevermore" we can find a specific connection with the signifier of the purloined letter in the short story Lacan thought worthy of such concentrated attention—a connection that strengthens the resonance between nineteenth-century author and postmodern theorist. The "Nevermore" behaves like the purloined letter: it indicates the positioning of subjects. The signifier "Nevermore," from the time it is spoken, defines the subject placement of the narrator; in Lacan's words, "the itinerary of a signifier" forms "the decisive orientation [of] the subject."[15] Like the signifier in "The Purloined Letter" that governs the placement of the subject, the signifier in "The Raven" casts the signifying nets by which the characters receive their identity. The "*insistence* of the signifying chain," one of Lacan's major conceptions, inheres in its power to determine intersubjectivity, for which, Muller and Richardson note, the "pivot is the 'pure signifier' of the 'purloined letter' that accounts for the automatism of repetition."[16]

In other words, upon the signifier turn the relationalities that establish intersubjectivities, or the ways subjects become positioned in regard to each other; also, the desire that demands language demands repetition because the very nature of the signifying chain is insistent.[17] Poe offers as pure a signifier in "Nevermore" as he does in the "purloined letter." The former proves more rarified and histrionic, perhaps, but altogether as useful, if not more so, for arranging the players in this oedipal game.

Of course, we must recognize that it is the raven and not the narrator who utters the initial "Nevermore"—the latter must learn it from the former; hence, the raven plays a fundamental role in starting the signifying chain that shapes the poem's complex relationalities. The principal players are the raven, the narrator, and Pallas Athena—one happy family whose intersubjectivities ineluctably enact the oedipal scenario.[18] Poe devotes the middle third of "The Raven" to characterizing this family as their relative positions are determined by the signifier. While the "saintly days of yore" mentioned by the narrator ostensibly refer to times long past, perhaps medieval, they also may refer to days of pre-oedipal, blissful union with the mother ("R," 366).

In the first stanza of the middle section of the poem, the narrator flings open the shutter to allow the fluttering raven ingress—the sounds of which may be the final gasps of the rhythmic, inarticulate *chora* giving over to the symbolic mode (the raven actually emerges from the shutter). With that action, we see the entrance of the paternal figure—the raven—who immediately perches atop the bust of Pallas. At this point in the poem, the gender of the raven remains indeterminate: the narrator imagines addressing the bird as either "Sir" or "Madam" and describes its "mien" as that of either "lord or lady" ("R," 365, 366). As the middle section progresses, gender begins to solidify as the narrator intermittently refers to the raven as "he" and "it." Interestingly, according to Lacan, one is not human, has no individuality, no identity—certainly no gender identity—until the advent of language. The signifier grants the subject his or her status as subject. Just so, with the first utterance of "Nevermore," gender begins to make a difference (and a *différance*). The narrator ponders the signifier offered by the raven by noting "*its* answer" (366, emphasis added); he still registers the bird as "it," but immediately after recording that the bird "spoke only/ That one word," he interprets it as an outpouring of "*his* [the raven's] soul" (367, emphasis added). Through the signifier the raven has become male, as the following line corroborates: "Nothing farther then *he* uttered—not a feather then *he* fluttered" (367, emphasis added). More importantly, two lines below, the narrator observes, "'On the morrow *he* will leave me, as my Hopes have flown before'" (367, emphasis original). Poe italicizes gender in this case, ostensibly as a way to emphasize that everyone sooner or later will desert the narrator but also as a way to solidify the narrator's sense of the raven's male identity.[19]

The male gender of the bird is significant because the raven operates as the father in a number of important ways. Literally, the raven embodies the conventional traits of a patriarchal authority figure in his "grave and stern decorum," a fitting description given that the father's traditional role entails introducing the child to the patterns of social decorum. Similarly, the narrator describes the raven as "'ghastly grim and ancient'" and, just to be sure the resonance is not missed, iterates almost comically that the raven is "'sure no craven'" ("R," 366). Further, the words "father" and "raven" share similar sounds, forming a kind of mnemonic image for each other. Even more compellingly, the term "raven" acts as a homonym, colloquial though it is, for "raving."[20] This raving performs exactly the kind of pronouncement of inchoate phonemes that the raven says with "Nevermore," signaling entry into the symbolic domain of the father. The most significant attribute of the raven as father, moreover, remains his ability to say "Nevermore"—a word he utters in answer to the narrator's question concerning his name (366). Here we have it, then: the Name of the Father is Nevermore.

In Lacan's oedipal scenario, the father's place is occupied not by the father but by the Name-of-the-Father, which keeps us within the realm of desire and language rather than biology. Given the patterns of desire identified in "The Raven," what better Name-of-the-Father could we find than Nevermore? The raven owns the pure signifier our narrator needs in order to be able to express his want-to-be—a want-to-be that pervades the poem, through profound images of lack, with the recognition of absence and the loss of oneness with the mother.

To further complicate matters, the father-raven who holds the key to the symbolic mode, relevant as he is, perches atop the statue of Pallas Athena. The bust, which largely has been ignored by twentieth-century critics but particularly spooked many nineteenth-century readers,[21] works powerfully as the manifestation of the narrator's want-to-be, a want-to-be that prompts the desire for language. Pallas completes the critical triangle of characters in the poem's drama of language and desire; she becomes the objectified Lenore—a stone corpse that hauntingly faces the narrator, standing in for his lost love. As is the case with virtually all Poe's fictional treatments of women, the narrator wants Lenore near him, preferably in an uncertain alive/dead state, so that his despair can be prolonged indefinitely. Pallas makes the ideal corpse-woman—conveniently present yet luminously absent. Though some critics have argued that the representation of Pallas exemplifies the killing of women into art,[22] it also can be interpreted as the objectification of the lost mother, the co-optation into the *Fort! Da!* game.

In an important way, we can see Pallas as the Lacanian spool that the narrator subjects himself to losing and finding over and over again. Pallas is not the mother but the reminder of the mother, an object the narrator might wish to make appear and disappear. The "Nevermore," spoken by the raven and learned by the narrator, must occur in the presence of the bust of Pallas that marks the absence of the mother (for whom Lenore in her turn substitutes). The narrator's want-to-be takes the form of a *Fort! Da!* expression—that is, "Nevermore"—as he begins to realize that signification signals an end to his prior bliss and oneness. Because of Pallas and the absence/presence she figures, he instates the beginning of language that makes desire human. Indeed,

Pallas seems to displace Lenore altogether once she is introduced.[23] Pallas is the perfect reminder of the want-to-be, for desire ultimately is not the desire for love but rather the desire to be desired by the other (*E*, 58). Given this conception, even the desire for a living partner (as Lenore once was, we take it) can never be gratified fully, let alone the desire for the partner who, as in the present case, is dead. This desire that cannot be requited is finally the want-to-be that initiates signification; the poem exemplifies how any speaking subject, once desire is loosed, becomes caught in the signifying chain and remains ensnared forevermore.

In the first stanza of the poem's middle section, Poe carefully sets up the scenario of desire and language by introducing the pale bust in juxtaposition to the "ebony" bird: "I made the bird alight on the bust of Pallas," he later explained, "for the effect of contrast between the marble and the plumage—it being understood that the bust was absolutely *suggested* by the bird" ("PC," 22). That the two of them appear together in this stanza cannot then be dismissed as coincidental: We need both before we can announce the arrival of the signifier. Each necessitates the existence of the other; in fact, Poe seldom pictures them separately, the mention of bird often prompting the mention of Pallas: "Bird or beast upon the sculptured bust above his chamber door,/ With such name as 'Nevermore'" ("R," 367).[24] It is not a bad encapsulation of the dawning of the entire oedipal schema—for both the raven and Pallas are further required to implicate the narrator in this relational drama.

Bird, bust, and narrator—the triangulation poses a dilemma, more precisely a dilemma of longing and language: Name-of-the-Father, spooled mother, and uncertain "I." The scene depicts the site of desire, of oedipal want-to-be. Lenore was simply a stand-in, and the grief the narrator feels is actually the grief for the absent mother whom the child desires because of her perceived phallus. By Lacan's lights, the child's want-to-be arises as the wanting to be the mother's phallus, which is of course what she lacks (*E*, 289). Lacan asserts that the phallus is "the signifier par excellence" of desire.[25] He distinguishes between having and being the phallus: only the father (real, imaginary, or symbolic) can have the phallus, never the mother, but apparently she can *be* the phallus (or be perceived as such) (*E*, 289). The bust in "The Raven" presents an apt figure for the mother perceived as (though lacking) a penis—the bust is itself in the shape of a phallus, a shape accentuated by the fact that Pallas Athena traditionally wears a helmet. Pallas, as Lacan might have it, is the phallus. If in studying *Hamlet* he can read the name "Ophelia" as "*O phallos*," then it is not difficult to imagine him reading "Pallas" as a similar *jeu de mot*.[26]

## 3

More interesting than wordplay in the current context, however, is the prominence of Pallas in the narrator's relinquishment of the prelingual drive for union with the mother in order to embrace the post-oedipal desire that marks the birth of language. This dynamic informs the third and last section of the poem. Whereas the middle section shows a bemused narrator who can continue "smiling" ruefully at his circumstance—bemused because he has not yet had to forfeit union with the mother—the last section dramatizes the traumatic experience of his attempted emergence into language. In the twelfth stanza, the last stanza of the middle section, the narrator, still dazed, "wheel[s] a cushioned seat in front of bird, and bust and door":

Then, upon the velvet sinking, I betook myself to linking
Fancy unto fancy, thinking what this ominous bird of yore—
What this grim, ungainly, ghastly, gaunt, and ominous bird of yore
        Meant in croaking "Nevermore."

("R," 367)

The cushion, a maternal presence, marks a crucial transition. By its agency we wheel from static triangulation to the dynamic of language acquisition in the third section.

---

If there were any doubt that the female figure in "The Raven" is the mother (and not Lenore, simply an understudy), we find it dispelled in the thirteenth stanza, which heads up the last section, where Poe italicizes the word "*She*." This "*She*" reminds the narrator of the mother figure, rather than Lenore, a reading supported by the introduction of the maternal presence in the stanza above, and even more by the description in this stanza of the "cushion's velvet lining." The narrator lies not on the outside of the cushion, as is customary, but on the lining, the inside. The feminine implications of birth space prove paramount as well as graphic here: he reclines his head on the "velvet-violet lining" and laments separation from the maternal body, grieving that "*She* shall press, ah, nevermore!" ("R," 368).[27] The narrator's want-to-be emerges as he notices the absence of the press of her velvet-violet lining, and now he no longer smiles, as he had in the stanza before. Whereas he then attempted to confront the dilemma with humor, he now begins to register the loss of his previous ecstatic merger with the mother; in this last section, the lengthy and arduous labor of bringing language to birth begins in earnest.

What remains is for the narrator himself to try the signifier; indeed, the entire poem funnels to his turn at saying "Nevermore." The final third opens with the silence of the narrator, who characterizes himself as "no syllable expressing" ("R," 367), and the fact that he expresses no syllable or, as yet, even an inchoate phoneme, becomes the burden of the poem. Though implicated in the *Fort! Da!* game of spool throwing—reporting repeatedly on the appearance of the bust, wheeling cushions in—he has yet to seize the Name-of-the-Father for his own. He needs ultimately to quote the "Nevermore," to orient himself within the chain of signification. Such quoting we expect as the climactic activity of "The Raven."

But the signifying chain has already started sliding: In the eighth stanza, when the raven first utters the "Nevermore," the word lights language and begins to orient the players to the world of the father. "Nevermore" starts a signifying chain reaction, so to speak. When the raven first announces the word, he claims his presence as proven by the existence of his name. When he says it the second time, the word threatens his absence, spoken as it is directly after the narrator expresses fear that he will leave, just as his "'[h]opes have flown before'" ("R," 367). These first two uses of the pure signifier indicate presence, then disappearance (again, *Fort! Da!*); as reiterations of "Nevermore" begin to point to different, even opposite, conditions, we see the signified becoming slippery in relation to the signifier. What was once pure signifier now begins to accrue meaning to itself. Lacan, in fact, understands signifiers as standing not for signifieds but for other signifiers. These signifiers for signifiers form a chain, the "rings of a necklace that is a ring in another necklace made of rings" (*E*, 153). That "Nevermore" is only (and powerfully) a signifier for other signifiers is made plain by the range of verbal possibilities, as the interpretive constructions of presence and disappearance exemplify.

"Nevermore" itself forms an oxymoron, simultaneously indicating both absence and desire—an antithetical combination of terms that others have noted with eloquence. J. Gerald Kennedy asserts, for example, that the compound word seems "on the one hand to manifest the desire to forget (the narrator will nevermore brood upon the lost Lenore) and on the other to serve (as it does for the speaker) as a nagging reminder of the irrevocability of death." Most relevant for the present argument is Jonathan Elmer's view of the signifier "Nevermore" as both arbitrary and meaningful: the poem, he suggests, is "simultaneously the depiction of the subordination of meaning to the senseless and arbitrary structure of the signifier and the apotheosis of meaning as the successful incorporation of that senseless signifier into a position from which it is made to signify grief—over a lost meaning as much as a lost Lenore."[28]

Poe plays with newfound possibilities for signification, remaining highly aware as he does so that he *is* playing. After finding the right sound for "Nevermore," as Poe reports in "The Philosophy of Composition," he proceeds to tinker with multiplicity of meaning:

And here it was that I saw at once the opportunity afforded for the effect on which I had been depending—that is to say, the effect of the *variation of application*. I saw that I could make the first query propounded by the lover—the first query to which the Raven should reply "Nevermore"—that I could make this first query a commonplace one—the second less so—the third still less, and so on—until at length the lover . . . [is] excited to superstition, and wildly propounds queries of a far different character—queries whose solution he has passionately at heart—propounds them half in superstition and half in that species of despair which delights in self-torture. ("PC," 19)

The narrator, who "experiences a phrenzied pleasure in so modeling his questions" that he might receive "from the *expected* 'Nevermore' the most delicious because the most intolerable of sorrow" ("PC," 19), understands that every signifier corresponds only to another signifier, and that the correspondence changes as relationalities change.

Possible meanings for "Nevermore" proliferate in the course of the poem. The following comprises a partial list of some of the most direct correspondences, in roughly the order they appear: the bird's name; the bird's status as guest, with perhaps a hint that he has overstayed his welcome; the bird's absence; a one-word language, or the (ontological) status of Lenore/mother; meaning, or the relevancy of the signified; scission from the mother; the (im)possibility of forgetting, or the difficulty of separating from the mother; the indeterminacy of truth, or the uncertainty that suffering will ever cease; life (or not) after death, or love (or not) after death, or the yearning to retain the mother and have language as well; departure ("'sign of parting'" ["R," 369]), or the possibility of writing; the non-closure of the process of grieving, or the inability of the son of the Name-of-the-Father to seize the word. Again, the list remains only partial. Elmer suggests that the potentialities of language that contribute to the pleasure also contribute to the pain of the narrator in his capacity as reader: "The pleasure here has to do with the formal qualities of language, that is, its ability to produce effects solely at the level of the signifier. But of course the narrator's pain has equally to do with the formal qualities of language, namely the fact that the signifier's incursion is experienced as irrevocably disarticulated from its signified."[29] The signifier's fluctuations call up the essential loss in language, that the signifier can never pin the signified.

There is nothing fixed or culminating about the "Nevermore"; it is a necklace that constitutes a growing web of identification by which the subject becomes human. In this web the narrator must situate himself by speaking the "Nevermore," a feat he almost manages several times. David Halliburton remarks that though the poem leaves us with the impression that the raven alone articulates the "Nevermore," actually the raven says the word six times and the narrator, five.[30] However, the narrator typically reports or thinks the word rather than *says* it—a small but telling distinction that comes through in Poe's careful use of quotation marks.

In "The Raven," the quotation marks trace the existence of signification. In stanza 8, the pure signifier first appears:

> Quoth the Raven "Nevermore."
> ("R," 366)

It is framed in quotation marks to show direct utterance, a pattern that all six of the raven's declarations will follow. (The original punctuation is retained in this and subsequent quotations to make the pattern clear.) The narrator's retellings of the word, though, take more varied forms. In the ninth stanza, for example, he mentions the word, but secondarily, as a recapitulation of what the raven has said:

> With such name as "Nevermore."
> ("R," 367)

The narrator makes a similar gesture at the end of stanza 12, when he again ponders the oddity of the raven's word, ponders what he

> Meant in croaking "Nevermore."
>
> ("R," 367)

The narrator toys with the word, dangles and spins it, but never claims it as his own. The signifier remains attached to the raven's utterance; that is, the narrator says or thinks it but not from within his own orientation. He only dispatches. In two other instances (lines 78 and 108), he nudges at the word but does not say it at all: it is neither capitalized nor in quotation marks. The second of these instances comprises the final line of the poem, and we shall return to that lowercase nevermore momentarily.

The fifth instance in which the narrator broaches the saying of the "Nevermore" constitutes the closest he comes to uttering his own signifier, but he stutters and stumbles over it. Taylor Stoehr, in an insightful treatment of saying and quotation marks in Poe's "Ligeia," sees as significant "the fact that the narrator reports his own exact words in quotation marks only once in the tale, at the very end when he stammers out [Ligeia's] name."[31] The following line at the end of the eleventh stanza of "The Raven" shows the narrator likewise stammering his own signifier:

> "Of 'Never—nevermore.'"
>
> ("R," 367)[32]

Here the narrator repeats the raven's expression but couches it within his own train of signifiers, seeking to claim the signifier—purloin it, if you will—from the raven. The marks within the marks trace the genesis of a speaking subject's own relation with language; ultimately, however, the narrator botches the gesture by stuttering—"'Never—nevermore'"—a movement that not only mars the signifier but renders its meaning redundant.[33] It is as if he mutilated his game of desiring peek-a-boo by saying *Fort! Fort! Da!* The narrator has not quite mastered the dichotomous swing yet, but he is close, very close. "The

Raven" tantalizes us with the closeness—promising us the position of witness to the birth of language and issuing, finally, in a kind of false labor.

Hence we are left in the last two stanzas at the birth site of language, our expectations high but unfulfilled. Instead of confidently taking the Name-of-the-Father as his own, the narrator has ended up only taking the Name-of-the-Father in vain. In the antepenultimate stanza, he exhorts the bird to depart and demands particularly, "'Leave no black plume as a token of that lie thy soul hath spoken!'" ("R," 369). What we might have anticipated as the narrator's legacy, the taking up of the writer's stylus (aptly figured, in light of Poe's style, by the black plume), becomes the legacy the narrator refuses altogether. The word that might have passed from father to son is denied by the narrator. The pungency of this scenario informs the otherwise rather overwrought line "'Take thy beak from out my heart, and take thy form from off my door!'" (369), which, given the workings of the narrator's desire *à la lettre*, renders the line a climax—and a stunning one at that, operating against all expectations.[34]

The last stanza of the poem leaves the narrator in the raven's shadow. Pallas is there, the Name-of-the-Father is there, and the narrator, who has failed to claim the signifier, exists merely as the wraith of a narrator. An electrifying stillness characterizes this scene: the dynamism we come to expect from the oedipal scenario has subsided to an excruciating passivity; all the kinetic workings of language formation have lapsed into a half-life of shadow and stillness. Every activity has been undertaken to facilitate the narrator's entry into language, and all that remains is for him to say the word. But he does not, or cannot. Instead, the stillness of the scene testifies to the stillbirth of language:

> And the Raven, never flitting, still is sitting, still is sitting
> On the pallid bust of Pallas just above my chamber door;
> And his eyes have all the seeming of a demon's that is
>     dreaming,

> And the lamp-light o'er him streaming throws his shadow
>     on the floor;
> And my soul from out that shadow that lies floating on the
>     floor
>                 Shall be lifted—nevermore!
>
>                                           ("R," 369)

The raven/father literally overshadows the narrator. Nothing moves; no one stirs. Again, the logical move—the only move—at this juncture is for the narrator to report his own declaration of the signifier, to take possession. And he almost does. It is the biggest joke in the poem—the last word is the "Nevermore," but simply, and without the fanfare of capitalization or quotation: the nevermore. Poe leaves the narrator, silent, as a shade of the father.

Just as Poe's composition of death and absence is a kind of decomposition, so his birth of language is a kind of stillbirth.[35] The signifier is always already stillborn in "The Raven." The characters are all "still" there, both unmoving and soundless—the pun catching up in its two meanings the sense of the language scenario that can go no further because of the narrator's refusal or inability to say the word. What the raven says negates and reconstitutes the narrator along the signifying chain. He can attain positioning only by speaking the word himself, by breaking the stillness. He must relinquish primordial union, that *jouissance* with the mother, in order to gain the Name-of-the-Father, the "Law of desire," so that he can articulate his want-to-be, but his attempt is faux. The narrator's desire *à la lettre* has taken us this far, to the ledge of the signifier. It is here that Poe leaves us—on the cusp of the quoting of the "Nevermore."

From *ESQ: A Journal of the American Renaissance*, 44, no. 4 (1998): 275-99. Copyright © 1998 by Washington State University. Reprinted with permission of Washington State University.

# Notes

1. Edgar Allan Poe, "The Raven," in *Collected Works of Edgar Allan Poe*, ed. Thomas Ollive Mabbott (Cambridge: Harvard Univ. Press, Belknap Press, 1969), 1:369. Hereafter, references to "The Raven" will be cited parenthetically as "R."

2. As countless commentators have observed, the French have preserved a linguistically sophisticated Poe for us until we were ready to reclaim him. American critics have been relatively quick to apply French theory to Poe's tales but have lagged in doing the same to his poems.

3. I am grateful to those critics who have begun an exploration of language and desire in "The Raven"; they include J. Gerald Kennedy, Mutlu Konuk Blasing, Michael J. S. Williams, Jefferson Humphries, and especially Jonathan Elmer. Kennedy sees importance in the name "Lenore," which "signifies the absence which afflicts [the narrator]." Blasing understands "Lenore" as representing a maternal, natural source language; basically, she offers a brief discussion of the poem as a Kristevan struggle between the maternal and paternal forces of language, between the names "Lenore" and "Nevermore." Williams argues that the "Nevermore" is essentially empty, that though it "seems to be a potential incursion of meaning from a supernal realm [it] is significant only in the context of the lover's narrative of loss." Humphries concludes his discussion of "Poe-eticity" (the title of chap. 2) by remarking that "*raven* is a name for the point at which signification breaks down and literariness, if it is to occur, will occur. It is the locus of the purely other, death, or whatever cipher one chooses to paste over its absence. It must be articulated in terms combining a tension of resemblance and difference, short of nothingness but sufficiently *different* so that the dialectic, or circuit, of signification is engaged, while it remains extraordinary, incongruous—in the extreme, grotesque." See Kennedy, *Poe, Death, and the Life of Writing* (New Haven: Yale Univ. Press, 1987), 68; Blasing, *American Poetry: The Rhetoric of Its Forms* (New Haven: Yale Univ. Press, 1987), 28-30; Williams, *A World of Words: Language and Displacement in the Fiction of Edgar Allan Poe* (Durham: Duke Univ. Press, 1988), 7; and Humphries, *Metamorphoses of the Raven: Literary Overdeterminedness in France and the South since Poe* (Baton Rouge: Louisiana State Univ. Press, 1985), 59.

Elmer explores, in greater detail, the trajectory of the signifier in "The Raven," proposing that the poem offers up "the very type of the arbitrary signifier" and at the same time records "the narrator's gradual assimilation to meaning of the bird's initially senseless repetition of the word." See *Reading at the Social Limit: Affect, Mass Culture, and Edgar Allan Poe* (Stanford: Stanford Univ. Press, 1995), 204-5. While I entertain intersections of disagreement with Elmer and the above critics, I nonetheless appreciate that their work opens up ways of thinking about "The Raven" as a twentieth-century text and acknowledges it as a sophisticated scenario of language.

4. Jacques Lacan, *Ecrits: A Selection*, trans. Alan Sheridan (New York: Norton, 1977), 303. All subsequent references will be designated within the text as *E*.

5. Edward H. Davidson, *Poe: A Critical Study* (Cambridge: Harvard Univ. Press, Belknap Press, 1957), 87.

6. There are other indications of a nonlinguistic state: Though the narrator is sur-

rounded by books, they all contain "forgotten lore," the erasure of words. As he turns each inked page, imaged as the "uncertain rustling of each purple curtain"—more veil than disclosure, more uncertainty than elucidation—the absence becomes more apparent ("R," 364, 365).

7. Julia Kristeva, *The Kristeva Reader*, ed. Toril Moi (New York: Columbia Univ. Press, 1986), 94.

8. Blasing, *American Poetry*, 32.

9. Edgar Allan Poe, "The Philosophy of Composition," in *Essays and Reviews*, ed. G. R. Thompson (New York: Library of America, 1984), 17-21, esp. 21; hereafter cited parenthetically as "PC."

10. Jacques Lacan, "Seminar on 'The Purloined Letter,'" trans. Jeffrey Mehlman, *Yale French Studies* 48 (1972): 39. The quotation appears in the introduction to *Ecrits* in the French original, though it is omitted from the English translation; see *Ecrits* (Paris: Editions du seuil, 1966).

11. John P. Muller and William J. Richardson, "Lacan's Seminar on 'The Purloined Letter': Overview," chap. 3 in *The Purloined Poe: Lacan, Derrida and Psychoanalytic Reading*, ed. Muller and Richardson (Baltimore: Johns Hopkins Univ. Press, 1988), 56, 68. The formulation of Freud's notion here comes from Muller and Richardson's paraphrase of Lacan's account.

12. Lacan, "Seminar on 'The Purloined Letter,'" 40.

13. Sigmund Freud, "Beyond the Pleasure Principle," in *The Standard Edition of the Complete Psychological Works of Sigmund Freud*, ed. and trans. James Strachey (London: Hogarth Press, 1964), 18:14-17, 15.

14. John P. Muller and William J. Richardson, *Lacan and Language: A Reader's Guide to "Ecrits"* (New York: International Universities Press, 1982), 22.

15. Lacan, "Seminar on 'The Purloined Letter,'" 40.

16. Muller and Richardson, *Purloined Poe*, 62; quoting Lacan.

17. Both Taylor Stoehr and Joseph Riddel comment that Poe's sense of reality is based on a kind of word reality. Stoehr notes that Poe "attempts a language that is absolutely literal. In his solipsistic world all reality will ultimately rest on words" ("'Unspeakable Horror' in Poe," *South Atlantic Quarterly* 78 [1979]: 331). Similarly, Riddel observes that "the power of words is no more than a power to move other words. Words are already secondary, and they repeat only an original abysm that marks their distance from any first law." Riddel further remarks that this "is a fable Poe obsessively retells, the wearying struggle to purify language through language, the poetic repetition of some idea of 'absolute perfection' or some idea of purity that in the same gesture reveals the mark of its own discontinuity with any original form, idea, truth, reality" ("The 'Crypt' of Edgar Poe," *boundary 2*, 7 [spring 1979]: 122). Both of these critics' suggestions are extremely helpful: I fully agree that Poe tries to create a sort of word reality that is literal or pure; I also think his reality is best interpreted within a Lacanian framework.

18. I prefer to use the phrase "oedipal scenario" rather than "oedipal dilemma" or "complex," so as to distance and even ironize somewhat the usage of the phrase. First, I suspect that language acquisition does not work this way for women, though it may well for men and for the male narrator of "The Raven." Second, and more important, I

want to emphasize the linguistic, as opposed to biological, propensities that operate here. Lacan claims to work only in the realm of language, but sometimes biologism seems to creep in. For instance, he states that both male and female infants experience the want-to-be—especially as he distinguishes between the "phallus" and the "penis" (as symbol vs. sexual organ)—and yet integral to his formulations is the assertion that the mother does not have the phallus or the penis. This is just one example of his claimed distinction between metaphor and biologism blurring into essentialism. As a metaphor for language, the oedipal movements work well to reveal desire; where Lacan clearly works with the metaphorical is the ground on which I wish to stand.

19. I should mention that the narrator refers to the raven as "it" again in line 62, presumably because the emergence of gender is difficult to apprehend all at once. In the final three lines of the poem, however, he twice uses masculine pronouns, making the bird's male gender strikingly clear ("R," 367, 369).

20. Humphries offers a useful discussion of the character of the word "raven": It contains "rave" and hints of "ravage" and, backwards, reads "never." Poe also chose "raven," he posits, for its "exotic ugliness and its association in many folk traditions with ill fortune." In addition, Mallarmé translated the word to the French, *corbeau*, which sustains a pun on *corps beau* (beautiful body, or beautiful corpse). The French *corbeau* means not only raven but also crow, a smaller, more common, less ominous bird (*Metamorphoses of the Raven*, 50-51). Hence, for French readers the *corbeau* has many overtones and slippages that the English word could never have. Mallarmé has Poe eating crow in several ways.

21. Nineteenth-century audiences focused on Pallas as an uncanny element in the poem. Note, for example, the following account by an English Miss Barrett: "I hear of persons haunted by the Nevermore, and one acquaintance of mine, who has the misfortune of possessing a bust of Pallas, never can bear to look at it in the twilight" (in P. Pendleton Cook, "Edgar A. Poe," in *The Recognition of Edgar Allan Poe: Selected Criticism since 1829*, ed. Eric W. Carlson [Ann Arbor: Univ. of Michigan Press, 1966], 23).

22. See Sandra Gilbert and Susan Gubar, *Madwoman in the Attic: The Woman Writer and the Nineteenth-Century Literary Imagination* (New Haven: Yale Univ. Press, 1979), 24-25. Gilbert and Gubar, noting Ann Douglas's study of the nineteenth-century cult of death, discuss women characters killing themselves into art. For a recent survey of scholarship concerning Poe's women, see Paula Kot, "Feminist 'Re-Visioning' of the Tales of Women," in *A Companion to Poe Studies*, ed. Eric W. Carlson (Westport, CT: Greenwood Press, 1996), 388-402. Kot describes the split between critics who see Poe as a misogynist, damned especially by his claim that the most poetical topic is a dead woman, and those who see him as commenting on his culture's representation of women. Kot notes that "[m]ore recently, critics argue that Poe did, indeed, know better, that he did not simply reinscribe conventional (repressive) attitudes toward women but that he critiqued these attitudes in his tales" (388).

23. Actually, Lenore does appear again in the fourteenth and sixteenth (the antepenultimate) stanzas. In the fourteenth, however, the narrator has distanced Lenore (by referring to the self that remembers her in the second person): "thy memories of Lenore" ("R," 368). In the antepenultimate, we seem to have the Lenore of the beginning, the

Lenore whom the angels have named. It is perhaps significant, though, that Poe claims to have written this stanza first ("PC," 20). Hence, it remains at least somewhat outside the dynamic progression of the oedipal drama that unfolds in the other stanzas.

24. The emphatic reliance upon the three elements of bird, bust, and chamber door may anticipate the triadic elements (of bird, star, and lilac) in Whitman's "When Lilacs Last in the Dooryard Bloomed." (Whitman may use the elements for oedipal resonances, too.)

25. Muller and Richardson, *Lacan and Language*, 280-81; paraphrasing Lacan.

26. Jacques Lacan, "Desire and the Interpretation of Desire in *Hamlet*," *Yale French Studies* 55-56 (1978): 20. Perhaps it is important that the raven perches atop the bust—that he, as phallus on phallus, *has* what she is only perceived to *be*; or perhaps Lacan would have it so.

27. I am grateful to my colleague Mark Richardson for pointing out the consonance of "velvet-violet" with a crucial word in this context, "vulva." Poe reported to his friend Mrs. Weiss that he considered the word "lining" a "blunder" but "was unwilling to sacrifice the whole stanza"; see Mabbott's note, *Collected Works*, 1:373. The "blunder" strikes me as one of those fortunate mistakes that reveals Poe's oedipal scenario; in any case, it is interesting that he felt he could not revise the one word without jettisoning the entire stanza.

28. Kennedy, *Poe, Death, and the Life of Writing*, 69; Elmer, *Reading at the Social Limit*, 205. Also see Humphries, who argues for a temporal disjunction: "*Never* is a negative name of eternity, pointing to past and future. *More* is similarly limitless, but acts as a positive and temporally specific limitation, a contradiction, of this negative infinity (never). The tension between the words establishes a difference between the past (a hypothetically pure anteriority) and the present, and it is this dialectical difference that the poem's analepses enact"; see *Metamorphoses of the Raven*, 62.

29. Elmer, *Reading at the Social Limit*, 206.

30. David Halliburton, *Edgar Allan Poe: A Phenomenological View* (Princeton: Princeton Univ. Press, 1973), 126.

31. Stoehr, "'Unspeakable Horror' in Poe," 321. Stoehr sees the narrator's quest in "Ligeia" as the quest for a name, the tale as a tale of *Logos*.

32. The double quotation mark at the start of the line is added for clarity's sake, given that the quotation began in a previous line. The first printing of the poem, in the *American Review: A Whig Journal of Politics, Literature, Art and Science* 1 (February 1845): 143-45, presents line 66 as follows:

That sad answer, "Nevermore!"
("R," 369-70)

This rendering involves the narrator in the saying of the signifier even less than the stuttered line, as again he only reports what the raven says. It should be noted that many variations of the poem exist, and that Poe continued to revise this much-reprinted poem for the rest of his life. Mabbott's edition (the one cited here) uses the version that appeared in the *Richmond Semi-Weekly Examiner* of 25 September 1849, "the last authorized version published during Poe's lifetime" ("R," 364).

33. Although the stutter occurs near the end of the second section, the occurrence does blur somewhat the tripartite division that does not have the narrator (almost) speaking until the third section. This discrepancy may account additionally for the stutter.

34. To the writer's activity—that of taking up the black plume—the raven/father replies with an enigmatic "Nevermore." This may or may not suggest the person of John Allan, Poe's adoptive father, who seemed to say "no" to many of Poe's most heartfelt pursuits.

35. Poe's uses of stillness are legion, not only in "The Raven" but in many of his poems.

# Baudelaire and Poe_____

Jonathan Culler

The relationship between the writings of Edgar Allan Poe and Charles Baudelaire is a tantalizing problem for literary history, literary criticism and, hence, for literary theory. Nowhere else in world literature, so far as I know, has a writer been so scorned by the literati of his own language and so celebrated by the best minds of another culture and language. In France, the most talented poets have praised Poe as a genius of the first order, although Baudelaire's *poète maudit* and master of the short story, Mallarmé's sublime poet, and Valéry's lucid theoretician of poetic effects are not exactly the same figure. English and American critics, on the other hand, have often deemed Poe, in Laura Riding's phrase, "a gloomy and sentimental hack," judging him a vulgar, adolescent poet and talented only as author of popular short stories (Riding, 252). American critics who in recent years have turned favorable attention on his stories have often been inspired to approach them by French theoretical discourses that belong to a tradition inaugurated by Poe's earlier French admirers. This unparalleled discrepancy—I can think of no other case where Francophone and Anglophone judgments of an English or American writer contrast so starkly—might lead one to suspect that there is some uncanny relation between Poe's texts and French readers, some deep and unexplained sense of the relevance of his work to their situation, for the admiration, while not universal, extends far beyond Baudelaire, Mallarmé, and Valéry. Verlaine wrote two poems entitled "Nevermore," and Rimbaud wrote "Les Corbeaux," putting in the plural the French title of Poe's "The Raven." A more extreme response, perhaps, but one which suggests that the poets were not alone in their strange receptivity to Poe, their sense of his peculiar pertinence, is the nineteenth-century French painter and engraver, Charles Meyron, whose work Baudelaire praised in the *Salon de 1859*. In a letter to Poulet-Malassis in 1860, Baudelaire reports that Meyron m'a demandé si j'avais lu les nouvelles d'un certain Edgar Poe. Je lui ai répondu que je les connaissais mieux que personne, et pour cause. Il m'a demandé alors, d'un ton très accentué, si je croyais à la réalité de cet Edgar Poe. Moi, je lui ai demandé naturellement à qui il attribuait toutes ses nouvelles. Il m'a répondu: "*A une société de littérateurs très habiles, très puissants et au courant de tout.*" (1966, I, 655)

He suspected this, he explained to Baudelaire, because these stories were about him. For instance: "'La *Rue MORGUE*. J'ai fait un dessin de la *Morgue*. Un *Orang-outang*. On m'a souvent comparé à un singe. Ce singe assassine *deux femmes, la mère et sa fille*. Et moi aussi, j'ai assassiné moralement *deux femmes, la mère et sa fille*. J'ai toujours pris le roman pour une allusion à mes malheurs'" (655). Meyron asked Baudelaire for a favor: "Vous me feriez bien plaisir si vous pouviez me retrouver la date où Edgar Poe (en supposant qu'il n'ait été aidé par personne) a composé ce conte, pour voir si cette date coïncide avec mes aventures" (655).

Although this reading of Poe is certainly strange, it ought not to be altogether unexpected, since the tales themselves frequently concern relations of this sort, where supposedly independent and external phenomena seem strangely to address and implicate those who encounter them—as the horse in the tapestry in Poe's "Metzengerstein" not only turns to glare at the Baron but destroys him. Poe's most famous poem, "The Raven," itself is precisely the story of a cultivated young man who gradually comes to believe that the croaking of a raven is "une allusion à mes malheurs," speaks to him of his own adventures, and specifically of his lost love. After several "Nevermores" the narrator is startled

> by reply so aptly spoken,
> "Doubtless," said I, "what it utters is its only stock and store
> Caught from some unhappy master whom unmerciful Disaster
> Followed fast and followed faster till his songs one burden bore."
> (Poe, 1984b, 84)

---

But as the "Nevermore" is repeated

> I betook myself to linking
> Fancy unto fancy, thinking what this ominous bird of yore—
> What this grim, ungainly, ghastly, gaunt, and ominous bird
>     of yore
> Meant in croaking "Nevermore."
> (Poe, 1984b, 84)

And finally he construes the bird as all-knowing emissary—
"'Prophet!' said I"—and begins asking it questions—"*Is* there balm in
Gilead?" Will "this soul with sorrow laden . . . , within the distant
Aidenn, . . . clasp a sainted maiden whom the angels name Lenore"?—
and he receives the devastating answer.

Poe's tales also frequently present circumstances in which an apparently independent creature or person proves to have an uncanny relation to the protagonist: in "William Wilson" the narrator slays an acquaintance who dogs him, only to be told that *"henceforward art thou
also dead . . . In me didst thou exist—and, in my death, see by this image, which is thine own, how utterly thou hast murdered thyself"*
(1984b, 356-7). Or again, in "Metzengerstein" the Baron is spellbound
by the figure of a horse in a tapestry which represents the murder by a
Metzengerstein of the horse's owner, an ancestor of the Baron's mortal
rivals, the Berlifitzings. The horse, he discovers, has altered its position and is staring straight at the Baron: "the eyes, before invisible,
now wore an energetic and human expression, while they gleamed
with a fiery and unusual red" (1984b, 137). As the Baron, "stupefied
with terror," flings open the door, "a flash of red light, streaming far
into the chamber, flung his shadow with a clear outline against the
quivering tapestry; and he shuddered to perceive that shadow—as he
staggered awhile upon the threshold—assuming the exact position,
and precisely filling up the contour, of the relentless and triumphant
murderer of the Saracen Berlifitzing" (1984b, 137). The representation

in the tapestry proves to have a decisive bearing on his life, as a mysterious, diabolical horse bears him to his death.

The effect of "The Raven," of such stories as "Metzengerstein," and others where women or cats uncannily resemble those who are thought to be dead, *should* be to produce precisely such readerly suspicions about uncanny resemblances between representations and one's own situation. When Baudelaire reports that the first time he opened a book by Poe, "j'ai vu, avec épouvante et ravissement, non seulement des sujets rêvés par moi, mais *des* PHRASES pensées par moi, et écrites par lui vingt ans auparavant" (1966, II, 386), he articulates an experience of the uncanniness of repetition that appears so often in Poe's stories, as when the narrator of "Morella" hears his daughter use the sentences of the dead mother: "above all—oh, above all—in the phrases and expressions of the dead on the lips of the loved and the living, I found food for consuming thought and horror" (1984b, 238). Or in "William Wilson", the narrator hears in the speech of his double "*the very echo of my own*" although, he says, "the imitation, apparently, was noticed by myself alone" (1984b, 344-5). Or there is "A Tale of the Ragged Mountains", pertinent because of the way events that occurred on one continent are uncannily produced on another fifty years later through the medium of writing: as Templeton in 1827 is writing an account of his adventures with a certain Oldeb in Benares in 1780, Dr. Bedloe is experiencing the same events in the mountains of West Virginia. The historical memoirs prove to be an exact account of the bizarre adventures in which Bedloe finds himself caught up.

The sense of finding oneself in a figure or representation that in principle is quite foreign is what much of Poe's writing is about. This contributes to what Jefferson Humphries calls, in seeking to explain Poe's French fortunes, his "enacting of the essential translatedness and nonintegrity of textuality" (Humphries, 5). That is, Poe's fate suggests that literature, in a sense, is always in translation, moving from text to text in a process of repetition and deferment. Long before the Civil War, before any actual loss, Poe incarnates the attraction of the American South to the French as "a site of loss, defeat, bereavement" (26) by using the means of life to create the effect of death (35)—an effect to which progressive Americans would remain cold. But this translation seems more plausible for Mallarmé and Valéry than for Baudelaire, who finds perversity rather than radical negativity in Poe, and whose image of the American South involves none of the metaphysics of defeat that post-Civil War generations would see there.

T. S. Eliot, looking at the attraction to Poe by the three great representatives of what he sees as the most interesting modern poetic tradition—Baudelaire, Mallarmé, and Valéry—open-mindedly advises "we should be prepared to entertain the possibility that these Frenchmen have seen something in Poe that English-speaking readers have missed" (Eliot, 28). He identifies this something as two central ideas of a poetic tradition in which increasing consciousness of language has as its theoretical goal *la poésie pure*: (1) that a poem should have nothing in view but itself, so that the poetic subject is above all a device permitting the poem to come into being, and (2) that the poet should strive for self-consciousness about the poetic production and poetic effects (39-40). This account does some justice to Mallarmé's and Valéry's readings of Poe. In speaking of Poe as "my great master" and "one of the most marvelous minds the world has ever known," or "le cas littéraire absolu," Mallarmé focused on a poet whose conception of poetry as musical play of the signifier was linked with a radical theory of the universe (Mallarmé, 531). Valéry admired above all else the theoretician of poetic effects, and indeed his response is principally what French eyes permit Eliot to see: the influence of Poe in "the development and descent of one particular theory of the nature of poetry"—which is primarily Valéry's conception of Poe. Eliot's account thus leaves the original and determining response to Poe as mysterious as ever, for Baudelaire came first to the tales and only later to the poems and poetic theory. He is scarcely infatuated with "The Philosophy of Composition," although he appreciates its "légère impertinence" and thinks "un peu de charlatanerie est toujours permis au génie" (Baudelaire, 1975, II, 335, 344).

It is on Baudelaire's encounter with Poe that I propose to focus. The significance of this encounter is one of the more puzzling problems in literary history—puzzling because unlike almost every other interesting problem in literary history, it seems as though it ought to be quite manageable. There seems no good way of deciding what romanticism means or ought to mean, or of working out what caused the rise of the novel, or even distinguishing in a principled way between modernism and post-modernism, but in the case of Baudelaire's encounter with Poe, we have two circumscribed bodies of writing, Poe's and Baudelaire's, and abundant statements by Baudelaire about what he saw in Poe. Yet it proves extremely difficult to calculate the nature and force of this encounter.

The question is how did Poe influence Baudelaire, and what did Baudelaire see in him, how did he read Poe? When one surveys the literature on this subject, one finds rather striking disagreements—striking in that neither of these questions seems to be one where different theoretical orientations would necessarily generate vastly differing conclusions, and thus one would expect a rather greater measure of agreement than one actually finds. On the character of Baudelaire's reading of Poe, for example, the claims run from Arthur Patterson's in *L'Influence de Edgar Poe sur Charles Baudelaire* that "Personne ne s'est jamais plus profondément pénétré des oeuvres d'un auteur que Baudelaire de celles de Poe" (Patterson, 8) to P. M. Wetherill's conclusion in *Charles Baudelaire et la poésie d'Edgar Allan Poe*: "Il serait difficile de trouver un autre exemple d'un homme si cultivé, d'un critique si pénétrant, poète lui-même, admirant avec tant d'enthousiasme un si médiocre poète" (Wetherill, 197). Marcel Ruff, on the other hand, maintains that although Baudelaire was profoundly moved by the man, whose unfortunate fate struck him as resembling his own, he expressed numerous and serious reservations about the particular writings supposed to have influenced him (Ruff, 67-75). The view that Poe decisively influenced Baudelaire is eloquently stated by Paul Valéry in his fine essay "Situation de Baudelaire": Baudelaire's natural gifts "n'eussent fait de lui qu'un émule de Gautier, sans doute, ou un excellent artiste du Parnasse, s'il n'eût, par la curiosité de son esprit, mérité la chance de découvrir dans les ouvrages d'Edgar Poe un nouveau monde intellectuel. . . . Son talent en est transformé, sa destinée en est magnifiquement changée" (Valéry, I, 599). However, Lloyd Austin, in his *Univers poétique de Baudelaire*, concludes that "L'influence de Poe sur Baudelaire a toutefois été moins grande qu'on ne l'a souvent dit" (Austin, 9).

The first aspect of this encounter is Baudelaire's attraction to Poe as an example of *le poète maudit*. It is clearly important to Baudelaire that Poe is a foreigner, not only a stranger to France but a stranger in his own country: "Les couleurs, la tournure d'esprit d'Edgar Poe tranchent violemment sur le fond de la littérature américaine" (Baudelaire, 1975, II, 253). Poe is "le Byron égaré dans un mauvais monde" (322) about whom Baudelaire's imagination constructs scenarios that might have figured in *Les Fleurs du Mal*: "les Etats-Unis ne furent pour Poe qu'*une vaste prison* qu'il parcourait avec l'agitation fiévreuse d'un être fait pour respirer dans un monde plus amoral . . ." (1975, II, 297, my italics). At the moment when Baudelaire discovered Poe, he had been championing Eugène Delacroix as the true romantic, vastly superior to Victor Hugo. The *Salon de 1846* argues that people have compared Delacroix to Hugo, but that this comparison is unfair to Delacroix, for Delacroix is essentially creative, the true romantic artist, while Hugo "est un ouvrier beaucoup plus adroit qu'inventif, un travailleur bien plus correct que créateur" (1975, II, 431). In seeking to eliminate Hugo from the scene, he celebrates Delacroix's paintings as "des poèmes, et de grands poèmes naïvement conçus, exécutés avec l'insolence accoutumée du génie" and which open "de profondes avenues à l'imagination la plus voyageuse" (431). He thus moves to conclude that whereas Hugo is merely a painter, "un peintre en poésie", Delacroix is the true romantic poet, "un poète en peinture" (1975, II, 432).

Although Baudelaire continues to champion Delacroix, the discovery of Poe enabled him to create another figure who actually wrote literature and whom he could attempt to set in the place of Hugo. Like Delacroix, "qui a élevé son art à la hauteur de la grande poésie, Edgar Poe aime à agiter ses figures sur des fonds violâtres et verdâtres où se révèlent la phosphorescence de la pourriture et la senteur de l'orage" (1975, II, 317-8). He wrote to Sainte-Beuve, "*Il faut*, c'est-à-dire je désire qu'*Edgar Poe*, qui n'est pas grand-chose en Amérique, devienne un grand homme pour la *France*" (1966, I, 343). But while Baudelaire's invention of Poe is part of an attempt to displace Hugo and leave a place for his own poetry, to create a great man who would resemble Baudelaire but in prose rather than poetry, this tells us little about his influence or Baudelaire's reading.

There are aspects of Baudelaire's poetry that were possibly influenced by Poe. In addition to echoing phrases from Poe's verse and short stories from time to time, Baudelaire makes heavy use of alliteration—more prominent in Poe than it had been in prior French poetry—and his use of internal rhyme and refrain may be linked with Poe's poetic practice; but much of his verse was written before he discovered Poe, and it is my contention that the most potent influence lies elsewhere.

Poe gave Baudelaire the idea for one project which he pursued, *Mon Coeur mis à nu*. Poe writes,

> If any ambitious man have a fancy to revolutionize, at one effort, the universal world of human thought, human opinion, and human sentiment, the opportunity is his own—the road to immortal renown lies straight, open, and unencumbered before him. All that he has to do is to write and publish a very little book. Its title should be simple—a few plain words—"My Heart Laid Bare." But—this little book must be *true to its title*. (1984a, 1423)

He concludes, however, in words that Baudelaire must have taken as a direct challenge, "No man dare write it. No man ever will dare write it. No man *could* write it, even if he dared. The paper would shrivel and blaze at every touch of the fiery pen" (1423). Baudelaire tried to do so, cultivating extreme thoughts—misogynistic, misanthropic, even anti-semitic—in the hope of producing this book, but the project remained unfinished.

Where Poe influenced Baudelaire most deeply, in my view, where Baudelaire proved an astute and powerful reader of Poe, is in Baudelaire's *Petits poèmes en prose*. Poe provided him with an aes-thetics of compression, and his example convinced him to abandon the project of writing short stories—he would not expect to outdo Poe in his chosen genre—but the example of prose writings exploring the mysterious, the uncanny, the exceptions of human life, was important, I suggest, in leading Baudelaire to undertake the prose poems. Poe's writing, he notes, "supprime les accessoires," "le sujet se découpe ardemment sur ces fonds nus" (1975, II, 282). The style is "serré, *concaténé*" (283). This effect was what he undertook to produce in the *Petits poèmes en prose*. One thing that helped make Poe's writing a possible model for prose poetry was the fact that in his reading and translation of Poe Baudelaire seems to have been insensitive to the ar-chaism of Poe's language—although in his verse Baudelaire did not hesitate to use a slightly archaic term or construction, especially in jux-taposition with something sardonic or low. His translations both of the few poems and especially of the stories put Poe into a vibrant, contem-porary French, while otherwise respecting syntax and meaning as scru-pulously as possible.

In "Notes Nouvelles sur Edgar Poe" Baudelaire wrote about the ad-vantages of Poe's form: "l'auteur d'une nouvelle a à sa disposition une multitude de tons, de nuances de langage, le ton raisonneur, le sarcastique, l'humoristique, que répudie la poésie, et qui sont comme des dissonances, des outrages à l'idée de beauté pure" (1975, II, 330). He describes the *Petits poèmes en prose* to his mother as seeking to join "l'effrayant avec le bouffon" (1966, II, 473). Baudelaire writes in his *présentation* of Poe's "Berenice", "ce qui fera son éternel éloge, c'est la préoccupation de tous les sujets réellement importants, et *seuls* dignes de l'attention d'un homme *spirituel*: probabilités, maladies de l'esprit, sciences conjecturales, espérances et calculs sur la vie ultérieure, analyse des excentriques et des parias de la vie sublunaire, bouffonneries directement symboliques" (1975, II, 289). This reading is the point of departure, or at least point of reference for the *Petits poèmes en prose*, which do most of these things, while generally leaving aside the *sciences conjecturales*—a side of Poe Baudelaire admired but for which he was scarcely gifted—and focusing instead on "des parias de la vie sublunaire" and "bouffonneries directement symboliques", not to say "maladies de l'esprit."

A story that sufficiently caught Baudelaire's attention for him to make it one of the eight he summarizes in his first article on Poe, "The Man of the Crowd", is one he praises again in "Le Peintre de la vie moderne" when discussing Constantin Guys: "Vous souvenez-vous d'un tableau (. . .) écrit par la plus puissante plume de cette époque, et qui a pour titre *L'Homme des foules?*" (1975, II, 689). The reading of it he offers here singles out the way in which the narrator, watching the passing crowds through a café window, "se mêle, par la pensée, à toutes les pensées qui s'agitent autour de lui. Revenu récemment des ombres de la mort, il aspire avec délices tous les germes et tous les effluves de la vie. . . . Finalement, il se précipite à travers cette foule à la recherche d'un inconnu dont la physionomie entrevue l'a, en un clin d'œil, fasciné. La curiosité est devenue une passion fatale, irrésistible" (1975, II, 690).

What is striking here is the way in which this description transforms Poe's story into something resembling Baudelaire's prose poem, "Les Foules", which focuses on the poet's "incomparable privilège" to enter "dans le personnage de chacun": "le promeneur solitaire et pensif tire une singulière ivresse de cette universelle communion." "Ce que les hommes nomment amour est bien petit, bien restreint et bien faible, comparé à cette ineffable orgie, à cette sainte prostitution de l'âme qui se donne tout entière, poésie et charité, à l'imprévu qui se montre, à l'inconnu qui passe" (1975, I, 291).

Poe's story (1984b, 388-96) is organized around a contrast between a first moment, when the narrator inside the café displays his analytic, classificatory powers, telling us how to recognize the various types who pass by and confidently reading "in that brief interval of a glance, the history of long years" (392), and a second moment when he follows a man of undecipherable countenance who continues to puzzle him ("'How wild a history,' I said to myself, 'is written within that bosom!'" (392)). Eventually he concludes that this "man of the crowd" who refuses to be alone is "the type and the genius of deep crime" (396) and that it is one of God's great mercies that so wicked a heart "lasst sich nicht lesen" (396). Although in "Les Fenêtres" Baudelaire takes up this trope of reading countenances, he transforms both the situation, placing the poet outside looking in, and the emphasis, which is not on the success or failure of reading the history but, with more than a touch of irony, on the narrator's self-satisfaction at constructing

> (. . .) l'histoire de cette femme, ou plutôt sa légende, et
> quelquefois je me la raconte à moi-même en pleurant.
>> Si c'eût été un pauvre vieux homme, j'aurais refait la
>> sienne tout aussi aisément.
>> Et je me couche, fier d'avoir vécu souffert dans d'autres
>> que moi-même.
>>> (1975, I, 339)

In "Les Foules", however, Baudelaire's reading of Poe emphasizes the *ivresse* of curiosity and participation, which is to be a central impulse of the *Petits poèmes en prose*. Even his translation, which in most respects is scrupulously faithful, at one point inflects the tale toward the "Multitude, solitude: termes égaux et convertibles pour le poète actif et fécond" of the prose poem (1975, I, 291) by translating Poe's phrase "the very denseness of the company around" as "la multitude innombrable qui les entourait" (Poe, 1965, 96). But the strangest, confirming moment of the direction of Baudelaire's reading comes in his summary of the story in his first article on Poe. Whereas the summary in "Le Peintre de la vie moderne" mentions the man of the crowd only as an object of the narrator's curiosity, the summary in "Edgar Allan Poe, sa vie et ses ouvrages" focuses exclusively on him, eliminating the narrator entirely, but despite this radical change of focus, the point for Baudelaire remains exactly the same: the *ivresse* of immersion in the crowd. While the other summary tells that the *narrator* "aspire avec délices tous les germes et tous les effluves de la vie" (1975, II, 690), here it is the man of the crowd who "se plonge sans cesse au sein de la foule; il nage avec délices dans l'océan humain" (1975, II, 277)— a description that points us toward the opening of "Les Foules": "il n'est pas donné à chacun de prendre un bain de multitude" (1975, I, 291). What Baudelaire preserves in both summaries, although they focus on different characters and different parts of the tale, is what he makes central to "Les Foules".

Another text in the *Petits poèmes en prose* is a reading of another aspect of Poe, the Gothic Poe of metempsychosis and uncanny doubles. "Laquelle est la vraie?", a story of two Bénédictas—the ideal Bénédicta whom the speaker buries and the bizarre figure who immediately appears to take her place, as a punishment for the narrator—is a parodic compression of two stories Baudelaire placed next to each other in his first volume of translations, *Histoires extraordinaires*: "Morella" and "Ligeia", where the anecdote of feminine doubling is played out in lugubrious detail. "Jai connu une certaine Bénédicta," begins Baudelaire, "qui remplissait l'atmosphère d'idéal, et dont les yeux répandaient le désir de la grandeur, de la beauté, de la gloire et de tout ce qui fait croire à l'immortalité" (1975, I, 342). Poe's two mysterious women, without pasts, are both passionately engaged with questions of immortality, and Ligeia's unparalleled beauty, "the beauty of beings either above or apart from the earth," which fills the atmosphere with ideality, comes especially from her eyes, whose extraordinary expression is "more profound than the well of Democritus" (Poe, 1984b, 264).

Baudelaire's next paragraph sardonically summarizes an aspect of Poe he saw only too clearly, as in the preface to *Histoires extraordinaires*, where he speaks of "ses femmes, toutes lumineuses et malades, mourant de maux bizarres" (1975, II, 318): in Poe, beauty exists so as to die. The prose poem continues, "Mais cette fille miraculeuse était trop belle pour vivre longtemps; aussi est-elle morte quelques jours après que j'eus fait sa connaissance, et c'est moi-même qui l'ai enterrée . . ." (Baudelaire, 1975, I, 342). Part of Poe's art of intensity is indeed to move immediately from the description of these beautiful and mysterious women to their death (sick beauties never recover): "Ligeia grew ill. The wild eyes blazed with a too—too glorious effulgence; the pale fingers became of the transparent waxen hue of the grave, and the blue veins upon the lofty forehead swelled and sank impetuously with the tides of the most gentle emotion. I saw that she must die" (1984b, 267).

In "Ligeia" the narrator then marries Rowena, whom he comes to loathe "with a hatred belonging more to demon than to man" (1984b, 272). He revels in recollections of his ideal Ligeia, as though he could call her back, and in fact as Rowena in turn sickens and dies, with horror he recognizes, in a lurid conclusion, Ligeia struggling to return in Rowena's body. In "Morella", the dead woman reappears in the daughter "to which in dying she had given birth": "And, hourly, grew darker these shadows of similitude, and more full, and more definite, and more perplexing, and more hideously terrible in their aspect" (1984b, 237-8). This tale concludes, "But she died; and with my own hands I bore her to the tomb; and I laughed with a long and bitter laugh as I found no traces of the first, in the charnel where I laid the second—Morella" (1984b, 239). Baudelaire's prose poem gives a comic rendition:

Et comme mes yeux restaient fichés sur le lieu où était enfoui mon trésor [i.e., the grave], je vis subitement une petite personne qui ressemblait singulièrement à la défunte, et qui, piétinant sur la terre fraîche avec une violence hystérique et bizarre, disait en éclatant de rire: "C'est moi, la vraie Bénédicta! C'est moi, une fameuse canaille! Et pour la punition de ta folie et de ton aveuglement, tu m'aimeras telle que je suis!"

Mais moi, furieux, j'ai répondu: "Non! non! non!" Et pour mieux accentuer mon refus, j'ai frappé si violemment la terre du pied que ma jambe s'est enfoncée jusqu'au genou dans la sépulture récente, et que, comme un loup pris au piège, je reste attaché, pour toujours peut-être, à la fosse de l'idéal. (1975, I, 342)

This little allegory, which suggests, perhaps, that Poe's narrators have truly put their foot in it, that their way of being attached to the ideal is like having their foot caught in a coffin, also narrates the relation between high and low feminine figures as a product of "folie" and blindness, translating Poe's gothic scenario into a more Baudelairian mode. But what I would stress here and return to later is the way in which this prose poem prosaicizes by literalizing figures and clichés, generating a narrative by taking literally the idea of being *attached* to one's ideal or *fastening* one's eyes on something (*ficher les yeux* sur quelque chose). Baudelaire's is a prosaicizing reading of Poe's supernatural. He prefers the lucid Poe.

Indeed, what Baudelaire reads in Poe, one might say, is a triad of qualities that he in effect sets against the revolutionary credo of his century: *Lucidité, Etrangeté, Perversité.*

(1) *Lucidité.* After describing the American milieu in its first section, Baudelaire's "Notes nouvelles sur Edgar Poe" begins its second section, "Car il ne fut jamais dupe" (1975, II, 321). He saw through the progressive platitudes of his century. This is the Poe who, with De Maistre, Baudelaire says taught him to think. It is also the Poe emphasized by Valéry in his brilliant "Situation de Baudelaire". Baudelaire's talents would have made him but a rival of Gautier if he had not discovered in the writings of Poe a new intellectual world.

Le démon de la lucidité, le génie de l'analyse, et l'inventeur des com-
binaisons les plus neuves et les plus séduisantes de la logique avec l'imagination, de la mysticité avec le calcul, le psychologue de l'exception,
l'ingénieur littéraire qui approfondit et utilise toutes les ressources de l'art,
lui apparaissent en Edgar Poe et l'émerveillent. Tant de vues originales et
promesses extraordinaires l'ensorcellent. Son talent en est transformé, sa
destinée en est magnifiquement changée. (Valéry, I, 599)

The attraction for Baudelaire lies above all in the combination of a romantic discourse with a lucidity permitting a critique of that discourse.

(2) *Etrangeté*. Baudelaire emphasizes that Poe's compositions are
"créées pour nous démontrer que l'étrangeté est une des parties
intégrantes du beau" (1975, II, 302). This is similar to the view he had
already taken in the Salon of 1846, emphasizing the need for novelty
and originality, but Poe gave him something that resembled a more set-
tled doctrine, linked to an account of the poetic faculty of imagination,
and by his practice Poe associated this *étrangeté* with the representation of the bizarre, of the pariahs and exceptions of human life.

(3) *Perversité*. Baudelaire found it possible to use Poe against Rous-
seau, as he used him against Hugo, in creating an alternative great
writer who shared some of his own conceptions and left him creative
space in which to work. In "Notes nouvelles sur Edgar Poe", the last of
his three essays, which reflects a much greater familiarity with Poe's
writings than do the other two, he insists on Poe's vision of the natural
perversity or depravity of man. "Mais voici plus important que tout",
he begins: "nous noterons que cet auteur, produit d'un siècle infatué de
lui-même, enfant d'une nation plus infatuée d'elle-même qu'aucune
autre, à vu clairement, à imperturbablement affirmé la méchanceté
naturelle de l'homme" (1975, II, 322). Baudelaire waxes eloquent
about the explanatory power of this concept, without which a host of
human actions cannot be understood: "la Perversité naturelle, qui fait
que l'homme est sans cesse et à la fois homicide et suicide, assassin et
bourreau" (323). The relevant text—perhaps the text which most in-

spired Baudelaire—is "The Imp of the Perverse", which Baudelaire placed at the beginning of the major collection of his translations of Poe, les *Nouvelles histoires extraordinaires*, and which he translates as "Le Démon de la perversité." That *imp* becomes *démon* is already characteristic of Baudelaire's reading of this text. Poe writes of "this overwhelming tendency to do wrong for the wrong's sake" (1984b, 827) which becomes in Baudelaire "cette tendance accablante à faire le mal pour l'amour du mal" (Poe, 1965, 51). I propose to focus on the reading of this story that Baudelaire undertakes in the *Petits poèmes en prose* through "Le Mauvais Vitrier"—a key text in that it shows how Baudelaire's reading of Poe transforms any suggestions picked up from Arsène Houssaye, to whom the book is dedicated, and who, he says, sought to capture the cry of the *vitrier* in a poetry of Paris.

Poe's story moves from a lengthy explanation of the principle of perverseness to examples that are surprising, in that they are scarcely what we expect to illustrate the idea of doing wrong for wrong's sake: "There lives no man who at some period, has not been tormented, for example, by an earnest desire to tantalize a listener by circumlocution" (1984b, 828). The description that follows is in fact quite wonderful, a circumlocutory dramatization, after which the next example, also vividly dramatized, is procrastination—against one's own best interests—and finally, the temptation to throw oneself over a precipice, because one knows one should not. We might, Poe concludes, "deem this perverseness a direct instigation of the Arch-Fiend, were it not occasionally known to operate in furtherance of good", to make a murderer confess, for example, against his own interests (1984b, 829).

Baudelaire's text begins not with a principle pushing us to procrastination but, inversely, with a principle perversely impelling procrastinators, contemplatives, or inoffensive dreamers to "les actes les plus absurdes et souvent même les plus dangereux", such as setting fire to a forest to see what would happen, lighting a cigar beside a powder-barrel to test fate, or suddenly embracing an unknown passer-by, who knows why (1975, I, 285). Baudelaire's speaker then proceeds to describe one "de ces crises et de ces élans" (286) of which he himself had been victim and which "nous autorisent à croire que des Démons malicieux se glissent en nous et nous font accomplir, à notre insu, leurs plus absurdes volontés" (286): he broke all the window panes of a poor *vitrier* plying his trade in the quartier. The narrator offers scant explanation, observing that "Il me serait d'ailleurs impossible de dire pourquoi je fus pris à l'égard de ce pauvre homme d'une haine aussi soudaine que despotique" (286), but what may appear unmotivated at a psychological level is allegorically motivated. The speaker tells us that he arose, "fatigué d'oisiveté, et poussé, me semblait-il, à faire quelque chose de grand, une action d'*éclat*" (286, my italics). What he does, then, is to produce precisely "le bruit *éclatant* d'un palais de cristal crevé par la foudre" (287)—"une action d'éclat" indeed. Calling the *vitrier* to come up to his room on the seventh floor, he chastises him for plying his trade in poor neighborhoods without "des verres de couleur", "des verres roses, rouges, bleus, des vitres magiques, des vitres de paradis"—"de vitres qui fassent voir la vie en beau" (287). The complaint is generated by a literalisation of the figure "voir la vie en beau"; clearly this requires a special sort of window pane. When the *vitrier* returns to the street, the speaker drops on him from a balcony "un petit pot de fleurs", his "engin de guerre" (287). Is it an accident that this *engin de guerre* is a "*pot* de fleurs", recalling the theorist of perversity? These may or may not be *des Fleurs du Mal*, but they are certainly *des Fleurs qui font du mal* to the poor *vitrier*, destroying "toute sa pauvre fortune ambulatoire" (287). The emphasis on *verres*—as in "verres de couleurs, verres roses"—suggests a connection with verses. Baudelaire is certainly thinking in these terms in 1859 when he writes to his editor Poulet-Malassis, "Nouvelles *Fleurs du Mal* faites. A tout casser, comme une explosion de gaz chez un vitrier" (1966, I, 568); and two weeks later he writes to the photographer and artist Nadar that for a frontispiece to his Poe articles he wants a portrait surrounded with allegorical figures representing Poe's principal conceptions and for the new edition of *Les Fleurs du mal* "un squelette arborescent" protecting several rows of "plantes vénéneuses, dans des petits *pots* . . ." (1966, I, 577, my italics).

But what does this have to do with "The Imp of the Perverse", one might ask? The perverse act of Baudelaire's speaker makes use of Poe according to a general principle sketched in quite different form in "The Imp of the Perverse." Poe's narrator explains that he had committed a cleverly-planned murder and had escaped all suspicion but would find himself "repeating, in a low undertone, the phrase, 'I am safe.'" Once, while murmuring these customary syllables, "In a fit of petulance, I remodelled them thus:—'I am safe—I am safe—yes—if I be not fool enough to make open confession!' No sooner had I spoken these words, than I felt an icy chill creep to my heart", knowing that the compulsion to perform the act would prove irresistible, as indeed it does (1984b, 831).

I suggest that it is from such tales, where an utterance or verbal formulation produces an event, that Baudelaire learned what would be one of the principal techniques of the *Petit poèmes en prose*—the generation of an allegorical narrative through the literalization of a phrase or a figure. It is striking that his prose poem which focuses on perversity is constructed on a version of the device that animates Poe's story, as word generates event. There is, of course, a difference between the two texts: whereas Poe's story articulates a theory of perversity to explain an event which is presented within the story as having been generated by language, adducing a psychological mechanism to move us away from the linguistic mechanism, Baudelaire's narrative leaves unexplained perverse events which seem to have been generated allegorically by language, thus foregrounding that semiotic mechanism, illustrating what the title of one of Poe's prose texts translated by Baudelaire calls "The Power of Words".

The *pot de fleurs*, the *action d'éclat*, the *vitres qui fassent voir la vie en beau* are examples of what Baudelaire called a "calembour en action". A vivid and perverse illustration appears in an incident that Asselineau reports: one when he and Baudelaire were visiting Verteuil, the secretary of the Théâtre-Français, Baudelaire nearly made the poor man faint with terror by describing to him, in minute and loving detail, the various tortures suffered by missionaries, as represented in an exhibition they had just visited at the Salle des Missions. "N'est-ce pas, Monsieur Verteuil, qu'il est beau de souffrir pour sa foi!" As the poor man tries to escape, Baudelaire offers the crowning example: "'Un de ces soldats chinois, poursuivait Baudelaire impitoyable, (. . .) ouvre la poitrine de la victime avec son poignard, lui arrache le coeur tout sanglant et l'avale! un calembour en action! vous comprenez, monsieur Verteuil?—pour se donner du cœur!'" Asselineau reports, "Baudelaire sortit radieux. Ce spectacle pour lui était si beau!" (Crépet, 297).

Well might Baudelaire identify with this *soldat chinois*, putting an expression into action, allowing it to generate a narrative. This is something he learned from Poe, whose story "Loss of Breath" is the tale of someone who literally loses his breath, cannot catch it; whose "Never Bet the Devil Your Head" explores the danger that what you metaphorically bet may be taken literally and literally taken; whose "The System of Doctor Tarr and Professor Feather" explores the possibility of producing cures through literalizing figures—holding your tongue, for example; whose "The Power of Words" represents the Earth as having been spoken into birth by a word. Some of Poe's tales are more interesting variations on the *calembour en action*, as when, in "The Black Cat", the narrator who tortures the cat finds that, "I knew myself no longer"—perhaps because he cut out its *eye*. And the literalization of representations is explored in other media as well, when the representation of a horse emerges from a tapestry and becomes deadly for baron Metzengerstein or when the compliment paid to the Oval Portrait in the tale of that name, a portrait so consummately done that one says "this is life itself", becomes literally true and takes the sitter's life: she drops dead as the portrait captures life itself.

Baudelaire put this technique to use in a range of prose poems, from the more obvious examples of "Le Galant Tireur", which is generated from the expression "Tuer le temps", to the narrativization of "le don de plaire" in "Les Dons des fées", to the more local and restrained literalization of puns in other prose poems: "Une mort héroïque" speaks of an "expérience physiologique d'un intérêt *capital*" which produces "capital" punishment, or of a "sifflet, rapide comme un glaive" which actually kills like a sword (1975, I, 320, 322); "Le Joueur généreux" explores the expression "bon diable". To explore these and other *calembours en action* is a task for another paper, but as readers of foreign language are inclined to notice or even to imagine puns, so it was, I think, in reading, in a foreign language he did not know very well, the author whose name seemed almost to make him the "*poè*te" *par excellence* and whose engagement with the fantastic enabled him to explore widely the literalization of figures, that Baudelaire found the germ for the allegorical method of the *Petits poèmes en prose*.

Poe even hints that there might be some special link between the *calembour en action* and the French language in his story "Berenice", a tale which certainly illustrates the force of a certain "démon de la perversité". The hero Egæus, who suffers from monomania, has an inclination "to muse for long unwearied hours with my attention riveted to some frivolous device on the margin, or in the typography of a book; . . . to repeat monotonously some common word, until the sound, by dint of frequent repetition, ceased to convey any idea whatever to the mind" (1984b, 227). He not only dwells upon forms of language, investing them with special import, but, as he reports, the object of his attention "was *invariably frivolous*, although assuming, through the medium of my distempered vision, a refracted and unreal importance" (1984b, 228). Egæus is betrothed to Berenice, who, like all Poe's women, is dying of mysterious ailments. She appears before him, emaciated and silent, but her thin and shrunken lips part and, "in a smile of peculiar meaning, *the teeth* of the changed Berenice disclosed themselves slowly to my view" (1984b, 230). The vision of these perfect teeth becomes his obsession ("Would to God that I had never beheld them, or that, having done so, I had died!" (230)). "In the multiplied objects of the external world I had no thoughts but for the teeth. For these I longed with a phrenzied desire" (231). The question of Berenice's *identity* becomes a dental obsession.

> I dwelt upon their peculiarities. I pondered upon their conformation. . . . I shuddered as I assigned to them in imagination a sensitive and sentient power, and even when unassisted by the lips, a capability of moral expression. Of Mad'selle Sallé it has been well said, "*que tous ses pas étaient des sentiments*," and of Berenice I more seriously believed *que tous ses dents étaient des idées. Des idées!*—ah here was the idiotic thought that destroyed me! (231)

The French phrase seems to provide him with a semiotic paradigm: if A's *pas* are feelings then perhaps B's *dents* are thoughts. That sign relation or "idiotic thought," as he correctly calls it, seems generated also by a verbal echo—*ses dents/des idées*—not a pun but a transformation of the signifier. "*Des idées!*—ah *therefore* it was that I coveted them so madly! I felt that their possession could alone ever restore me to peace, in giving me back to reason" (1984a, 231). When he hears that Berenice is dead, the association produced by the verbal equivalence, *ses dents/des idées*, joined with a Latin proverb which instructs that visiting the grave of friends will lighten one's cares, mysteriously impels him, in a stupor, to rob the grave and pull out all of the teeth of the woman who, it turns out, had been buried alive while in an epileptic trance.

That French phrase, "que tous ses dents étaient des idées", lurid and bizarre, now seems to suggest that what Poe was trying to do had to be put into French, as if it were the medium in which such relations belong, and while this is scarcely an explanation of Baudelaire's *Petits poèmes en prose*, it serves as allegorical indication of Poe's perverse affinity for the French, which became, in Baudelaire's writing, a representational strategy.

## Bibliography

Austin, Lloyd, *L'Univers poétique de Baudelaire*, Paris, 1956.

Baudelaire, Charles, *Correspondance* (Bibliothèque de la pléiade), 2 vols, Paris, 1966.

_____, *Œuvres complètes* (Bibliothèque de la pléiade), 2 vols, Paris, 1975.

Crépet, Eugène, *Charles Baudelaire, Etude biographique*, Paris, 1928.

Eliot, T. S., "From Poe to Valéry", *To Criticize the Critic*, New York, 1965.

Humphries, Jefferson, *Metamorphoses of the Raven: Literary Overdeterminedness in France and the South Since Poe*, Baton Rouge, Louisiana, 1985.

Mallarmé, Stéphane, *Œuvres complètes* (Bibliothèque de la pléiade), Paris, 1945.

Patterson, Arthur, *L'Influence de Edgar Poe sur Charles Baudelaire*, Grenoble, 1903.

Poe, Edgar Allan, *Essays and Reviews* (Library of America), New York, 1984 (= 1984a).

_____, *Nouvelles Histoires extraordinaires*, trans. Ch. Baudelaire, Paris, 1965.

_____, *Poetry and Tales* (Library of America), New York, 1984 (= 1984b).

Riding, Laura, "The Factor in the Case of Monsieur Poe", in *Contemporaries and Snobs*, New York, 1928.

Ruff, Marcel, *L'Esprit du mal et l'esthétique baudelairienne*, Paris, 1955.

Valéry, Paul, *Œuvres* (Bibliothèque de la pléiade), 2 vols, Paris, 1957.

Wetherill, P. M., *Charles Baudelaire et la poésie d'Edgar Allan Poe*, Paris, 1962.

# Poe and Frances Osgood, as Linked Through "Lenore"_____

Burton R. Pollin

All accounts of the Della Cruscan poetic exchanges and of the highly publicized "year-long" relationship of Poe and Mrs. Frances Sargent Osgood seem to concentrate on the beginning of 1845. Poe then started his climb to the co-editorship of the *Broadway Journal* and early exercised discretion over the selection and printing of the poems from contributors, including her dozen verse tributes to Poe or love confessions printed under various pseudonyms or anonymously.[1] However, in a curious way the antiphonal exchanges of published poems preceded the year 1845, and certainly the relationship continued afterwards even into the postlude of Poe's life—for a further eight months, until Mrs. Osgood's death in May 1850. The latter, newly estimated extension, thanks to the discovery of the early (December 1849) publication by Mrs. Osgood of her elegy on and reminiscences of Poe, has recently been presented in detail.[2] With a re-evaluation of certain interrelated poetic and prose works, the pre-1845 Poe-Osgood link becomes stronger and more significant.

There are two "inspirational episodes" in this intellectual connection. The first involves a poem by Mrs. Osgood entitled "Leonor," first appearing in her book *A Wreath of Wild Flowers from New England* (London: Edward Chutton, 1838). It also was reprinted in the popular annual *The Token and Atlantic Souvenir . . . 1839*, published in 1838, for the Christmas gift trade.[3] It is strange that a prior poem with a name and, in a sense, a theme so close to that of Poe's 1843 "Lenore" should apparently not have been examined for links. Although it is also available in the 1846 *Poems* of Mrs. Osgood (pp. 151-153) and the final "collection," *Poems* (1850; issued in December 1849), it needs to be read for comparison.[4]

## Leonor

1   Leonor loved a noble youth,

2   But light was Leonor's maiden truth;

3   She left her love for wealth forsooth.

4          Faithless Leonor!

5   Now she paces a palace-hall.

6   Lords and ladies await her call,—

7   Wearily Leonor turns from all.

8          Haughty Leonor!

9   Leonor lies on a couch of down

10   The jewel-light of a ducal crown

11   Gleams through her tresses of sunlit brown.

12          Beautiful Leonor!

13   Leonor's robe is a tissue of gold.

14   Flashing with splendour in every fold;

15   Bracelets of gems on her arms are rolled.

16          Radiant Leonor!

17   Diamonds sparkle in Leonor's zone,

18   With a star-like glory in every stone;

19   But the heart they smile o'er is cold and lone.

20          Joyless Leonor!

21   To be free once more she would give them all,—

22   The crown, the couch, and the sculptured hall,

23   And the robe with its rich and shining fall.

24          Poor, poor Leonor!

25   Like a captive bird, through her cage's bar

26   Of gold she looks on her home afar,

27   And it woos her there like a holy star.

28          Vainly, Leonor!

29   Leonor's lip has lost its bloom.

30   Her proud blue eyes are dark with gloom.

31   She will sleep in peace in her early tomb.

32          Lonely Leonor![5]

---

This effusion is obviously one of the numerous poems derived from the very popular "Lady Clara Vere de Vere" in Tennyson's *Poems* of 1833 (issued 1832), in which the proud "daughter of a thousand earls" smiles at the youth "of a country heart." He predicts: "You pine among your halls and towers;/ The languid light of your proud eyes/ Is wearied of the rolling hours" and will be "sickening of a vague disease" (stanza 7). Poe had already treated the theme tangentially in the early "Paean" in his unnoticed *Poems* of 1831, in that a proud maiden has married into great wealth, has sickened and has died amid hostile heirs or false friends (Mabbott, *Works*, I, 204-207). He knew Osgood's later presentation of the theme via *The Wreath*, of 1838, and probably also via *The Token* of the same year. He incorporated several of her points into his revised and much strengthened version of "Paean," which he called "Lenore," changing the name of the dead girl from "Helen."[6] Moreover, implicitly Helen's "pride" had come from her wealth, evidenced by her "gaudy bier" and "costly broider'd pall," but "Leonor" has probably served to add "the jewel-light of a ducal crown" (line 10) in the reference to "Lenore's" "vacant coronet."[7]

Since Poe's awareness of Mrs. Osgood's works and physical presence is usually assumed to date from 1845, it is essential to note that both writers had appeared in the important anthology of 200 poems by Americans collected by George Pope Morris, eminent librettist for popular songs and also co-editor with Willis of leading American journals. This 1840 volume, *National Melodies of America*, was reviewed as *American Melodies* by Poe in the December 1839 issue of *Burton's Gentleman's Magazine* (pp. 332-333). It was an article of great importance in the development of Poe's concept of the desirable quality of "indefinitiveness" in poetry and in music, and from it he largely quoted twice: first, in the December 1844 "Marginalia 44" discussing Tennyson and "true musical expression" and, second, in expanded form, in the April 1849 "Marginalia 202."[8] Poe's contribution to the Morris anthology was his major poem "To One in Paradise," which had first appeared as part of the text of "The Visionary," in *The Lady's Book* for

January 1834 (later *Godey's Lady's Book*); in Morris's volume it bore the Byronic title of "To Ianthe in Heaven" as a lingering evidence of the chief narrative element of the matrix-tale.[9] Frances Osgood's contribution was "Your Heart Is a Music-Box, Dearest!" Surely, Poe read carefully through the volume as a reviewer and contributor, paying attention to Osgood's work, as he had done previously in *The Wreath of Wild Flowers*. He tacitly admits this when commenting on the reprint of her "Music-Box" poem in her *Poems* of 1846, declaring its "melody and harmony" as "absolutely perfect," directly after quoting it verbatim in his review.[10] Poe's ample comments on her London 1838 *Wreath* in this article clearly indicate a long acquaintance with her works and fame. A strong evidence lies also in his December 13, 1845, *Broadway Journal* review of her *Poems*, several of which, he writes, come from *The Wreath*. Since there is no dating or earlier printing indicated in the anthology, his knowledge could spring only from prior reading, or, less likely, a careful collation of the two volumes.[11]

In another of his articles on Mrs. Osgood, "The Literati" papers of September 1846 in *Godey's Lady's Book*, Poe evidences his having followed her prolific output as it was issued in various popular journals; he is lamenting the incompleteness of her 1846 collection, *Poems*, noting the nonappearance of "The Daughter of Herodias."[12] This happened to be issued in *Graham's Magazine* (21 [August 1842], pp. 14-15), two months after Poe's leaving the editor's chair. He may have had little to do with the acceptance of Osgood's works beforehand, such as her sentimental story "May Evelyn" in the March 1842 issue (pp. 145-149), or choosing her highly didactic poem "Venus and the Modern Belle" (20 [May 1842], 274), printed a few pages beyond his own "Mask of the Red Death" in the same issue (pp. 257-259), the last of Poe's editorship.[13] Certainly, Poe's keen interest in the magazine, especially after Griswold sat in the editor's chair, would have guaranteed his reading others: her long poem "Truth," in the December 1842 magazine, or, in successive issues for the first half of 1843, the long "nouvelle" in five "chapters," "The Coquette," with its interspersed poems by Osgood and Tennyson (pp. 24-28) and preceding Poe's "Conqueror Worm" by only four pages; her poem "The Flowers and Gems of Genius" (p. 82); "The Soul's Lament for Home" (p. 194); "First Affection" (p. 214) and "Little Red Riding Hood" (p. 296). Clearly their awareness of each other's work must have been growing more weighted and anticipatory in the rather limited and gossipy circles of the New York literati.

It could not have been totally accidental, therefore, that Osgood's "To Lenore" was one of her new works in the *Poems* (1846), which first appeared in the *Broadway Journal* of May 31, 1845 (p. 347) as by "Clarice." As will appear, it is full of themes and approaches reflecting a tale and poem of Poe. This important segment of the Poe-Osgood exchange came soon after Poe's reprint in the May 10 issue (p. 295) of "To One in Paradise," the verse section of his "Assignation," which Poe printed in the number directly after the one with Osgood's poem based on the tale's conclusion (June 7, pp. 357-360). There, of course, it bore the original fifth stanza.[14] (His stress on the poem of "Clarice" is shown in that his review in the December 13, 1845, *Broadway Journal* quotes it in full, under the title "Lenore.") With the continuation of the love-poem exchanges, we find Poe, after consolidating his control of the journal, reprinting his "Lenore" on the first page of the August 16 issue (p. 81). Despite his extensive coverage of sources and suggestions for "Lenore" (*Works*, I, 330-334), Mabbott omits Mrs. Osgood's use of another form of the name in the 1838 "Leonor" and Poe's responsive use here. Indeed, only John E. Reilly (pp. 138-139, 145 [n. 13]) senses and hints at a connection of the *three* poems of that name before the late dating of Osgood's second and Poe's reprinting of his poem in the *Broadway Journal* of August 16 induces him finally to reject the fruitful idea.

Poe had printed his "Lenore" (well after Osgood's "Leonor" of 1838) at least twice in 1843 as well as twice at the beginning of 1844, and three times in 1845: in Lowell's widely read sketch of Poe, in the February 1845 *Graham's Magazine* (appearing in January), and later in the *Broadway Journal* of August 16 and his volume of poems. His girl's name, "Lenore," was available at the beginning of 1845 in the widely circulated and recited "Raven," so that Osgood could easily attach it to her new poem, where it forms no part of the text at all, being simply the unaccountable title.[15] It is the content which is the strongest tie to Poe, i.e., to his early tale "The Visionary" of January 1834, retitled "The Assignation" in the July 1835 *Southern Literary Messenger*, the 1839 *Tales of the Grotesque and Arabesque*, and the June 7 *Broadway Journal*. The chief features of the plot and setting, basic to Osgood's "To Lenore," require specification. Poe's narrator describes his "ill-fated and mysterious hero," who proves to be Byron, although unnamed, in his "Palladian palace" overlooking a canal in Venice. He then shifts to the late evening when he witnesses the hero rescue the baby of the Marchesa Aphrodite, which has fallen into the waters, and he overhears a whispered message between the Marchesa and the hero. He escorts "Byron" home, and accepts the invitation to visit early the next morning. He finds the "palazzo" to be of "fantastic pomp" and his host's apartment to be filled with incredibly rich and rare art works. The tear-stained manuscript of a love poem (actually Poe's inserted "To One in Paradise" or "To Ianthe in Heaven") reveals to the narrator his "Italian" friend's English identity and prior love-acquaintance with Aphrodite before her marriage to an old, dissolute Venetian nobleman. The last stanza (published only in the tale) also encapsulates the "plot" of Poe's later "Lenore."[16] Finally, "Byron" drinks from a glass of wine in toast to a portrait of the angel-winged Marchesa on the wall and to the "land of real dreams whither I am now rapidly departing." The horrified narrator finds him "riveted in death" just as a servant of Aphrodite brings the news of her simultaneous self-poisoning. The "cracked and blackened goblet" reveals the truth of the double suicide (*Works*, II, 148-169). The final action rests on a widespread folk-belief, best (and appropriately) expressed by the real Lord Byron in *The Two Foscari* (V, 1): "Our Venetian crystal has/ Such pure antipathy to poison, as/ To burst, if aught of venom touches it."

We must note, preliminarily, in Mrs. Osgood's "Lenore" her epitomized use of several key elements of the tale, such as "the pomp of those palaces" of Venice and the shattering effect of love, when "wild Passion"[17] threatens to supersede the restrictions of society and discretion. While it is a theme purveyed by several of the poems in the exchanges of Poe and Frances Osgood (then separated from Samuel Osgood), the allusions to elements in Poe's tale suggest that the note of a doomed marriage in both poems about "Lenore" puts her poem, composed early in 1845 and printed in the *Broadway Journal* of May 31 (p. 347) into the stream of sentimental and even erotic addresses to Poe.[18]

### To Leonore

Oh! fragile and fair, as the delicate chalices,
    Wrought with so rare and so subtle a skill;
Bright relics, that tell of the pomp of those palaces,
    Venice—the sea-goddess—glories in still!

Whose exquisite texture, transparent and tender,
    A pure blush alone from the ruby wine takes;
Yet ah! if some false hand, profaning its splendor,
    Dare but to taint it with poison—it breaks!

So when Love pour'd thro' thy pure heart his lightning
    On thy pale cheek the soft rose-hues awoke—
So when wild Passion, that timid heart frightening,
      Poison'd the treasure—it trembled and broke!

It is surely significant that Poe singled out this twelve-line poem to typify various merits of Osgood's poetry, such as "grace of expression," "facility in illustration," and "her epigrammatism." This was in the *Broadway Journal* of December 13, 1845. In his *Godey's Lady's Book* review of her *Poems*, in March 1846, he limits himself to mentioning this poem's "passionate sadness" as a sign of her growing creative maturity. Moreover, in his "Literati" sketch of Osgood, of September 1846, he again cites the whole poem as exemplifying her "ingenuity," "her exactitude and facility at illustration,"[19] and her "*epigrammatism*," to use his own self-conscious coinage. Poe vacillates about this quality, "in which she excels." He recognizes the kinship of this poem with the "class of allegorical or emblematical verses," which "no poet can admit to be poetry at all." However, "in its better phase, that is to say, existing apart from the allegory," he cites "To Lenore" as an "exquisite specimen" of her verse.[20] But in his glowing appreciation of Mrs. Osgood, in the *Southern Literary Messenger* of August 1849, which closely follows the "Literati" sketch, he omitted "To Lenore" and all reference to it. His firmly rooted distaste for allegory, so well wrought in the central images of "To Lenore," must have finally reduced his partiality—that, and the fact that by the end of 1846 there was a cooling of the "wild Passion" that the writer and probably the silent "Byron" of the situation had been experiencing from early 1845 into late 1846. Both continued to be interested in each other's activities and publications, as shown in articles, reviews, and poems—most poignantly in her "Dirge" for Israfel (October 13, 1849) and her "Reminiscences of Poe" (December 8, 1849); also revealing is her booklet *A Letter about the Lions* (1849).[21]

Even during January 1850 Mrs. Osgood, sorely stricken with tuberculosis, could not resist expressing her own gloominess over approaching death through a powerful verse metaphor taken from one of Poe's most memorable and characteristic poems, "A Dream within a Dream." Poe had published it in the Boston *Flag of Our Union* on March 31, 1849. It was a journal well known to Mrs. Osgood; moreover, the poem was again readily available to her in the two volumes of Griswold's edition of *Poe's Works* (II, 40), issued early in January 1850. The striking resemblances justify quoting several of Poe's lines:

"Take this kiss upon the brow!
And, in parting from you now,
Thus much let me avow—
You are not wrong, who deem
That my days have been a dream.

. . . . . . . . . .

*All* that we see or seem
Is but a dream within a dream."
[concerning the grains of sand creeping through his fingers]
"O God! can I not save
*One* from the pitiless wave?
Is *all* that we see or seem
But a dream within a dream?"

(ll. 1-5, 10-11, 21-24)

Mrs. Osgood contributed her poem to the well-known pages of Sartain's *Union Magazine of Literature and Art*, issued by John Sartain, the loyal friend of Poe, first in New York City and now in Philadelphia. It was prominently printed at the head of the February issue as one of the plate articles, immediately after a full-page picture of a cloaked man under a twisted oak tree, watching a deer at the edge of a river. The picture and poem are called "The Melancholy Jacques; or, A Dream of Life," with the pertinent lines cited as epigraph from *As You Like It* (II, 3, 31-33). Her opening quotes directly from Poe:

"A dream within a dream. I fell asleep
Holding a picture of the dreamer, Jacques,
And musing upon life's vicissitudes:—
I dreamed that life itself was but a dream;
This stern, dark, terrible life, with all its fears,
Its wrong and sin and suffering and despair—
That it was all, only a long night's sleep."

After a maudlin section about lying down at her "dear Father's feet' in heaven she concludes:

> " . . . With a start
> Of horror, which was death I woke
>
> . . . . . . . .
>
> And knew I had but dreamed . . . .
> There was another wakening. Worn and faint
> With years of suffering, I unclosed my eyes
> And saw and felt the dread reality
> Of life around me still."

Clearly the language, mood, idea, and conclusion are similar for the "melancholy" Poe and Frances Osgood, and she is rather obviously proclaiming her continuing interest in the dead poet in this uncollected and, as yet, unstudied poem.

As for Poe's interest in her, his long *Messenger* appreciation of Osgood, which he left to his literary executor as a substitute for the original "Literati" sketch, and many references in his criticism speak about his continued tenderness. But the "Passion" was clearly gone after 1846; moreover, public expression of it before his death was embarrassing to both participants, especially with the return and acceptance of Samuel Osgood into Frances Osgood's home.

Her seeming submission to the dominating and, probably, philandering husband is belied somewhat by her once publishing verses somewhat different in theme from the breakable chalice image of "To Lenore." On April 8, 1848, a married women's property-rights bill, climaxing almost a decade of strong agitation and close "wins," as in the 1846 Constitutional Convention, passed the New York State Assembly and Senate and was signed into law.[22] Frances Osgood sent her individualistic response to it for printing in the New York *Tribune* of April 17 (VIII, no. 7, p. 4).[23] Griswold, her literary counsellor and editor of her large-volume collected *Poems* of late 1849 (which Poe had often advised her to arrange), clearly rejected the work from the canon.[24] In consequence, no modern student of her life and works has commented on this evidence of her awareness of the major women's-rights legislation. By implication the poem bears on her basic attitudes. She was now, clearly, no resigned victim of Passion (as in her verses "To Lenore"), or of the slander of gossips or of envious Poe courtiers,[25] or even of the former virtual desertion by Samuel Osgood, perhaps intimated in these verses. Obviously, Mrs. Osgood foresees the need for a true equality of respect and dignity between husband and wife, over and above property rights.

For the New-York Tribune

LINES

Suggested by the announcement that "A Bill for the<br>
Protection of the Property of Married Women has<br>
passed both Houses of our State Legislature"

Oh, ye who in those Houses hold
    The sceptre of Command!
Thought's sceptre, sunlit, in the soul,
    Not golden, in the hand!
Was there not one among ye all,
    No heart, that Love could thrill,
To move some slight amendment there,
    Before you passed the bill?
Ye make our gold and lands secure;
    Maybe you do not know,
That we have other property,
    We'd *rather* not forego.
There *are* such things in woman's heart,
    As fancies, tastes, affections;—
Are no encroachments made on these?

Do *they* need no "protections?" [sic]
Do we not daily sacrifice,
    To our lords—and Creation's,
Some darling wish—some petted whim,
    Ah, me! in vain oblations!
These "cold realities" of life,—
    These men, with their intrusions;
Do they not rob us, one by one,
    Of all our "warm illusions?" [sic]
These highway robbers, prawling [sic] round,
    Our "young affections" stealing.
Do they not take our richest store
    Of Truth and Faith and Feeling.
Our "better judgment," "finer sense,"
    We yield with souls that falter,—
A costly, dainty holocaust
    Upon a tyrant's altar;
We waste on them our "golden" hours,
    Our "real estate" of Beauty,
The bloom of Life's young passion-flowers—
    And still they talk of "Duty."
Alas for those, whose all of wealth
    Is in their souls and faces,
Whose only "rents" are rents in heart,
    Whose only tenants—graces.
How must that poor protection bill
    Provoke their bitter laughter,
Since they themselves are leased for life,
    And no *pay-day* till after!
By all the rest you fondly hope,
    When ends this lengthened session,
That household peace, which Woman holds
    Thank heaven! at *her* discretion.

---

Poe and Frances Osgood

If a light of generous chivalry,
    This wild appeal arouses,
Present a truer, nobler bill!
    And let it pass–*all houses*!

Frances S. Osgood[26]

## Notes

1. For good accounts of this 1845 "year"—obviously at least eighteen months of mutual interest, dating from March well into the "Literati" period, of mid-1846—see the studies of Mary G. DeJong, "Lines from a Partly Published Drama: The Romance of Frances Sargent Osgood and Edgar Allan Poe," in *Patrons and Protégées* (Rutgers University Press, 1988), pp. 31-58; John E. Reilly, "Mrs. Osgood and the *Broadway Journal*," *Duquesne Review*, 12 (Fall 1967), 131-146; the information of T. O. Mabbott in *Works*, I, 556-558, 560, and his commentaries on Poe's poems "exchanged" with those of Mrs. Osgood, via his Index; and Kenneth Silverman, *Edgar A. Poe* (New York: HarperCollins, 1991), pp. 280-293.

2. See Burton R. Pollin, "Frances Sargent Osgood and *Saroni's Musical Times*: Documents Linking Poe, Osgood and Griswold," *Poe Studies*, 23 (December 1990), 27-36.

3. Edited by S. G. Goodrich for the Boston firm of Otis, Broaders and Co., this reputable annual each year engaged leading American authors and was widely reviewed in the periodical press. Poe must have known it well. There was also an American imprint of *A Wreath of Wild Flowers* soon after the London issue, which was reviewed in the *North American Review* of January 1839. Poe does not, however, seem to indicate awareness in several references to the book (see James A. Harrison, *The Complete Works of . . . Poe* [New York: Crowell, 1902]), XIII, 17, 105-125, 186-187; XV, 96-100).

4. I am citing the text of the London edition, of which the plates were also used for the American issue, according to the Bibliography of American Literature. Mrs. Osgood introduced changes into the punctuation and wording in *The Token*. The latter alterations are indicated after the slash—8: Haughty/Languid; 14: with splendour in every fold/in every graceful fold; 19: o'er/over; 24: Poor, poor/Poor, lost; 25: her cage's bar/the beaming bar; 32: Lonely/Suffering. The changes of *The Token* were not carried over into the *Poems* of 1846 and 1850.

5. Despite her great prolificity and celerity in composition Mrs. Osgood paid at-

tention to details of punctuation and wording in reprinting this poem. Nothing substantive was altered between the various book-publications, but in *The Token* (pp. 116-117) we find: 1.8, Haughty/ Languid; 1.14, with splendour in every fold/ in every graceful fold; 1.15, Bracelets of gems on her arms/ And braided gems on her arms.

6. In *Works*, I, 330-334 Mabbott discusses many possible sources for the change to another form of "Helen" but strangely omits any reference to Osgood's "Leonor." He suitably cites Poe's manuscript notes of 1848 on the margin of the *Broadway Journal*, showing the equivalents: "Helen, Ellen, Elenore, Lenore." Osgood showed her awareness of the equivalence in using "Ellen" as a pseudonym for "To the Evening Star" in the March 1845 *Columbian Magazine*, to which Poe refers in his editorial inquiry, "Is there no hope of our hearing from 'Ellen' of the *C.M.*?" in the *Broadway Journal* of March 22, p. 191.

7. The two printings of "Lenore" of 1843 were in Lowell's magazine, *The Pioneer of February* (p. 60), and in the Philadelphia *Saturday Museum* of March 4; in both, Poe, like Osgood, clearly intended Lenore's marriage to be for greater wealth and for a noble title: "Yon heir, . . . sees only, through/ Their [his eyes'] crocodile dew,/ A vacant coronet" (*Collected Works*, I, 334); in Poe's further revisions of the poem, of 1844-1850, he eliminated the "vacant coronet." It is curious that the new introduction of the name "de Vere" in the jilted lover, "Guy de Vere," is also perhaps a reflection of Tennyson's "lady Clara Vere de Vere," in which the aristocratic (and then extinct) title, implying "true," is used only for its panache. In his note on the name (p. 338, n.3) Mabbott ignores Tennyson's poem, as I did not do in my brief study "Poe's Use of the Name De Vere in 'Lenore'," *Names*, 23 (March 1975), 1-5. It is noteworthy that Mrs. Osgood introduces stanzas from Tennyson's "Lady Clara" into her narrative of "The Coquette" in the January 1843 *Graham's Magazine*, including the celebrated lines: "'Tis only noble to be good,/ Kind hearts are more than coronets." Significantly, to the section of *The Raven and Other Poems* (1845) called "Poems Written in Youth," Poe attaches a short prefatory note about these poems as antedating "the date of Tennyson's first poems" without giving any exact date at all; this raises the suspicion that some of these works did indeed derive from Tennyson's. For the full text, see Harrison, *Works*, VII, xlix.

8. See the "Marginalia" texts and commentary-notes in Pollin, *Writings of Poe*, II, 153-156, 337-344. The first item appeared in the *Democratic Review*, the second in the *Southern Literary Messenger*.

9. The volume was *National Melodies of America* (Philadelphia: H. F. Anners, c. 1840), pp. 186-187; it was reprinted with the same plates save for the title-page in 1841 by Linen and Finnell of New York, with an apparent second issue in 1850, to judge from a review in the London *People and Howitt's Journal*, 10 (1850), 102-104.

10. *Godey's Lady's Book*, March 1846, q.v. in Harrison, *Works*, XIII, 105-125, specifically, pp. 115-116.

11. For the article by Poe and for my commentary-notes, see Pollin, *Writings of Poe*, III, 328-333 and IV, 248-249. Poe's strong interest in her and her works leads him to promise to "resume this subject—to us a truly delightful one—. . . in the more ample pages of Godey's Magazine," since Poe's magazine was now nearing its termination.

12. Osgood, *Poems* (New York: Clark, Austin). The article is reprinted in Harrison,

*Works*, XV, 94-105, specifically, p. 100. Osgood stressed the inordinate length of her share in the papers very graphically when she described the unfolding of the long roll of his manuscript in her "Reminiscences of . . . Poe," published in the *Musical Times* of December 8, 1849 (q.v. in Pollin, *Poe Studies*, 23 [December 1990], 27-36, specifically pp. 31-32).

13. Arthur H. Quinn, *Poe* (New York: Appleton-Century-Crofts, 1941), p. 330, mentions her works of March and July as published by Poe's "arrangement." Concerning the choosing of contributions—Poe wrote to Lewis J. Cist, on September 18, 1841: "I merely write the Reviews, with a tale monthly, and read the last proofs" (*Letters*, I, 182), but this statement may have been a tactical excuse to an aggrieved or disappointed contributor. Surely Graham consulted him frequently, especially about contributed poems.

14. It might be worth noting that in the copy of the magazine that Poe eventually gave to Mrs. Whitman, in 1848 (now in the Huntington Library), he sidelined this stanza.

15. Note, in her "Ida Grey," in the August 1845 *Graham's Magazine* (pp. 82-84), her casual insertion of "only that and nothing more," in describing the heroine—a clear indication of the omnipresence of "The Raven" in her thoughts during 1845.

16. Since "Lenore" is invariably printed ending with the "entrancing" fourth stanza, we might wish to see the fifth stanza of the version in the tale: "Alas! for that accursed time/ They bore thee o'er the billow/ From me [or Love]—to titled age and crime,/ And an unholy pillow—/ From Love [or me], and from our misty clime/Where weeps the silver willow!" (*Works*, I, 215; II, 163). The alternatives for "me" and "Love" were Poe's own variations in different printings of the tale.

17. Osgood's association of "wild" love with and from Poe is made clear later in her "Echo-Song" of September 6, 1845, in the *Broadway Journal* (p. 129): "I know a noble heart that beats/ For one it loves how 'wildly well!'" The version of "Israfel" available before the approaching issuance in *The Raven and Other Poems*, that is, in the October 1841 *Graham's Magazine* (p. 183), furnished "wildly well" (l. 3) and singing "so well" and "so passionately" in the last stanza. See also John Reilly, pp. 139-140, who stresses rather "the lethal effects of gossip."

18. It was signed "Clarice" in the magazine. The two who have most amply and cogently presented the Poe-Osgood relationship differ about this poem. John Reilly (pp. 138-139) thinks it unlikely that Poe's poem influenced hers, "written before" she met Poe. Mary DeJong mentions "angel named Lenore" in "The Raven," the opening of "Lenore": "Ah, broken is the golden bowl" for its parallel image of shattering, and Poe's later review space devoted to it (pp. 37-38). She does not develop earlier themes used from the poems of both poets, however.

19. He finds weak only the metrics of the poem, which he called "false and inadmissible" anapaests in 1845 and "false dactyls" in September 1846. (Poe is in error; they are merely irregular iambs.)

20. This is in the "Literati" sketch of Osgood in the September 1846 issue of *Godey's*, q.v. in Harrison, *Works*, XV, 94-105, specifically p. 100.

21. For the details, see my account in *Poe Studies* of December 1990, especially n. 14 for the booklet.

22. For an excellent account of the background of the bill, including the leading political and literary figures for and against its measures, see Norma Basch, *In the Eyes of the Law: Women, Marriage and Property in Nineteenth-Century New York* (Ithaca, New York: Cornell University Press, 1982), Chapter 5, pp. 136-137, "For Good or for Evil: The 1848 Statute." Mary DeJong (p. 34) notes that the popular "lady poet" then did not "meddle with politics nor evince an unfeminine desire for fame." Even in this ambiguous comment on the bill and in her 1849 collecting of her works we may see evidence of Osgood's move toward independence, in the two years before her anticipated death.

23. I found it only through the clue presented in the *Williamsburgh Gazette* (of Brooklyn) of April 18, 1849 (vol. 13, no. 13), which printed all stanzas with an attribution to the *Tribune*. It does not seem to have received widespread reprinting.

24. Griswold, closely involved with his friend Horace Greeley, surely must have read her new poem in the *Tribune*. It may have been excluded, however, from the volume by Mrs. Osgood herself, as indecorous or too occasional.

25. See John Reilly, pp. 139-141.

26. With her puns on "property," "rents," "lease" and "pay-day" Osgood manages a bitter jest on the "chattel" status of women and on their continuing lack of claim to their own wages, if employed (a glaring fault in the 1848 bill). This is a talent for wit which was displayed in the *Letter about the Lions* and accounted for the "epigrammatic" element of which Poe often half complained. Is she here nibbling at the broad field of what we would call wife-abuse and also "harassment"? Her main point in her "Reminiscences of Poe" is to exonerate him of such "intrusions" (q.v., in *Poe Studies*, 23 [December 1990], 31-32).

# Poe and the Brownings_____

Francis B. Dedmond

In the early and mid-1840s, Edgar Allan Poe was determined to have his works published in England and was determined, moreover, to bring them to the attention of influential members of the British literary gentry who had what he called "extensive home reputation[s]" (*Works*, ed. Harrison, 11:250 [hereafter cited as *W*]), such as Charles Dickens, Robert and Elizabeth Browning, and Alfred Tennyson. Thus, in early March 1842, Poe—seizing the available opportunity and with a plan clearly formulated to achieve his desired ends—met with Dickens in the old United States Hotel in Philadelphia. In his letter requesting permission to call, Poe enclosed his playful, before-the-fact review of *Barnaby Rudge*, which had been published in the *Saturday Evening Post* for 1 May 1841. The "prospective review"—to use Poe's term—was an attempt on his part to predict the outcome of the story from only the first serialized episode of the novel as it had appeared in *Bentley's Miscellany* for 13 February 1841. However, Poe did not send Dickens a copy, as he could well have done, of his lengthy, but uncomplimentary review of the completed *Barnaby Rudge* from the February 1842 issue of *Graham's Lady's and Gentleman's Magazine*—a review containing a frontal assault on "the present absurd fashion of periodical novel-writing" (*W* 11:54). Rather, armed with the two-volume edition of his *Tales of the Grotesque and Arabesque* (1840), Poe came to his meeting with Dickens and extracted from him a promise that he would try to interest a London publisher in a volume of his tales.[1]

But when Dickens failed in the "mission" Poe had charged him with,[2] Poe—in what was and would continue to be, for some time, his characteristic *modus operandi* in such matters—carefully set the stage for his on-going, undaunted venture by writing yet another review—as he had done in the case of Dickens—that could be used as a Poesque means of introduction and that should provide, if it accomplished its purpose, the occasion for asking yet another favor of yet another British author. Thus, in the March 1844 number of *Graham's*, Poe published a review of the fourth edition of Richard Hengist Horne's epic allegory, *Orion*—a review from which Poe later lifted the chief arguments of his "The Poetic Principle." To borrow a phrase used later by Elizabeth Barrett, the review of *Orion* demonstrated Poe's characteristic pattern of folding in on one another "the two extremes of laudation and reprehension" (*Let RB and EBB* 1:307). On the one hand, Poe was extravagant in his praise of the poem, declaring that "'Orion' will be admitted by every man of genius, to be one of the noblest, if not the very noblest poetical work of the age. Its defects are trivial and conventional—its beauties intrinsic and *supreme*" (*W* 11:275). On the other hand, Poe accused Horne of being infected by a "junto of dreamers" who caused him to attempt to commingle "the obstinate oils and waters of Poetry and Truth" (*W* 11:254) rather than to listen to the dictates of his own soul and thereby write a poem "*solely for the poem's sake*" (*W* 11:258). Nevertheless, Poe wrote, "in all that regards the loftiest and holiest attributes of true Poetry 'Orion' has *never* been excelled. Indeed we feel strongly inclined to say that it has never been *equaled*. Its imagination—that quality which is all in all—is of the most refined—the most elevating—the most august character" (*W* 11:266).

On 15 March, with the review in hand, Poe wrote Cornelius Mathews, a friend of Horne, asking for Horne's address and mentioning that he had "a letter and small parcel" for Horne (1:245). The parcel contained a manuscript of Poe's tale "The Spectacles,"[3] but *not* his review of *Orion*. Again Poe chose—by design—to hold back his mixed review of "laudation and reprehension" until after he had made his initial contact. But in the letter, now lost, Poe may well have mentioned the review and may have repeated selectively in the letter, again consistent with his manner and pattern, something of what he had written in the review—that he was, for instance, an early and earnest admirer of Horne's work, especially of *Orion* (*W* 11:250)—for Horne, in his reply on 16 April, thanked Poe "for the noble and generous terms in which you speak of my works": but as to Poe's request that he seek to place "The Spectacles" in a British journal, Horne pointed out that he was not in critical favor at the time and could likely be of little assistance to Poe. But he would try, nonetheless, to place "The Spectacles" where Poe would be "fairly remunerated."[4]

However, before receiving Horne's letter of 16 April, Poe—following up what he no doubt hoped had been a "successful" introduction—forwarded then to Horne a copy of his review of *Orion*. In his reply of 27 April, Horne informed Poe that Cornelius Mathews had told him of the forthcoming review well before its appearance in *Graham's*. "My friend Miss E. B. Barrett," Horne wrote, also had sent him a note about the publication of the review of *Orion* (*W* 17:168).

But that Miss Barrett was a friend of Horne came as no surprise to Poe. He knew well before their exchange of letters began that Elizabeth Barrett had been—along with Horne, Wordsworth, Leigh Hunt, and others—"a contributor . . . to 'Chaucer Modernized'" (*W* 11:250), a work edited by Horne.[5] And, it should be noted, moreover, that at the very time Poe was preparing to send his parcel to Horne, he was awaiting the first American publication of "The Spectacles," which would appear, in a matter of days, in the 27 March issue of the *Dollar Newspaper*. What Poe was asking then of Horne—the placing of only a single tale that no doubt would have already been published before Poe's parcel reached London—was a far cry from what he had asked of Dickens. Did Poe then have another purpose in mind, other than what might appear on the surface, for "singling out Horne?"[6] Was Poe planning, all the while, to "use" Horne as an intermediary, but expedient means of bringing his works to Miss Barrett's notice, something that to Poe was doubtless, at the time, of far greater importance than the publication of a lone tale that had already appeared in print? Indeed, such seems to have been the case; but it took Horne some little time to realize the method in Poe's madness.

No doubt Poe knew—even with the unwitting Horne as his go-between—the method he would use to bring himself and his works to

Miss Barrett's attention. It had worked with Dickens; it had worked also with Horne. First of all, there must be the review with its "two extremes of laudation and reprehension." The review would then be sent with or would follow shortly after the posting of a personal introductory letter that would contain a milder critique of the work in question than was the case with the published review—a technique apparently designed to soften the impact of the "reprehensible" aspects of the review. With the letter, Poe would also send a manuscript or a published piece of his work. Thus, as the first step in his patterned approach, Poe published his "Personal Notices of Elizabeth Barrett" in the *New York Weekly Mirror* for 7 December and followed it on 4 January and 11 January 1845 with his two-part review, in the nascent *Broadway Journal*, of Miss Barrett's *The Drama of Exile and Other Poems*.

Poe opened the first installment of the review on 4 January by complaining that American critics had heaped nothing but praise on Miss Barrett's little volume of poems. While his review would contain, Poe made clear in the beginning, his usual mixture of praise and blame, he sought to soften the strictures that would follow by asserting that nonetheless "the fair author" would likely find no one with a "more enthusiastic reverence and admiration of her genius, than the author of these words" (*W* 12:2-3). Even so, Poe declared the plot of "The Drama of Exile" to be worse than incongruous and with "a continuous mystical strain of ill-fitting and exaggerated allegory—if, indeed, allegory is not much too respectable a term for it" (*W* 12:8). And even the best one of the twenty-eight sonnets that followed "The Drama of Exile" was flawed by "its extreme artificiality," Poe stated. In fact, Poe concluded that Miss Barrett lacked "a well-controlled dexterity of touch" that sonnet writing required (*W* 12:14). Poe, however, praised her poem "The Cry of the Children" for its "horror sublime" (*W* 12:16) and declared that he had never read "a poem with so much of the ethereal fancy, as the 'Lady Geraldine's Courtship,' of Miss Barrett," with the exception of Tennyson's "Locksley Hall." Indeed, Poe said, "Lady Geraldine's Courtship" is "a very palpable imitation" of "Locksley

Hall" (*W* 12:16); yet "Lady Geraldine's Courtship" is "the only poem of its author which is not deficient, considered as an artistic whole" (*W* 12:19). Poe complained also of Miss Barrett's many affectations, of her far-fetched imagery, and of her inattention to rhythm.

But six-sevenths of the way into the review, Poe called for "an end of our faultfinding" and declared that thereafter he would "speak, equally in detail of the *beauties* of this book" (*W* 12:29). But he had already said too much of a pejorative nature about the book to make adequate amends. Thus, he sought to gloss over his remarks by heaping praise, though often qualified, on the poetess. "That Miss Barrett has done more in poetry, than any woman, living or dead, will scarcely be questioned:—that she has surpassed all her poetical contemporaries of either sex (with a single exception)[7] is our deliberate opinion" (*W* 12:32), Poe stated. Then he added: "Her poetic inspiration is the highest—we can conceive nothing more august. Her sense of Art is pure in itself, but has been contaminated by pedantic study of false models" (*W* 12:34). In his conclusion, Poe sought to excuse—not very gallantly, to be sure—her poetic weaknesses on the basis of her ill health which, he baldly stated, had "invalidated her original Will—diverted her from proper individuality of purpose—and seduced her into the sin of imitation" of Tennyson (*W* 12:35).

Although the review was not a *fait accompli*, Poe would still have to wait another two weeks until he could secure advanced sheets of "The Raven" from *The American Review* for February 1845 before he would be ready, according to plan, to write Horne again.[8] However, Poe's letter of 25 January, now lost, was not received by Horne until late April upon his return from an extended visit to Germany. But from Horne's reply to Poe from London on 17 May, it is clear that Poe had sent Horne his review of Miss Barrett's *The Drama of Exile* along with a personal letter to Horne, which consisted largely of a toned-down critique of Miss Barrett's book of verse. Since, as Horne put it, "your letter to me contained more of the bright side of criticism than the 'Broadway Journal'" (*W* 17:208), Horne—inadvertently aiding and abetting Poe in perfecting his strategy—decided to send *only* the letter and "The Raven" to Elizabeth. Within the space of a few days, she returned the letter, as Horne would inform Poe, "with a note, half of which I tear off, and send you (*confidentially*) that you may see in what a good and noble spirit she receives the critique—in which, as you say, the shadows do certainly predominate" (*W* 17:208-209). Miss Barrett, Horne reported, had read "The Raven" and found in it "a fine lyrical melody" (*W* 17:209).

It should be pointed out, however, that Horne's reply on 17 May was not written until after he had received two other letters from Elizabeth and not until she had received from Horne or from someone else the *Broadway Journal* review. On 12 May she had written Horne from 50 Wimpole Street:

> Your friend, Mr. Poe, is a speaker of strong words "in both kinds." But I hope you will assure him from me that I am grateful for his reviews, and in no complaining humour at all. As to the "Raven" tell me what you shall say about it! There is certainly a power—but it does not appear to me the natural expression of a sane Intellect in whatever mood. . . . There is a fantasticalness about the "sir or madam," and things of that sort, which is ludicrous, unless there is a specified insanity to justify the straws. Probably he—the author—intended it to be read in the poem, and he ought to have intended it. The rhythm acts excellently upon the imagination, and the "nevermore" has a solemn chime with it. . . . And I am of opinion that there is an uncommon force and effect in the poem. (*W* 17:385-386)

But immediately upon sending this letter to Horne, Miss Barrett had evidently been smitten with qualms of conscience; and on the same day—12 May—she followed it with a second letter to him:

> You will certainly think me mad, dear Mr. Horne, for treading upon my own heels . . . in another letter. But I am uncomfortable about my message to Mr. Poe, lest it should not be grateful enough in the sound of it. Will you

tell him what is quite the truth,—that, in my opinion, he has dealt with me most generously. . . . Also, the review is very ably written,—and the reviewer has so obviously and thoroughly *read* my poems, as to be a wonder among critics. Will you tell Mr. Poe this . . . or to this effect, dear Mr. Horne—all but part of the last sentence. . . . (*W* 17:387)

Horne, in his letter to Poe, did as Elizabeth had directed and added that he too was "of the same opinion as Miss Barrett about the 'Raven'; and it also seems to me," he continued, "that the poet intends to represent a very painful condition of mind, as of an imagination that was liable to topple over into some delirium or an abyss of melancholy, from continuity of one unvaried emotion" (*W* 17:209).

But before closing his 17 May letter, Horne could not refrain from expressing his surprise that Poe in his 25 January letter had indicated an interest in cultivating, obviously with Horne's help, something of the same kind of relationship with Tennyson that, through Horne's good offices, was now budding with Elizabeth Barrett. "It is curious that you should ask for opinions of the two poets with whom I am especially Intimate," Horne wrote. "Most of the others I am acquainted with, but am not upon such terms of intellectual sympathy and friendship as with Miss Barrett and Tennyson" (*W* 17:209). Undoubtedly, at last, Horne began to see what Poe was about, and he obviously determined that he would not be used in the same manner a second time. Thus, at this point, Horne evidently withdrew as go-between, leaving Poe to pursue his designs as best he could. But Victorian social amenities had been taken care of; Poe and Elizabeth Barrett were now sufficiently "acquainted" so that they could write each other directly. Therefore, Poe had little or no need of Horne anymore as he went about his plans for his big play.

Thus on 19 November 1845, Poe's little volume *The Raven and Other Poems* was published in New York and was dedicated "To the noblest of her sex—Elizabeth Barrett Barrett." Exactly how Elizabeth found out about the dedication is not known, and she apparently did not know how to take or what to make of what someone had apparently told her; for in a letter to Robert Browning, 1 December 1845, she wrote:

And think of Mr. Poe, with that great Roman justice of his (if not rather American!), dedicating a book to one and abusing one in the preface to the same. He wrote a review of me in just that spirit—the two extremes of laudation and reprehension, folded in on one another. You would have thought it had been written by a friend and foe, each stark mad with love and hate, and writing the alternate passages—a most curious production indeed. (1:307)

It was not, however, until 9 January 1846 that Elizabeth actually received from someone a copy of the book. On that day she wrote Robert Browning that she had "just received Mr. Poe's book—and I see that the deteriorating preface which was to have saved me from vanity-fever produceable by the dedication, is cut down and away—perhaps in this particular copy only!" (1:384).[9] Browning on 15 January, in reply to her letter, requested that she "let Mr. Poe's book lie on the table on Monday . . . that I may read what he does say, with my own eyes" (1:400).

For some reason, Browning did not see "Mr. Poe's book" on Monday; and Elizabeth decided to send the volume on to him. In her letter of 26 January that accompanied the little book, she assured Browning that she did not know Poe, had never heard from him directly, and had never written to him, although, she said, people had plied her with Poe's works, especially with copies of "The Raven" from no fewer than "*four* different quarters . . . when it had only a newspaper life." She was sending him the volume of poems; but she was, she told Robert, much more excited about "a most frightful extract from an American magazine sent me yesterday . . . no, the day before . . . on the subject of mesmerism—and you are to understand, if you please, that the Mr. Edgar Poe who stands committed in it, is my dedicator."[10] She wanted Robert to decide "whether the outrageous compliment to E.B.B." or "The Facts of M. Valdemar's Case" "goes furthest to prove him mad . . . —and in my opinion," she continued, "there is more faculty shown in the account of that horrible mesmeric experience (mad or not mad) than in his poems. Now do read it from the beginning to the end," she admonished. "That 'going out' of the hectic, struck me very much . . . and the writing *away* of the upper lip. Most horrible!—Then I believe so much of mesmerism," she confessed, "as to give room for the full acting of the story on me . . . without absolutely giving full credence to it, understand" (1:428).

Then in February 1846, Wiley and Putnam published as a compound volume Poe's *The Raven and Other Poems* and his *Tales* (first published in June 1845). And Poe himself would shortly send Miss Barrett a copy. But before it arrived, she wrote Robert on 7 March that her friend John Kenyon—"in an immoderate joy . . . about Mr. Poe's 'Raven' as seen in the *Athenaeum* extracts"—[11] had dropped by "to ask what I knew of the poet and his poetry" and had taken away with him her copy of *The Raven and Other Poems* (1:537). When her copy of *The Raven and Other Poems and Tales* from Poe finally did arrive on 20 March, Elizabeth immediately wrote Kenyon: "Today Mr. Poe sent me a volume containing his poems and tales collected, so now I must write and thank him for his dedication. What is to be said, I wonder, when a man calls you the 'noblest of your sex'? 'Sir you are the most discerning of yours'" (*Let EBB*, ed. Kenyon 1:249).[12]

Within a few weeks, Miss Barrett—no longer able to communicate with him through Horne but freed now from Victorian strictures against corresponding with strangers—wrote her first letter to Poe. The dedication, she said, was "too great a distinction, conferred by a hand of too liberal generosity." She assured Poe that "The Raven" had "produced a sensation, a 'fit horror,' here in England. Some of my friends are taken by the fear of it and some by the music," she wrote. "I hear of persons haunted by the 'Nevermore,' and one acquaintance of mine who has the misfortune of possessing a 'bust of Pallas' never can bear to look at it in the twilight." And Miss Barrett was also sure that Poe would like to know that "our great poet, Mr. Browning, the author of 'Paracelsus,' and 'Bells and Pomegranates,' was struck much by the rhythm of that poem." Although, as Elizabeth pointed out, "The Facts in the Case of M. Valdemar" was missing from the volume Poe had sent her,[13] she nonetheless could not resist the urge to inform Poe that his tale of mesmerism was "throwing us all into 'most admired disorder,' and dreadful doubts as to whether 'it can be true,' as the children say of ghost stories. The certain thing in the tale in question is the power of the writer, and the faculty he has of making horrible improbabilities seem near and familiar" (*W* 17:229).

Poe could not keep Miss Barrett's effulgent praise to himself. He spread the work abroad.[14] And, as a consequence, Miss Barrett received within weeks the first of several letters from Americans who came to know or fancied they knew of her interest in Poe. On 7 May 1846, she received a letter and a book—probably *The Poetry of Flowers and the Flowers of Poetry* (1841)—from Mrs. Frances Sargent Osgood, whom Poe first met in March 1845 and with whom he had carried on a literary flirtation and courtship in the *Broadway Journal* later that year. On the day Elizabeth received the book, she wrote Browning: "Today I had a book sent to me from America by the poetess Mrs. Osgood. Did you ever hear of a poetess Mrs. Osgood? . . . and her note was of the very most affectionate, and her book is of the most gorgeous, all purple and gold—she tells me . . . ah, she tells me . . . that I ought to go to New York, only 'to see Mr. Poe's wild eyes flash through tears when he reads my verses.' It is overcoming to think of, even . . . isn't it?" (2:133).

Elizabeth and Robert Browning eloped, were married on 19 September 1846, and fled to Italy. But even in their sanctuary there, they were not beyond the reach of well-meaning Americans who came bearing as their entrée memories or mementos of Poe from earlier days. In early October 1854, John Reuben Thompson, under whom Poe had worked on the *Southern Literary Messenger* twenty years before, sought out the Brownings with a letter of introduction from Owen Meredith:

> My dear Browning[.]
>
> Will you allow me to introduce to you a very intimate friend of Edgar Poe, and also an old friend of mine. Mr. Thompson of Virginia for whom Poor Poe wrote his last Poem of Annabel Lee? He will tell you much about that love Pleiad.
>
> Ever fondly yr<br>R. Lytton (95-96)[15]

"I sent you an American," Meredith again wrote the Brownings in late 1854, "who came back to me and said you had been kind to him. So let me tell you how I thank you, for he was kind to me in the U.S. . . . and thinking too, his acquaintance with Poor Edgar Poe might make him interesting to you, I yielded to his request" (99).

Two years later, Thompson, according to John H. Ingram in his biographical sketch of Poe in *Edgar Allan Poe: A Memorial Volume* (1877), wrote James Wood Davidson that he had had "a long conversation in Florence with Mr. Robert and Elizabeth Barrett Browning, concerning Poe. The two poets, like yourself, had formed an ardent and just admiration of the author of 'The Raven' and feel a strong desire to see his memory vindicated from moral aspersion" (34).[16]

Then in 1860, Mary Katherine Field—daughter of Joseph J. Field, an American actor and later editor of the St. Louis *Reveille*, in which he editorially defended Poe during the so-called "War of the Literati"—[17] was studying music in Florence. Kate, as she was familiarly known, proudly treasured the letter Poe had written her father on 15 June 1846, in which Poe had copied—with some embellishments—the choice statements from Elizabeth's April 1846 letter to Poe from 5 Wimpole Street.[18] When Miss Field called on the Brownings, she, of course, brought with her the letter; and when she reviewed Mrs. Browning's *Essays on the Greek Christian Poets and English Poets* (1863) in the

July 1863 issue of the *Christian Examiner*, she could not refrain from reminiscing about "that day at Casa Guidi, when we carried to the Brownings a letter of Edgar Poe's addressed to a friend, in which Poe had copied for his reading the warm praise that 'the world's greatest poetess, Elizabeth Barrett,' had awarded him. 'Did Poe write this of me?' exclaimed Mrs. Browning, looking up with glistening but unbelieving eyes; 'he was kind.'" When Mrs. Browning had finished reading what Poe had copied of her remarks about "The Raven"—about its having produced a "fit horror" in England, about persons being haunted by the "Nevermore" and about Robert Browning's enthusiastic admiration of its rhythm—Kate quoted Mrs. Browning as saying, "I am so glad I wrote that." Robert Browning too expressed his pleasure at seeing the letter. "It was a noble sight to us," Kate noted, "this mutual homage, and we rejoice that the curious accident of the letter should have made us witness to it" (40-41).

But Robert Browning was far from pleased in 1876 when John H. Ingram began to bombard him with queries about Poe and Mrs. Browning. Browning was piqued at Ingram because Ingram had discovered that the gap between the ages of Elizabeth the elder and Robert the younger had been much greater than they had led the world to believe, and Robert was therefore inclined to be uncooperative with the meddlesome Ingram. For instance, on 10 February 1876, he curtly wrote Ingram: "I have never heard anything whatever from my wife on the subject of Poe, or her contributions (if any there were) to his magazine" (*Let RB Collected TJW* 169). Browning must have been bothered somewhat by the tone and substance of his 10 February letter, for the next day he wrote Ingram again, admitting that, "as to our great admiration for Poe's power, that anybody who cared to question my wife or myself on the subject would be certain to hear" (170). But on the question of Poe's debt in "The Raven" to Elizabeth's "Lady Geraldine's Courtship," Browning was almost vehement in his denial of *any* debt. Ingram had apparently reminded Browning of what the novelist Buchanan Read was purported to have told Browning—that Poe himself had described to him "the whole process of the construction of his poem, and declared that the suggestion of it lay wholly in a line from 'Lady Geraldine's Courtship'" (*EAP: His Life, Letters, and Opinions* 1:276). Browning responded to Ingram's suggestion: "The notion that 'The Raven' was derived from 'Lady Geraldine's Courtship' is truly absurd and I consider the statement of Poe himself, that he had really so derived any particle of it (except perhaps the measure, which belongs to whoever can manage it) as equally absurd" (*Let RB Collected TJW* 170).[19]

There is no evidence that any of Poe's works were published in England because of any contact he had with any of his contemporaries among the English poets. But no doubt he succeeded, far beyond his expectations, in bringing his poetry and prose to the abiding attention of the Brownings.

## Notes

1. Probably the best account of the Dickens-Poe meeting is in Allen, 423-424.

2. On 27 November 1842, Dickens wrote Poe: "I am, however, unable to report any success. I have mentioned it to publishers with whom I have influence, but they have, one and all, declined the venture" (*W* 17:125).

3. For a detailed account of the fate of the manuscript of "The Spectacles" that Poe sent Horne and the publishing history of the tale at home and abroad, see "Poe's 'The Spectacles,'" ed. Moldenhauer, 179-234.

4. Horne's holograph letter of 16 April 1844 is in the Boston Public Library. It is partially published in "Poe's 'The Spectacles,'" ed. Moldenhauer, 184.

5. The work published in 1841 was entitled *The Poems of Geoffrey Chaucer Modernized* (London: Whittaker & Co., 1841). Edited by Horne, the book contained "modernizations" by Robert Bell, Elizabeth Barrett, Leigh Hunt, Thomas Powell, William Wordsworth, Z.A.Z., and Horne himself. An unpublished letter from Elizabeth Barrett to Horne, 19 February 1841, concerning the "modernizations," is in the University of Iowa Library.

6. Over thirty years later, Horne wrote: "During a certain period of Poe's troubled circumstances, he wrote to me, I being in London, and inclosed a manuscript saying

that he had *singled me out, though personally a stranger,* to ask a friendly service of handling a certain story to the editor of one of the magazines" (*EAP: A Mem. Vol*, 82; italics added).

7. The exception is Tennyson.

8. Thomas Ollive Mabbott points out that "'The Raven' . . . was printed off before the issue [of the *American Review* for February 1845) was completed" (1:143-145).

9. The volume here referred to as "Mr. Poe's book" was not sent to Miss Barrett by Poe. Miss Barrett was misinformed about there having been a "deteriorating preface."

10. "The Facts of M. Valdemar's Case" was first published in *The American Review: A Whig Journal* 2 (December 1845): 561-565 and was reprinted on 5 January 1846 in the London *Morning Post*. Whether Miss Barrett's "frightful extract" was from *The American Review* or the *Morning Post* is not clear. She may have been referring to the reprinted tale since it was copied, so the "extract" said, from "an American magazine." Poe changed the name of the tale to "The Facts in the Case of M. Valdemar" when he reprinted the tale in the 20 December 1845 issue of the *Broadway Journal*.

11. *The Athenaeum* on 28 February 1846 published "The Raven" in its entirety. The introductory and concluding comments were scurrilously abusive. The critic said, "It is Mr. Poe's fancy to be original. . . . The instinct of borrowing must be unconquerable amongst a people who borrow even their *originality*" (215).

12. Frederic Kenyon had this letter incorrectly dated "about Jan.-Mar. 1845" (1:249). It should have been dated a year later. (See Varner, 244.) The date Elizabeth received the book can be dated specifically from a letter Elizabeth wrote Robert Browning on 20 March 1846: "Mr. Poe has sent me his poems and tales—so now I must write to thank him for his dedication. Just now I have the book" (1:565).

13. The reason "The Facts in the Case of M. Valdemar" did not appear in this volume was that this composite volume was made up from sheets of earlier printings which did not contain the tale.

14. Poe no doubt showed the letter around among his friends. He also lifted portions of it and included them in letters to Joseph M. Field (15 June 1846) and Philip P. Cooke (9 August 1846). (See *Letters* 2: 318-320 and 2: 327-330.)

15. Owen Meredith was the pseudonym of Robert Bulwer, first Earl of Lytton.

16. It is interesting that when Ingram was checking his "facts" a year earlier—11 February 1876—Browning wrote him that he did not remember "the Mr. Thompson you quote from, but am quite sure that 'strong desire to see Poet's memory vindicated from moral aspersion' must have been simply an echo of a desire of his own" (*Let RB Collected TJW* 170). Ingram, however, no doubt convinced that Browning was just being difficult, stuck with the Brownings' reported statement.

17. See Sidney P. Moss, *Poe's Major Crisis: His Libel Suit and New York's Literary World* (Durham: Duke University Press, 1970). Field's article on Poe from the *Reveille* appears on pp. 21-24.

18. The letter is published in *Letters* 2: 318-320 and partially published in Whiting, 21-23.

19. T. O. Mabbott says, however, that "unquestionably the cardinal source of the final stanzaic form of Poe's poem was Elizabeth Barrett's 'Lady Geraldine's Courtship'" (1:356).

# Works Cited

Allen, Hervey. *Israfel: The Life and Times of Edgar Allan Poe*. New York: Rinehart & Co., 1949.

Browning, Elizabeth Barrett. *Letters of Elizabeth Barrett Browning*. Ed. Frederick G. Kenyon. 2 volumes. New York: The Macmillan Co., 1897.

_____. *Letters of Elizabeth Barrett Browning Addressed to Richard Hengist Horne*. 2 volumes. Ed. S. R. Townshend Mayer. London: Richard Bentley and Son, 1877.

Browning, Robert. *Letters of Robert Browning Collected by Thomas J. Wise*. Ed. Thurman L. Hood. London: John Murray, 1933.

Browning, Robert, and Elizabeth Barrett. *Letters of Robert Browning and Elizabeth Barrett Browning, 1845-1846*. 2 volumes. New York: Harper, 1898.

[Field, Kate]. "Mrs. Browning's Essay on the Poets." *The Christian Examiner*, 75 (July 1863): 40-41.

Ingram, J. H. "Edgar Allan Poe: A Biographical Sketch." *Edgar Allan Poe: A Memorial Volume*. Ed. Sara S. Rice. Baltimore: Turnbull Brothers, 1877.

_____. *Edgar Allan Poe: His Life, Letters, and Opinions*. 2 volumes. London: John Hogg, 1880.

Meredith, Owen. *Letters from Owen Meredith to Robert and Elizabeth Barrett Browning*. Ed. A. B. Harland and J. L. Harland, Jr. Waco: Baylor University Press, 1936.

Poe, Edgar Allan. *Collected Works of Edgar Allan Poe*. Ed. Thomas Ollive Mabbott. 3 volumes. Cambridge: Harvard University Press, 1969.

_____. *Complete Works of Edgar Allan Poe*. Ed. James A. Harrison. Virginia Edition. 17 volumes. New York: Thomas Y. Crowell, 1902.

_____. *Letters of Edgar Allan Poe*. Ed. J. W. Ostrom. 2 volumes. Cambridge: Harvard University Press, 1948.

_____. "Poe's 'The Spectacles': A New Text from Manuscript." Ed. Joseph J. Moldenhauer. *Studies in the American Renaissance, 1977*. Ed. Jose Myerson. Boston: Twayne Publishers, 1978.

Review of *The Raven and Other Poems*, by Edgar Allan Poe. *The Athenaeum* no. 957 (28 February 1846): 215-216.

Rice, Sara S., ed. *Edgar Allan Poe: A Memorial Volume*. Baltimore: Turnbull Brothers, 1877.

Varner, J. G. "Poe and Miss Barrett." *The Times* (London) *Literary Supplement*, 11 April 1935: 244.

Whiting, Lilian. *Kate Field: A Record*. Boston: Little, Brown and Co., 1899.

# Poe's Composition of Philosophy:
## Reading and Writing "The Raven" _____

Leland S. Person, Jr.

For most readers "The Philosophy of Composition" is less important as an account of how Poe actually wrote "The Raven" than as a
statement of his general poetic theories. Kenneth Burke, for example,
carefully distinguishes between Poe as the author of "The Raven" and
Poe as critic of the poem, in order to argue that the essay represents a
significant "guide for critics"—indeed, "the ideal form for an 'archi-
tectonic' critic to aim at."[1] Although Burke does not go as far as Edward H. Davidson, who maintains that to appreciate the essay "one
need not know the poem at all," like many other critics, he does separate the essay from the poem.[2] Since few critics consider the essay in a
context that includes "The Raven," the unfortunate result is that Poe's
"Philosophy" is commonly disjoined from the "composition" that
forms its pretext.

In this essay I should like to rejoin Poe's philosophy and his composition by examining the intriguing relationship between the essay and
the poem. As early as 1850 George Washington Peck suggested that in
"The Philosophy of Composition" Poe "carried his analysis to such an
absurd minuteness, that it is a little surprising that there should be any
[one] verdant enough not to perceive that he was 'chaffing.'" Peck
even compared the essay to Poe's "harmless hoaxes," at the end of
which the author "cries 'sold!' in our faces."[3] Much like "The Purloined Letter," which Poe published just prior to "The Raven," and
which has been exhaustively analyzed for its intricate doublings of
texts and authors, I think "The Philosophy of Composition" can be regarded, although in a different sense than Daniel Hoffman has suggested, as a "put-on": ostensibly a critical essay that becomes another
version of the work it purports to critique.[4] By conflating the processes
of reading and writing so that reading becomes rewriting, Poe subverts
the very sort of scientific or mathematical certainty that he seems to be

praising and illustrating in his essay. Put another way, he deconstructs not only his own "philosophy of composition," but philosophy itself—making philosophy essentially synonymous with composition.[5] Furthermore, the deconstruction to which Poe subjects "The Raven" in "The Philosophy of Composition" can also be observed in the poem itself. Reading the raven, no less than reading "The Raven," means writing, or composing, a philosophy.

I

The "philosophy of composition" that Poe describes in his essay depends upon a perfect, logical relationship between authorial intention and what he calls "effect." The intention to produce an effect is always matched immediately, he would have us believe, by the perfect word. In explaining his famous organic theory of poetry (as a "metre-making argument"), Ralph Waldo Emerson had written in "The Poet" that "the thought and the form are equal in the order of time, but in the order of genesis the thought is prior to the form."[6] Emerson was trying to resolve a paradox, of course. Thoughts must exist in some form in order to be thoughts at all; a thought without a form would not be a thought. Yet Emerson wishes to distinguish hierarchically between thoughts according to the propriety of their forms. To do this he posits a gap in the order of genesis between thought and form and so raises the possibility of alternative forms, as well as the possibility of better or worse, more natural or less natural, forms. But in Poe's philosophy of composition, the effect or form of a thought must somehow precede the thought itself. "Nothing is more clear," he claims, "than that every plot, worth the name, must be elaborated to its *denouement* before anything be attempted with the pen. It is only with the *denouement* constantly in view that we can give a plot its indispensable air of consequence, or causation, by making the incidents, and especially the tone at all points, tend to the development of the intention."[7]

The denouement, or effect, must be in view before the intention to produce it and the plot that precedes it can be developed; the effect, as it were, produces the intention. Poe's claims are both tautological and ironic: tautological because he claims that every plot must be imagined, or written, before it can be written; ironic because, as he notes, "consequence, or causation," is only an "air," or illusion. In considering the essay a "put-on," Daniel Hoffman says that "as critics, as analysts of literature, even, sometimes, as poets, we find it *a convenient fiction* to assume that this is indeed the way that poems are made."[8] In fact, in writing such an elaborate, step-by-step anatomy of his own compositional process, Poe parodies the critical or analytical process. It is not poems that are "composed" through the process Poe describes, after all, but critiques of poems—in other words, readings, rather than writings, of poems. Retrospectively discovering his intentions by deducing them from their effects—that is, from the words already elaborated to their denouement—"The Philosophy of Composition," not "The Raven," is Poe's true example of what he calls writing "backwards" (193).

Poe says in the essay that "The Raven" "may be said to have its beginning—at the end, where all works of art should begin" (202). But it is more likely that "The Philosophy of Composition" alone truly began at the end—at the end of the poem—ostensibly describing the beginnings of a process that is already over. Prescribing the parameters of the poem, as Poe does in the essay, really means describing rather than reconstructing the poem already written. Given that fact, he can claim without fear of contradiction that his "plot" possesses an "indispensable air of consequence, or causation." He can also fulfill his intention "to render it manifest that no one point in [the poem's] composition is referable either to accident or intuition—that the work proceeded, step by step, to its completion with the precision and rigid consequence of a mathematical problem" (195).[9] The essay cannot be wrong about the "points" in the poem's composition or about the poet's intentions simply because the poem's "effects" are already known. They precede the intentions that Poe "reconstructs." The result, as a matter of course, is an "indispensable air of consequence, or causation," if not causation it-self.

If we take Poe at his word, however, his intentions in "The Philoso-phy of Composition" include debunking the common Romantic notion that poems are composed "by a species of fine frenzy—an ecstatic in-tuition" (194)—and substituting a logical, mathematically precise model of the creative process. Interestingly, those intentions are at odds with the philosophy of Auguste Dupin in "The Purloined Letter," for Dupin is intent upon revealing the limitations of mathematical rea-son and upon illustrating the virtues of a synthetic reason—that is, a reason that combines mathematical logic and poetic intuition.

As another of Poe's readers, however, Dupin can shed some light on "The Philosophy of Composition," for his philosophy of reading re-sembles the philosophy of composition that Poe describes. Unlike the Prefect of Police, who is only a mathematician, Dupin is both a mathe-matician and a poet, and, like the schoolboy in his "even and odd" guessing game (and like Poe in "The Philosophy of Composition") he can identify perfectly with his adversary, the Minister D—. As the schoolboy explains,

'When I wish to find out how wise, or how stupid, or how good, or how wicked is any one, or what are his thoughts at the moment, I fashion the expression of my face, as accurately as possible, in accordance with the expression of his, and then wait and see what thoughts or sentiments arise in my mind or heart, as if to match or correspond with the expres-sion.'[10]

With only a slight shift in context, the boy's remarks compose a phi-losophy of perfect reader response—the closing, or "defacing," of the gap between expression and interpretation, writing and reading, and thus the elimination of indeterminate or multiple meanings in a text. In other words, the detective-reader can understand the writer's inten-tions by becoming the writer, by making his expression coincide with the writer's. He can read the text by rewriting, or re-expressing, it. Writing and reading are the same because they inscribe the same words, the same expression. Poe's explanation in "The Purloined Letter," furthermore, resembles the one he gives in "The Philosophy of Composition": like Dupin and the schoolboy, he studies the "effect" in order to understand the "intention" that produced it. To put it precisely, the writer (the boy's opponent) begins with an intention (to say either even or odd) and then produces an effect or expression (the intended even or odd); the reader (the boy) matches that expression (in effect, by writing it on or in himself) and then beholds the original thought or sentiment arise in his own mind or heart. And so in "The Philosophy of Composition": as writer, Poe produces "The Raven"; as reader of the poem—that is, as the detective who would discover his own original intentions—he writes the essay, beginning with the "effect" or expression (the poem itself as already elaborated to its denouement), and so discovers the thoughts and sentiments that arose in his own heart and mind as he produced the poem. Through this process of reconstruction, the readerly and writerly become one and the same.

Given those alleged intentions and Poe's alleged "philosophy" of composition, it is ironic that the actual process of composition which he goes on to describe should be so illogical and intuitive. Again and again in the essay, Poe describes himself making decisions instantaneously, as if in a flash of inspiration—in other words, as if in a moment of "fine frenzy." Contemplating the ideal length for a poem, he says that he "reached at once" the proper length of 100 lines (197). Seeking what he calls "some pivot upon which the whole structure might turn," he perceived "immediately that no one had been so universally employed as that of the *refrain*." Trying to decide on the proper refrain, he was led "at once" to the use of a single word (199). And searching for the perfect "*character* of the word" to embody the sonorous mood he wanted (199), he says that "it would have been absolutely impossible to overlook the word 'Nevermore.' In fact, it was the very first which presented itself" (200). The "next *desideratum*" being the "pretext for the continuous use of the one word 'never-more'," Poe claims that the idea of a "*non*-reasoning creature capable of speech" arose in his mind "immediately" (200). Introducing the bird through the window was "inevitable," he maintains (204); the bust of Pallas, furthermore, was "absolutely *suggested* by the bird" (205). Again and again, in other words, Poe belies his own scientific method. Like lightning arcing between earth and sky, the words of the poem "arc" between effect and intention—so immediately that it is impossible to tell in which direction they actually move. No wonder that "The Philosophy of Composition" possesses an "indispensable air of consequence, or causation."

Having laid out in meticulous detail the ratiocinative process by which he composed "The Raven," Poe undermines everything he has said at the end of the essay. He admits that "in subjects so handled, however skilfully, or with however vivid an array of incident, there is always a certain hardness or nakedness, which repels the artistical eye. Two things are invariably required—first, some amount of complexity, or more properly, adaptation; and, secondly, some amount of suggestiveness—some under-current, however indefinite, of meaning" (207). In other words, in the final analysis poems such as "The Raven" resist precisely the sort of scientific reconstruction that Poe has just performed.

Having demystified the compositional process, Poe proceeds to remystify it and thus to transform the essay he is still in the process of composing into a parody. It is only the worst works of art, it turns out, that can be reconstructed; the meaning of the best works remains indeterminate. Poe goes on, in fact, to say that it is the "*excess* of the suggested meaning—it is the rendering this the upper instead of the under current of the theme—which turns into prose (and that of the very flattest kind) the so called poetry of the so called transcendentalists" (207-08). In order to prevent such flatness of prose—ironically, a flatness that Poe's essay would seem to confirm in the poem—he maintains that he added the two concluding stanzas of the poem. Their "suggestiveness," he says, "being thus made to pervade all the narrative which has preceded them" (208).

Just as the concluding paragraphs of the essay re-mystify the process of composition, the concluding stanzas of the poem cast a spell of suggestiveness, or indeterminacy, back over the preceding stanzas. Poe thus belies his promise to reconstruct his intentions, to "render it manifest that no one point in [the poem's] composition is referable either to accident or intuition—that the work proceeded, step by step, to its completion with the precision and rigid consequence of a mathematical problem." The poem was not completed that way; its *denouement* was not kept constantly in view, because its denouement, he now admits in the essay, was added at the end, not the beginning, of the process. The final effect of the poem was not present at the beginning as an originating idea, and therefore Poe's intentions are present (and thus available for "reconstruction") only at the end as well. As he himself coyly admits at the end of the essay, "it is not until the very last line of the very last stanza, that the intention of making [the raven] emblematical of *Mournful and Never-ending Remembrance* is permitted distinctly to be seen" (208).

Poe had also admitted that "the case is by no means common, in which an author is at all in condition to retrace the steps by which his conclusions have been attained" (195), but he does just that in the essay, which becomes a literal "retracing" of the poem—"step by step." Indeed, in order to suggest that the essay possesses the same "air of consequence" as the poem, Poe even makes sure that reading each of them has the same consequence by having each of them reach the same conclusion. They end with the same words—literally, with the same stanza:

> And the Raven, never flitting, still is sitting, still is sitting,
> On the pallid bust of Pallas, just above my chamber door;
> And his eyes have all the seeming of a demon's that is
>     dreaming,

And the lamplight o'er him streaming throws his shadow
  on the floor;
And my soul from out that shadow that lies floating on the
  floor
       Shall be lifted—nevermore.

                (208)

Before the final stanza Poe had maintained that "With the *denoue-ment* proper—with the Raven's reply, 'Nevermore,' to the lover's final demand if he shall meet his mistress in another world—the poem, in its obvious phase, that of a simple narrative, may be said to have its completion" (206). But the effect of the essay's echoing of the poem is to eclipse that "other world" of transcendental meanings, with an infinitely regressive doubling. That is, the poem and the essay are "doubles," and they exist together in a hermeneutic loop. They interpret or "read" each other, at least in the sense that interpretation, or reading, has become a reiteration, or echo—a rewriting. "The Philosophy of Composition" both parodies the creative process and doubles it. The essay becomes a kind of demonic double, or "spectre" in the path of our access to the poem. Much like the second William Wilson, it is the conscience of the poem and opposes through an act of pre-emption the free play of a writerly reading of the poem.


II

It may be simply a coincidence that the raven first appears in stanza seven of the poem and that Poe first mentions "The Raven" in the seventh paragraph of the essay, but, ironically, the essay does finally point us in the right direction for reading the poem, because the poem, too, is double and, like the essay, "about" itself—that is, about reading and writing the raven. Mutlu Konuk Blasing says that the "poem is 'about' the process of its own development, for its narrative content reduces to the operations of its form," but there is a more obvious way in which the poem is about writing itself and thus about a "philosophy of composition."[11]

As readers, for example, our relationship to "The Raven" parallels the student's relationship to the raven, which figures in the poem as a kind of primitive "speaking" text.[12] At the most basic level, both the reader outside the text and the student inside it are trying to read "The Raven." The raven, like the poem with which it is synonymous, utters a word whose meaning must be interpreted, although this is not to say that the raven is the author of the word "Nevermore." The bird is really identical with the word it speaks, since it possesses no intentionality and no other words. Poe himself, in fact, explicitly links the student with the reader, maintaining that the "revolution of thought, or fancy, on the lover's part [near the end of the poem], is intended to induce a similar one on the part of the reader—to bring the mind into a proper frame for the *denouement*—which is now brought about as rapidly and as *directly* as possible" (206). David Halliburton calls the relationship between the bird and the student a "reciprocity," but the relationship is not truly reciprocal, since the student controls the meaning of the bird's utterance—what Poe calls the "effect of the *variation of application*" (201).[13]

Furthermore, in the poem as in the essay Poe demonstrates that the student's attempt to "read" and understand the raven's word (or "philosophy") involves him necessarily in an effort to rewrite, or "compose," the raven. While the raven ("The Raven") utters only a word—only itself—the student (the reader) manipulates the text in order to make it mean what he wants it to mean.[14] The "effect" or meaning of the word "Nevermore," like the meaning of the poem, varies according to the pretext of its utterance. As Poe himself almost perversely puts it, "Perceiving the opportunity thus afforded me—or, more strictly, thus forced upon me in the progress of the construction—I first established in mind the climax, or concluding query—that to which 'Nevermore' should be in the last place an answer—that in reply to which this word 'Nevermore' should involve the utmost conceivable amount of sorrow and despair" (202). What Poe found "forced" upon him was, first, the necessity of knowing the answer before he propounded the question (the answer "Nevermore" precedes and determines the query to which it is the answer) and, second, the importance of knowing the last question in his series before he asked the first. Questions and answers go around and around, each preceding the other in a microcosmic variation of the hermeneutic loop formed by the poem and the essay. The answer precedes the question in the order of composition, while the question precedes the answer in the order of reading.

Beginning in the first stanza, when the student concludes that the "tapping" he hears represents "some one gently rapping" and then "some visitor," Poe foregrounds questions of interpretation, or reading, and emphasizes the subjectivity of the student's conclusions.[15] Although the "text" that the student interprets is composed of a single word, he persistently imposes, or inscribes, meaning on what he sees and hears under the guise of ascribing it. His reading becomes writing. Since the student's investigation of the tapping, his "opening wide the door," reveals only "Darkness there and nothing more," his initial interpretation proceeds virtually without an object, and he is left in stanza 3 to stand "repeating" his conclusion (spoken in line 5) that the noise is made by "some visitor." For "some visitor," however, the student then substitutes "Lenore" in stanza 5. Based on nothing more than a tapping sound, the student has progressed through a series of putative interpretations (moving from "some one" to "some visitor" to "Lenore")—all in the absence of a text and in the context of an "unbroken" silence and a stillness that "gave no token." As the student himself seems to recognize,

> And the only word there spoken was the whispered word,
>   "Lenore?"
> This I whispered, and echo murmured back the word,
>   "Lenore!"
>     Merely this and nothing more.

The student has read and interpreted this most primitive text (a sound that comprises even more primitive a text than the "A" in *The Scarlet Letter*) in the context of his own desire. Under the guise of interpretation he has projected his own obsession—the dead Lenore. Put another way, the essentially blank text (an unbroken silence or stillness that gives no sign even of itself) is written over by the student's own word "Lenore"—the "only word there spoken."[16] Ironically, as the speaker-writer of the poem in which he figures as a character, the student has done what Poe describes himself as doing in "The Philosophy of Composition." He has concluded (before he has even encountered the raven) with "Lenore" and thus with the death of his beautiful woman. The raven follows this conclusion (in the poem, although not necessarily in the student's experience that precedes the poem) much as "The Raven" follows the effect Poe has decided to achieve (in the essay, although not necessarily in the writing of the poem).

In the next section of the poem (stanzas 7-12), the student interrogates the raven, which, like he himself in stanza 5, speaks "only/ That one word"—"Nevermore." In this section, too, Poe foregrounds the problem of interpretation in order to underscore the subjective character of the student's reasoning, and in the process he emphasizes the gap between word and meaning—text and interpretation. "Much I marvelled this ungainly fowl to hear discourse so plainly," says the student in response to the raven's first utterance of "Nevermore," "Though its answer little meaning—little relevancy bore." When the raven responds "Nevermore" to the student's muttered "'Other friends have flown before—/ On the morrow *he* will leave me, as my Hopes have flown before,'" the student feels startled that the reply is "so aptly spoken." This opening line of stanza 11 represents the turning point of the poem because on the student's presumption of "aptness" the rest of the poem depends. Out of coincidence—the accidental "aptness" of successive words—he creates meaning. Much as Poe will do in "The Philosophy of Composition," he reasons backward from effect to cause.

Behind effect (the word "Nevermore") he discovers intentionality. Indeed, he speculates immediately that the raven's single utterance encodes the story of its "author," the

> unhappy master whom unmerciful Disaster
> Followed fast and followed faster till his songs one
>  burden bore—
> Till the dirges of his Hope that melancholy burden bore
>  Of "Never-nevermore."

The same hermeneutic process—text plus readerly context equals meaning—is repeated in the crucial last section of the poem, especially in stanzas 14-17 where the student tortures himself about Lenore. Climactically, in stanzas 16 and 17, "Nevermore" signifies his eternal separation from Lenore and his eternal hauntedness by the raven that will never leave his "loneliness unbroken." Although J. Gerald Kennedy argues that the poem "enacts the struggle to escape solipsism through a recovered connection with the Other," Poe seems to deny the possibility of such recovery by emphasizing the interpretive solipsism, as it were, of the student's composition of the poem.[17] Each time, the meaning of the text ("Nevermore") depends entirely upon the pretext of its utterance; the meaning, or "relevancy," of the raven's "discourse," therefore, is utterly arbitrary because utterly subject to the student's own interpretive and interpreting design. While he cannot alter the raven's discourse, he could easily alter and even invert its meaning, if he wished, for example, to promise himself a reunion with Lenore.

By placing the student in the position of reader as well as writer, Poe implies that a poem is also a kind of "stillness" that gives "no token" of itself until a word is spoken or written by the reader. The poem, like the raven, becomes an "echo" that "murmurs" the words read or written into it by the reader—"merely this and nothing more." In this respect, too, Poe casts himself in a position very similar to the student's: both of them confront a raven. Like the poem, the raven utters or echoes the speech of someone behind itself. Neither the bird nor the poem possesses any intentionality of its own; each only represents the "effect" of another's speaking. Words have been inscribed in the raven, just as they have in "The Raven"; in both cases, the intentions of the inscriber are hidden and unknown. The student has no clearer idea about who trained the raven to speak than the reader of the poem has about the writer who wrote the poem. Moreover, the student, like the reader of the poem, must provide a context, or metalanguage, in which the raven's utterance will have any meaning at all, because by itself—that is, unheard or unread—the raven's ("The Raven"'s) word makes no sense. But the act of hearing or reading constitutes a reinscription, an echo of the words uttered or perceived on the printed page; the reader takes the place of the student just as the student takes the place of the raven. David Halliburton points out that the human speaker uses the word "nevermore" almost as often as the bird—"five times to the raven's six," but in fact the student utters the word every time.[18] As the speaker of the poem, the student describes himself in the act of writing the poem and so in the act of reinscribing the raven's words, but of course, when spoken, the raven's utterance also affects or completes the meaning of the student's words. Like Poe, the student begins with an "effect" (the word "Nevermore") and by causing the bird to repeat that word in response to different statements, he actually creates the "intentions," as it were, behind those words. That is, those intentions are simply the product, or effect, of what the student says: they answer a question he has posed. Iteration is reiteration, the poem makes clear, and the essay insists upon the larger point that reading "The Raven" (like understanding the raven) is an act of re-writing it, an "echo." *Re*iteration is also iteration, however, because the reader, like the student, plays out his own identity theme and makes interpretation coincident with desire, even with "self-torture." Poe says that the student "experiences a phrenzied pleasure in so modeling his questions as to receive from the *expected* 'Nevermore' the most delicious because the most intolerable of sorrow" (202). As a critic, in other words, the student is guilty of the "affective fallacy"; in Poe's own terms, he confuses "effect" with "intentions." Or, as the student himself admits in stanza 12,

> Then, upon the velvet sinking, I betook myself to linking
> Fancy unto fancy, thinking what this ominous bird of yore—
> What this grim, ungainly, ghastly, gaunt, and ominous bird
>     of yore
>        Meant in croaking "Nevermore."

Not simply the effect of the raven's utterance, but its meaning derives from the subjective process of "linking fancy unto fancy." Michael Williams has observed that "in 'The Raven,' as in Poe's works generally, [the ideal sign] is revealed as a function of interpretive desire."[19] The same thing can be said about "The Philosophy of Composition," for in the process of reading and rewriting the poem in that essay, Poe makes it clear that the intention, or effect, of both reading and writing is an "air of consequence." Poe notes at one point in the essay that the "next *desideratum* was a pretext for the continuous use of the one word 'nevermore,'" but in fact the only "pretext," at least for the raven's speech, is the poem or composition—actually a series of compositions—in which the word is inscribed. Pretext and text become the same.

In his analysis of *Eureka* Joseph Riddel notes that Poe distinguishes between the "created universe," or "plot of God," which is an "inimitable perfection," and the "plots of man," which are "secondary metaphors, discontinuous and indeed inadequate to the only original." Furthermore, he says, the "'plot' of God would be a kind of poem; the 'plots' of men, interpretations." Most importantly, Riddel argues that Poe's "strategy is to forget the origin—even the 'creation,' which could only have occurred once in all its completeness, and can never be repeated—and hence the 'fall' implied in God's plot; then to conceive of man's plots, in all their imperfections, as a metaphoric play evoking, by repetition, a God-like supplement to his machine."[20] Although "The

Philosophy of Composition" does not pretend to be a philosophy in this sense, the relationship between "The Raven" and the essay (the poem and the interpretation, in Riddel's terms) does resemble that between God's "plot" and man's. Instead of feeling as if his interpretive plot were supplemental to the original, however, Poe enjoys the privilege of playing both God and man—of composing the original which he then interprets. Indeed, the essay is really closer to the origin of the poem than the poem itself, because Poe plays himself as creator in the act of "reconstructing" his creation. The "man" in "The Raven," on the other hand, is the one who repeats or echoes his creator's word without knowing, much less forgetting, the origin of what he repeats. In that sense, Poe's interpretation becomes the original, while the original becomes the interpretation. So, too, Poe's "philosophy" is ultimately, originally, a "philosophy of composition"—that is, a "composition of philosophy," a writing as much as a reading.

## Notes

1. Kenneth Burke, "The Principle of Composition," *Poetry* 99 (1961) 49, 51. Burke credits Poe with recognizing the critic's responsibility to discover the principles, or philosophy, which every literary work embodies, but, he argues, Poe mistakenly tried to explain those principles "in terms of a purely 'genetic' (narrative, temporal) series" (51).

2. Edward H. Davidson, *Poe: A Critical Study* (Cambridge: Harvard University Press, 1957) 66. Davidson considers the essay "more an attempt to outline Poe's view of what poetry should be and should do than . . . a forthright demonstration of how 'The Raven' came to be" (84). "The analysis or reconstruction is not the poem," he concludes; "each is a separate exercise, one of the imagination, the other of the skeptical intellect" (66).

3. Peck's essay from the *American Whig Review* (March 1850) is included in *Edgar Allan Poe: The Critical Heritage*, ed. I. M. Walker (London and New York: Routledge & Kegan Paul, 1986): 342-56; quotation from p. 350.

4. Daniel Hoffman, *Poe Poe Poe Poe Poe Poe Poe* (Garden City, N.Y.: Doubleday, 1972) 79. For Hoffman's analysis of the essay as a "put-on," see pp. 82-96.

5. Poe is increasingly viewed as a metafictionist, a writer about writing—in Joseph N. Riddel's terms, a writer who "abandons nature for the image," whose "world becomes a text, or a library of multiple texts" ("The 'Crypt' of Edgar Poe," *boundary 2* 7 [Spring 1979] 120). Also see John T. Irwin, *American Hieroglyphics: The Symbol of the Egyptian Hieroglyphics in the American Renaissance* (1980: Baltimore: Johns Hopkins University Press, 1983), and especially the excellent recent book by Michael J. S. Williams, *A World of Words: Language and Displacement in the Fiction of Edgar Allan Poe* (Durham: Duke University Press, 1988).

6. "The Poet," *The Essays of Ralph Waldo Emerson*, ed. Alfred R. Ferguson and Jean Ferguson Carr (Cambridge: Harvard University Press, 1987) 224-25.

7. "The Philosophy of Composition," *The Complete Works of Edgar Allan Poe*, ed. James A. Harrison, 17 vols. (New York: Thomas Y. Crowell, 1902) 14:193.

8. Hoffman 94.

9. John T. Irwin's characterization of narrative voice in Poe's tales could also apply to Poe himself as "narrator" of "The Philosophy of Composition": Poe's "rule seems to be that the more incredible the story or the more indeterminate the experience to be evoked, then the more 'scientifically' exact the narrative and descriptive apparatus, so that, by defining its own boundaries in the clearest possible imagery, linguistic discourse defines as well the opposing limits of what lies beyond language and reason" (*American Hieroglyphics* 117).

10. "The Purloined Letter," *Collected Works of Edgar Allan Poe*, ed. Thomas Ollive Mabbott, 3 vols. (Cambridge: Harvard University Press, 1969) 3:984-85.

11. Mutlu Konuk Blasing, *American Poetry: The Rhetoric of Its Forms* (New Haven: Yale University Press, 1986) 27.

12. Numerous critics have analyzed the raven as an emblem or symbol. Edward H. Davidson, for example, compares the bird to the scarlet letter and to Moby Dick as a symbol of the imaginative "reach toward a further understanding of the illusion of reality and the painful awareness of nothing on the 'other side' of reality" (*Poe: A Critical Study* 90, 91). David Ketterer says that the "raven represents the quest of the intellectual for knowledge" (*The Rationale of Deception in Poe* [Baton Rouge: Louisiana State University Press, 1979] 169). Kent Ljungquist considers the bird a "daemonic agent, deriving some of its power from ancient associations" (*The Grand and the Fair: Poe's Landscape Aesthetics and Pictorial Techniques* [Potomac: Scripta Humanistica, 1984] 178). The most ingenious and exhaustive attempt to analyze the raven's allegorical meaning is Barton Levi St. Armand, "Poe's Emblematic Raven: A Pictorial Approach," *ESQ: A Journal of the American Renaissance* 22 (1976): 191-210. My purpose in this essay is not to refute the claim that the raven stands for something outside the poem, but to underscore Poe's own emphasis on the dynamics of the poem-making process for which the raven offers the pretext.

13. David Halliburton, *Edgar Allan Poe: A Phenomenological Approach* (Princeton: Princeton University Press, 1973) 127.

14. As Michael Williams notes, "The narrator is trapped in his inability to recognize the essential emptiness of the word, 'Nevermore.' What seems to be a potential incursion of meaning from a supernal realm is significant only in the context of the lover's narrative of loss" (7).

15. "The Raven," *Collected Works of Edgar Allan Poe*, 1:364-69.

16. Blasing assumes that the raven repeats the word "Lenore" in stanza 5, even though Poe writes that an "echo" murmured back the word (32). This assumption helps to warrant her case that the raven and Lenore are "coeveal opposites," the raven embodying a "mechanical, pornographic reproduction of . . . language" and Lenore offering the pleasures of an "oral mother tongue, of memory and repetition." Thus, she concludes that the raven's "Nevermore" both "echoes and drowns out" the student's "Lenore," and thereby "prevents union with the poetic source, and thwarts the very life of poetry" (29).

17. J. Gerald Kennedy, *Poe, Death, and the Life of Writing* (New Haven: Yale University Press, 1987) 68.

18. Halliburton 126.

19. Williams 7.

20. Riddel 130-31.

# "The Poetess" and Poe's
# Performance of the Feminine_____

Eliza Richards

> . . . forms that no man can discover
> For the tears that drip all over . . .
>
> Poe, "Dream-Land"

Poe's aesthetic discourse registers a crisis of masculine literary sentiment sparked by the influx of women poets to the American marketplace in the 1830s and '40s. At this time, white, middle-class women, supposed embodiments of the emotions associated with privatized domestic life, gained greater sanction not only to write but also to publish in the most "intimate" of forms, lyric poetry. "The whole tendency of the age is Magazine-ward," Poe proclaims in 1846, and women poets were invited to cultivate this potentially wayward public medium with genteel literary sentiments ("Marginalia" 139). Concerned that this emerging group might be more constitutionally suited to write poetry than they, male writers sought to define a specifically masculine literary sensibility. Stabilizing the shifting ground of aesthetic authority required delicacy, however, in order not to alienate female readers; for just as women entered the market in unprecedented numbers as producers of literature, they were also gaining influence as a powerful class of literary consumers.[1]

Poe's solution to the dilemma of women's encroachment in the literary domain did not lie in a simple dismissal of female achievement, because women's attention, both personal and literary, was extremely important to his poetic practices. Instead, he imagined women poets in ways that seek to reconcile their multiple roles: muse, literary competitor, and audience for his own poetry. While designating women as the "natural" site of poetic utterance, Poe also argues that poetic "truth" lies in a theatrical performance of the feminine.[2] Identifying women poets with his poetic images of women, Poe enacts a drama of evacua-

258                                                            Critical Insights

tion within his poems in which he drains women of their poetic potency while claiming that the transfer of powers is in the spirit of feminine mimicry. For an audience of women poets, Poe himself performs a "feminine" poetry which simultaneously mirrors and upstages their own practices. He extends and consolidates these aesthetic claims in his criticism, an almost exclusively male genre in the 1840s. Reappraising the impact of these forgotten women poets upon a canonical figure presents new ways to understand the work of canonical writers, the canonization process, and the structure and habits of American literary criticism.[3]

Imagining women as the power generators of poetic discourse, Poe's critical interest in their work is extensive and sustained. Although his reviews of women poets outnumber those of male poets in his later criticism, they are rarely treated in studies of his poetics.[4] When not ignored altogether, these frequently positive reviews are usually dismissed as either a display of vapid gallantry or an aberration in taste bearing little relation to his more serious considerations of male peers such as Hawthorne and Longfellow. In his own time, however, Poe was considered a leading—and by far the most rigorous—critic of female writers, discriminating at one point between "poetesses (an absurd but necessary word)" and female poets worthy of admiration and serious critique ("Marginalia" 58-59). To the second category belonged writers like Frances Sargent Osgood, Sarah Helen Whitman, Elizabeth Barrett, Amelia Welby, and Elizabeth Oakes Smith. In a review of Barrett's *Drama of Exile*, Poe laments that "the inherent chivalry of the critical man" results in the "unhappy lot of the authoress to be subjected, time after time, to the downright degradation of mere puffery" (*Complete* [*The Complete Works of Edgar Allan Poe*] 12: 1). Poe promises, in contrast, to pay Barrett the respect of telling her "the truth" about her work (2). While proving Poe's critical pronouncements "sincere" at any juncture would be a hopeless task, his critical treatment of women poets is comparable to that of their male counterparts.

Poe's critical pronouncements on women's poetry are torn between delimiting a separate character for female genius and rewarding poetesses by welcoming them into the male world of the "poet." Poe trounces anthologist Rufus Griswold, for example, for elevating "aristocrats" over "poets" in his *Poets and Poetry of America*, and for relegating certain worthy writers, men and women alike, to the desultory category of "various authors." Poe laments the disservice done to poets such as Sarah Josepha Hale, Horace Greeley, John Quincy Adams, and Frances Osgood ("one of our sweetest of poetesses") by "throwing openly the charge of their incompetency to sustain the name of Poets, and implying that they were only occasional scribblers[.] (This and of such men, is again from Rufus Wilmot Griswold!)" (*Complete* 11: 241). More than once, Poe includes women, and even "poetesses," under the rubric of "such men" and "Poets." He compares Elizabeth Barrett favorably to Tennyson; he also says that "The Sinless Child" demonstrates that its creator, Elizabeth Oakes Smith, had the potential, even if she lacked the discipline, to have written "one of the best, if not the very best of American poems" (*Complete* 12: 16; 13: 85).

While Poe often measures everyone against a single aesthetic standard, he also attributes superior artistic powers to the woman poet. He defends Maria Brooks against Charles Lamb's claim that her poem "Zóphiël" was so good that a woman could not have written it:

> As for Lamb's pert query—"was there ever a woman capable of writing such a poem?"—it merely proves that Lamb had little understanding of the true Nature of Poets—which, appealing to our sense of Beauty, is, in its very essence, feminine. If the greatest poems have not been written by women, it is because the greatest poems have not been written at all. (*Collected Writings* [*The Collected Writings of Edgar Allan Poe*] 358)

For Poe, the "true" "essence" of poetry is its "feminine" appeal to the reader's aesthetic sense. Designated as the natural location of feminine Beauty, women possess an innate capacity for poetic expression.

While both Lamb and Poe were certainly familiar with the romantic commonplace that poetic accomplishment in men arises from their feminine aspect, Poe perceives a new dilemma: if one accepts a female claim to poetic authorship, one must recognize that women ostensibly contain more of that feminine element from which poetry emerges than men.[5]

Rufus Griswold tries to work through this problem in the introduction to his popular anthology *The Female Poets and Poetry of America* (an 1848 sequel to *Poets and Poetry of America* that newly segregates women poets in a separate volume—an organizational scheme which itself indicates male anxiety over female poetic achievement): "It does not follow, because the most essential genius in men is marked by qualities which we may call feminine, that such qualities when found in female writers have any certain or just relation to mental superiority. The conditions of aesthetic ability in the two sexes are probably distinct, or even opposite" (16). While Griswold's formulation reserves the domain of the feminine for the male writer, elsewhere he insists that the woman writer should emanate a pure essence of femininity, an accomplishment belonging preeminently to Frances Sargent Osgood: "All that was in her life was womanly, 'pure womanly,' and so is all in the undying words she left us. This is her distinction" (qtd. in Hewitt 16). In Griswold's aesthetic hierarchy, this ultrafeminine poetry takes a diminutive second place to men's accomplishments. His writings thus register an irreconcilable contradiction: if the feminine is the indispensable ingredient in poetry, then why isn't women's poetry, which supposedly contains a purer essence of femininity, superior to that of men?

This potential threat to male poetic accomplishment was partially neutralized through a frequent identification of antebellum women with poetic "song": light, spontaneous-seeming amateur verse that "elevates" the reader's taste in preparation for more serious forms of literature. While feminine sensibility infused men's intellects, it resided in women's hearts, from which poetry emanated as naturally as a heartbeat (DeJong, "Fair" 269). Critic George William Curtis says, for example, that Sarah Helen Whitman's poetry exudes "pure and holy and feminine feeling, as if the singer's heart were a harp so delicate that even chasing sun and shadow swept it into music" (qtd. in Whitman, *Hours* x).[6] Women poets were frequently characterized as fonts of authentic, unmediated emotion. The lyric, therefore, was the privileged vehicle for female poetic expression; however, because women's song was a natural extension of womanhood, by definition it was not art.

For both Poe and his contemporaries, then, female verse inextricably linked the personal and the poetic, and the physical body and poetic form: Poe goes so far as to say at one point that "a woman and her book are identical" (*Complete* 12: 1). But for Poe, more than other purveyors of female verse such as Griswold, a woman's duplication of her book may be construed doubly: her book may record the expressions of the heart, or the heart may also lend itself to the expressions of the book. In a review of Frances Osgood's "Elfrida, a Dramatic Poem, in Five Acts," Poe celebrates this transitive relation: "There is a fine feeling blending [sic] of the poetry of passion and the passion of poetry" (*Complete* 13: 110). Emphasizing the harp over the heart in the conventional formulation of female poetic ability, Poe highlights the natural capacity of women to produce art. If women and poems are equally sources of beauty, then the woman poet displays artful rather than artless emotions. Thus, while much literary commentary of the period stressed the naturalness of women's poetic utterance, Poe emphasized the female poet's natural capacity for the artistic. This difference helps explain Poe's broad appeal for the women poets of his generation, who, regardless of self-effacing proclamations, energetically sought fame and literary acclaim.

Poe's theory of female artistry emphasizes women's dramatic abilities: if the body is drama's primary instrument, and women's bodies are naturally artistic, then women must make exceptional actors. For Poe (whose mother was a successful actress and his father a failure upon the stage), women possessed an uncanny ability to imbue their poems with the aesthetic impression of an emotional presence which was often emphatically not their own. Poe's association of the dramatic with both the woman and the poet is clear in a review of a performance by actress Anna Cora Mowatt, whom he greatly admired: "her seemingly impulsive gestures spoke in loud terms of the woman of genius— of the poet deeply imbued with the truest sentiment of the beauty of motion" (*Complete* 12: 187-88). Mowatt is admirable not because she is naturally impulsive, but because she can *feign* spontaneity so convincingly. Poe's syntax equates acting with both the woman of genius and the poet, implying that male poets must transform themselves into theatrical women if they wish to be poetic geniuses.

This homogeneous relation between women and art inevitably produces the dramatic lyric, a sincere form of theater, and Poe praised women's dramatic lyric performances as well. He voiced particular enthusiasm for "Lady Geraldine's Courtship" by Elizabeth Barrett, spoken in the voice of a male poet who has fallen in love with an aristocratic woman; an elegy by Amelia Welby, written from the point of view of a young man who mourns the death of his wife, and Elizabeth Oakes Smith's "The Sinless Child," a story of a modern, blameless "Eva" told in the third person. All the poems evoke an author figure obliquely, as the object of the narrative rather than the speaking subject. Any strictly autobiographical reading is impossible, even while autobiographical speculation is encouraged. For Poe, the woman was the ultimate poet, or poem. The seamless performance, the very difficulty in distinguishing the artist from the production, or the woman from her role as artist, is the sign of poetic genius.

Poe participated in public literary romances with two of the poets he esteemed, Sarah Helen Whitman and Frances Sargent Osgood, because he valued their status as embodiments of poetic sentiment. This formulation counters the more familiar view that he flattered their poetry because he was blinded by their personal charms. Exchanging love poems with Whitman and Osgood in the pages of the literary journals and newspapers of the late 1840s, Poe participated in full-scale dramatic productions of personal life. Of Anna Blackwell Poe inquires: "Do you know Mrs. Whitman? I feel deep interest in her poetry and character. . . . Her poetry is, beyond question, *poetry*—instinct with genius" (qtd. in Ticknor 49). Due to the inextricable link between female "character" and poetry, Poe's poetic romances generate romantic poetry: he engages Beauty in dialogue in hopes of absorbing some of its power.

Of all the women poets, Frances Osgood, with whom Poe carried on a literary flirtation in the pages of the *Broadway Journal* while he was editor, symbolized poetry incarnate: "Mrs. Osgood was born a poetess only—it is not in her nature to be anything else. Her personal, not less than her literary character and existence are one perpetual poem" (*Complete* 13: 105). For Poe, Osgood was so poetic that she was incapable of writing anything else, namely any species of prose:

> She begins with a desperate effort at being sedate—that is to say, sufficiently prosaic and matter-of-fact for the purpose of a legend or an essay; but in a few sentences we behold uprising the leaven of the unrighteousness of the muse; then, after some flourishes and futile attempts at repression, a scrap of verse renders itself manifest; then another and another; then comes a poem outright, and then another and another and another, with little odd batches of prose in between, until at length the mask is thrown fairly off, and far away, and the whole article—*sings*. (*Complete* 15: 104)

In an ironic reversal, the "mask" of prose, associated with the real (the "prosaic"), is thrown off to expose the more artful genre, which is Osgood's true form of expression. Combining aspects of both genius and muse, Poe posits Osgood as a passive creator, the fecund site where wild poetry breeds and escapes into the world, even against her will. However, "the warm *abandonnement* of her style," which makes her the visible manifestation of poetic process, prevents her from becoming a premier poet. Her amateurism reconfirms a poetry of presence, never to be matched by poetic output. With "more industry, more method, more definite purpose, more ambition," Mrs. Osgood "might have written better poems; but the chances are that she would have failed in conveying so vivid and so just an idea of her powers as a poet" (*Complete* 13: 175). While Osgood's amorphous relation to poetry relegates her to the realm of eternal amateur, her "astonishing facility" also renders her capable of emitting poetry in any vein, and of imitating the signature verse of another. Poe took Osgood's talent so much to heart that, when he felt incapable of producing a new poem to read before the Boston Lyceum, he asked her to write "a poem that shall be equal to my reputation" (qtd. in Silverman 286).

By emphasizing Osgood's incompleteness as a poet, Poe creates a space for himself to finish what she so energetically starts. Osgood's work only "affords us glimpses . . . of a capacity for accomplishing what she has not accomplished and in all probability never will" (*Complete* 13: 176). The ambiguous phrasing suggests that Osgood affords Poe glimpses of his own capacity for accomplishing what remains a mirage in her own work. Poe imagined women poets as sites of poetic ore that he might mine, a theme that is familiar from his poems and tales, which often take as their source and center the death of a beautiful young woman. J. Gerald Kennedy has said that "in calling poetry the 'rhythmical creation of beauty,' and then designating the death of a *beautiful woman* as the most poetical of topics, Poe established an implicit metaphorical relationship between the death of beauty and poetic texts" that "dramatize[s] the writer's problematic relationship" to his work (75). The "metaphorical relationship" is more properly between the death of a beautiful woman and Poe's generation of a poetic text. This equivalence implies a convertibility between the terms: not only do poetic texts thematize the deaths of beautiful women, but beautiful women generate poetic texts. Poe's poems dramatize the writer's relation to women poets by acting out the transfer of energy from female poetic wellsprings to his own poems.[7] Poe himself encouraged a tendency among his critics, which Kennedy's formulation exemplifies, to read women symbolically. Draining women of substance in his poems, encouraging them to stand as markers for other things, Poe transforms his all-too-present female poetic rivals into marmoreal emblems, momentarily quieted so that his own work might take center stage.

Rather than rejecting the feminine, Poe becomes an expert in the field, out-feminizing the feminine in a masculine rendition that inverts female poetic practice and thus exoticizes the banal performativity of the female poet. Countering a poetry of presence, Poe roots his alternative poetics in a drama of evacuation, which takes as its explicit subject the process of conversion that makes a woman's poem into a man's. "To Helen," Poe's funereal portrait of Sarah Helen Whitman, "clad all in white, upon a violet bank," celebrates the "poetry of [her] presence" even while highlighting its conversion to the presence of his poem (*Collected Works* [*The Collected Works of Edgar Allan Poe*] 443). In the initial image of Whitman among her flowery creations ("roses that grew in an enchanted garden"), poet and poems, equally embodied, share one landscape: "I saw thee half reclining; while the moon/ Fell on the upturn'd faces of the roses,/ And on thine own, upturn'd—alas, in sorrow!" Almost immediately, however, the speaker sees the roses die of an excess of sameness: even their odors "died in the arms of the adoring airs." The speaker dismantles both the landscape ("in an instant, all things disappeared") and Whitman ("thou, a ghost amid the entombing trees/ Didst glide away") until "*Only thine eyes remained.*" Her eyes—"two sweetly scintillant Venuses, unextinguished by the sun"—stay behind because they serve as the illuminating force for the speaker's poetic landscape. The juxtaposition of the lingering eye-stars and the departed Whitman recalls the need for the integrity of even a ghostlike body, returning the reader to the recalcitrant problem of Poe's poetic dilemma: he needs her to stay, in order to provide the materials for his poem, and he needs her to go in order to make his poem anew.

Poe's evacuative aesthetic is most clearly propounded, as well as performed, in "The Raven" and its critical companion piece, "The Philosophy of Composition." The pairing of poem and critique resonates with Poe's attempts to elaborate a poetics of absence. While "The Philosophy of Composition" works as an extension of the poem it interprets (and I will discuss this effect presently), "The Raven" serves as a study of composition, particularly as it relates to the interplay of gender and genre. Poe explores issues of feminine influence within the poem by working from an identifiable female rhythmic prototype, "Lady Geraldine's Courtship" by Elizabeth Barrett.[8] Highlighting her influence, Poe dedicated his volume *The Raven and Other Poems* (1845) to Barrett. He also encouraged readers to compare his poem with its most obvious precursor by publishing a review of Barrett's *Drama of Exile* in January 1845, shortly before the first publication of "The Raven," which pays special attention to "Lady Geraldine's Courtship":

> With the exception of Tennyson's "Locksley Hall," we have never perused a poem combining so much of the fiercest passion with so much of the most ethereal fancy, as the "Lady Geraldine's Courtship," of Miss Barrett. We are forced to admit, however, that the latter work is a very palpable imitation of the former, which it surpasses in plot or rather in thesis, as much as it falls below it in artistical management, and a certain calm energy— lustrous and indomitable—such as we might imagine in a broad river of molten gold. (*Complete* 12: 16)

The dueling referential "its" contribute to the reader's uncertainty about what status "the palpable imitation" holds, and which qualities adhere to the original and which to the copy. By highlighting Barrett's derivative qualities shortly before he presents his own imitation of her poem, Poe demonstrates his solidarity with a second-comer and consolidates his identification with the female poet seeking to establish legitimacy within a male tradition.

Taken together, the two poems work as variations upon a theme, encouraging a contemplation of the differences between Barrett and Poe, and, more broadly, between models of female and male poetic achievement. A comparison of just two lines highlights this process:

BARRETT:

> With a murmurous stir uncertain, in the air, the purple curtain
> Swelleth in and swelleth out around her motionless pale brows.

(Browning 105)

POE:

> And the silken sad, uncertain rustling of each purple curtain
> Thrilled me—filled me with fantastic terrors never felt before.

(Collected Works 364)

In both poems, a male poet speaks of his unattainable love. However, while Barrett's poet records his close observation of Lady Geraldine's queenly presence, framed and enhanced by the swelling curtains, which register her unspoken passion, Poe's poet notes his lover's absence in passing, and then shifts to an observation of his own sensations about the curtains. While thrushes and songbirds, emblems of poetic musicality, fill Barrett's lines, Poe populates his poem with a single "croaking" bird that can only repeat human words learned from its previous owner. Even this scant comparison suggests that "The Raven" parodies its own reliance upon imitation of a feminine precursor, and asserts itself as original by highlighting its mirror-like reflexivity.

Poe also leaves traces within his poem to suggest that he enacts a symbiotic—or, with the presence of the scavenger bird, an explicitly parasitic—model of creation in "The Raven"'s composition. Aligned with the raven, the poet-speaker replaces female inspiration by drawing from it. Whereas the beautiful woman inspires the poem, her evacuation is prerequisite to its existence. Contemplating the memory of his departed loved one, the speaker sits in the velvet chair that was her habitual resting place in order to compose his poem: "This and more I sat divining, with my head at ease reclining/ On the cushion's velvet lining that the lamp-light gloated o'er,/ But whose velvet violet lining with the lamp-light gloating o'er,/ *She* shall press, ah, nevermore!" (368). Not only does Lenore's absence inspire the poet to link "fancy unto fancy," but he literally occupies her vacated space while composing his poetic tribute. The speaker thus underscores rather than hides the fact that Lenore's death provides him with an opportunity for poetic generation.

Caught in an insoluble dilemma, the speaker cannot completely erase Lenore and still retain the poem's reason for being: the elegiac occasion of *"Mournful and Never-ending Remembrance"* ("Philosophy" 373). He professes his need to remember Lenore, the center and source of his imagining, even while asserting his need to forget her in order to assert his poetic primacy. As a result, the speaker simultaneously asserts his desire to forget and stimulates his desire in remembering by repeating the tantalizing word Lenore, an ambivalent marker for a banished presence, or a presence of banishment: "'Respite—respite and nepenthe from thy memories of Lenore;/ Quaff, oh quaff this kind nepenthe and forget this lost Lenore.'/ Quoth the Raven 'Nevermore'" (*Collected Works* 368; 82-84).[9]

Highlighting his appropriation of the feminine, the speaker encourages readers to ponder the implications of an aesthetic that foregrounds its exploitative tendencies. Although in "The Philosophy of Composition" Poe states that the tone of "The Raven" is characterized by sadness, this contemplation of "the death of a beautiful woman" ultimately results in vicarious titillation, offering a rare opportunity to experience "the most delicious because the most intolerable of sorrow" ("Philosophy" 369). The speaker promotes himself to the reader as an expert on suffering who has achieved heightened sensibility through Lenore's death, which provides him with an occasion not only to experience but also to give guided tours through "fantastic terrors never felt before." The speaker stresses the ways that his poem provides an occasion for novel entertainment: "For we cannot help agreeing that no living human being/ Ever yet was blessed with seeing bird above his chamber door—/ Bird or beast upon the sculptured bust above his chamber door,/ With such name as 'Nevermore'" (367; 51-54). The collective pronoun aligns the speaker with the reader in admiration of his brand-new, never-before-seen amalgamation. The poet thus makes himself into an observer of his own performance who celebrates its vicarious qualities as the basis of readerly identification. At a dramatic remove from the incident of even a fictional lover's death, the narrative is concerned with the thrill that the theatrical portrayal of a loss would evoke in an audience, to which the speaker himself belongs. Voyeur to the speaker's preoccupation with his own sensation, the reader never gains insight into the memory of a dead lover, unless she understands the speaker's narcissistic aestheticization of grief as an attempt to block the memory of the loved one. Against the backdrop of a feminine poetics imbued with heartfelt emotion, Poe's speaker openly disowns his grief, transforming it into a show for the viewer's pleasure.

The vicarious quality of Poe's poetry was not lost upon his contemporaries. Some readers even literalized their impressions, accusing Poe of killing his wife in order to have a fitly mournful subject for "The Raven." With "passions controlled by the presence of art until they resembled sculptured flame," according to one published accusation, Poe "deliberately sought [Virginia's] death that he might embalm her memory in immortal dirges" (qtd. in Whitman, *Edgar* 42-43). This peculiar type of character assault, which hovered around Poe, found its starting point in his own poems, which encouraged scandalous readerly fantasies. Such accusations ignore the distinction between material and poetic worlds that underpins the poetic conflation. In "The Raven," as in other poems ("Ulalume," "The Sleeper"), a dead woman stands in for a publicized robbery of feminine forms. Not surprisingly, a woman poet, Sarah Helen Whitman, recognized this distinction and defended Poe against the charge of wife-killing in the name of art: "A serious objection to this ingenious theory may perhaps be found in the 'refractory fact' that the poem was published more than a year before the event

[Virginia's death] which these persons assume it was intended to commemorate" (*Edgar* 42-43). Whitman's eloquent and influential defense testifies to the paradoxical power of Poe's poetic crime scenes to mobilize female sympathy.[10]

Underscoring its recycled qualities and proudly confessing its poetic secondariness, "The Raven" echoes "Lady Geraldine's Courtship" as well as any number of other precursors. While I have focused on this single pairing, Poe frequently embeds identifiable fragments or aspects of poems written by women within his own forms. In "Ulalume," the speaker replicates the plot of Elizabeth Oakes Smith's "The Summons Answered," in which a reveler arrives unwittingly at his wife's tomb. Buford Jones and Kent Ljungquist have recently argued that Frances Osgood's "The Life Voyage" is a model for Poe's "Annabel Lee" (275-80).[11] Contemporaries would have been able to identify many of these "plagiarisms," particularly if they were part of a select group who followed each other's work in the literary journals. Wearing rather than hiding his female influence, Poe generates a masculine poetics of flattery that particularly appeals to an audience of female poets.

There is substantial evidence to support the hypothesis of Poe's special appeal for women poets, particularly in the context of the New York literary salons of the mid 1840s where he recited "The Raven" and other poems (Silverman 280). Elizabeth Oakes Smith, a poet who frequented the salons, recalls the special attraction Poe held for women:

He did not affect the society of men, rather that of highly intellectual women with whom he liked to fall into a sort of eloquent monologue, half dream, half poetry. Men were intolerant of all this, but women fell under his fascination, and listened in silence. (Smith 88)

Though women imagined themselves as Poe's captive audience, they were voluble in describing the event. Their fascination lies in the ways that his poetic self-presentation mirrors their own. Elizabeth Barrett reportedly told Frances Osgood that "it was worth a trip to New York to see Poe's 'wild eyes flash through tears' when he read Barrett's poems" (qtd. in Silverman 287). The image of Barrett coming from afar to listen to her own verse emerge from Poe's mouth is a decidedly narcissistic fantasy, and women also analyzed this appeal. Smith remarked upon Poe's "chameleon-like temperament, by which he assimilated to those with whom he associated, and thus each analyzer of Poe gives us a glimpse of his own idiosyncrasies rather than a revelation of this unique wonderful creation" (qtd. in Ljungquist and Nickels 243).

Women poets confirm Poe's poetry as a powerful site of female identification by making him over to look like themselves. The mirror-like qualities of his poems inspired reciprocity, generating echoic responses in his female contemporaries. Among others, both Osgood and Whitman wrote elegies to Israfel, the angelic poet of Poe's own verse (Osgood 465-66; Hewitt 163-64). Like his poetic sisters' harp-like hearts, Israfel's "heart-strings were a lute." However, the poet who speaks in Poe's poem is *not* Israfel, but an earthly poet who laments his distance from that ideal: "If I could dwell/ Where Israfel/ Hath dwelt, and he where I,/ He might not sing so wildly well/ A mortal melody,/ While a bolder note than this might swell/ From my lyre within the sky" (*Collected Works* 175-77). In making Poe into Israfel, the women poets render him closer to the ideal of the Poetess whose heartstrings sing effortlessly. This conversion process suggests that they read his poetic performances of writerly and emotional blockage—one speaker's vicarious detachment in "The Raven," another speaker's anxious dismemberment of Helen—as a plea for female assistance.

Just as he once asked Frances Osgood to write his poem, Poe calls upon the loquacity of the poetess to give voice to his unspoken feelings, which, he implies, are also her own. Smith records just such a moment:

I noted his [Poe's] delicate organization—the white, fine skin of a face that had upon it an expression of questioning like that of a child, a shade of anxiety, a touch of awe, of sadness; a look out of the large, clear eyes of intense solitude. I felt a painful sympathy for him, just as one would feel for a bright, over-thoughtful child. I said at once: "Ah, Mr. Poe, this country affords no arena for those who live to dream." (116-17)

Convinced that she has read his expression properly, Smith gives sympathetic voice to his imagined plight. She and Poe take their cues in this mutual performance from Poe's poetry. Women feel moved to translate for the angelic Israfel whose "voice, all mute" cannot be discerned by less ethereal beings. But their voluble assistance only reaffirms Poe's need to render the ladies mute in turn. Together they participate in a dynamics of reciprocal translation in which women poets give voice to Poe's imagined suffering (which resembles their own), and Poe's lyric personae speak for the mute (sleeping, dead) women in their poems.

Poe's poetry displaces women's poetry by offering a masculine rendition of the feminine which draws attention to its own "crime" by encasing the evidence, the female corpse, within the poem that has absorbed the female spirit. Furthermore, these poems take as their primary audience the "poetesses" whose materials they borrow. Critics have been too quick to diagnose Poe in the terms he himself presented in his poetic self-portrait of an isolated, tortured artist, cast out from society, plagued by loss, deprived of a loving woman's nurture. In fact, Poe was one of the most successful among his contemporaries in enlisting the attention of accomplished women, in part because of the appeal of this pathetic self-portrayal. Orphaned as an infant, Poe casts himself as a sufferer of incurable loss; his perpetual mourning fuels his spiritual quests to the netherworld in search of female solace beyond the grave. Ironically, Poe's inconsolable mourning serves as a powerful draw for female sympathy: his primary audience consists of women who are moved at the plight of men who are unloved by women. Some of the seemingly more peculiar traits of Poe's poetry are variations on conventional themes in American Victorian poetry, particularly in the poetry of women, who were most intimately associated with the period's poetic practice. Rather than evidence of social isolation, the themes in Poe's poetry are signs of cultural engagement, an aspect of Poe's work that is just beginning to receive significant amounts of attention.[12]

If within his poetry Poe establishes a cross-gendered identification with women poets even as he attempts to upstage them, in his critical essays he negates that relation in order to establish an affective tie with the "race of critics" who "are masculine—men" (*Complete* 12: 1). Poe hypermasculinizes the traditionally masculine genre of the critical essay, advertising its analytical hold over the poetic realm of feminine feeling. His titles alone drive home this point: "The Rationale of Verse," "The Poetic Principle," and "The Philosophy of Composition" all celebrate the critic's ability to arrive at distilled truths of art which are invisible to readers and common authors alike. This gesture towards dominating the terrain of poetry with an alien rhetorical force, however, becomes Poe's attempt to extend his poetic claims by expanding his performance of emotional distance via the poetic feature of voice. Linked to his lyric speakers by the power of authorial association, Poe's critical voice offers a lens through which to gaze at the agony of the poet from a distance enforced not by lack of feeling, but by excess.[13] In Poe's critical scenario, a tortured soul finds relief in the realm of thought, but blankly recalls, like one in shock, the source of pain: the poem. This overlay of ironic distance upon an image of a suffering soul creates a model of emotional suppression, a powerful and enduring constellation signifying masculine literary sentiment that Poe helped to organize. Rather than a separate genre, Poe's essays are more accurately demonstrations of poetic mastery which seek to relocate the ground of affective authenticity from the heart of the poetess to the page of the critical essay.[14]

As the companion piece to "The Raven," "The Philosophy of Composition" offers the clearest example of this process. Published in *Gra-*

*ham's Magazine* in April 1846, the essay rode the wave of the poem's tremendous success. Poe reminds his readers that he is the author of the poem that many had found haunting, even as he adopts an incongruous critical voice that offers to "render it manifest that no one point in the poem's composition is referable to either accident or intuition" (365).[15] Numerous people who had heard one of Poe's many public readings of the poem had testified to the uncanny quality of the event; by revealing that impression to be a mere product of the reader's imagination, perhaps Poe hoped to create a second sensation. The vast difference between Poe's critical and poetic voices enhances the mystique of Poe the author, for in trying to reconcile the disparity between the essay and the poem, readers must posit an author outside the two texts who stands behind both.

Overdubbing the voice of the young scholar, Poe's philosopher voice displays and disowns the emotions of his poem's speaker, who has already displayed them to the poem's readers. While the essay purports to tell the tale of the poem's purely rational construction—"which proceeded, step by step, to its completion with the rigid consequence of a mathematical problem"—more accurately, the critic decomposes the poem into its elements, exposing in the process the fictional nature of the poem's speaker ("Philosophy" 365). "Commencing with a consideration of an effect," Poe relocates the source of melancholy regret from the poem's speaker to a universal reader who would agree that "the death . . . of a beautiful woman is, unquestionably, the most poetical topic in the world—and equally is it beyond doubt that the lips best suited for such a topic are those of a bereaved lover" (364, 369). Ironically, however, this disavowal of sentiment closes the distance between Poe, the living breathing poet, and the *"Mournful and Never-ending Remembrance"* evoked in the poem (373). For once the speaker is gone, who else but Poe might own "the lips . . . of a bereaved lover"?

Poe contrasts this emotionally detached state—which paradoxically signifies greater emotional authenticity—favorably against that of other poets who make claims to "ecstatic intuition," a description that recalls his profile of Fanny Osgood and other "poetesses." Like a showman, Poe opens the curtains on the theatricality of lyric: "Most writers—poets in especial—prefer having it understood that they compose by a species of fine frenzy—an ecstatic intuition—and would positively shudder at letting the public take a peep behind the scenes" (364). Reversing the feminine terms of evaluation, Poe exposes the theatricality of the poet's performance of the natural, and naturalizes theatricality as the poet's authentic environment. His gesture of sincerity is to expose their fraudulent version of it. Poe lets the public look, even stare "at the wheels and pinions—the tackle for scene-shifting—the step-ladders and demon-traps—the cock's feathers, the red paint and the black patches, which, in ninety-nine cases out of the hundred, constitute the properties of the literary *histrio*" (364-65). Whereas other poets would shrink at the idea, Poe purports to tell precisely how he composed "The Raven." Ironically, the poet's mental processes consist of nothing but a banal process of recombining clichéd images into elaborate, tantalizing new forms. Poe speaks of "originality" as an "obvious" and "easily attainable . . . source of interest" (364). Nor does he "pretend" to "originality in either the rhythm or the meter of the 'Raven'" (370). Instead, the secret of the poem's success lies in the "originality of combination" (370). Indeed, his poetic method is original only in its extreme lack of any claim to originality. Poe posits a purified theater that, in highlighting its own artifice, is more genuine than the "seemingly natural" theater of his female contemporaries. Removing the site of authenticity from the female poet's body to the masculine critical gaze, Poe engineers a critical lens that finds validity in absence and distance rather than presence and proximity.

Poe's aesthetic model methodically inverts his portrayal of his female competitors' practices. Instead of arising from the spontaneous, the mystical, and the unquantifiable, originality in verse is characterized by the crafted, the banal, and the mechanically deducible. While emotion dictates the form of women's utterance, Poe selects through analytical process the most "*universally* appreciable" focus at every stage of composition. Whereas he characterizes the poetess as a font of poetic language and feeling ("The poetess speaks because she feels, and what she feels—but what she feels is felt only by the truly poetical"), Poe starts as far away from the lyric self as possible, working backwards, not even from the poem's end, but from the "effect" he imagines that the poem might have on its readers (*Complete* 13: 115; "Philosophy" 364). The perverse opposite of those of his female contemporaries, Poe's critical practices must have instilled an odd sense of familiarity in their 180-degree difference, as if he encouraged the reader to recognize the image and the influence of the feminine in the labor he invests in reversing it.

This reversal further suggests that Poe's aesthetic system is designed to convert the poetess from the ideal producer of poetry into an ideal consumer of his own. Poe's rendition heightens the narcissistic, self-performative aspects latent in female-identified verse forms. By down-playing the relationship of the lovers within the poem, however, Poe foregrounds an intimate relationship between himself and his female contemporaries. In "The Raven" (as well as in many of his other poems) Poe's speaker adopts the role of the feminized man that was a popular figure in the poems of his female contemporaries: the poet-speaker of "Lady Geraldine's Courtship," for example. This casting decision encourages the tendency to equate poet with poetic speaker, because, like his speakers, Poe was a male poet. He thus encourages his female contemporaries to fantasize that he is the living embodiment of their poetic image, attentive to his lover even beyond the grave. Poe must imagine readers in the image of the woman poet, the ultimate home of Beauty, when he tries to ascertain what sorts of things might be "*universally* appreciable," and arrives at the conclusion that "'the death . . . of a beautiful woman is, unquestionably, the most poetical topic in the world—and equally is it beyond doubt that the lips best suited for such a topic are those of a bereaved lover.'" This formulation makes a captive audience of one sector of Poe's literary competition. For it was undoubtedly seductive for women to imagine themselves into the position of Poe's lost love and the object of his poetic tributes. The multiple bids for the role of the inspiration of "Annabel Lee" are well-known: at least three women, two of them poets, believed the poem was written for her alone.[16] If the most poetical topic is a male lover's longing for his female lover, then women would have difficulty imagining themselves into the role of poet in Poe's poetic system with the same level of authenticity that Poe, himself a male poet, could claim. For while we have seen that Poe was particularly drawn to poems by women told from the perspective of a bereaved male lover, in his criticism, Poe naturalizes the link between himself and that figure.

Positioning women in the role of audience and himself in the role of poet with superior claims to emotional authenticity, Poe's critical essays stabilize the fluid, imitative play of cross-gendered poetic exchange. Rather than a systematic attempt to disenfranchise women poets, however, Poe's negotiations of the critical genre seek to carve out a specifically masculine poetic space. By annexing the critical essay to the "province of poetry," Poe creates a hybridized model of masculine literary sentiment. Rather than a separate sphere of discourse, his essays overlay his poetry in order to create a composite portrait of an authentic male artist. Confirming and extending this aesthetic fusion of critic and poet, influential critic (and poet) Daniel Hoffman locates the key to Poe's artistic sensibility at the point of a generic comparison. "A remarkable achievement *in candor*," "The Philosophy of Composition" offers the second half of a confession that begins in Poe's poems (91):

What is the relation between his claim that imagination is a rational and orderly premeditated process and his need to drape it in crepe at the bier of a beautiful woman? What is the connection but that the straitjacket method enables the poet to deal with his obsessive and inescapable subject by compelling him to think about something else, something other than the woe vibrating within him which to think of would overcome him. So the method of his art enables the madness of his matter to be spoken. (92)

"The woe vibrating within" Poe is made visible through generic juxtaposition: his critical assertions of aesthetic rigor complement and authenticate the obsessive crepe-draping of the poems. If the strength and rigidity of the "straitjacket method" betray the power of the contained emotion, then criticism is a more radical form of artistic self-containment than poetry-writing, and is thus, paradoxically, the location of authorial self-revelation.

Present in Poe but missing from his descendants is an acknowledgment of his aesthetic exchange with his female contemporaries. Following cues from Poe's essays while ignoring the evidence from his poems, critics have consolidated a tradition of Poe scholarship in which the figure of the woman poet has suffered an ever more radical absorption into the figure of the male poet. Baudelaire's mid-century interpretations of Poe have played a key role in this process. In appropriating Poe for his own poetico-critical project, Baudelaire suppresses Poe's expressions of female identification and indebtedness, while exaggerating his literary misogyny. Looking to Poe in order to ask how to write an elite poetry within a market economy, Baudelaire finds an answer in the exorcism of female influence.

In his 1856 introduction to his first volume of translation of Poe's works, Baudelaire portrays a monstrous America, founded at a point of civilizational decline that is articulated in its democratic organization, whose unchecked impulses and enormous energy find their outlet in indiscriminate productivity. In the American literary marketplace, excessively prolix writers proliferate: "America babbles and rambles with an astonishing volubility. Who could count its poets? They are innumerable. Its bluestockings? They clutter the magazines" (122). Deprived of the protective milieu surrounding his aristocratic European forebearers, the great American poet confronts an innumerable throng of profit-oriented writers whose dubious poetic projects stand on equal footing with great literary works. The productivity of "the money-making author" mimics the mindless generativity of mass production and threatens to drown the true artist (Poe), adrift in the modern world.

Baudelaire finds Poe's theatrical strategies successful in combating the encroachment of literary materialists in this "maelstrom of mediocrity": Poe distinguishes himself "as a *caricature*" (122, 123). The prototype for his "charlatanry" is also its audience: the writers whom he conquers through his duplicative and dismissive play. Baudelaire contrasts the masculine artificiality of Poe's work with the natural femininity of those writers aligned with market forces. Taking his cue from Poe, Baudelaire links Poe's masculine literary style to an artificial performance of the feminine. He says of "Marginalia"'s advocacy of an analytical approach to writing: "The lovers of a fine frenzy will perhaps be revolted by these cynical maxims; but everyone may take what he wishes from them. . . . After all, a little charlatanism is always permitted to genius, and is even proper to it. It is, like rouge on the cheeks of a naturally beautiful woman, an additional stimulus to the mind" (156). Whereas Karen Halttunen argues that antebellum theatricality opposes sincerity and embodies the threat of hypocrisy, Baudelaire suggests that theatricality is a form of transparency that sets off natural beauty. He maps this set of associations onto literary styles, associating the inferior "fine frenzy" with the rougeless female, and Poe's "deliberate," premeditated style with both theatricality and the made-up woman.

The logical conclusion of Baudelaire's argument would be that Poe is a literary transvestite whose charms are superior to the "naturally beautiful" women he imitates. And indeed, he advances precisely this claim, revealing in the process that the ultimate threat to the male writer's autonomy is the female writer, the spirit not of the home, but of the marketplace. Poe's rendition of the feminine beats the literary women on the very terms that they should excel: intensity and sincerity of emotion. Baudelaire's logic is associative:

As for [Poe's] intense preoccupation with the horrible, I have noticed among a number of men that it was often the result of an immense unused vital energy, or sometimes of a stubborn chastity, or of a deeply repressed sensibility. The unnatural pleasure that a man may feel on seeing his own

blood flow, brusque and useless movements, loud cries uttered almost in-
voluntarily are analogous phenomena. Pain relieves pain, action rests one
from repose. Another characteristic of his writing is that it is completely
anti-feminine. Let me explain myself. Women write and write, with an ex-
uberant rapidity; their hearts speak and chatter in reams. Usually they
know nothing of art, or measure, or logic; their style trails and flows like
their garments. . . . In the books of Edgar Poe the style is concatenated; the
prejudice or the inertia of the reader cannot penetrate the meshes of this
network woven by logic. All his ideas, like obedient arrows, fly to the same
target. (78-79)

Baudelaire suggests that we read Poe's narcissistic preoccupation
with self-inflicted pain as a sign of his heightened capacity for strong
feeling, presumably repressed into such perversions in order to protect
himself from his less sensitive contemporaries. Baudelaire links Poe's
unnaturally heightened sensibility to his "anti-feminine," highly
crafted writing style which counters the "natural" feminine writing
style. After likening Poe's preoccupation with the horrible to men who
enjoy "seeing their own blood flow," Baudelaire repeats this image in
transmuted form when describing feminine style, which "trails and
flows like their garments." The striking parallel, caused by the repetition of similar images and an identical word, articulates the difference
between feminine and masculine styles in terms of control. Women's
lack of control is superficial, advertised in their flowing clothing. Inter-
nalizing their fashion accessories, women's writing reveals the same
careless superficiality. The male writer, on the other hand, is a detached
observer of his own uncontrol, which registers not superficially, in his
clothes, but crucially, on his body. His writing style uniquely combines
ultimate detachment and intense engagement.[17]

While Baudelaire draws a stark contrast between men and women,
ultimately he casts masculinity as a theatricalized extension of femininity. Poe's emotional distress is repressed into a physical symptom
that expresses a desire for suicide, a pleasure in seeing blood come to

the surface. The analogy—that blood is to man as clothing is to woman—implies that bleeding, as an externalized expression of bodily and mental agony, is men's way of becoming feminine. A man bleeding from a cut is the hysterical equivalent of a woman menstruating. A perverse masculine miming of womanhood, men's flowing blood is an unregenerative, even deadly version of women's fertility. To Baudelaire, Poe's lack of emotional receptivity is the sign of a "deeply repressed sensibility," and his mechanistic tendencies (his "concatenated" style) are a sign of "unused vital energy": both aspects of his style symbolically substitute for what is not there. As I have argued in relation to "The Philosophy of Composition," Baudelaire believes that Poe's theatricality contributes to the reader's impression of his sincerity rather than undercutting it. Canonical values lie in a reaction to a female-identified aesthetic of proximity to the marketplace; however, the masculine performance of distance as a sign of heightened emotional sensitivity contains all the traits of the poetess in inverted form.

Baudelaire thus advances a hypermasculine version of a Poe aesthetic, heavily reliant upon his critical statements, that has profoundly influenced not only the American reception of Poe, but also the development of an American canonical aesthetic which has all but entirely screened out nineteenth-century women poets (Emily Dickinson is the only retention). Critics continue to read Poe as Baudelaire read him: the embattled, heroic artist awash in a sea of female poetry which was indistinguishable from marketplace motions and which therefore appealed, far more readily than his own work, to the popular taste. But in investing Poe with the feminine, Baudelaire and, even more radically, the canon-minded critics who follow, have divested literary history of the significance of women poets, whose presence, a mixed blessing for Poe, is a pure evil for Baudelaire, and an incomprehensibility for later scholars. Hoffman awards Poe the position of "the first critic in this country to insist that literary work be measured by literary standards alone," but in the same breath expresses bafflement about Poe's peculiar interest in poetesses:

> True, [Poe's] own standards were not only high but a little odd: he couldn't keep himself from overpraising poetesses who wrote elegies to dead lovers, finding in the effusions of such nobodies as Mrs. Amelia Welby and Elizabeth Oakes Smith the nearly articulated intimations of the theme which became the sole burden of his own verse, and its undoing. But when I read Poe's notes on poetry—not on contemporary poems . . . Poe on poetic principles makes a lot of good sense. (94)

Hoffman suggests that Poe overestimates the extent to which women poets offered "nearly articulated intimations" of his own work. Echoing Poe's critical gesture of female exorcism, Hoffman identifies with Poe and dismisses his female contemporaries on the basis of his "poetic principles" as distinct from his book reviews.

In forgetting the women, Hoffman and others have divested the canonical male writer of his ties to a market-based dynamics of literary exchange in order to render him an impermeable critic of those forces. That external vantage point, as Poe more than his followers might readily acknowledge, is a fiction constructed by the writers themselves. In order to cast Poe as "great," critics have needed to forget that Emerson called him "the jingle man," thus aligning him with "the female poetasters," those "anti-poetic influences of Massachusetts" that the great writer must struggle against.[18] Often, critics have needed to forget Poe's poetry entirely in order to make of him "a brilliant analyst of a market he was never able fully to exploit"; generally speaking, the canonical (and masculine) Poe is the prose Poe of fiction and criticism (Douglas 84).

Although some scholars have located the systematic dismissal of female literary achievement in the antebellum period, in truth antebellum writers, as we see from the case of Poe, were more open to considerations of the literary merit (not simply the saleability) of women's poetry, than later generations of critics. And while writing was obsessively categorized according to supposedly gendered qualities, cross-gendered literary interactions were pervasive among writers who considered themselves peers. Poe's struggles (and those of his critics) testify that women poets played a formative role in the creation of literary tastes in the antebellum period, rather than serving as a repulsive force that impels great writers to create works of art in sheer resistance to mass mediocrity.[19] Later critics have tended to accept as accurate the dismissive characterization of the antebellum female poet promulgated in the period by literary competitors. When looking for the reasons why women poets of the nineteenth century have been forgotten, we should consider the lyric voice of the critical essay as much as its aesthetic pronouncements, and reconsider the impact of the "poetess" in an often recognizably reactive rhetoric. Rather than peripheral, trivial, or obviously frivolous, women poets in the antebellum period posed a truly central aesthetic challenge. This case study of Poe's work helps to indicate that their work profoundly influenced canonical as well as forgotten literary movements, and any historical understanding of the poetic practices of the period requires a thorough re-evaluation of the significance and influence of the female poets and poetry of America.

## Notes

1. Publisher N. P. Willis voices a common sentiment: "It is the women who read. . . . It is the women who give or withhold a literary reputation. . . . It is the women who exercise the ultimate control over the Press" (qtd. in Douglas 103). Baym notes that at least eighty women published books of poems between 1800 and 1850; over double that number published poems in newspapers and magazines (297). Pattee claims that "the American literary 'female' as seen in the 1830s and the 1840s, was a writer of verse" (50), while Ostriker notes that poetry and the poetess were associated with moral uplift in the early nineteenth century (30).

2. Arguing that writing is "a public gesture, not a private act," Railton defines "literary performance" as "how writers conceive of and address themselves to an audience" (4, 12). Because authors are important members of each other's audience in the antebellum period, I suggest that these categories overlap. Moreover, I find that the

"drama of literary creation" is a drama of collaboration among writers rather than a one-man show, as Railton suggests (4).

3. Recent studies have reproduced elements of canonical structure in their challenges to it by positing discrete men's and women's literary traditions, with the men's dominant (e.g., Walker 57 and Ostriker 28-37). This circumscription model curtails the possibility of women's influence on larger literary and cultural movements. Some recent works have begun exploring cross-gender literary exchanges; see Marchalonis.

4. For one example of a dismissal, see Hoffman (93-94). In his edition of Poe's works, Harrison includes a number of reviews of women poets, but his introductions refer only to reviews of male poets such as Lowell, Bryant, and Longfellow (introductions, *Complete*, vols. 8-13). In "Amorous Bondage," Dayan notes "Poe's serious attention to women writers," including Elizabeth Barrett, yet dismisses his reviews of Frances Sargent Osgood and Lydia Sigourney as "cloying and sentimental" without explaining why we should pay attention to some reviews and ignore others (199). See also Dayan's "Poe's Women" (3). Countering the critical dismissal of Osgood, DeJong has argued convincingly for a "literary alliance" between Osgood and Poe ("Lines").

5. Ellison explores the association of the feminine with the male romantic. Her chapters on Margaret Fuller treat the female romantic critic's attempts to reconfigure the gendered paradigms of romanticism (pt. III).

6. Wendorff's dissertation explores the legacy of the "Poetess Ideal" for late-nineteenth-century women poets. See also Walker (27). Wendorff's study de-links that ideal from female writerly identity by arguing that women poets adapted the convention to their expressive needs. Indeed, whether the poetess is more than an ideal for any poet or critic of the time is unclear. On this point I differ with DeJong who asserts that Poe shares "the prevalent view" that Osgood (as well as women poets in general) was "a natural 'singer'—not a creative artist" ("Fair" 269).

7. Cushman's useful notion of poetic "fictions of form" has informed this essay throughout. In "Amorous Bondage," Dayan argues that Poe "repeats, exaggerates, and transforms the immutable, romanticized attributes white women are granted by men. He dramatizes the fact of appropriation, and thereby undefines the definitions that mattered to civilized society" (190). If one grants that women writers were not entirely circumscribed by men's idealization, then one may also grant that Poe uses these definitions to appropriate female achievement. In "Poe's Women," Dayan argues that Poe's inhabitance of women's place is "no mere appropriation: the 'possession' is reciprocal" (9). While I agree on this point, I do not agree that "Poe is after nothing less than an exhumation of the lived, but disavowed or suppressed experiences of women in his society" (10). It is not women's place in patriarchy, but more specifically the intimacy with lyric (and art more broadly) which that place enables that concerns Poe. Imagining women as literary competitors, Poe imitates women's poetry in order to gain access to their poetic power. For an exploration of woman as medium for conversions, see Dayan's *Fables of Mind* (ch. 3). For a psycholinguistic reading of Poe's dead women, see Bronfen. For a related argument on female absorption in Victorian men's artwork, see Christ (144, 146).

8. See Mabbott's comments on the relationship between the two poems (*Collected Works* 411). My argument draws upon Bloom's notion of the "anxiety of influence," a

generational psychodrama between men in which the younger poet wrests power from the older by repeating his practices in an altered manner while denying his influence. By emphasizing gender and audience factors in systems of poetic influence, I offer a system of contemporaneous, cross-gendered poetic influence and exchange.

9. Kennedy notes that the speaker "wishes both to forget and to remember" and attributes the dilemma to "a conflict between memory and denial" at the center of the logic of bereavement and writing (68).

10. Brown argues that Poe's fiction relies upon a "single-minded prohibition of female generativity in order to produce evidence of a particular instance" of "individual consciousness" (341-42). I argue, to the contrary, that Poe's work enacts a male indebtedness to a female intellectual productivity imagined to be superior.

11. See Mabbott's comments on "The Summons Answered" (*Collected Works* 411) and Reilly's rebuttal of Jones and Ljungquist. The idea that Poe embeds identifiable fragments of others' works within his poems evokes Riffaterre's notion of the hypogram. In Poe's work, however, one does not have to go hunting for the source, for it is identifiable within the poem which "steals" it.

12. The image of Poe as an isolated, tortured artist underpins much of the finest Poe criticism, which follows in the psychoanalytic tradition (Baudelaire, Blasing, Bonaparte, Hoffman, and Silverman). While recent studies place Poe in his cultural context, his exceptionalism survives. Elmer's provocative study explains Poe's "double history" in literary studies as the originator of many mass cultural genres and as the hermetically sealed high artist. While this work powerfully demonstrates Poe's engagement with certain "cultural logics" of his day, it minimizes the collaborative aspects of Poe's work and their gender logic (aspects which challenge a mass-individual dichotomy, even as it is played out within one author's opus) that I emphasize here. See also Allen, Fisher, and Rosenheim and Rachman.

13. Cameron argues that Emerson advances a model of sincere affect based upon the evacuation of identifiably elegiac feeling: he mentions his son's death at the outset of "Experience," and then drops the subject. This model, in which profound mourning is defined by personal reticence, is especially comprehensible as a reaction to contemporary elegiac modes that identify sincere mourning with an outpouring of grief.

14. A number of critics have noted that Poe's critical essays, particularly "The Philosophy of Composition," serve as extensions of his poetic endeavor, though the characterizations of that continuous model differ (Elmer 210-13; Pease 184).

15. One review called "The Raven" "wild and shivery," and an observer noted that readers were "electrified by the weird cry of Nevermore" (Silverman 237; also 237-38, 278-79).

16. Sarah Helen Whitman, Sarah Anna Lewis, and Elmira Shelton. Whitman and Lewis were poets. Others have suggested that Frances Osgood, Virginia Poe, or Nancy Richmond were the objects of tribute. See Mabbott (Poe, *Collected Works* 468-77).

17. Elmer posits a related formulation of Poe's critico-poetical affect in "The Philosophy of Composition": Poe "acts out *and* reflects, he both repeats *and* critiques the workings of his poem" (211). I argue that this combination is a quality of criticism as a poetic genre, which Poe helped to found, rather than a resistance to criticism as a genre, as Elmer claims.

---

18. Pearce echoes Emerson's characterization approvingly (139).

19. A recent example of this distinction appears in Gilmore: "The split between elite and mass culture . . . appears to be confirmed in the actual literary market. While the romantics were still producing the masterpieces still read today, domestic novels written by women commanded the enthusiasm of the antebellum public" (7). Elmer complicates this distinction in provocative ways by defining it as a dynamic of ambivalence that goes on within the individual artist (and also within the social body); still, the dichotomy remains.

## Works Cited

Allen, Michael. *Poe and the British Magazine Tradition.* New York: Oxford University Press, 1969.

Baudelaire, Charles. *Baudelaire on Poe.* Trans. and ed. Lois and Francis Hyslop. State College: Bald Eagle Press, 1952.

Baym, Nina. "The Rise of the Woman Author." *Columbia Literary History of the United States.* New York: Columbia University Press, 1988. 289-305.

Blasing, Mutlu. *American Poetry: The Rhetoric of Its Forms.* New Haven: Yale University Press, 1987.

Bloom, Harold. *Anxiety of Influence: A Theory of Poetry.* New York: Oxford University Press, 1987.

Bonaparte, Marie. *The Life and Works of Edgar Poe.* Trans. John Rodker. London: Hogarth Press, 1949.

Bronfen, Elisabeth. *Over Her Dead Body: Death, Femininity and the Aesthetic.* Manchester: Manchester University Press, 1992.

Brown, Gillian. "Poetics of Extinction." Rosenheim and Rachman 330-44.

Browning, Elizabeth Barrett. *Elizabeth Barrett Browning: Selected Poems.* Ed. Margaret Foster. Baltimore: Johns Hopkins University Press, 1988.

Cameron, Sharon. "Representing Grief: Emerson's 'Experience.'" *Representations* 15 (Summer 1986): 15-41.

Christ, Carol. "Painting the Dead: Portraiture and Necrophilia in Victorian Art and Poetry." *Death and Representation.* Ed. Elisabeth Bronfen. London: Johns Hopkins University Press, 1993. 133-51.

Cushman, Stephen. *Fictions of Form in American Poetry.* Princeton: Princeton University Press, 1993.

Dayan, Joan. "Amorous Bondage: Poe, Ladies and Slaves." Rosenheim and Rachman 179-209.

_____. *Fables of Mind: An Inquiry Into Poe's Fiction.* New York: Oxford University Press, 1987.

_____. "Poe's Women: A Feminist Poe?" *Poe Studies* (June/Dec. 1993): 1-12.

DeJong, Mary. "Her Fair Fame: The Reputation of Frances Sargent Osgood, 'Woman Poet.'" *Studies in the American Renaissance.* Ed. Joel Myerson. Charlottesville: University Press of Virginia, 1987.

_____. "Lines From a Partly Published Drama." Marchalonis 31-58.

Douglas, Ann. *Feminization of American Culture*. New York: Knopf, 1977.

Ellison, Julie. *Delicate Subjects: Romanticism, Gender, and the Ethics of Understanding*. Ithaca: Cornell University Press, 1990.

Elmer, Jonathan. *Reading at the Social Limit: Affect, Mass Culture, and Edgar Allan Poe*. Stanford: Stanford University Press, 1995.

Fisher, Benjamin Franklin, ed. *Poe and His Times: The Artist and His Milieu*. Baltimore: The Edgar Allan Poe Society, 1990.

Gilmore, Michael. *American Romanticism and the Marketplace*. Chicago: University of Chicago Press, 1985.

Griswold, Rufus, ed. *Female Poets and Poetry of America*. Philadelphia: Moss and Co., 1863.

Halttunen, Karen. *Confidence Men and Painted Women: A Study of Middle-Class Culture in America, 1830-1870*. New Haven: Yale University Press, 1982.

Hewitt, Mary, ed. *Laurel Leaves: Woven by the Friends of the Late Mrs. Osgood*. New York: Lamport, Blackman and Law, 1854.

Hoffman, Daniel. *Poe Poe Poe Poe Poe Poe Poe*. Garden City: Doubleday, 1972.

Jones, Buford, and Kent Ljungquist. "Poe, Mrs. Osgood, and 'Annabel Lee.'" *Studies in the American Renaissance*. Ed. Joel Myerson. Charlottesville: University Press of Virginia, 1983. 275-80.

Kennedy, J. Gerald. *Poe, Death, and the Life of Writing*. New Haven: Yale University Press, 1987.

Ljungquist, Kent, and Cameron Nickels. "Elizabeth Oakes Smith on Poe: A Chapter in the Recovery of His Nineteenth-Century Reputation." In Fisher. 235-46.

Marchalonis, Shirley, ed. *Patrons and Protégées: Gender, Friendship, and Writing in Nineteenth-Century America*. New Brunswick: Rutgers University Press, 1988.

Osgood, Frances Sargent. *Poems*. Philadelphia: Carey and Hart, 1850.

Ostriker, Alicia. *Stealing the Language: The Emergence of Women's Poetry in America*. Boston: Beacon Press, 1986.

Pattee, Fred Lewis. *The Feminine Fifties*. New York: D. Appleton and Co., 1940.

Pearce, Roy Harvey. *The Continuity of American Poetry*. Princeton: Princeton University Press, 1962.

Pease, Donald A. *Visionary Compacts: American Renaissance Writings in Cultural Context*. Madison: University of Wisconsin Press, 1987.

Poe, Edgar Allan. *The Collected Works of Edgar Allan Poe*. Ed. T. O. Mabbott. Vol. 1. Cambridge: Belknap Press of Harvard University Press, 1969.

_____. *The Collected Writings of Edgar Allan Poe*. Ed. Burton Pollin. Vol. 3, pt. 1. *Broadway Journal Prose*. New York: Gordian Press, 1986.

_____. *The Complete Works of Edgar Allan Poe*. Ed. James Harrison. New York: AMS Press, 1965.

_____. *Marginalia*. Ed. John Carl Miller. Charlottesville: University Press of Virginia, 1981.

_____. "The Philosophy of Composition." *Selected Poetry and Prose of Edgar Allan Poe*. Ed. T. O. Mabbott. New York: Modern Library, 1951. 363-74.

Railton, Stephen. *Authorship and Audience: Literary Performance in the American Renaissance*. Princeton: Princeton University Press, 1992.

Reilly, John. "Mrs. Osgood's 'The Life-Voyage' and 'Annabel Lee.'" *Poe Studies* 17.1 (1984): 23.

Riffaterre, Michael. *Semiotics of Poetry*. Bloomington: Indiana University Press, 1978.

Rosenheim, Shawn, and Steven Rachman, eds. *The American Face of Edgar Poe*. Baltimore: Johns Hopkins University Press, 1995.

Silverman, Kenneth. *Edgar A. Poe: A Mournful and Never-ending Remembrance*. London: Weidenfeld, 1993.

Smith, Elizabeth Oakes. *Selections from the Autobiography of Elizabeth Oakes Smith*. Ed. Mary Alice Wyman. Lewiston, ME: Lewiston Journal, 1924.

Ticknor, Caroline. *Poe's Helen*. New York: Charles Scribner's Sons, 1916.

Walker, Cheryl. *The Nightingale's Burden: Women Poets and American Culture Before 1900*. Bloomington: Indiana University Press, 1982.

Wendorff, Laura. "Race, Ethnicity, and the Voice of the 'Poetess' in the Lives and Works of Four Late-Nineteenth-Century American Woman Poets." Diss. University of Michigan, 1992.

Whitman, Sarah Helen. *Edgar Poe and His Critics*. New York: Rudd, Carleton, 1860.

_____. *Hours of Life and Other Poems*. Boston: Houghton, Osgood and Co., 1879.

# Edgar Allan Poe's Control of Readers:
## Formal Pressures in Poe's Dream Poems_____

James Postema

In his "Philosophy of Composition," Edgar Allan Poe is clearly concerned with how the word-choices, sounds, and rhythms of "The Raven" might control the way readers respond to that poem. Many writers have either supported or denied Poe's claims that he wrote "The Raven" with the reader in mind, but to a surprising extent the discussion of Poe's intended effects on readers has remained largely within the bounds set up by his own theoretical works; at least in the area of criticism, Poe has in fact controlled readers' responses.[1] Instead of arguing about Poe's intentions in the "Philosophy of Composition," however, we can look to the formal structures of Poe's poems themselves and see that several of them do indeed limit the information they give to readers, thereby governing the roles that readers may play in interpretation of the poems. "Dream-Land" and "Fairy-Land" provide two instructive examples: each poem opens into a fantastic world which defies any interpretations that are based upon readers' everyday experiences, but each poem also offers readers a logical, formal structure that pushes interpretation in a particular direction.

Fifteen years separate these poems; the first version of "Fairy-Land" was published in 1829, while "Dream-Land" appeared in 1844. But they begin with the same premise: in each we see nearly identical images of misty, mystical landscapes obscured by "tears that drip all over,"[2] scenes which somehow open into larger, more easily visible worlds. The cause of the tears is unclear; they may be evidence of the poetic personae's own unhappiness, or they may simply be metaphorical descriptions of some foggy, rainy state.

What is clear is that because the tears obscure "forms we can't discover" ("Fairy-Land," line 3) readers must trust the speaker's description of what lies behind the tears. Each of these works is a dream poem, and Poe's dream poems in particular control readers quite strictly: because such poems depict worlds that differ greatly from the "real" world, they do not allow readers to use everyday logic. We cannot rely on our experience of natural laws to understand "Ulalume" or "The City in the Sea," for example. We are forced to suspend disbelief more fully in these poems than in other poems.

Readers know from the very beginning of "Fairy-Land" [I] that events in the poem do not operate on normal rational principles. Instead, Poe replaces cause-and-effect logic with metonymic connections: things are related simply because he puts them together. The landscape obscured by tears begins the poem, followed by a scene in which "Huge moons . . . wax and wane." But the poem then seems to jump from one discrete scene to another: the moons and other images in the poem don't seem to be obscured by tears; rather, the tears and the moons are only related sequentially, by appearing in the same poem.

The description of the moons begins a chain of metonymic imagery that stretches throughout "Fairy-Land." In lines 9-10 the moons acquire faces, from which they can "put out the star-light"; a concealed metaphor here equates star-light with a candle, which can be blown out by a breath. In lines 12-14 the moons decide by "trial" which of them is "the best," with the winner described as "more filmy than the rest." And in the rest of the poem Poe relates the moon to drapery, to a "labyrinth of light" that "buries" the world beneath, to a "moony covering" which soars with storms in the skies, to a yellow albatross, and to a tent. In the final lines the moon breaks into a shower of "atomies" that come to rest on butterflies' wings.

Poe's reasons for using such metonymic associations may be related to his opinion of the relative imaginative qualities of various figures of speech. Studying Poe's practical criticism, Robert D. Jacobs concludes that "Poe had claimed that metaphor was more imaginative than simile, but he had also suggested that an imaginative poet rarely used figurative language" (282). And Jacobs explains that for Poe, "A figure of speech, insofar as it specifies resemblance between objects, belongs to the real world, the phenomenal world that can be perceived by the

senses. . . . Poe would have had the imagination soar completely beyond actuality" (243). By using metonymic associations, Poe could attempt to do just that, since he could disregard the normal ways in which
objects acted and interacted in the world of ordinary experience. But
these metonymic deviations make some particular kinds of interpretation difficult, if not impossible: we cannot explain why any one event
or image is connected to another, the way we might be able to in a realistic work, nor can we predict any actions or images that will appear
next in the poem. The poem cuts itself off from interpretations based
on cause-and-effect logic.

Poe further removes the poem from the realm of everyday logic by
the use of personification. Butterflies are "never-contented" because
the speaker gives them that quality; the moons meet together to decide
who will be chosen for the descent to earth because the speaker says
they do. It is easy for readers to accept, but impossible to predict, these
personifications; we must simply accept Poe's description of the butterflies as malcontents and go on to try to form some interpretation on a
different level.

It is possible to do so because Poe presents these images in a literary
structure, a plot of sorts. The poem opens with a potential conflict for
readers, if not for the speaker, when we first realize that this is a dream
poem: the tears of the opening scene (which may or may not be the
speaker's tears) obscure the forms of the landscape, imposing blindness and uncertainty on the reader, the protagonist, or both. But the
poem progresses from that state to a calm, peaceful description of the
moon's setting: its "wide circumference/ In easy drapery falls." In the
next few lines we see a catalogue of things lighted by the moon, as it
sets

> Over hamlets, over halls,
> Wherever they may be—
> O'er the strange woods—o'er the sea—
> Over spirits on the wing—

Over every drowsy thing—
And buries them up quite
In a labyrinth of light—

After the peaceful moonset, this catalogue helps resolve the poem's initial crisis of uncertainty. Even with the connotations of burial in a "labyrinth of light," the description seems purposefully drawn out to resolve some of the tensions of that initial scene. In the next section, too, the speaker implies that people are going about their usual business in an everyday manner; the moon's dissolution above this normal scene could be interpreted as the coming of daylight and the restoration of clear vision, adding another step in the progression from metonymic uncertainty to a state of resolution.

The catalogue in the center of the poem helps diminish tension in another way, for despite the metonymic string of imagery, the description of the moon's setting in lines 16-24 brings some images together for more clearly rhetorical reasons. A moon could quite naturally appear to settle on the peak of a mountain. This is one of the few images that can correspond realistically to the natural world, providing readers with a more familiar scene. Further, the rest of the catalogue is made up of opposites, so that the name of one in each pair matches the other: poor hamlets suggest rich halls, woods form a parallel to seas, and "spirits on the wing" contrast with drowsy things. With the possible exception of flying spirits, all of these make logical sense when seen in a picture of moonlight, for the moon's spreading light is an image large enough to contain them all. The sense of completeness that this catalogue creates balances much of the uncertainty of the obscuring tears at the beginning: although we are in a different world, we seem to be able to see that world as a whole.

By using this catalogue and the progression of scenes, Poe provides readers with a logical structure that allows a certain kind of understanding of the poem. Readers do not have to accept this structure as a key to the poem's meaning; nor would I argue that all readers will accept it. But by eliminating interpretations based upon ordinary experience, and by providing these literary structures, Poe (whether consciously or not) puts formal pressures on readers to understand "Fairy-Land" in certain ways.

One of those ways is to lessen the reader's sense that he or she must arrive at any one interpretation of this poem. The calmness of the imagery gives the impression that, even if we misinterpret what the speaker is describing to us, nothing will be hurt; we can be wrong without any dire consequences. In everyday life we do not normally see the moon breaking up into a shower of atomies, but when it does so here the result is not cataclysmic upheaval; instead, we see a piece of that moon resting on the "quivering wings" of a rather harmless butterfly. When the moon sets over hamlets and halls, the speaker says, "then, how deep!—O, deep!/ Is the passion of their sleep." But this potentially threatening image is resolved in the next line: "In the morning they arise."[3]

"Fairy-Land" [I] thus begins in tension and obscurity but progresses to an essentially peaceful state, and in doing so the poem reduces the importance of getting any exact interpretation correct. Instead, we are left with an impression that the poem is a complete narrative sequence of imaginative events in a pleasantly unreal world. The meaning of those events is not completely clear, but neither is the need for attaching a specific meaning to them.[4]

"Dream-Land," on the other hand, is a much darker poem. Like "Fairy-Land," it begins by letting readers know clearly that they are in an unreal world, but here Poe's poetic persona says so directly. Poe does not use metonymy so heavily in this poem; in the introduction he states that this is a world "Out of Space—out of Time," a kingdom ruled by Night. Poe even calls that Night an "Eidolon," making sure that readers know they are in ideal, unreal surroundings. After describing tears that obscure vision, as in "Fairy-Land," the speaker takes us through an unsettled landscape, scenes constructed differently from those in "Fairy-Land." All the images in this part of

"Dream-Land" come from the natural world, yet nothing here has any natural bounds—we see "bottomless vales" and "lakes that endlessly outspread." The unbounded elements constantly intermingle as well: the poem describes "Seas that restlessly aspire,/ Surging, unto skies of fire," and "Mountains toppling evermore/ Into seas without a shore."

This world not only exists outside the realm of our experience, but is contradictory to what we know; we can put together the words *boundless* and *seas*, as Poe has, but our minds cannot comprehend boundless seas, let alone shoreless seas with mountains falling into them. While Poe as poet can form such antithetical constructions, for us as readers, according to Roy Harvey Pearce, the words he uses are still "ineradicably tainted by the reality of the things and states to which they [refer]" (150). The fantastic world here does not rely on metonymy, as it does in "Fairy-Land," but the effect of those oxymorons is the same for readers as with metonymy: because ordinary logic does not apply, we have to look elsewhere for clues to an interpretation of the poem.

Poe heightens our sense of unreality in this realm with his description of mountains "toppling evermore," suggesting an existential insecurity and impermanence—there is quite literally no firm ground here. Yet by making the mountains topple eternally, Poe not only creates that insecurity but gives it a sort of permanence: readers can be sure that the mountains always will be falling. However, knowing this doesn't give readers any alternate structure for understanding the poem; rather, it reinforces the impression of anxiety. The idea of constancy in the mountains' constant falling reminds us that we can conceive of some sort of stable, permanent state in which we could rest, some rational interpretation of the poem; yet the constant falling also reassures us that such rest is completely unreachable. Unlike the moons in "Fairy-Land," which eventually coalesce into a single moon, the recurrences here do not allow us any sense of closure or intellectual security.[5]

After this section, however, the poem moves back into more conventional imagery, with shrouded and white-robed figures walking around doing things that shrouded forms are supposed to do: "forms of friends long given,/ In agony, to the Earth," they "start and sigh." These symbols are less powerful than earlier scenes because they already fit into widely accepted schemes of what death and the dead are like, in Poe's time as well as our own. But readers also can feel a little more secure in contemplating such figures because, even though the ghosts are in a morbid world, the idea of ghosts already exists in a context outside of the speaker's personal vision. They allow readers to feel again that they can see a larger, more coherent picture of this strange realm.[6]

Less clear than the symbolism of these figures is the reason why the traveler "May not—dare not openly view" this world. We learn that the unseen King of "Dream-Land" has decreed that "Never its mysteries are exposed/ To the weak human eye unclosed," perhaps suggesting that only the dead may look with impunity on sad waters and skies of fire. Yet the speaker is presumably human, if not alive, again creating self-contradictions in the speaker's statements. The "fringed lid" and "darkened glasses" necessary here also return us to less conventional images, ones that can carry some of the speaker's anxious view of this world without seeming trite (as some of the ghost imagery does). Again, these images remove the poem from the world of everyday experience, eliminating one kind of interpretation.

Yet, as he does in "Fairy-Land," Poe includes in "Dream-Land" some structures that give readers direction for interpretations. The tone of these contradictory images is fairly consistent: while we cannot understand the world here logically, we can say that it is—uniformly— not a pleasant one. From the insecurity of "mountains toppling" to the projected emotions of "lone waters," the poem has a dark, morbid tone. If this is indeed the realm of Night and of death, such morbid images make sense. So does the illogical nature of the region: visual perception breaks down at night, just as our experiential wisdom cannot understand the world of the dead. The poem thus turns on itself: the qualities that make it hard to understand end up serving as clues for interpretation; because we cannot interpret the poem's existential insecurity on an experiential level, we can see it as a statement about a world that is not secure and does not submit itself to everyday logic—the realm of Death. The poem's illogic becomes logical.

In the conclusion, Poe repeats the first six lines of the poem almost identically. In some ways nothing has changed since the beginning of the poem; the static, yet dynamic, world of the poem is apparently continuing in its cycles of destruction, but we still have no idea of how the narrator could survive in such a strange world.

By repeating these lines, Poe also creates a structure that allows no closure in the poem, even though the speaker has returned safely. He does not show a progression of images that comes to a close, as in "Fairy-Land," nor does he even relate the frame of the introduction and conclusion directly to the interior of the poem (in Mabbott's edition, as well as in others, they are separated by spaces). Instead, we see a speaker returning (again) from a strange land, suggesting a cycle that will be repeated, just as the mountains fall again and again into "boundless floods." But this lack of closure implies a kind of closure, an insecure security, as does the uncertain certainty of "mountains toppling evermore." The structure of "Dream-Land" does not allow any narrative closure, as "Fairy-Land" does; nor does it let us arrive at a final meaning. But that is in itself a meaning. The poem is about a "Dream-Land," one that cannot be dealt with on ordinary logical terms nor, as Poe here suggests, on conventional literary terms.

"Dream-Land" is harder for readers to deal with than "Fairy-Land" because the formal structures it offers to readers are thinner. While "Fairy-Land" presents a coherent plot that arrives at a resolution, this poem has no formally concluded narrative: the speaker simply ends the poem by stopping in the middle of an impossible description of a weird landscape, saying that now he or she has returned from that world. "Fairy-Land" offers the rhetorically structured catalogue of opposites that are all included in the moon's setting light, but here in "Dream-Land" the rhetoric itself is undermined by syntactic contradictions like "boundless floods." The only structures that readers may use to build an interpretation of "Dream-Land" are the poem's consistent inconsistencies: its morbid tone, its lack of a logical structure.

In this poem, then, Poe controls readers and their interpretations by default. He denies readers the use of experiential knowledge in understanding the world of "Dream-Land," and he builds the poem around a journey that seems never to come to an end, thus eliminating any resolution on a formal level. The only interpretation available to us is simply to take his word that this is a world "Out of Space—Out of Time," and to leave it at that: we can make no interpretation, other than what he gives us, because nothing in the poem allows us to agree or disagree with what the speaker says. Poe thus creates the kind of controlling structure in "Dream-Land" that in "The Philosophy of Composition" he said he wanted to create: a poem that limits readers so severely that they must accept *his* interpretation. In effect, readers do not interpret here; they simply read.

From *Essays in Literature* 18, no. 1 (1991): 68-75. Copyright © 1991 by Western Illinois University, Department of English & Journalism. Reprinted with permission of Western Illinois University.

## Notes

1. To my knowledge, the only two critics who go beyond restatement to consider Poe's ideas about his readers as readers are Robert D. Jacobs and George Kelly. Jacobs discusses Poe's normative psychology in making assumptions about a mass audience of journal readers (*Poe* 436). Kelly sees Poe's movement of "the point of critical focus away from the work of art to its interpreter" as a "drift toward subjectivism"; Kelly uses his own description of this drift as an opening statement, against which he contrasts what he sees as the objective strategies by which Poe "contravened" such a drift (35).

Edward H. Davidson (esp. 67-75), Charles Feidelson, Jr., Albert Gelpi, T. S. Eliot, and Allen Tate discuss on a general level Poe's ideas about the power of language and the limits he could not overcome.

2. Texts for both poems are taken from Thomas Ollive Mabbott's edition of Poe's texts.

3. Compare Davidson's remarks on "Fairy-Land": "nothing happens; no one really dies or lives; the moon and sun remain the same; only the protagonist who has 'seen'

these things is changed" (31). While one might question whether or not the protagonist changes (if we see enough of this person even to call him or her a protagonist), Davidson and other critics generally agree about the light tone of this poem. Kent Ljungquist, Jacobs, and Mabbott all comment on its humor as well.

4. I have been using the first version of "Fairy-Land," which Poe wrote in 1829. He revised this poem in 1831, soon after the first version was published; the short time between revisions suggests that he was unhappy with his first drafts. As Mabbott remarks in his introduction to the second version, "Fairy-Land" [II] is "virtually a new poem, with an effect of its own" (161) because of Poe's many changes. It is interesting to note that one of his major changes was to anchor the description of "tears that drip all over" in a scene where the persona speaks to a woman named Isabel; the poem becomes in part a description of a vision addressed to her. Isabel's presence brings the poem closer to the realm of everyday experience, though the speaker wonders whether or not the spot where they sit and where the moon-beam fell is "all but a dream." Poe also adds another interpretive level to the poem this way, since the relation between the speaker and this woman gives readers more grounds for speculation.

5. Critics have offered various interpretations of the imagery in this poem. Davidson sees "Dream-Land" as "a place where everything that exists is in a state of disintegration, as though all matter and form were returning to its primordial condition of mere atomicity" (82). While this view is consistent with the tone of the poem, it fails to emphasize the eternal quality of the disintegration. Arthur Hobson Quinn remarks that Poe "produces the effect of vastness and desolation by his usual methods of denying limitations" (416).

6. William M. Forrest and Mabbott (346) also see some Biblical imagery in "Dream-Land," especially in this latter half. Forrest cites, for example, "the spirit that walks in shadow" (line 41) and "Behold it but through darkened glasses" (line 50) as derived from scripture (171). While Killis Campbell doubts the likelihood of Poe's direct borrowing from the Bible (547), images such as spirits and shadows are at any rate common in our culture.

## Works Cited

Campbell, Killis. *The Mind of Poe and Other Studies.* Cambridge: Harvard UP, 1957.

Davidson, Edward H. *Poe: A Critical Study.* Cambridge: Belknap P of Harvard UP, 1957.

Eliot, T. S. "From Poe to Valéry." *The Hudson Review* 2 (1949): 327-42.

Feidelson, Charles. "Poe." *Symbolism and American Literature.* Chicago: U of Chicago P, 1953.

Forrest, William M. *Biblical Allusions in Poe.* New York: Macmillan, 1928.

Gelpi, Albert. *The Tenth Muse: The Psyche of the American Poet.* Cambridge: Harvard UP, 1975.

Jacobs, Robert D. *Poe: Journalist & Critic.* Baton Rouge: Louisiana State UP, 1969.

_____. "The Self and the World: Poe's Early Poems." *The Georgia Review* 31 (1977): 638-68.

Kelly, George. "Poe's Theory of Unity." *Philological Quarterly* 37 (1958): 34-44.

Ljungquist, Kent. "Poe's 'The Island of the Fay': The Passing of Fairyland." *Studies in Short Fiction* 14 (1977): 265-71.

Pearce, Roy Harvey. "Poe." *The Continuity of American Poetry*. Princeton: Princeton UP, 1961. 141-53.

Poe, Edgar Allan. *Poems*. Vol. 1 of *Collected Works of Edgar Allan Poe*. 3 vols. Ed. Thomas Ollive Mabbott. Cambridge: Belknap P of Harvard UP, 1969.

Quinn, Arthur Hobson, *Edgar Allan Poe: A Critical Biography*. New York: Appleton, 1941.

Tate, Allen. "The Angelic Imagination: Poe and the Power of Words." *Kenyon Review* 14 (1952): 455-75.

# Poe and the Position of the Poet in Contemporary Japan_____

Keiji Minato

In the United States, no other author's image has been more exploited as a convenient eye-catcher than that of Edgar Allan Poe. With the skull, the raven, and other gruesome icons, his macabre features never stop plaguing the popular imagination. This prevalence itself might not be deplorable but the imbalance between his popular and literary usage certainly is. The case is slightly different in Japan. Poe's image has its place in the popular imagination, but at the same time it has influenced a number of literary endeavors. Here, we look at six poems by six Japanese poets; each use images of Poe or from Poe's work. All except the first were written after the 1970s, and what is notable is the variety both of style and theme and the boldness of the literary challenges they take on. Reading them will show how Japanese literature has made use of Poe to develop itself, especially, in articulating the position of the poet in society.[1]

Hagiwara Sakutaro (1886-1942), the founding father of genuinely modern poetry in Japan, regarded Poe as a guiding figure. He even named his massive study on poetry *Shi no Genri* [The Poetic Principle] (1928) after Poe's essay. Edogawa Rampo (1894-1965), the most influential detective fiction writer in Japan, took his pseudonym after the father of the genre. Important novelists such as Tanizaki Junichiro (1886-1965), Mishima Yukio (1925-1970), and Sakaguchi Ango (1906-1955) praised Poe's humor, which seems to have been largely disregarded or overlooked in his home country.[2]

This remarkable popularity largely stemmed from the fact that French literature had the strongest influence among Japanese writers in the Meiji (1886-1910) and Taisho (1910-1925) eras.[3] In the development of modern literature in Japan, French Symbolism, with praise of Poe by such poets as Charles Baudelaire, Stéphane Mallarmé and Paul Valéry, permeated into the deepest grain of Japanese modern poetry. So

much so that, in the manifesto of the *Arechi* [Waste Land] school he belonged to, Ayukawa Nobuo, the most powerful poet-critic in post-
WWII Japan, had to express a need "to reject an idea which emerged
from the past of *our* poetry, that is, the fixed idea of poetry established
by symbolist poets from Poe and Baudelaire through Mallarmé to
Valéry."[4]

In order to see how ingeniously Poe was ingrained into modern Japanese poetry, let us examine an early poem by Miyoshi Tatsuji (1900-
64), a disciple of Hagiwara and himself a great poet who remained influential all through the pre-war, war-time, and post-war eras.[5] Its title
"*Torigo*" [The Bird Words] (1930) suggests that the poem is a kind of
pastiche of Poe's "The Raven" (1845). The speaker boards in the house
of a French family which has lived in Japan for many years. In his
room, "there is a parrot," whose cry sounds like a French phrase, "*J'ai
tué . . .*" [I killed . . .]:

> In a birdcage hanging in the window of my room, there is a parrot which,
> all day gnawing the rings of a rusty old chain tied to its leg, sometimes all
> of a sudden cries the only phrase it seems it knows, as if perceiving some
> emptiness in an indefinite distance:
> —*Watashi wa Hito o Koroshita no daga . . .*
>     [I once killed a man . . .]
> To tell the truth, it is a shriek in French, a simple phrase, *J'ai tué.* . . . So
> when I translate it in this way, much of it is shared by my fanciful imagina-
> tion. Yet I have some reason for this vagary.[6]

Listening to the cry so many times, the speaker variously interprets
it by translating it into Japanese or adding French words to it. At first,
that is only for fun, but he comes to know, or he thinks he comes to
know, the truth behind the sinister phrase: the old master actually killed
someone and fled successfully but was tormented by his conscience
until his death:

At first, I with my wit added some words to it: *J'ai tué . . . le temps.* The phrase didn't bother me so much, and everyday I went on with my desultory reading. That is,

—*Kinou mo Kyo mo Watashi wa Muda ni Hi o Sugosu.*

[Everyday, I just kill my time.]

was her phrase, with which she innocently leaned her head by my window. It was much later that I came to realize a sinister connotation behind the phrase, suggested in a casual conversation with Rose, a tall, lean maid of the house.[7]

The speaker's act of translation becomes compulsive. At last, he reaches the point where he cannot distinguish between his psyche and the imagined sin-burdened mind of the old master, just as the speaker in Poe's "The Raven" takes the raven's cry "nevermore" into his mind:

As I listen to it, the phrase has somehow seeped into my heart so deeply and mixed with my own memories. And now it has come to the point that, if someone accuses me of a murder I might have committed a long time ago, I will not deny it at all. Still today, as I am reading desultorily before dahlias in full bloom at the window, the bird overhead repeats the phrase.—Why don't you come to my room and listen to the bird, if you have no memory of murdering someone but nonetheless want to have vague remorse for it.[8]

With its aestheticism, atmosphere of decadence, morbid sensibility of the modern, and half-comical use of a refrain, the poem shows how Japanese poetry digested Poe's poetics in its best form.

WWII and the defeat of Japan forced many Japanese poets to reconsider their assumptions about poetry and their own position in society. Ono Tosaburo (1903-1996), a socialist-realist poet, was one of them. He criticized traditional Japanese lyricism nurtured in the rhythms of *tanka*, a traditional form of poetry in Japan, consisting of 31 (5-7-5-7-

7) syllables, regarding it as a fermenter of the fascist regime in wartime Japan and the lingering feudalist mentality after the war.[9] At the same time, he repudiated the asocial aestheticism of Miyoshi's generation and also rejected the imported communist ideal of his contemporaries. In *"Kamoyama-Kou"* [An Essay on Mt. Kamo] (1974), Ono metaphorically describes his search for an ideal form of society:

An Essay on Mt. Kamo

In the drizzle,
The Omori silver mine
Looks like a ghost town.
Passing streets without a soul,
I take a mountain road with *kudzu* vines hanging over it
    like dew grass.
With a piqué hat on, Saito Mokichi sits
On the passenger's seat.
The other of our party, napping on the rear seat,
Is Edgar Allan Poe.
As I wipe the front shield,
Streaming in is a road in the Iwami mountains I have run
    for the first time.
Mokichi, checking out road signs
And opening a folded map,
Tries to give me directions.
Although his days are long, long gone,
His memory is very precise.
Though we just took the wrong road
And had some difficulty turning the car,
The overall direction must be right.
Deep in the deepest mountain area of the San'in region.
Even in this middle of nowhere,
There are rice fields and villages,

Where big blue hydrangea flowers are in full bloom.

They are the same

As those the poet of "Eureka" saw on the way

Through the mountains in Carolina

To reach the valleys of Arnheim.

Out of a village,

There are only bushes of *kudzu* vines on both sides of the
road.

I don't know how far this is going to last.

"Are you sure this is the right way?"

". . . . . ."

Before I know it,

Mokichi with his piqué hat

Has disappeared from beside me.

Turning my head, I cannot see Poe, either.

The two companions of my journey suddenly disappeared.

Only myself left.

With nothing besides *kudzu* vines sprawling over

Mountains, cliffs, and valleys along the road

Without a visible end.

In the slanting sunlight,

Deep in the deepest mountains of the Iwami region,

I go round bends

And pass through tunnels,

Often hampered by cliffs and brooks.

Listening to voices of *higurashi* cicadas,

I am so alone.[10]

In the poem, the speaker drives a car with two passengers. One of the company is Saito Mokichi (1882-1953), the most important *tanka* writer of the pre-war era, and the other is none other than Edgar Allan Poe.[11] They drive in the Iwami mountains of the San'in region, which used to produce a large amount of silver but rapidly declined after

WWII. The landscape with its indigenous vines is a metaphor of Japan entangled in its feudalist social structure and mentality. Saito tries to give the speaker directions through his memory of the past, which still has certain validity but never helps find a new landscape (that is, a new form of society). Poe, who just "sits in the rear seat napping," is no use either, though, seeing "big blue hydrangea flowers," the speaker thinks of "the valleys of Arnheim." "Arnheim" is the name of the landscape garden a young aristocratic millionaire named Ellison builds with his incredible inheritance in Poe's "The Domain of Arnheim" (1846). Yet the destination for the speaker of Ono's poem doesn't appear before him as easily as Arnheim does for the narrator of Poe's tale. The fact that even a social-realist poet like Ono used Poe's image shows how prevalent Poe's influence in Japan was.

\* \* \*

Yoshioka Minoru (1919-90) has gained a unique position in the history of Japanese poetry with surrealist imagery crystallized to the extreme in his earlier poems and post-modernistic plays of citations in his later work.[12] In the early stage of his career, he tried to exclude external references, concentrating on his inner imagery. It was around the time he wrote the poem cited here, "*Irei-sai*" [A Memorial Service for Not-Us] (1974), that he began to open up his poetry to intertextuality with citations from and references to various literary figures. This poem hasn't had so much attention paid to it, but Yoshioka published a booklet with the same title, which shows he considered it a poem of importance. It has eight sections in all; below is the latter half:

> 5
> You can pick up a theme in advance
> But the destiny of a creature is
> Too dark to see like a scar in fur
> A black dot that flaws Redon's copperplate engraving

If it's a masked man who
Rings the bell then
Who is it who is crying?
Tied eternally with a twisted rope
Allan
Peek into the large mouth of a masked soldier
There is no red greasy tongue
In that deep dark bowl but
An iron ball sticking out
Allan
Get drunk
With sulky brothers
Unheard bells!
Soon the snow will fall on our city
So it seems that
Solemnly
The exit is closed
If pushed from inside by force
It will break into two
And several spring doves will fly out
Allan
Do you feel tickled
On the place where the panels of a door with gothic
    ornaments
Meet each other a bough touches slightly

6

What lasts lasts
What doesn't last doesn't last
That might be true
From what lasts
To what doesn't last
Changing forms

Changing languages
Changing colors
Allan
Your work late at night meets
A miserable poor cucumber
You make of the unfortunate life of your wife
A beautiful story
Flowers of eggplants bloom in violet
Please make the lipstick dark
Faces of the dead have
Their own life you know
On "smoke in the figure of a horse"
You ride your wife
Allan
You are approaching
Your father's frozen land

7

You do the work you hate
For a living
With cunning inconceivable for us
Allan
You concoct *The Concologist's First Book*
Shellfish without shells
And coral-colored membranes that never stop
Giving birth to humongous things
A study of a horrible shellfish that conceives
Every kind from heroes to psychopaths
In order to forget sinful analyses
Allan
We put on overcoats and
Go out to drink
Looking for a crouching cat . . .

A barefooted

Maroon-colored hairy virgin

Ellie!


8

Those who live modestly

In the shade of a lotus leaf

Those who defend a nation

Hanging ears of rabbits

Aren't those ideal ways of life among us

Meaningful misunderstanding indeed

Such worldly-living creatures

Will fall on their backs

On stones if there are stones

Allan

You will go wandering

Out of the world of ideas where the blade of a scythe
　　shines

Looking for the thing itself

"Which looks like a shadow"

On roads with coiling poisonous snakes

Where it has another dimension

Allan

You and I

Why don't we try for a while

"Hopscotch on top of a mountain"—[13]

Yoshioka uses images from Poe's work and real life, transforming them into his own eerie psychological drama. He calls Poe "Allan," the name of Edgar Poe's foster family, which the American poet himself loathed in his adult life. The reason why Yoshioka does this seems to correspond with the part in which the clearest reference to Poe's biographical fact occurs and ironically demonstrates Poe's frustrated life.

In the sixth part, the speaker writes: "You do the work you hate/ For a living/ With cunning inconceivable for us/ Allan/ You concoct *The Concologist's First Book.*" It might be surprising to find the title of such a rare volume as *The Concologist's First Book* (1839) in a poem of a Japanese near-contemporary. Although we now know that the book was not written by Poe and that he just let his name be used, Yoshioka's reference to this obscure detail suggests he was much interested in Poe's life. Himself a poet who made a living as an employee of a publishing company, he shows a considerable sympathy for the destiny of the American poet. Yoshioka usually shuns direct speech, so it sounds touching when he concludes the poem with a surprisingly intimate call to a fellow poet.

\* \* \*

Irisawa Yasuo (b. 1931), a prolific poet and lucid theorist, translated many of Poe's poems in the 1960s.[14] Against the dominant view that poetry is a form of self-expression for an individual, Irisawa repeatedly asserts that it is a kind of artifact, constructed with conscious manipulation. Irisawa's poem "Mare Tenebrarum–*Baltimore no Noroi kara Takumini Nogareru tameno Jumon*" [Mare Tenebrarum—An Incantation for Escaping the Curse of Baltimore Ingeniously] was published in 1974 in the Edgar Allan Poe special issue of *Eureka*, a leading poetry magazine in Japan. The subtitle makes clear the self-referential quality of the poem and also evokes the Romantic view of poetry as an incantation by a cursed poet:

Mare Tenebrarum—An Incantation for Escaping
the Curse of Baltimore Ingeniously

1

The sea of tar     congealing below a plume like a petal

2

In the center of a city a rusted funnel and a flask dented with teeth

3

Below thirteen moons     *Lycopodium*     *Rubiaceae*

4

In the gondola of a balloon     too much salt

5

Beside a bottle of laudanum     a violet heart lying

6

On a forehead a marriage ring     on fingers a flower crown and a coleopteron from a caldera

7

Over the threshold of the gate to dreams     the ghost of an orangoutang

8

Wandering on a northern shore     a rooster larger than a camel

9

We were two    No three    No alas we were eight
hundred eighty seven

10

High and high and high above the sea of milk    seven
rings of light![15]

Composed of ten one-liners with pared-down imagery, the poem allows multiple interpretations but can be considered to describe the speaker's trip from Japan to Baltimore and back to Japan. The first line is the scene of a flight over the Pacific ocean at night, and the lines that follow describe Baltimore, probably including the exhibition in the Poe House. Irisawa ingeniously mixes mythic images about Poe, images from Poe's work, and his own minute observations to achieve both the realistic and the surrealistic ambiance for the poem. The speaker has a nightmare as the result of staying in Baltimore (line 7). Line 8 is unclear but it probably depicts big advertisements on the seashore: Wild Turkey, a bourbon whiskey, and Camel, a cigarette. The phrase "We were two" in the next line derives from Stéphane Mallarmé's poem, and with it the speaker tries to evoke a quasi-double relation with a great precursor against the mass commercial environment.[16] The connotation of the number 887 is not obvious but it certainly signifies the failure of an attempt to separate himself from the crowd around him. The last line is a scene from the return flight to Japan. "Seven rings of light" must be the stars of the Big Dipper in the northern sky, used to ascertain direction at night. The passage from the image of "thirteen moons" in line 3 to "seven rings of light" seems to symbolize a successful escape. Here, Poe is used as a prototype of the *poète maudit*. Turning life into a series of congealed images is for the speaker, and probably for Irisawa, a way of escaping from a similar destiny.

Miyoshi, Ono, Yoshioka, and Irisawa all belong to different streams of Japanese contemporary poetry: aesthete-traditional lyricist, socialist realist, modernist-postmodernist, and academic theorist. It is quite surprising that Poe has served for such different poets to probe their position in society and to develop their ideas of poetry writing.

\* \* \*

However, it seems that Poe's influence has rapidly lost its power after the 1970s. This mainly stems from the wane of Euro-centrism and of the general sense of backwardness of Japan as a nation. Poe's name is gradually fading away from the surface of Japanese poetry in common with many of the western poets once fervidly referred to by the Japanese under westernization and modernization. References to foreign poets and writers in general have lost a larger part of their appeal to contemporary Japanese. As early as the 1970s, one contemporary poet-critic wrote: "Although our history of thoughts and literature will still be awakened and enlivened through contacts with the ideas of 'other countries' or other cultures, I think, today, the idea of the advanced-ness [of European countries] has completely lost its validity."[17]

The poet who wrote the above passage, Kitagawa Toru (b. 1935), is one of the most trenchant critics of poetry in today's Japan and a poet who has published many controversial books of poetry.[18] From the beginning of his career, he has constantly tried to question the basis of his own position as a poet and of poetry itself. His book of poetry published in 1988, entitled *Po wa Doko made Kawareru ka* [How Far Can Po Change?], is full of wordplays and other post-modernist devices that force the reader to ask what poetry is (in Japanese the pronunciations and spellings of "Po" and "Poe" are the same). One of the poems in it is:

## Po no Love Song [A Love Song of Po]

I'm raising Po
It's half a year since I began to raise Po
It's not easy to raise Po
Po multiplies endlessly
Hey Po      Jump      Po jumps
Then look      Po is now two Po
Jump again      Jump one more time      Jump Po
Two Po jump
Then two Po are now four      then eight      and then sixteen
Is Po human      or a domestic animal      or a *hato-poppo*
   [cuckoo-dove]
Surely not Po[e] of The House of Usher or
Mr. Rampo of The Golden Mask I hope
Po never knows itself
Po just keeps jumping      responding to my voice
Opening the legs wide      Po keeps multiplying
Laughing in the rainbow colors

Po is raising me
It's half a year since Po began to raise me
It's not easy to be raised by Po
Po haughtily orders me
To jump      Jump      You jump
I jump against my will
On every jump I am torn up
Why do I have to be torn up      by a curious cat
By an old woman with a fox-like face      by a tomato and a
   goofy bottle opener
By a clown with no head      by a king of broken china
With desperate cries      uncountable I keep multiplying
I cannot count myself
Any more

Po has a strong sexual urge     with wet lips
Always sexually aroused
Countless I too     have a fever every high tide
And make love with someone     hate someone
I want Poe strangled     with my own hands
Po too     I think     wants to bury me in the ground
Ha-ha     It's too late     No way out
Po never stops jumping     Nothing can stop it
I is a self-multiplying machine that multiplies against its will
Which I is Po
Which Po am I
Po unknown and I unknown
Under a sky unknown     in a city unknown
Have a hug unknown and a kiss unknown
Sing a song unknown
Die a death unknown     which is . . .[19]

In this book, which contains poems in various forms and styles, the speaker is obsessed with, or haunted by, something called "Po." Although the poem above says that "Po" is "Surely not Poe of The House of Usher," we are never sure because this "Po" takes so many different forms. It is sometimes male, sometimes female, sometimes "I," the speaker, and sometimes not human at all. It is also possible that it is a metaphor of poetry or just a sound without any meaning. Therefore, we could say that it might also be Edgar Allan Poe. What is certain is that here the name of Poe is buried among incessant plays of sounds and images and loses his status as the authority figure he held in past literary history. The poem reveals the contemporary situation in which there is no fixed anchorage for reading literature. With protean "Po(e)," the speaker and also the reader are here involved in a thorough deconstruction of human subjectivity and of literature itself.

Many regard Yoshimasu Gozo (b. 1939) as the most important poet in Japan today since he succeeds in bringing out the many-layered potentials of Japanese as a language.[20] He expresses the influence of Emily Dickinson and often directly borrows phrases from her poems, but his references to Poe are rare. In one essay, however, he says: "For my book of poetry entitled *Hanabi no Ie no Iriguchi de* [At the Threshold of the House of Fireworks] (2001) . . . , I sort of plagiarized the rhythm of Edgar Poe's The Fall of the House of Usher."[21]

The title of the first poem in the book *Asha no Ié é* [To the House of the Dumb] (first published in 1986) is a kind of pun on the "House of Usher," but the poem has more relevance to Poe's tale than the wordplay. Its speaker, recovering from an illness, tries to tap into the world beneath ordinary reality and elicit the undercurrents of suppressed voices with his sharpened senses. This reminds us of the narrator in Poe's "The Man of the Crowd" (1840) and, of course, Roderick Usher with his "morbid acuteness of the senses." However, the acuteness of the senses in Yoshimasu's poem is far from being "morbid." Look at the beginning and the ending of the poem:

> < You go out and dance?
> < Well . . . But already.
>
> Softly, a bank, asked, the river goddess, in a whisper.
> (Splendid, . . . . . .). Roots of a tree, under a tree, (. . . . . .,)
> in a hallway, a few steps, . . . . . . the day when I was
> finally able to walk. Hearing the sound,
>
> A green ant, on a corner of a pebble, I saw it take a rest.
>
> A hill of trillions of light years seemed to shine softly in
>    the shade of trees.

There is a sound of paper torn up. Will a "deep sound"
   follow it? "I / the author" never knows.

[. . .]

Sound of the galaxy in the window-for-gods of the house
   of the dumb. For a while.

Far away, it goes. A small maelström. A snake with no
   name stood upright entangled with the universe.

Leaning, a little

Farther it goes

Sound of the galaxy in the window-for-gods of the house
   of the dumb, for a while

(Stars, to heavy

"words of the river goddess, . . . .

Listen in "bushes" of (the hill of,) voices

of

"Oars / of the night"

"It's so quiet"

(Yeah, sounds moving now
(Yeah, sounds moving now[22]

Whereas the world in "The Fall of the House of Usher" (1839) is on the verge of decay, the world in "The House of the Dumb" is at the threshold of rebirth. The line "There is a sound of paper torn up. Will a 'deep sound' follow it? 'I / the author' never knows" shows the poem will go beyond the limits of human subjectivity and authorial control. Despite this, Otherness in Yoshimasu's poetry is remarkably free from the morbidity of the modern, which is a persistent theme in Japanese modern-contemporary poetry and seems to be the main source of its fascination with Poe. While "The House of the Dumb" reflects some elements of "The Fall of the House of Usher," the difference between the two shows a paradigm shift on a large scale in the history of literature.

* * *

The image of Poe has helped Japanese poets reconsider their relation, as poets, to reality and to poetry itself. Especially, after WWII, they were forced to be conscious of their standing in society and needed to reconceptualize the idea of poetry. It appears that most of them used Poe as a negative for their own image, thinking that he belonged to the past. For poets in post-war Japan, the ideas of poetry that Poe's image suggests to them should be overcome and yet dialectically synthesized into their own poetics.

The number of references to Poe's name and works seems destined to decline, since the influence of overseas writers on Japanese literature is losing most of the importance it had had in the past. It is unlikely that Poe is going to preserve the privileged status he had in Japanese literature. At least we are sure that his presence will always be firmly stamped onto Japanese poetry through such example works as we looked at in this consideration of Poe's image in contemporary Japanese poetry. Written by influential poets, these poems certainly indicate Poe's great contribution to Japanese literature, and they, in return, are the greatest tributes of Japanese poets to their American precursor.

## Notes

The author thanks the poets cited in this article for their permission to quote extensively from their work.

1. The vast influence of Poe and the endless references to him have been chronicled by Noriko Mizuta Lippit in the Japan chapter in Lois Davis Vines, ed., *Poe Abroad: Influence, Reputation, Affinities* (Iowa City: U of Iowa P, 1999) and more recently by Miyanaga Takashi in his massive volume *Poe to Nihon Sono Juyou no Rekishi* [Poe and Japan: The History of the Reception of Poe in Japan] (Tokyo: Sairyu-sha, 2000).

2. Sakaguchi's short story "Kaze-hakase [Dr. Wind]" (1931) is a superb pastiche of Poe's "X-ing a Paragrab" (1849). In this essay, I write Japanese names except mine in the traditional order (the family name followed by the first name).

3. Because of Poe's "French connection," early Poe studies in Japan tended to be carried out by scholars of comparative literature like Shimada Kinji and Sadoya Genshin. See Shimada Kiniji, *Poe to Baudelaire* [Poe and Baudelaire] (Tokyo: Eveningstar-sha, 1948) and Sadoya Shigenobu, *Poe no Meikai-Gensou* [The Otherworldly Imagination of Poe] (Tokyo: Kokushokankou-kai, 1988).

4. Ayukawa Nobuo, "*Gendai-shi towa Nanika*" [What Is Contemporary Poetry?] in *The Waste Land Poetry Anthology* [Arechi Shishu, 1951] (1951, rpt. Tokyo: Kokubun-sha, 1975), 30.

5. Miyoshi began writing poetry as an aesthete, highly successful in incorporating European decadent aestheticism into Japanese poetry. He later turned to a more traditional lyricism of Japan and led the *Shiki-ha* [Four-Seasons School], one of the most influential groups of poets during and after WWII. His work includes *Sokuryou-sen* [The Surveying Ship] (Tokyo: Daiichi-Shobou, 1930) and *Itten-shou* [One Hour] (Tokyo: Sogen-sha, 1941).

6. Miyoshi Tatsuji, *Miyoshi Tatsuji Zenshu* [The Complete Works of Miyoshi Tatsuji] Vol. 1 (Tokyo: Chikuma-Shobo, 1964), 32. All translations in the paper are mine.

7. Miyoshi, 32-3.

8. Miyoshi, 37.

9. Ono began his career as an anarchist writer, influenced by American working-class poets like Carl Sandburg, and kept this political attitude through WWII. He is renowned and much respected for his realistic style and firm political concerns. His books of poetry include *Fuukei Sishou* [Landscape Poems] (Osaka: Koubun-sha, 1943) and *Kyozetsu no Ki* [The Tree of Rejection] (Tokyo: Shicho-sha, 1974). His influential essays on poetry are collected in *Shiron+ Zoku-Shiron+ Souzou-ryoku*: *Tanka-teki-Jojou no Hitei* [Essays on Poetry+ More Essays on Poetry+ Imagination: The Negation of Tanka-esque Lyricism] (Tokyo: Shicho-sha, 1976).

10. Ono Tosaburo, *Ono Tosaburo Chosakushu* [The Collected Works of Miyoshi Tatsuji] Vol. 1 (Tokyo: Chikuma-Shobo, 1990), 572-3.

11. Saito advocated realism as a leader of the Araragi school, the mainstream faction in *tanka* writing. He wrote many pro-nationalist *tanka* during WWII and was harshly criticized after the war. "An Essay on Mt. Kamo" is the title of an essay of his from 1934, which refers to the place of Kakinomoto-no Hitomaro's death. Kakinomoto is a poet who lived from the seventh to the eighth century and is sometimes called the Saint of Tanka.

12. Yoshioka is the most idiosyncratic poet but is greatly respected and influential in Japan. He grew up in a non-academic environment, taught himself how to write, and developed a singular style in which he crystallized surrealistic imagery to the extreme. He later changed his style to a freer one with many plays on citations. Many regard him as the best fruit of modernism and postmodernism in Japan. Some of his works are translated into English. See Ooka Makoto and Thomas Fitzsimmons, ed., *Play of Mirrors: Eight Major Poets of Modern Japan* (Rochester, MI: Katydid Books, 1987), Yoshioka, *Celebration in Darkness: Selected Poems of Yoshioka Minoru* (Rochester, MI: Katydid Books, 1985) and *Lilac Garden: Poems of Minoru Yoshioka* (Chicago: Chicago Review Press, 1976). Eric Selland translated the whole of one of the books of poetry by Yoshioka, *Kusudama* [Kusudama] (1983), into English. Yoshioka, *Kusudama*, trans. Eric Selland (Vancouver: Leech, 1991).

13. Yoshioka Minoru, *Yoshioka Minoru Zen-Shishu* [The Complete Poems of Yoshioka Minoru] (Tokyo: Chikuma-Shobo, 1996), 376-80.

14. Irisawa is one of the most theoretical poets in today's Japan. With ample knowledge of European and Japanese literature, he keeps producing keenly self-referential and subtly political texts. He constantly asserts that poetry is a kind of artifact, not self-expression as in the Romantic view of literature. His books of poetry include *Waga Izumo Waga Chinkon* [My Izumo, My Reqiem] (Tokyo: Shicho-sha, 1968) and *Tooi Utage* [The Faraway Banquet] (Tokyo: Shoritsu Yamada, 2002). His two theoretical books on poetry, *Shi no Kouzou ni Tsuiteno Oboegaki* [Notes on the Structure of Poetry] (Tokyo: Shicho-sha, 1968) and *Shi no Kankei ni Tsuiteno Oboegaki* [Notes on the Relation of Poetry] (Tokyo: Shicho-sha, 1979), are regarded as monumental works in the history of Japanese contemporary poetry.

15. Irisawa Yasuo, *Irisawa Yasuo <Shi> Shusei 1951-1994* [The Collection of the <Poetry> of Irisawa Yasuo 1951-1994], Vol. 2 (Tokyo: Shicho-sha, 1995), 38-40.

16. Stéphane Mallarmé, *Oeuvres complètes* [Complete Works] (Paris: Gallimard, 1945), 55-57.

17. Kitagawa Toru, *Netsu Aru Houi* [The Direction with Heat] (Tokyo: Shicho-sha, 1976), 55.

18. Kitagawa, one of the most acute critics of poetry in contemporary Japan and himself a prolific poet, is deeply conscious of the position of the poet in society and continues with bold experiments both in style and content. Since the 1980s, he has criticized the traditional image of the poet, asserting that it is irrelevant to today's postmodern society. His work includes *Me no Inritsu* [The Meter of the Eyes] (Gifu: Okada-shoten, 1968) and *Ouka-ron* [An Essay on Yellow Fruit] (Tokyo: Sunagoya-shobou, 2000). He has also published more than twenty books of criticism on poetry.

19. Kitagawa Toru, *Po wa Doko made Kawareruka* [How Far Can Po Change] (Tokyo: Shicho-sha, 1988), 64-67.

20. Yoshimasu began his career as a young revolutionary poet in the 1960s, writing in a style almost like auto-writing with unsorted vocabulary. He later changed his style to a more serene, many-layered one. Today, by way of his experimental style, he tries to tap into undercurrents of suppressed voices, as is shown in the title of his latest book of poetry, *The Other Voice* [The Other Voice] (Tokyo: Shicho-sha, 2002). Some of his poetry is translated into English. See Thomas Fitzsimmons and Yoshimasu Gozo, ed., *The New Poetry of Japan—the 70s and 80s* (Santa Fe: Katydid Books, 1993) and Yoshioka, *Osiris, the God of Stone* (Laurinburg, NC: St. Andrews Press, 1988) and *A Thousand Steps—and More: Selected Poems and Prose 1964-1984* (Rochester, MI: Katydid Books, 1987).

21. Yoshimasu Gozo, *Moeagaru Eigagoya* [The Movie Theater in Fire] (Tokyo: Seido-sha, 2001), 51.

22. Yoshimasu Gozo, *Hanabi no Ie no Iriguchi de* [At the Threshold of the House of Fireworks] (Tokyo: Seidosha, 2001), 6-19.

# RESOURCES

| | |
|---|---|
| 1809 | Edgar Poe is born in Boston on January 19 to David Poe, Jr., and Elizabeth Arnold Poe (née Hopkins). |
| 1810 | Poe's sister, Rosalie, is born on December 20. |
| 1811 | On December 8, Elizabeth Arnold Poe dies in Richmond, Virginia. David Poe dies a few days later. Orphaned, Edgar is taken into the home of John and Frances Allan of Richmond. Rosalie is taken in by Mr. and Mrs. William Mackenzie. Poe's brother, Henry (born 1807), remains with his grandparents in Baltimore. |
| 1812 | Poe is christened as "Edgar Allan Poe." |
| 1815 | The Allan family, with Poe, travel to England. |
| 1815-1820 | Poe attends the schools of Misses Dubourg and later Manor House School. |
| 1820 | Poe and family return to Richmond, Virginia. |
| 1821-1823 | Poe continues his education at the school of Joseph H. Clarke and then the school of William Burke. |
| 1824 | Poe serves as a lieutenant of the Richmond Junior Volunteers. |
| 1825 | John Allan inherits some money and moves the family into a mansion called Moldavia. Poe becomes engaged to childhood sweetheart Elmira Royster. |
| 1826 | Poe enters the University of Virginia in Charlottesville. Elmira, at her parents' insistence, breaks off her engagement to Poe and becomes engaged to Alexander B. Shelton. |
| 1827 | After arguing with John Allan over gambling debts, Poe leaves the Allan home and travels to his family in Baltimore. He eventually enlists in the U.S. Army under the name Edgar A. Perry. His battery is sent to Fort Moultrie in Charleston, South Carolina. *Tamerlane, and Other Poems* is published. |

| | |
|---|---|
| 1829 | Poe is promoted to sergeant major. Frances Allan dies. Poe is granted leave from the army and returns to Richmond. Poe's second book, *Al Aaraaf, Tamerlane, and Minor Poems*, is published. |
| 1830 | John Allan marries Louisa Patterson. Poe enters the U.S. Military Academy at West Point. |
| 1831 | Poe is court-martialed and dismissed from service. The collection *Poems* is published. Henry Poe dies in Baltimore. |
| 1833 | Poe moves in with his aunt Maria Clemm in Baltimore. He receives a prize from a Baltimore magazine for the short story "MS. Found in a Bottle." |
| 1834 | John Allan dies in Richmond. Poe is left out of Allan's will and inherits nothing. |
| 1835 | Poe moves to Richmond and becomes editor of Thomas W. White's *Southern Literary Messenger*. Poe publishes critical reviews, poems, and stories. |
| 1836 | Poe marries Virginia Clemm (age thirteen) in Richmond. |
| 1837 | Poe leaves his position as editor of the *Southern Literary Messenger* and moves to New York City. |
| 1838 | Poe moves to Philadelphia. His novel *The Narrative of Arthur Gordon Pym* is published by Harper & Brothers. |
| 1839 | Poe becomes editor of *Burton's Gentleman's Magazine*. |
| 1840 | Poe's short-fiction collection *Tales of the Grotesque and Arabesque* is published. The story "The Journal of Julius Rodman" is published in *Burton's Gentleman's Magazine* and is mistaken by many for an actual account of an expedition. |
| 1841 | "The Murders in the Rue Morgue" is featured in *Graham's Magazine*. |

| 1842 | Poe meets Charles Dickens, who is touring the United States. Poe leaves his position at *Graham's Magazine* and is replaced by Rufus W. Griswold. |
|---|---|
| 1843 | "The Gold-Bug" and *The Prose Romances of Edgar Allan Poe* are published. Poe begins his lectures on American poetry. |
| 1844 | Poe moves to New York, where he begins working as a member of the staff of the newspaper the *Evening Mirror*. |
| 1845 | "The Raven" is published in the *Evening Mirror*. Poe becomes an editor of the *Broadway Journal*; he eventually becomes owner as well. *Tales* and *The Raven, and Other Poems* are published. |
| 1846 | The *Broadway Journal* ceases publication. Poe publishes "The Literati of New York City: Some Honest Opinions at Random Respecting Their Authorial Merits, with Occasional Words of Personality" in *Godey's Lady's Book*. |
| 1847 | Virginia Poe dies of tuberculosis. |
| 1848 | Poe's prose poem *Eureka* is published. Poe becomes engaged to Sarah Helen Whitman; Whitman later calls off the engagement. |
| 1849 | Poe begins a lecture tour in the southern United States and meets up with the now widowed Elmira Royster Shelton; the two eventually become engaged. On October 7, Edgar Allan Poe dies in Baltimore. He is buried in his grandfather's plot in the Westminster Burying Ground. |

# Works by Edgar Allan Poe

**Poetry**

*Tamerlane, and Other Poems*, 1827
*Al Aaraaf, Tamerlane, and Minor Poems*, 1829
*Poems*, 1831
*The Raven, and Other Poems*, 1845
*Eureka: A Prose Poem*, 1848
*Poe: Complete Poems*, 1959 (Richard Wilbur, editor)
*Poems*, 1969 (Thomas Ollive Mabbott, editor)

**Long Fiction**

*The Narrative of Arthur Gordon Pym*, 1838

**Short Fiction**

*Tales of the Grotesque and Arabesque*, 1840
*The Prose Romances of Edgar Allan Poe*, 1843
*Tales*, 1845
*The Short Fiction of Edgar Allan Poe*, 1976 (Stuart Levine and Susan Levine, editors)

**Drama**

*Politian*, 1835-1836

**Nonfiction**

*The Letters of Edgar Allan Poe*, 1948 (2 volumes; John Ward Ostrom, editor)
*Literary Criticism of Edgar Allan Poe*, 1965 (Robert L. Hough, editor)
*Essays and Reviews*, 1984 (G. R. Thompson, editor)

**Miscellaneous**

*The Complete Works of Edgar Allan Poe*, 1902 (17 volumes)

# Bibliography

Ackroyd, Peter. *Poe: A Life Cut Short*. New York: Doubleday, 2008.

Alexander, Jean. *Affidavits of Genius: Edgar Allan Poe and the French Critics, 1847-1924*. Port Washington, NY: Kennikat Press, 1971.

Allen, Hervey. *Israfel: The Life and Times of Edgar Allan Poe*. New York: Rinehart, 1949.

Allen, Michael. *Poe and the Magazine Tradition*. New York: Oxford University Press, 1969.

Alterton, Margaret. *Origins of Poe's Critical Theory*. Iowa City: University of Iowa, 1925.

Bailey, J. O. "The Geography of Poe's 'Dream-Land' and 'Ulalume.'" *Studies in Philology* 45.3 (1948): 512-23.

Baudelaire, Charles. *Baudelaire on Poe*. Trans. and ed. Lois and Francis E. Hyslop, Jr. State College, PA: Bald Eagle Press, 1952.

Bittner, William. *Poe: A Biography*. Boston: Little, Brown, 1962.

Bloom, Harold. "The Inescapable Poe." *New York Review of Books* 11 Oct. 1984.

_____, ed. *Edgar Allan Poe*. New York: Chelsea House, 1985.

Bonaparte, Marie. *The Life and Works of Edgar Allan Poe: A Psycho-analytic Interpretation*. Trans. John Rodker. London: Imago, 1949.

Buranelli, Vincent. *Edgar Allan Poe*. New York: Twayne, 1961.

Campbell, Killis. *The Mind of Poe and Other Studies*. Cambridge, MA: Harvard University Press, 1933.

Carlson, Eric W. "Symbol and Sense in Poe's 'Ulalume.'" *American Literature* 35.1 (March 1963): 22-37.

_____, ed. *A Companion to Poe Studies*. Westport, CT: Greenwood Press, 1996.

_____, ed. *Critical Essays on Edgar Allan Poe*. Boston: G. K. Hall, 1987.

_____, ed. *The Recognition of Edgar Allan Poe: Selected Criticism Since 1829*. Ann Arbor: University of Michigan Press, 1966.

Davidson, Edward H. *Poe: A Critical Study*. Cambridge, MA: Harvard University Press, 1957.

Dayan, Joan. "Amorous Bondage: Poe, Ladies, and Slaves." *American Literature* 66.2 (1994): 239-73.

_____. "From Romance to Modernity: Poe and the Work of Poetry." *Studies in Romanticism* 29.3 (1990): 413-37.

_____. "Poe's Women: A Feminist Poe?" *Poe Studies/Dark Romanticism* 26 (June/Dec. 1993): 1-12.

Dykman, Aminadav A. "Poe's Poetry in Israel (and Russia)." *Poe Studies/Dark Romanticism* 33.1-2 (2000): 33-40.

Eliot, T. S. "From Poe to Valéry." *To Criticize the Critic and Other Writings*. New York: Farrar, Straus and Giroux, 1965. 27-42.

Elmer, Jonathan. *Reading at the Social Limit: Affect, Mass Culture, and Edgar Allan Poe*. Stanford, CA: Stanford University Press, 1995.

Fisher, Benjamin F. *The Cambridge Introduction to Edgar Allan Poe*. New York: Cambridge University Press, 2008.

_____, ed. *Poe and His Times: The Artist and His Milieu*. Baltimore: Edgar Allan Poe Society, 1990.

Fletcher, Richard M. *The Stylistic Development of Edgar Allan Poe*. The Hague: Mouton, 1973.

Forrest, William M. *Biblical Allusions in Poe*. New York: Macmillan, 1928.

Godden, Richard. "Edgar Allan Poe and the Detection of Riot." *Literature and History* 8.2 (1982): 206-31.

Halliburton, David. *Edgar Allan Poe: A Phenomenological View*. Princeton, NJ: Princeton University Press, 1973.

Hansen, Thomas S., and Burton R. Pollin. *The German Face of Edgar Allan Poe: A Study of Literary References in His Works*. Columbia, SC: Camden House, 1995.

Hayes, Kevin J., ed. *The Cambridge Companion to Edgar Allan Poe*. New York: Cambridge University Press, 2002.

Hoffman, Daniel. *Poe Poe Poe Poe Poe Poe Poe*. Baton Rouge: Louisiana State University Press, 1998.

Howard, Leon. "Artificial Sensitivity and Artful Rationality: Basic Elements in the Creative Imagination of Edgar Allan Poe." *Poe Studies/Dark Romanticism* 20.1 (1987): 18-33.

Humphries, Jefferson. *Metamorphoses of the Raven: Literary Overdeterminedness in France and the South Since Poe*. Baton Rouge: Louisiana State University Press, 1985.

Hutchisson, James M. *Poe*. Jackson: University Press of Mississippi, 2005.

Hyneman, Esther F. *Edgar Allan Poe: An Annotated Bibliography of Books and Articles in English, 1827-1973*. Boston: G. K. Hall, 1974.

Jackson, Virginia. "Poe, Longfellow, and the Institution of Poetry." *Poe Studies/Dark Romanticism* 33.1-2 (2000): 23-28.

Jacobs, Robert D. *Poe: Journalist and Critic*. Baton Rouge: Louisiana State University Press, 1969.

_____. "The Self and the World: Poe's Early Poems." *Georgia Review* 31 (1977): 638-68.

Jones, Buford, and Kent Ljungquist. "Poe, Mrs. Osgood, and 'Annabel Lee.'" *Studies in the American Renaissance* (1983): 275-80.

Joseph, Gerhard J. "Poe and Tennyson." *PMLA: Publications of the Modern Language Association* 88 (1973): 418-28.

Kelly, George. "Poe's Theory of Beauty." *American Literature* 27 (1956): 521-26.

_____. "Poe's Theory of Unity." *Philological Quarterly* 37 (1958): 34-44.

Kennedy, J. Gerald. *A Historical Guide to Edgar Allan Poe*. New York: Oxford University Press, 2001.

_____. *Poe, Death, and the Life of Writing*. New Haven, CT: Yale University Press, 1987.

Kenyon, Joseph P. "Auber and Avernus: Poe's Use of Myth and Ritual in 'Ulalume.'" *Poe Studies/Dark Romanticism* 36.1-2 (2004): 58-67.

Knapp, Bettina L. *Edgar Allan Poe*. New York: Frederick Ungar, 1984.

Krutch, Joseph W. *Edgar Allan Poe: A Study in Genius*. New York: Russell & Russell, 1926.

Lawlor, James. "Daemons of the Intellect: The Symbolists and Poe." *Critical Inquiry* 14.1 (1987): 95-110.

Lawrence, D. H. "Edgar Allan Poe." *Studies in Classic American Literature*. 1923. New York: Penguin, 1977. 83-88.

Levin, Harry. *The Power of Blackness: Hawthorne, Poe, Melville*. New York: Alfred A. Knopf, 1958.

Ljungquist, Kent. *The Grand and the Fair: Poe's Landscape Aesthetics and Pictorial Techniques*. Potomac, MD: Scripta Humanistica, 1984.

Mabbott, Thomas Ollive, ed. *Collected Works of Edgar Allan Poe*, vol. 1, *Poems*. Cambridge, MA: Harvard University Press, 1969.

Meyers, Jeffrey. *Edgar Allan Poe: Life and Legacy*. New York: Macmillan, 1992.

Omans, Glen A. "Intellect, Taste, and the Moral Sense: Poe's Debt to Immanuel Kant." *Studies in the American Renaissance* (1980): 123-68.

_____. "Victor Cousin: Still Another Source of Poe's Aesthetic Theory?" *Studies in the American Renaissance* 7 (1982): 1-27.

Parks, Edd Winfield. *Edgar Allan Poe as Literary Critic*. Athens: University of Georgia Press, 1964.

Peeples, Scott. *Edgar Allan Poe Revisited*. New York: Twayne, 1998.

Phillips, Elizabeth. *Edgar Allan Poe, an American Imagination: Three Essays*. Millwood, NY: Associated Faculty Press, 1986.

Pollin, Burton R. "Poe's 'Von Kempelen and his Discovery': Sources and Significance." *Études anglaises* 20.1 (1967): 12-23.

Quinn, Arthur Hobson. *Edgar Allan Poe: A Critical Biography*. Baltimore: Johns Hopkins University Press, 1998.

Quinn, Patrick F. *The French Face of Edgar Poe*. Carbondale: Southern Illinois University Press, 1957.

Regan, Robert, ed. *Poe: A Collection of Critical Essays*. Englewood Cliffs, NJ: Prentice-Hall, 1967.

Richards, Eliza. *Gender and the Poetics of Reception in Poe's Circle*. New York: Cambridge University Press, 2004.

_____. "Lyric Telegraphy: Women Poets, Spiritualist Poetics, and the Phantom Voice of Poe." *Yale Journal of Criticism: Interpretation in the Humanities* 12.2 (1999): 269-94.

Riddel, Joseph N. "The 'Crypt' of Edgar Poe." *boundary 2* 7.3 (Spring 1979): 117-44.

Rosenheim, Shawn, and Stephen Rachman, eds. *The American Face of Edgar Allan Poe*. Baltimore: Johns Hopkins University Press, 1995.

Silverman, Kenneth. *Edgar A. Poe: Mournful and Never-Ending Remembrance*. New York: HarperCollins, 1991.

Sova, Dawn B. *Edgar Allan Poe, A to Z: The Essential Reference to His Life and Work*. New York: Facts On File, 2001.

Stoehr, Taylor. "'Unspeakable Horror' in Poe." *South Atlantic Quarterly* 78 (1979): 317-32.

Stovall, Floyd. "The Conscious Art of Edgar Allan Poe." *College English* 24.6 (1963): 417-21.

Tate, Allen. "The Angelic Imagination: Poe and the Power of Words." *Kenyon Review* 14 (1952): 455-75.

Thomas, Dwight, and David K. Jackson. *The Poe Log: A Documentary Life of Edgar Allan Poe, 1809-1849*. Boston: G. K. Hall, 1987.

Thorpe, Dwayne. "Poe's 'The City in the Sea': Source and Interpretation." *American Literature* 51.3 (1979): 394-99.

Vines, Lois Davis, ed. *Poe Abroad: Influence, Reputation, Affinities*. Iowa City: University of Iowa Press, 1999.

Waggoner, Hyatt A. *American Poetry from the Puritans to the Present*. Boston: Houghton Mifflin, 1968.

Walker, I. M., ed. *Edgar Allan Poe: The Critical Heritage*. London: Routledge & Kegan Paul, 1986.

Whalen, Terence. *Edgar Allan Poe and the Masses: The Political Economy of Literature in Antebellum America*. Princeton, NJ: Princeton University Press, 1999.

Zimmerman, Brett. *Edgar Allan Poe: Rhetoric and Style*. Montreal: McGill-Queen's University Press, 2005.

# CRITICAL
# INSIGHTS

# About the Editor

**Steven Frye** is Professor of English at California State University, Bakersfield. He served as the guest editor (with Eric Carl Link) of a double issue of *Poe Studies/ Dark Romanticism: History, Theory, Interpretation* in honor of the journal's founder, G. R. Thompson. He is the author of *Understanding Cormac McCarthy* (2009) and *Historiography and Narrative Design in the American Romance: A Study of Four Authors* (2001). In addition, he is the author of numerous essays on the American fiction and short fiction of the nineteenth and twentieth centuries in journals such as *American Literary Realism*, *Studies in American Naturalism*, *American Studies*, *The Southern Quarterly*, *The Centennial Review*, *Leviathan*, *The Midwest Quarterly*, and *The Kentucky Review*. His work in the American romance tradition deals primarily with the relationships among history, religion, aesthetics, and narrative technique.

# About *The Paris Review*

*The Paris Review* is America's preeminent literary quarterly, dedicated to discovering and publishing the best new voices in fiction, nonfiction, and poetry. The magazine was founded in Paris in 1953 by the young American writers Peter Matthiessen and Doc Humes, and edited there and in New York for its first fifty years by George Plimpton. Over the decades, the *Review* has introduced readers to the earliest writings of Jack Kerouac, Philip Roth, T. C. Boyle, V. S. Naipaul, Ha Jin, Ann Patchett, Jay McInerney, Mona Simpson, and Edward P. Jones, and published numerous now classic works, including Roth's *Goodbye, Columbus*, Donald Barthelme's *Alice*, Jim Carroll's *Basketball Diaries*, and selections from Samuel Beckett's *Molloy* (his first publication in English). The first chapter of Jeffrey Eugenides's *The Virgin Suicides* appeared in the *Review*'s pages, as well as stories by Rick Moody, David Foster Wallace, Denis Johnson, Jim Crace, Lorrie Moore, and Jeanette Winterson.

*The Paris Review*'s renowned Writers at Work series of interviews, whose early installments include legendary conversations with E. M. Forster, William Faulkner, and Ernest Hemingway, is one of the landmarks of world literature. The interviews received a George Polk Award and were nominated for a Pulitzer Prize. Among the more than three hundred interviewees are Robert Frost, Marianne Moore, W. H. Auden, Elizabeth Bishop, Susan Sontag, and Toni Morrison. Recent issues feature conversations with Salman Rushdie, Joan Didion, Norman Mailer, Kazuo Ishiguro, Marilynne Robinson, Umberto Eco, Annie Proulx, and Gay Talese. In November 2009, Picador published the final volume of a four-volume series of anthologies of *Paris Review* interviews. *The New York Times* called the Writers at Work series "the most remarkable and extensive interviewing project we possess."

*The Paris Review* is edited by Philip Gourevitch, who was named to the post in 2005, following the death of George Plimpton two years earlier. A new editorial team has published fiction by André Aciman, Colum McCann, Damon Galgut, Mohsin Hamid, Uzodinma Iweala, Gish Jen, Stephen King, James Lasdun, Padgett Powell, Richard Price, and Sam Shepard. Poetry editors Charles Simic, Meghan O'Rourke, and Dan Chiasson have selected works by John Ashbery, Kay Ryan, Billy Collins, Tomaž Šalamun, Mary Jo Bang, Sharon Olds, Charles Wright, and Mary Karr. Writing published in the magazine has been anthologized in *Best American Short Stories* (2006, 2007, and 2008), *Best American Poetry*, *Best Creative Non-Fiction*, the Pushcart Prize anthology, and *O. Henry Prize Stories*.

The magazine presents two annual awards. The Hadada Award for lifelong contribution to literature has recently been given to Joan Didion, Norman Mailer, Peter Matthiessen, and, in 2009, John Ashbery. The Plimpton Prize for Fiction, awarded to a debut or emerging writer brought to national attention in the pages of *The Paris Review*, was presented in 2007 to Benjamin Percy, to Jesse Ball in 2008, and to Alistair Morgan in 2009.

*The Paris Review* was a finalist for the 2008 and 2009 National Magazine Awards in fiction, and it won the 2007 National Magazine Award in photojournalism. The *Los Angeles Times* recently called *The Paris Review* "an American treasure with true international reach."

Since 1999 *The Paris Review* has been published by The Paris Review Foundation, Inc., a not-for-profit 501(c)(3) organization.

*The Paris Review* is available in digital form to libraries worldwide in selected academic databases exclusively from EBSCO Publishing. Libraries can contact EBSCO at 1-800-653-2726 for details. For more information on *The Paris Review* or to subscribe, please visit: www.theparisreview.org.

# Contributors

**Steven Frye** is Professor of English at California State University, Bakersfield. His books include *Understanding Cormac McCarthy* (2009) and *Historiography and Narrative Design in the American Romance: A Study of Four Authors* (2001), and he has published essays in *American Literary Realism, Studies in American Naturalism, American Studies, The Southern Quarterly, The Centennial Review, Leviathan, The Midwest Quarterly,* and *The Kentucky Review.*

**Mark Minor** was Professor of English at Westmar College in Le Mars, Iowa.

**Juliet Lapidos,** a culture editor at *Slate,* has written for that publication as well as for *Bookforum, The New York Observer,* and the *New York Sun.* She is also the author of "The *Paris Review* Perspective" in the Critical Insights volume on Bram Stoker's *Dracula.*

**Brian Yothers** is Assistant Professor of English and Director of Graduate Studies in Literature at the University of Texas at El Paso. He is the author of *The Romance of the Holy Land in American Travel Writing, 1790-1876* (2007) and a coeditor of *Journeys: The International Journal of Travel and Travel Writing.* He has published on Poe in *Poe Studies* and in *Approaches to Teaching Poe's Prose and Poetry* (2008). He is also a contributor to *Melville's Marginalia Online* and is working on book projects dealing with Herman Melville's critical reception and representations of religious pluralism in Melville's work.

**Jeffrey Scraba** teaches in the Department of English at the University of Memphis. He has published articles on Washington Irving and on Walter Scott, and he is currently working on a book about memory and the production of the local in nineteenth-century literature.

**Matthew J. Bolton** is Professor of English at Loyola School in New York City, where he also serves as the Dean of Students. He received his doctor of philosophy degree in English from the Graduate Center of the City University of New York (CUNY) in 2005. His dissertation at the university was titled "Transcending the Self in Robert Browning and T. S. Eliot." Prior to attaining his Ph.D. at CUNY, he also earned a master of philosophy degree in English (2004) and a master of science degree in English education (2001). He did his undergraduate work at the State University of New York at Binghamton, where he studied English literature.

**Robert C. Evans** earned his Ph.D. from Princeton University in 1984. In 1982 he began teaching at Auburn University Montgomery, where he has been named Distinguished Research Professor, Distinguished Teaching Professor, and University Alumni Professor. External awards he has received include fellowships from the ACLS, the APS, the NEH, and the Folger, Huntington, and Newberry Libraries. He is the author or editor of more than twenty books and of numerous essays, including recent work on nineteenth-century American writers.

**Dave Smith** is Elliot Coleman Professor of Poetry and Department Chair of The Writing Seminars at Johns Hopkins University. Concentrating in the English language and contemporary poetry, he has been the editor of *The Southern Review* and is currently the editor of the *Southern Messenger Poetry Series* at Louisiana State University. He is the author of *Hunting Men: Reflections on a Life in American Poetry* (2006) and *Little Boats, Unsalvaged* (2005) and the editor of *The Essential Poe* (1991) and *The Pure Clear Word: Essays on the Poetry of James Wright* (1981).

**G. R. Thompson** is Professor Emeritus of English and Comparative Literature at Purdue University. Known primarily for his works on poet Edgar Allan Poe, he has published the *Norton Critical Edition of Edgar Allan Poe* (2004), *Essays and Reviews of Edgar Allan Poe* (1984), and *Poe's Fiction: Romantic Irony in the Gothic Tales* (1973).

**Richard Godden** is Professor of English at the University of California, Irvine. His essay "Maximizing the Noodles: Class, Memory, and Capital in Sergio Leone's *Once Upon a Time in America*" won him the Arthur Miller Prize in 1998. He is also the author of *William Faulkner: An Economy of Complex Words* (2007).

**Daneen Wardrop** is Professor of English at Western Michigan University, where she teaches primarily in American literature from the nineteenth century to the present. In addition to authoring two books of literary criticism, she has published one book of poetry, *The Odds of Being* (2008). Her poetry has earned her the Poetry Society of America Robert H. Winner Memorial Award, the Bentley Prize for Poetry, and two Pushcart Prize nominations.

**Jonathan Culler** is Professor of English and Comparative Literature at Cornell University. Currently completing a term as President of the American Comparative Literature Association, he focuses his teaching on nineteenth-century French literature, literary theory, and historical lyricism. His publications include *Flaubert: The Uses of Uncertainty* (1985), *The Pursuit of Signs: Semiotics, Literature, Deconstruction* (1981), and *Structuralist Poetics: Structuralism, Linguistics, and the Study of Literature* (1975).

**Burton R. Pollin** is Professor Emeritus of English at the City University of New York. He has published more than 145 articles and books on Edgar Allan Poe and has lectured worldwide on the poet's life and works. He is the editor of *The German Face of Edgar Allan Poe: A Study of Literary References in His Works* (1996) and *The Collected Writings of Edgar Allan Poe* (1981).

**Francis B. Dedmond** is Professor Emeritus of English at Catawba College, where he also served as Chair of the English Department. Over the course of his career, he published articles on Poe, Emerson, Thoreau, and the Civil War in journals such as *Modern Language Quarterly* and *American Literature*.

**Leland S. Person, Jr.**, is Professor of English and Senior Associate Dean for Academic Affairs at the University of Cincinnati. In addition to contributing articles to the *Nathaniel Hawthorne Review*, the *Edgar Allan Poe Review*, and the *New England*

*Quarterly*, he has published seven books, most recently *Henry James and the Suspense of Masculinity* (2003). He is also the editor of the Norton Critical Edition of *The Scarlet Letter and Other Writings* (2005) by Nathaniel Hawthorne.

**Eliza Richards** is Professor of English and Comparative Literature at the University of North Carolina. She is the author of *Gender and the Poetics of Reception in Poe's Circle* (2004) and various essays and chapters on nineteenth-century American and British literature and poetry. She is currently working on her next book, *Hearing Voices: Lyric Representation in Nineteenth-Century America.*

**James Postema** is Associate Professor of English and Associate Dean for Faculty Development and Resources at Concordia College in Minnesota. His research interests are in folk literature and the temporal structures in Robert Frost's poems. His essays have been published in such scholarly journals as the *North Dakota Quarterly*, the *Journal of Presbyterian History*, and *Essays in Literature.*

**Keiji Minato** is a scholar of English literature and American and Australian contemporary poetry. He is the author of the poetry book *Garasu no me/ Nuno no hifu* (2004).

# Acknowledgments

"Edgar Allan Poe" by Mark Minor. From *Critical Survey of Poetry*, Second Revised Edition. Copyright © 2003 by Salem Press, Inc. Reprinted with permission of Salem Press.

"The *Paris Review* Perspective" by Juliet Lapidos. Copyright © 2011 by Juliet Lapidos. Special appreciation goes to Christopher Cox, Nathaniel Rich, and David Wallace-Wells, editors at *The Paris Review.*

"Edgar Allan Poe and the Nightmare Ode" by Dave Smith. From *Southern Humanities Review* 24, no. 1 (1995): 1-10. Reprinted in *Hunting Men: Reflections on a Life in American Poetry* by Dave Smith. Copyright © 1995 by Dave Smith. Reprinted with permission of the author.

"The Visionary Paradox: Poe's Poetic Theory" by G. R. Thompson. From *Circumscribed Eden of Dreams: Dreamvision and Nightmare in Poe's Early Poetry* (1984). Copyright © 1984 by the Enoch Pratt Free Library. Reprinted with permission of the Enoch Pratt Free Library and the author.

"Poe and the Poetics of Opacity: Or, Another Way of Looking at That Black Bird" by Richard Godden. From *English Literary History* 67, no. 4 (2000): 993-1009. Copyright © 2000 by the Johns Hopkins University Press. Reprinted with permission of the Johns Hopkins University Press.

"Quoting the Signifier 'Nevermore': *Fort! Da!*, Pallas, and Desire in Language" by Daneen Wardrop. From *ESQ: A Journal of the American Renaissance* 44, no. 4 (1998): 275-99. Copyright © 1998 by Washington State University. Reprinted with permission of Washington State University.

"Baudelaire and Poe" by Jonathan Culler. From *Zeitschrift für Französische Sprache und Literatur* 100 (1990): 61-73. Copyright © 1990 by Jonathan Culler. Reprinted with permission of the author.

"Poe and Frances Osgood, as Linked Through 'Lenore'" by Burton R. Pollin. From *Mississippi Quarterly: A Journal of Southern Culture* 46, no. 2 (1993): 185-197. Copyright ©1993 by Mississippi State University Press. Reprinted with permission of Mississippi State University Press.

"Poe and the Brownings" by Francis B. Dedmond. From *American Transcendental Quarterly* 1 (1987): 111-122. Copyright © 1987 by the University of Rhode Island. Reprinted with permission of the University of Rhode Island.

"Poe's Composition of Philosophy: Reading and Writing 'The Raven'" by Leland S. Person, Jr. From *Arizona Quarterly* 46, no. 3 (1990): 1-15. Copyright © by the University of Arizona. Reprinted by permission of the Regents of the University of Arizona.

"'The Poetess' and Poe's Performance of the Feminine" by Eliza Richards. From *Arizona Quarterly* 55, no. 2 (1999): 1-29. Copyright © 1999 by the Arizona Board of Regents. Reprinted with permission of the Arizona Board of Regents and the author.

Humboldt, Alexander von, 30
Humphries, Jefferson, 183, 191
Hunt, Freeman, 78
Huxley, Aldous, 13, 57, 84
Hyneman, Esther F., 87

Imagery, 29, 111, 291; ghosts, 42,
    134, 266, 296; religious, 25, 299;
    shadows, 28, 38, 46, 104, 123,
    129, 135, 182, 190, 299
*Incidents of Travel in Egypt, Arabia
    Petraea, and the Holy Land*
    (Stephens), 21
Ingram, John H., 236
"Irei-sai" (Yoshioka), 306
Irisawa Yasuo, 310, 320
Irving, Washington, 20
Irwin, John T., 256
"Israfel" (Poe), 6, 25, 121, 224, 272

Jacobs, Robert D., 139, 291, 298
James, Henry, 13, 82
Johnson, Barbara, 44
Jones, Buford, 271

"Kamoyama-Kou" (Ono), 304
Kant, Immanuel, 118, 125
Kelly, George, 298
Kennedy, J. Gerald, 177, 252, 265, 286
Ketterer, David, 256
Kitagawa Toru, 313, 320
Kot, Paula, 185

Lacan, Jacques, 163, 177
"Lady Geraldine's Courtship" (Barrett),
    229, 267
"Lake, The" (Poe), 6, 133, 141
Lawrence, D. H., 83
"Leonor" (Osgood), 210
"Letter to B——" (Poe), 5, 22, 64, 114,
    126

"Ligeia" (Poe), 24, 30, 162, 180, 199
Ljungquist, Kent, 256, 271, 299
Loss, 6, 34, 44, 53, 63, 131, 145, 173,
    191, 206, 270
Lowell, James Russell, 77

Mabbott, Thomas Ollive, 27, 54, 87,
    137, 223, 239, 285, 299
Mallarmé, Stéphane, 5, 81, 185, 192,
    301, 312
"Man of the Crowd, The" (Poe), 197,
    316
"Mare Tenebrarum" (Irisawa), 310
McGill, Meredith, 41, 54
Melancholy, 15, 35, 47, 76, 109, 136,
    157, 166, 232, 275
Memory, 35, 43, 48, 63, 123, 129, 144,
    154, 270, 306
Metaphors, 4, 13, 27, 120, 126, 185,
    217, 265, 290
Meter, 43, 51, 58, 66, 72, 87, 102,
    147, 153, 163, 224
Milton, John, 67, 138
Miyoshi Tatsuji, 302
Morris, George Pope, 77, 212
Motifs, 131, 161
Mourning, 34, 43, 47, 53, 146, 162,
    273, 286
Music, 4, 14, 63, 72, 111, 113, 120,
    124, 212

Names, 39, 45, 59, 151, 159, 161,
    172, 178, 183, 212, 223, 309
Neal, John, 76

"O, Tempora! O, Mores!" (Poe), 23
Odes, 100
Omans, Glen A., 139
Ono Tosaburo, 303, 319
Osgood, Frances Sargent, 210, 235, 261,
    264, 271, 286

Otherworldliness, 25, 110, 117, 130
"Oval Portrait, The" (Poe), 206

Pearce, Roy Harvey, 86, 287, 295
Peck, George Washington, 79, 241
Phillips, Elizabeth, 88
"Philosophy of Composition, The"
    (Poe), 4, 14, 34, 44, 99, 124, 148,
    166, 177, 192, 241, 256, 266, 274,
    278, 290
Pindaric ode, 100
"Po no Love Song" (Kitagawa), 313
Poe, Edgar Allan; and Elizabeth Barrett,
    76, 228, 259, 267; childhood, 8, 105;
    as critic, 4, 113, 125, 243, 255, 259,
    274; critical reception of poetry, 41,
    56, 75, 99, 188; education, 8;
    innovation in poetry, 44, 72, 87;
    literary career, 8, 13, 19, 40, 226;
    and Frances Sargent Osgood, 210,
    235, 264; as outsider, 105; on poetry,
    5, 14, 22, 35, 63, 109, 123, 140
Poe, Virginia Clemm (wife), 9, 271
"Poetic Principle, The" (Poe), 4, 14, 22,
    53, 63, 109, 116, 119, 227, 274
Pollin, Burton R., 28
Polonsky, Rachel, 35
"Power of Words, The" (Poe), 108,
    136, 139, 205
Puns, 139, 152, 182, 185, 207, 225, 316
"Purloined Letter, The" (Poe), 152, 166,
    241, 245

Quinn, Arthur Hobson, 26, 299

"Rationale of Verse, The" (Poe), 4, 125,
    274
"Raven, The" (Poe), 4, 7, 15, 29, 34, 56,
    61, 99, 124, 147, 163, 170, 189, 231,
    234, 239, 241, 266, 290; critical
    reception, 41, 76

Raven, and Other Poems, The (Poe), 77,
    140, 232
Refrains, 14, 44, 149, 166, 195, 245,
    303
Rhyme, 14, 41, 58, 64, 72, 86, 102, 148,
    165, 195
Rhythm, 43, 64, 72, 78, 82, 88, 102,
    120, 147, 154, 159, 165, 230, 235,
    267, 290, 316
Richards, Eliza, 34
Ricoeur, Paul, 36
Riddel, Joseph N., 184, 254
Robinson, Edwin Arlington, 82
Romantic poetry, 3, 14, 21, 80, 99,
    108, 138, 193, 264
Rowe, John Carlos, 30

Said, Edward, 20
Saintsbury, George, 83
Saito Mokichi, 305
Samson Agonistes (Milton), 68
Shadows, 28, 38, 46, 104, 123, 129,
    135, 182, 190, 299
Shakespeare, William, 64
Shaw, George Bernard, 82
Shelley, Percy Bysshe, 122, 130
Silverman, Kenneth, 41, 54
Siriwardena, Regi, 31
Smith, Elizabeth Oakes, 260, 271
"Sonnet—To Science" (Poe), 6
"Spectacles, The" (Poe), 228
Stephens, John Lloyd, 21
Stoehr, Taylor, 180, 184
Stovall, Floyd, 86
Swift, Jonathan, 70
Symbolist movement, 7, 31, 58, 83, 301

"Tamerlane" (Poe), 24, 37, 141
Tamerlane, and Other Poems (Poe), 5, 8,
    13, 23, 112, 131
Tate, Allen, 86, 101